Library of
Davidson College

Socialist Albania since 1944

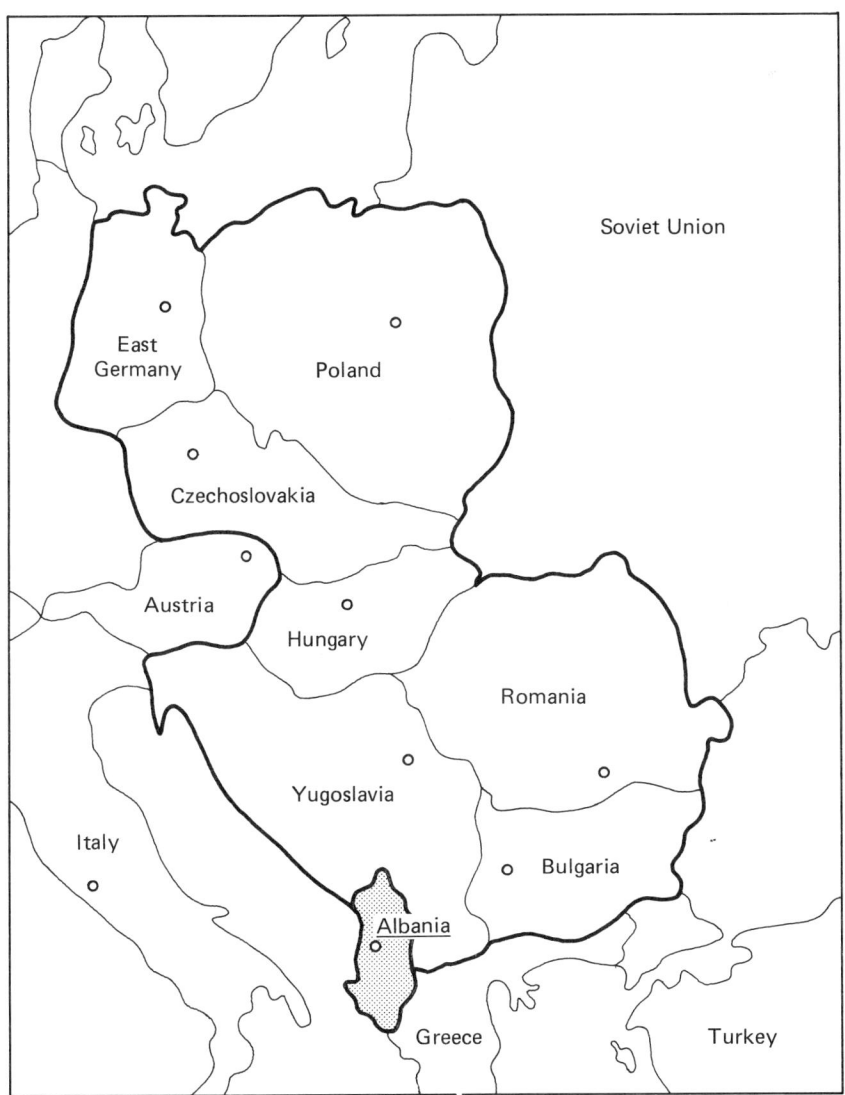

Albania and Communist East Europe

Studies in Communism, Revisionism, and Revolution (formerly Studies in International Communism), William E. Griffith, general editor

1. Albania and the Sino-Soviet Rift, William E. Griffith (1963)
2. Communism in North Vietnam, P. J. Honey (1964)
3. The Sino-Soviet Rift, William E. Griffith (1964)
4. Communism in Europe, Vol. 1, William E. Griffith, ed. (1964)
5. Nationalism and Communism in Chile, Ernst Halperin (1965)
6. Communism in Europe, Vol. 2, William E. Griffith, Ed. (1966)
7. Viet Cong: The Organization and Techniques of the National Liberation Front of South Vietnam, Douglas Pike (1966)
8. Sino-Soviet Relations, 1964–1965, William E. Griffith (1967)
9. The French Communist Party and the Crisis of International Communism, Francois Fejitö (1967)
10. The New Rumania: From People's Democracy to Socialist Republic, Stephen Fischer-Galati (1967)
11. Economic Development in Communist Rumania, John Michael Montias (1967)
12. Cuba: Castroism and Communism, 1959–1966, Andrés Suárez (1967)
13. Unity in Diversity: Italian Communism and the Communist World, Donald L. M. Blackmer (1967)
14. Winter in Prague: Documents on Czechoslovak Communism in Crisis, Robin Alison Remington, ed. (1969)
15. The Angoian Revolution, Vol. 1: The Anatomy of an Explosion (1950–1962), John A. Marcum (1969)
16. Radical Politics in West Bengal, Marcus F. Franda (1971)
17. The Warsaw Pact: Case Studies in Communist Conflict Resolution, Robin Alison Remington (1971)
18. The Transformation of Communist Ideology: The Yugoslav Case, 1945–1953, A. Ross Johnson (1972)
19. Radical Politics in South Asia, Paul R. Brass and Marcus F. Franda, eds. (1973)
20. The Canal War: Four-Power Conflict in the Middle East, Lawrence L. Whetten (1974)
21. The World and the Great-Power Triangles, William E. Griffith, ed. (1975)
22. The Angolan Revolution, Vol. 2: Exile Politics and Guerrilla Warfare (1962–1976), John A. Marcum (1978)
23. Socialist Albania since 1944: Domestic and Foreign Developments, Peter R. Prifti (1978)

Socialist Albania since 1944
Domestic and Foreign Developments

Peter R. Prifti

The MIT Press
Cambridge, Massachusetts, and London England

Copyright © 1978 by
The Massachusetts Institute of Technology

All rights reserved. No part of this book may be reproduced in any form or by any means, electronic or mechanical, including photocopying, recording, or by any information storage and retrieval system, without permission in writing from the publisher.

This book was set in IBM Composer Press Roman by The Blue Ridge Group, printed and bound by Halliday Lithograph Corporation in the United States of America.

Library of Congress Cataloging in Publication Data
Prifti, Peter R
   Socialist Albania since 1944.
   (Studies in communism, revisionism, and revolution ; 23)
   Includes bibliographical references and index.
   1. Albania—History—1944— I. Title.
II. Series.
DR977.P74   949.65'03   78-1728
ISBN 0-262-16070-6

To my parents
Ralph and Parashqevi Prifti

Contents

Map of Albania and Communist East Europe   iii

Preface   x

List of Abbreviations   xiv

Administrative Map of Albania   xvi

1   A Sketch of the Country and the People   1

2   How the Partisans Seized Power   9

3   The Nature of the Albanian Communist Party   22

4   The Socialization of the Economy   52

5   The Movement for Women's Emancipation   90

6   The Evolution of the Arts   113

7   The Cultural Revolution (1966-1969)   143

8   The Abolition of Religion   150

9   The Party *vs.* the Intelligentsia   167

10   The Developments in the Armed Forces   195

11   The Albanian Minority in Yugoslavia   222

12   The Foreign Policy Line   242

Epilogue   257

Notes   263

Index   301

Preface

It is the consensus of scholars that Albania is one of the least known countries of Europe in the West. Lack of familiarity with this ancient Balkan nation is unfortunate because it impoverishes our understanding of that country and in addition tends to distort our overall image of the Balkans. It is a defect that applies especially to domestic developments in contemporary Albania. The foreign relations of postwar Albania have attracted some attention in the West, largely because of the role Albania has played in the Sino-Soviet conflict. As a result this aspect of her society has been dealt with in a number of studies, in particular by William E. Griffith in his *Albania and the Sino-Soviet Rift* (1963) and Nicholas Pano in *The People's Republic of Albania* (1968). When we look at the domestic scene, however, we find a notable gap in the literature on Albania. With the exception of Stavro Skendi's *Albania* (1956), the standard work on the country as a whole, no comprehensive study of domestic developments in Albania has appeared. My primary motive, therefore, in writing this book was to help fill this gap.

The choice of the topics for the study was based on two or three considerations: One of these was to include topics such as Albania's cultural revolution, the developments in the armed forces, and the Albanian minority in Yugoslavia, about which the reading public and even many scholars know the least. Another was to discuss areas of Albanian life in which most scholars and nonscholars alike seem to take the greatest interest. In this group fall the chapters on the background of the Albanian people, the Albanian Communist Party, and the question of religion in the country. Third, the choice of topics reflects also my personal bias as to what developments in socialist Albania are of interest and significance and deserve to be discussed in a work of this kind. The chapters on the evolution of the arts, the movement for women's emancipation, and the role of the artistic intelligentsia reflect especially that bias or preference.

As is often the case, the chapters in this volume are not of uniform length. The length of the chapters was dictated by the purpose and needs of each individual unit and by the overall objectives of the book. If one were to judge by the titles of the chapters, one could conclude, I suppose, that nearly all of them deal with domestic matters. But in fact all of the chapters combine discussions of both domestic and foreign policies. Apart from the chapters on foreign policy and on the Albanian minority in Yugoslavia, the foreign affairs element is especially evident in the chapters on the economy, the cultural revolution, and the developments in the armed forces. Nearly all of the chapters have a historical perspective and a summary section. They are thus largely self-contained and can be read either in isolation or in conjunction with the other units in the volume.

With regard to notes, the titles of books in foreign languages have been given in both the original and English. However, in the interest of space requirements, the titles of articles in foreign languages appear only in their English translations. Contrary to current practice in the West, the spelling of the name of Albania's capital has been given as Tiranë, rather than Tirana. The indefinite form is the one generally used in Albania in the spelling of names of towns, and I saw no compelling reason to make an exception in the case of the capital city.

This book contains considerable data. In using the data, I adopted what might be called the "dialectical" rather than the "static" approach. My main interest was not to give statistical information about Albanian institutions, or to describe the organization and structure of Albanian society, but to view the data as part of a dynamic process. I thought this was the best approach to take in writing about contemporary Albania, a society in transition that is experiencing rapid and radical change in every area of life. Seen from this angle, this book is mostly the story of the tensions between the Albanian Communist Party and the Albanian population. It is the story of the continually evolving relationship between a Stalinist state leadership bent on modernizing a notoriously backward society, in accordance with the leadership's own blueprint, and the resistance to that leadership by various segments of the population. In telling the story, I have expressed both sympathy with and criticism of the Albanian leadership, depending on my evaluation of its policies and actions. I have tried to be objective in my evaluation, and I hope I have succeeded in this aim.

Nearly all of the research and writing of this study was done at the Center for International Studies of the Massachusetts Institute of Technology. In 1974, however, I benefited from the use of the library facilities at the University of California at Berkeley, during a two weeks' visit in the area. Similarly, I profited from research at the Library of Congress, during a short stay in Washington, D.C., in the spring of 1976.

Some of the material in this volume appeared earlier, in the form of articles, in a number of publications. I express my appreciation to the parties concerned for permission to use these articles. They are "The Albanian Party of Labor and the Intelligentsia," *East European Quarterly* 7, no. 3 (Fall 1974): 307-335; "Albania—Towards an Atheist Society," chapter in Bohdan R. Bociurkiw and John W. Strong, eds., *Religion and Atheism in the USSR and Eastern Europe*

(New York: Macmillan Co., 1975), pp. 388-404; "The Albanian Women's Struggle for Emancipation," *Southeastern Europe* 2, pt. 2 (1975): 109-129; and "The Albanian Party of Labor," which is scheduled for publication in a volume on the communist parties of Eastern Europe, Stephen Fischer-Galati, ed. All of the articles were revised in accordance with the needs of the manuscript.

The American Council of Learned Societies funded part of the research on the book, and I am grateful to it for its generous grant.

Many people helped me with this book. I acknowledge with thanks the constant support and assistance of William E. Griffith, Senior Research Analyst and Director of the project on communist studies at the MIT Center for International Studies (CENIS). Robin Remington, Professor of Political Science at the University of Missouri at Columbia, Missouri, edited much of the manuscript, and I benefited immensely from her perceptive criticism and encouragement. I was fortunate to work closely with her and Griffith over a period of several years at MIT. Professor Eugene Skolnikoff, Director of CENIS at MIT, and two members of his staff, Amelia C. Leiss and Jessie R. Janjigian, were most helpful in making available the valuable facilities of the Center for my research. I thank them for their consideration and patience. Rada Vlajinac of the CENIS Department of Publications provided useful source material. It was a pleasure to work with her.

Others at MIT who assisted me in research were William Presson, the genial Associate Librarian of the Dewey Library; and Karel Kovanda, at the time a Ph.D. student at the university. I profited greatly from the cooperation and constructive suggestions of Arshi Pipa of the University of Minnesota. Peter S. H. Tang of Boston College was very helpful with his sympathetic comments about my work on Albania in general. Dhimitri Nikolla (Trebicka), editor of the Albanian-American weekly, *Liria*, in Boston contributed to the research by providing me with valuable original source materials from Albania. I express my thanks to him for his unfailing cooperation. I wish also to commend Sher Brewer of San Diego for the conscientious and competent work she did in typing the entire manuscript. She showed initiative and took pride in her work, and I am grateful to her.

Finally, I have sought with this book on Albania to sum up three decades in the life of the country—three decades, at that, of the most rapid and far-reaching political, social, economic, and cultural transformations in the history of the country. In the course of this inquiry and summing-up, I have attempted to answer two of the questions people ask most frequently about Albania:

First, why did Albania remain the lone stronghold of Stalinism in Europe, in spite of the post-1956 thaw in Eastern Europe and the era of détente in East-West relations? Second, how did the smallest country in Europe ally itself with the largest country in Asia, namely, communist China, and what caused the rift in the Albanian-Chinese alliance in 1977? I hope I have achieved a fair degree of success in dealing with these and other questions raised in the book. Above all, I trust that the book will stimulate other people to embark on further and more fruitful studies on Albania and in this manner raise the current level of scholarship on the country.

Peter R. Prifti
The University of California at San Diego
La Jolla, California

List of Abbreviations

ACP
Albanian Communist Party

ANLA
Albanian National Liberation Army

APL
Albanian Party of Labor

BK
Balli Kombëtar (The National Front)

COMECON
Council for Mutual Economic Assistance

CP
Communist Party

CPC
Communist Party of China

CPSU
Communist Party of the Soviet Union

D. K.
Dokumenta Kryesore (Main documents)

LAWA
League of Albanian Writers and Artists

LYUA
Labor Youth Union of Albania

NATO
North Atlantic Treaty Organization

NLF
National Liberation Front

PLA
People's Liberation Army (of Communist China)

PPSH
Partia e Punës e Shqipërisë (Albanian Party of Labor)

Abbreviations

TUA
Trade Unions of Albania

UAW
Union of Albanian Women

YCP
Yugoslav Communist Party

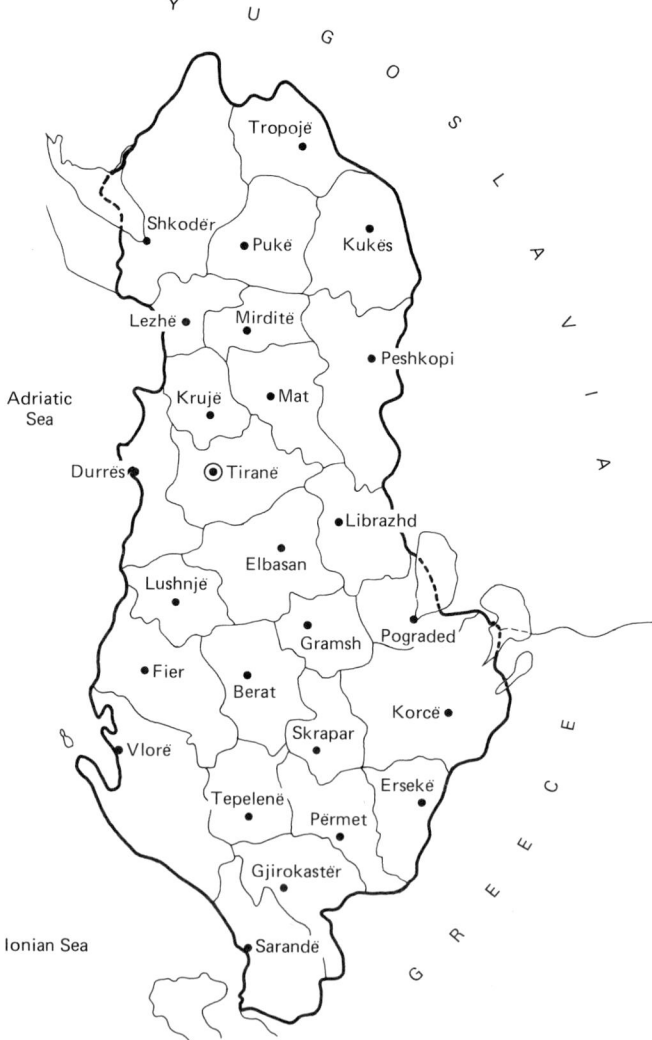

Administrative Map of Albania

1
A Sketch of the Country and the People

Albania has a reputation as a land of great natural beauty and romantic remoteness. These two characteristics have made it all the more attractive, mysterious, forbidding, challenging, or exasperating to outsiders, be they travelers, scholars, diplomats, or merchants. For example, in a work he published in 1913, the Croatian scholar Milan von Sufflay called Albania *regio mirabilissima*, "a most singular country" or "a most marvelous country."[1] Others have referred to it as the "Switzerland of the Balkans" or as the "rock garden of southeastern Europe." On the other hand, the country's uncommon isolation from the world, arising generally from its rugged, mountainous terrain, has led foreigners to speak of it as "the Tibet of Europe" or as a country more mysterious than central Africa. It is an attitude that has had currency for centuries. We find it, for instance, in the writings of Edward Gibbon, the great eighteenth-century British historian. Speaking of Albania, Gibbon said that it is "a country within sight of Italy, which is less known than the interior of America."[2]

The remoteness and isolation of the country became practically legendary and all too frequently gave rise to reports and descriptions of the land and the people—even in books and encyclopedias—that were closer to legends than to reality. Perhaps because of its romantic remoteness and other reasons, Albania has exerted a continuous fascination on artists, including poets, playwrights, composers, and more recently film makers and producers of television programs. Shakespeare set his comedy *Twelfth Night* in Illyria—the name by which Albania was known in former times. Lord Byron, who visited southern Albania in 1810, wrote some stirring lines about her landscape in his poem *Childe Harold*.

Morn dawns: and with it stern Albania's hills . . .
Robed half in mist, bedewed with snowy rills.

In Mozart's comic opera *Così fan tutte* the principal male characters, Ferrando and Guglielmo, appear for the most part in disguise as two "Albanian noblemen" in a clever scheme to test the love of their fiancées. [The women fail the test when they succumb to the charms of the Albanians but succeed nevertheless in winning back the love of their men.] In our own time, we find that Peter Ustinov—taking a cue from Shakespeare—set one of his comedies, *Romanoff and Juliet*, in post-World War II Albania. Ustinov's Albania is a somewhat fanciful land but serves him well as a neat laboratory to grapple with and overcome the Cold War enmities between American and Soviet diplomats stationed in that country. Three films dealing with Albania and

Albanians are *Five Fingers*; *Action of the Tiger*; and *The President's Analyst*. All three are action films involving intelligence operations, but the last two lack artistic merit and—as is so often the case where Albania is concerned—tend to give a misleading picture of the country.³

What then, are the "basic facts" about Albania, as far as we have knowledge of them? The smallest country in the Balkan Peninsula, Albania is bordered on the north and northeast by Yugoslavia, on the southeast by Greece, and on the west and southwest by the Adriatic and Ionian seas. It lies less than 100 km (60 mi) from Italy at the nearest point of the Strait of Otranto. In area, the country encompasses 28,000 km² (11,000 mi²), yet it is bigger than Massachusetts (8,200 mi²) or any state in New England with the exception of Maine.⁴ Its population in 1976 was about 2,500,000; again, not large at all, yet larger than the combined populations of the three New England states of Vermont, New Hampshire, and Rhode Island, which totaled 2,130,000.⁵ The capital of Albania, Tiranë, had a population of 190,000 in 1973; all the rest of the nation's cities had populations under 60,000.

For a small country, Albania has a remarkably diverse climate: a semi-tropical zone along the seacoast, warm enough to grow oranges and other citrus fruit, eucalyptus and palm trees; and a hinterland region that is subject to cold, Continental weather patterns, including heavy snowfalls and blizzards in the winter. Most of the country is mountainous, with some of the mountains reaching altitudes of 2,700 m (over 8,000 ft). The mountain ranges that cover the land have served as a protective shield for the preservation of the nation's ethnic integrity through several millennia.

Albania is an unusually homogenous nation, from the viewpoint of the ethnic composition of her population. According to the 1961 census, slightly over 95 percent of the population consists of ethnic Albanians. The remainder included 40,000 Greeks (2.4 percent), 15,000 Macedonians and Montenegrins (0.9 percent), 10,000 Vlachs (0.6 percent), and about 10,000 Gypsies.⁶ In terms of their physical characteristics, most Albanians are said to belong to the Dinaric group, which is found on the western part of the Balkan Peninsula. As such, they are generally tall, have dark eyes and dark hair and straight or curved noses. These traits are found especially among northern Albanians, formerly known as Gegs; they are less common among southern Albanians, formerly called Tosks.⁷ Before the Second World War, the northern part of the country was very backward compared with the southern part which, owing in some measure to wider contacts with the outside world, stood at a higher social and economic level. Since the war, however, Albania has made progress in eradicating the imbalance in the development of the two regions.

The Albanians are believed to be the descendants of the Illyrians, who inhabited the Balkans as far back as the second millennium B.C. Many scholars affirm that the Albanians are the oldest of the Balkan peoples.[8] Their ancestors, the Illyrians, were in the Balkans centuries before the Slavs began to migrate into the area.[9] The consensus of scholars at present is that the Illyrians were indigenous in the Balkans and not—as some writers have argued in the past—a people who migrated there from another part of the world.[10] Ethnically, the Albanians are neither Slavs nor Greeks but a distinct ethnic group, although like their neighbors they are a part of the great family of European peoples.

A curious item about Albania is her very name, that is, the etymology of the word "Albania." The country was known as Illyria in ancient times and until the eleventh century A.D. Since the name "Albania" appears in thirteenth-century Latin dictionaries, the term probably was in use even earlier. During the Middle Ages the Albanians called their country Arbër or Arbën and referred to themselves as Arbëresh or Arbënesh. To this day, there are communities of Albanians who migrated to Greece and Italy, in the wake of foreign invasions and pressures, who know themselves by those names.[11] According to the Albanian scholar Konitza, the term "Albania" did not displace "Illyria" completely until the end of the fourteenth century.[12] The term is believed to derive from "Albanoi," the name of an Illyrian tribe in what is now north-central Albania, which was first mentioned in the second century A.D. by Ptolemy, the Alexandrian astronomer. The term slowly spread to other Illyrian tribes until its usage became universal among all the Albanian people.

Still more curious is the fact that the Albanians today call themselves Shqiptarë rather than Albanians, and their country Shqipëri rather than Albania. The two terms came into use following Albania's occupation by the Turks in the fifteenth century, but why and in what manner this occurred is still a mystery.

The Albanian language is a part of the Indo-European family of languages. It is not a Slavic, Latin, or Germanic language, nor is it related to the Greek. It forms instead a subgroup of its own, in the same manner as the Armenian and Iranian languages constitute subgroups of their own, within the larger, all-inclusive Indo-European group. Opinions vary concerning the exact origin of the Albanian language, but there is practically no dispute over the thesis that it is related to the Illyrian and Thracian languages.[13]

Until late in the nineteenth century, the teaching and publication of the Albanian language were forbidden by the Turkish authorities and Greek ecclesiastics who collaborated with them during the Turkish occupation of the country. As a consequence, most outsiders, including some respected authors in the West, had the mistaken notion that the Albanian people lacked a literary tradition; in other words, that they had no written language. But in fact the Albanian language has a literary history that goes back to the Middle Ages. A fourteenth-century Dominican friar, Father Brocardus, noted in a pamphlet he published in 1332 that "the Albanians have a language quite other than the Latins," but "they use the Latin letters in all their books."[14] Apart from a fragmentary document in Albanian, published in 1462 by Pal Engjëlli (Paulus Angelus), archbishop of Durazzo (Durrës), the first book in the Albanian language—as far as we know—was published in 1555. Its author was Dom Gjon Buzuku, and it bears the title *Meshari* (Missal). The book is a compendium of church rituals. A copy of it is housed in the Vatican Library in Rome. In 1935, Frano Bardhi (Franciscus Blancus) published in Rome his *Dictionarium latino-epiroticum*, the first known Latin-Albanian dictionary. The evidence shows, moreover, that the "study of Albanian grammar has a tradition of 350 years"[15] and includes works by Bardhi (1606-1643), Andre Bogdani (1600-1685), Nilo Katalanos (1637-1694), and others.

Writings in Albanian were scanty in the eighteenth century but increased considerably in the last century with the advent of the national awakening among the Albanians in Italy, Egypt, Romania, Greece, and Bulgaria. Until the twentieth century, this literature was published in a variety of foreign scripts, most of it in Latin and Greek. In 1908, however, leaders of the Albanian national and cultural revival held a congress in Monastir—now Bitola in the Yugoslav part of Macedonia—that laid the basis for the adoption of the Roman alphabet currently in use in Albania.

Like her language and people, a number of Albania's cities and towns bear witness to the antiquity of the country. For example, the nation's leading seaport, Durrës, was founded in 627 B.C. Known in antiquity as Dyrrahion or Epidamnos, the town was the site of the decisive battle in 48 B.C. between Julius Caesar and Pompey. It is alleged, moreover, that Saint Paul preached there in the course of his missionary work in the Balkans.[16] Two other very old towns are Shkodër (Skodra in antiquity) in northern Albania, which dates from the fourth century B.C. and was at one time the capital of Illyria; and the seaport of Vlorë in the south, whose bitumen mines have been in operation since the days of the Roman Empire, when the town was known as Aulon. Pojan, a mere village today near Vlorë, was an important center of culture and education in pre-Christian Albania. A city-state, it had then a population of some 40,000. Apollonia, as Pojan was known in its days of power and renown, was founded in 588 B.C. in honor of Apollo, god of beauty, poetry, and music. Aristotle mentions it in his *Politics* (book 4, chapter 4), saying that in Apollonia "the freemen . . . rule over the many who are not free"; in other words, the city had an oligarchic form of government.

In their long history the Albanians and their Illyrian ancestors were victims of numerous invasions and occupations by foreign armies. The Romans conquered Illyria in 167 B.C. and ruled it for over five and a half centuries, until A.D. 395, when the Roman Empire was partitioned into East and West, and Illyria became a part of the Byzantine Empire. The consequences of Roman rule are evident in the Albanian language, which was strongly influenced by Latin, and in the traces of the celebrated Via Egnatia that extended from Durrës to Ohrid, then to Salonika, Byzantium (Istanbul), and finally to Jerusalem. A few miles of this road reportedly are still in use in modern Albania, a testimony to the engineering genius of Rome. On the other hand, the Illyrians, too, exerted their influence on the Roman Empire. For nearly one hundred years (A.D. 247-361), emperors of Illyrian origin, among them Claudius II, Aurelian, Diocletian, and Probus, ruled the empire.[17]

For an interval between the fall of the Roman Empire in A.D. 476 and the fall of the Byzantine Empire in 1453, Albania gained recognition for the first time in her history as a distinct political entity under her own name. This happened in the thirteenth century, when Charles I of Anjou (1227-1285), king of Naples, marched his army across the Adriatic and occupied Durrës in 1272. He then formed the "Regnum Albaniae" (kingdom of Albania) and assumed for himself the title of "Rex Albaniae" (king of Albania). His kingdom lasted for nearly a century.[18]

The most brilliant chapter in the history of Albania was written in the middle of the fifteenth century, when Gjergj Kastrioti Skënderbeu (George Castrioti Scanderbeg, 1405-1468), Albania's National Hero, waged a successful 25-year-long struggle against the Ottoman Turks. Rebelling against the Turkish occupation of Albania, Skënderbeu seized power in 1443 and with the combined support of the nobility and the peasants, plus foreign aid, kept Albania largely free of Turkish control until his death in 1468. The foreign aid came from "the Papacy, the Kingdom of Naples, the Venetian Republic and the City of Ragusa—in short, the entire Catholic world whose cause he championed."[19] During this period, he repulsed two major expeditions that were led in person by two great sultans: the first, by Murad II in 1439-1450; and the second by Mehmed II—the Conqueror of Constantinople (1453)—in 1466-1467. The heroic resistance of the Albanians attracted widespread attention in Europe and led Pope Nicholas V (1447-1453) to call Skënderbeu "Champion of Christendom." The admiration of the Vatican for Albania's brilliant soldier-statesman is reflected also in the remark by Pope Calixtus III (1453-1458) that ". . . he stopped the fury of the Turkish tide and prevented it from overrunning Christian Europe."[20]

The high estimation of Skënderbeu by Catholic Rome was not without foundation. For after crushing organized Albanian resistance in 1479, "about 10 thousand Turkish soldiers started from Vlorë and landed in Italy, where they captured the citadel of Otranto" in the kingdom of Naples.[21] The Turks were driven out of Otranto in 1481.

During the nearly five centuries of life under the Turks, the Albanian people continued to take up arms from time to time against the occupiers. At the same time, many Albanians took advantage of opportunities available to them to rise to positions of great power and influence in the administration of the Ottoman Empire. At least twenty-seven grand viziers or "prime ministers" of the empire were of Albanian origin—a remarkably large number in proportion to the size of the Albanian population when measured against the total population of the empire.[22]

The modern Albanian state dates from 1912, when the venerable aristocrat Ismail Qemal Bey proclaimed Albania independent from the Turks in the city of Vlorë on November 28 of that year. A stirring cry went up from the delegates who had assembled there from all parts of the country as Qemal raised Albania's flag, the same flag under which Skënderbeu had fought the Turks nearly five centuries earlier.[23] Following recognition of the new state by the Great Powers of Europe in 1913, Wilhelm Wied, a German prince and Prussian army captain, was installed as Albania's ruler. The prince arrived in Albania in March 1914 but left six months later in the wake of the turmoil created in the Balkans and Europe by the outbreak of the First World War. The new nation experienced the trauma of the invading armies of Serbia, Greece, Italy, and Austria during the war and threats of dismemberment after the war.

In June 1924, roughly ten years after Prince Wied quit his throne, Bishop Fan S. Noli, an American-educated clergyman from Boston and founder of the Albanian Orthodox Church in America, was proclaimed prime minister of

Albania. But like Wied's, Noli's reign came to an end six months later (December 1924) when Ahmed Zog, a tribal leader from the Mati region in north-central Albania, drove the bishop out of the country. In 1928 Zog proclaimed himself king of Albania and ruled the country until 1939. On April 7, 1939, Benito Mussolini, to whom he had become increasingly indebted economically and militarily, ordered Italian troops into Albania and forced King Zog into exile. He died in Paris in 1961, leaving behind Queen Geraldine and their only heir, Leka, who is currently the pretender to the Albanian throne.

We will conclude this sketch of Albania and her people with a note on the religion and character of Albanians. Christianity appeared on Albanian soil about the second century, when mention is made of the existence of underground Christian groups in Dyrrahion (Durrës) and Aulon (Vlorë). It was therefore "during the Roman rule that Christianity was introduced into Albania."[24] For a while, the new religion had to compete with the cult of Mithra, the Persian god of light, which had spread into Albania. By the fourth century, however, Christianity emerged victorious and became the official religion of the land. The event reflected the triumph of the Christian faith over all the Roman Empire, in consequence of Emperor Constantine's proclamation of Christianity in 313 as the official religion of the empire.

Although Albania became a part of the Eastern (Byzantine) Roman Empire in 395, it belonged to the Roman see until 734 when Leo I, emperor of Byzantium, detached it from Rome and gave it to the partriarchate of Constantinople. In the course of the centuries that followed, Constantinople's hold on Albania weakened progressively, with the result that by the fifteenth century "Albania was preponderantly Roman Catholic."[25] In other words, when Skënderbeu rebelled against the Turks, Albania was a Catholic country. During the Ottoman occupation of their country, Albanians turned increasingly to the Islam faith. By the twentieth century, the majority of the Albanian population had become Moslem, a condition that is unique among the nations of Europe. According to the 1945 census in Albania, 72.8 percent of the country's population was Moslem, 17.1 percent Orthodox Christian, and 10.1 percent Catholic.

The character of the Albanian people is the product, of course, of many forces: historical, political, geographic, social, and economic. The mountain fastness of their land tended to isolate them from social and commercial intercourse with the outside world. This, plus the fact that they lived largely free of control by a central government through most of their history, helped to breed in them a strong spirit of independence and individualism. According to Konitza, individualism is "the most conspicuous characteristic of the Albanians, and one without the knowledge of which their history remains a mystery."²⁶ The fact, too, that Albania has experienced waves of conquests and domination by foreign powers through many centuries has made Albanians highly suspicious of neighboring states and sensitive to the slightest threats to their independence and ethnic identity.

Yet, on a person-to-person level, Albanians are known for their hospitality to strangers, as well as to one another. Edith Durham, an English author, illustrates this character trait of the Albanians with a story from personal experience. While traveling in northern Albania in the early part of our century, she visited the mud hut of a poor mountaineer. She was greeted with courtly grace by her ragged host, who said to her: "We are poor. Bread, salt, and our hearts is all we can offer, but you are welcome to stay as long as you wish."²⁷

A century earlier, another English author, the poet Lord Byron, wrote from southern Albania to friends back home that he found the Albanians to be "brave, unquestionably honest and loyal," and that Albanian women were "very beautiful." Indeed, Albanians have a reputation for their sense of loyalty, as well as of pride and honor. It was not by chance that Albanians were chosen to serve as the bodyguards of the sultans of Turkey. This refined sense of honor of the Albanian people, which they call *besa*, is rooted in the customs and traditions of their society. It is based on the Code of Lek Dukagjin, a fifteenth-century Albanian feudal lord and contemporary of Skënderbeu, who formulated the body of unwritten, customary laws that governed the lives of Albanian highlanders until recent times.

To be sure, Albanians are afflicted with vices as well, as their detractors have been quick to point out. The late Soviet leader Khrushchev, for example, complained of the stubbornness of the Albanians, using as evidence his dealings with Albania's communist leaders. Others have accused them of being a mercenary people, quick-tempered, violent, ruthless, boorish, and unforgiving toward those who offend or injure them.

Whatever the accuracy or validity of this tableau of Albanian character traits, the significant fact is that, despite their small numbers, they have managed to preserve their language, culture, and ethnic identity; in short, to survive as a distinct ethnic group in the face of overwhelming odds. If survival is a virtue, that is no small achievement. In any case, it is probably just this particular mixture of attractive and unattractive qualities, of virtues and vices, in the makeup of their character that makes the Albanians a people of more than usual interest and fascination to the outside world.

2
How the Partisans Seized Power

The Albanian people have hacked their way through history, sword in hand.

Enver Hoxha

The contemporary Albanian state grew out of a fierce and costly Partisan struggle during World War II. Albania became a socialist state via a successful guerrilla resistance against the Italian and German occupation armies and the defeat of domestic opposition forces, including nationalist, monarchist, and factional leftist groups. Albania was the only country in Eastern Europe where not a single Soviet soldier set foot in the course of the Red Army's rollback of Nazi power on the eastern front and in the Balkans. It was only in August of 1944, just four months before the liberation of the country, that an advisory military mission from Moscow arrived in Albania at the invitation of the Partisans.[1]

It may be asked: How and why did a communist revolutionary movement in a minor theater of war triumph over its enemies, both foreign and domestic, whose combined resources in men and arms were much superior to its own? In other words, how did the Partisans seize power in Albania? The question whether Albania would remain in the Western sphere of influence or become a potentially hostile outpost of the socialist bloc in the Balkans depended largely on the outcome of the civil war that raged in the country during the Second World War. The fact that Albania became a socialist country, thus coming under the influence of a totalitarian, anti-West power bloc, is of some consequence for the politics of the Balkans and the Mediterranean area, as well as for East-West relations in general in postwar Europe. Albania's geographic and strategic importance has long been recognized by statesmen and military leaders, from the time of the Roman Empire, through the Crusades, the dominion of the Ottoman Turks in Europe, down to the modern era. The country is a natural gateway to the Balkans and moreover commands the entrance to the Mediterranean from the Adriatic Sea.

The Political Situation Prior to the Formation of the Albanian CP

The fact that communist underground activity began in Albania in the early 1930s, some ten years before the founding of the Albanian Communist Party (ACP),[2] and grew steadily through the decade signaled an emerging contradiction in Albanian society; namely, the increasing alienation of various segments of the population from the government headed by King Zog. In the social order during Zog's rule, political power rested with the land-owning beys, the tribal chieftains or *bairaktars*, and a few wealthy merchants. The balance of power between "the establishment forces" on the one hand and dissident elements on the other hand, including communists, social democrats, pro-Fascists, and others, rested heavily in favor of the former, as long as Zog was the head of state.

The situation changed when Italy invaded Albania in 1939, forcing King Zog to flee his throne. With the expulsion of Zog, the coalition of forces on which his power rested quickly collapsed, leaving the country without a cohesive political institution, which might have served as a rallying point for resisting the invaders and as a foundation for the political system that was to emerge following the regaining of liberty and independence. A power vacuum was thus created, which the various anti-Italian and anti-Zog forces sought naturally to fill. The stage was set for an internal power struggle in the country.

For some three years following the Italian invasion, this struggle was mostly a war of words among the contending parties, and it was perhaps an open question at this point whether the struggle would be resolved peacefully or through a violent civil war. The nature of the struggle was conditioned by a variety of factors, among them the programs, organization, and leadership of the contending parties. Yet, important as these were, it was the external factors, brought into being by World War II, that played the more significant role in the development and outcome of the struggle. As a consequence of the global conflict, the power struggle within Albania became a part of the larger conflict between the Allies and the Fascist powers and brought into play forces that in the end decided the outcome of the struggle in favor of the Partisans.

Above all, Hitler's attack on the Soviet Union in June 1941 caused great indignation among Albanian communists and furnished them with a compelling motive to organize into a single political force. For until then, the Albanian communist movement consisted of some eight minuscule groups that were badly split among themselves. Albanian ideologists have noted that "The entry of the Soviet Union in the war accelerated the founding of the Albanian Communist Party...."[3] In fact, less than five months after the entry of the USSR in the war, the more influential of the communist groups—particularly the Korçë and Shkodër groups—submerged their differences and in November 1941 founded the Albanian Communist Party, a momentous event in the history of the Albanian nation. In this task, the Albanian communists received considerable help from the Yugoslav Communist Party (YCP). The leadership of the YCP calculated that it would be to its advantage to have an anti-Axis resistance movement in Albania, led by an Albanian CP.

Let us consider then, how the communist-led Partisan movement developed—with hardly any awareness by the outside world—to become, within three years, the supreme and unchallenged political force in Albania.[4]

The Partisan Movement

According to the Albanian communists, the two major tasks the newly founded Communist Party set for itself were the liberation of the country from the Fascist occupiers and the destruction of the feudal-bourgeois social order— Zog's power base—to be followed by the establishment of a democratic government of the people.[5] Both of these objectives were to be accomplished through an uncompromising guerrilla-type warfare, a method of war eminently suited to the rugged terrain of Albania. The all-out armed struggle thus encompassed a national goal (the liberation of the country) and a political goal (the seizure of power by the communists).

The occupiers were first the Italian invaders and later—following Italy's surrender in September 1943—the German army. The feudal-bourgeois opposition was represented, in the view of the communists, by *Balli Kombëtar* (The National Front), a conservative group opposed to both communists and monarchy; *Legaliteti* (Legality), which favored the return to power of Albania's prewar monarch, King Ahmed Zog; and the various Albanian puppet governments that served Italian and German occupation forces. The communists had also to struggle against the Trotskyist Left; namely, the *Zjarri* (Fire) group and elements of a larger and more powerful faction known as *Të Rinjtë* (Youth).

In embarking on their drive for power, the communists carried on a relentless struggle on three fronts: the political, the diplomatic, and the military. The three fronts meshed together, but the political struggle generally took priority over the other two, serving at all times as the rationale and guiding principle for all military actions and diplomatic activities.

The Political Struggle

The political war took the form of an energetic and well-organized propaganda campaign, carried out by dedicated Party cadres and aimed at popularizing the armed struggle against the Fascist enemy, discrediting opposition groups such as *Balli*, building up the image of the Soviet Union, advertising the victories of the Red Army against the Nazis, and generating sympathy and support for the communist cause.[6] This "war of words" was carried on in towns and villages, at public gatherings, and in private homes, not infrequently in face-to-face competition with representatives of *Balli*, the communists' only serious rival for power.[7] In the grim propaganda war, which often made enemies of neighboring villages and turned members of the same family against one another, the communist missionaries pressed their case with fanatic zeal, using persuasion and intimidation to great effect.[8] Communist agitation cadres presented the Partisans as the true patriots and as the country's only hope for liberation from Fascism. While armed struggle against the Fascist occupiers was the main theme of the communist agitators, they also told their listeners that victory for the Partisans would mean political power for the people, confiscation of "the large estates of the feudal chiefs and the accumulated wealth of merchant speculators, and ... land reform."[9]

Beginning in 1942, the Party's struggle on the political front gathered momentum, drawing increasing numbers of people into the Partisan movement. Communist sources note that the stream of volunteers included intellectuals, women, and shopkeepers, but most of all peasants and workers. According to Shehu, currently Albania's prime minister:

The bulk of those who filled the ranks of [the Partisan] army were peasants ... and workers. This was not casual [accidental]. This was the logical consequence of the age-long oppression of the peasants and workers. [They] had borne the greater share of the cruel oppression of the former regimes and fascism.[10]

In line with classic communist theory, the Party strategy for victory called for the alliance of the working class with the peasantry. Party historians affirm that the worker-peasant alliance constituted the foundation of the Partisan movement, both politically and militarily, with the peasants providing the bulk of the manpower for the movement, while the workers provided the leadership. A distinguishing and highly significant feature of the worker-peasant movement was its youthfulness, for communist cadres succeeded in attracting into the movement the overwhelming majority of the youth, first within the cities and later in the countryside. The youth became the most active force of the National Liberation War.

Following the formation of the Party in 1941, perhaps the most important development on the political front was the holding of the "National Liberation

Conference" on September 16, 1942. The conference was held at Pezë, a village near Tiranë. Invitations were sent to all nationalist leaders in the country, with the intention of forming a common, popular front embracing all the forces that were committed to the liberation of the country from the Italian occupiers. Although influential nationalists like Midhat Frashëri and Ali Këlcyra did not attend, the Pezë conference succeeded in creating the National Liberation Front (NLF), with a leadership which included communists as well as several influential noncommunist figures, among them Abas Kupi, a powerful chieftain from north-central Albania. The conference essentially confirmed the leading role of the communist-led Partisans in the liberation struggle and has been hailed by communist historians as the Party's first great political victory. As a consequence of the Pezë conference, there was a rapid increase in the flow of volunteers to the Partisan formations—a sign that the Party's struggle on the political front was bearing fruit.

Diplomatic Maneuvers
The second component of the communist plan for seizing power in Albania related to the diplomatic front. Albanian communist leaders realized from the beginning of their drive for power that they could not hope to reach their objective if they fought an insulated war, depending solely on their own efforts and resources for victory over their enemies. They were conscious of the need, at the very least, for the moral and psychological support of allies in order to cope successfully with the armed confrontation that loomed ahead. The struggle on the diplomatic front, therefore, called for efforts by the Party to link the Partisan movement with other popular liberation movements in the Balkans and, in addition, to obtain recognition by the Allied powers of England, the United States, and the Soviet Union. Accordingly, the first proclamation to the Albanian people issued by the Albanian Communist Party in November 1941 stressed the need to promote close collaboration with the Balkan peoples, particularly the Serbian, Greek, Montenegrin, and Macedonian peoples who had risen against the Italian-German invaders.[11]

The most important link, by far, that the Albanian Partisans forged with their Balkan neighbors was with the Yugoslav Partisans, led by J. B. Tito. Albanian sources admit that "close links were established between the Communist Party of Albania and the Communist Party of Yugoslavia."[12] Published Yugoslav accounts on relations between the Yugoslav and Albanian Partisan movements maintain in general that Tito's political and military representatives wielded great influence in the hierarchy of the Albanian Party.

Hoxha himself reportedly acknowledged the important role played by the Yugoslav communists in the successful struggle for power by the Albanian Communist Party. He is quoted as saying in 1944 that the "valuable advice" and "unceasing aid" given by YCP was "a chief factor in the formation, development, and strengthening of [the Albanian] Party."[13]

This does not necessarily mean that without the aid of the Yugoslavs there would have been no Albanian CP. In fact, Dušan Mugoša, Tito's personal emissary to Albania, said in an interview in May 1972 that while the Yugoslavs were helpful "in establishing ... cooperation among the various [Albanian] communist groups" this should "not be interpreted to mean that the Albanians could not accomplish this task themselves."[14] He added that Albanian communist leaders "would have, in time, solved their administrative problems"; in other words, they would have buried their differences and formed the Albanian CP. Even the organ of *Balli Kombëtar* in exile stated in an article published in late 1976 that the arrival of two top YCP emissaries in wartime Albania, Popović and Mugoša, "hastened the unification of the [various communist] groups ... into one party,"[15] thus implying that the ACP would in time have been founded, even without direct outside assistance.

Following the break with Tito in 1958, however, Tiranë revised drastically the history of wartime relations between Albanian and Yugoslav communist parties and challenged the validity of Yugoslav claims that the YCP gave extensive aid to the Albanian communists, in the form of political guidance and the organizing and training of Partisan guerrilla units.[16] Tiranë nevertheless acknowledged the presence in wartime Albania of such YCP leaders as Svetozar Vukmanović-Tempo, Miladin Popović, and Velimir Stojnić but mentioned with approval only Popović, secretary of the Regional Committee of Kosovo. Popović was "an international communist" who fought heroically to the end for the Albanian people and Party.

By the end of 1942, Albanian Partisans had made a strong enough impact in the Balkan theater of war to attract favorable attention from the leaders of the Allied coalition. Thus, in a statement issued in December 1942, Cordell Hull, then U.S. secretary of state, said: "The struggles of the various partisan units operating in Albania against the common foe have given rise to our highest admiration and esteem."[17] Similar statements were issued by British and Soviet government spokesmen. The communist-led Partisans had won a major diplomatic victory. These expressions of solidarity by the Allied leaders boosted the morale of the Partisans and subsequently led to military aid to the NLF from the Allied Mediterranean Command.

The Military Buildup

The third component of the communist strategy for victory in the internal power struggle concerned the military buildup of the Partisan movement. In a practical sense, the struggles on the political and diplomatic fronts were but two aspects of the military front, for in the end it was military might that was going to count most in the Partisan drive for power. Indeed, the chief task entrusted to the National Liberation Front, following its establishment, was the development of the military power of the Partisans.

In line with this strategy, the Communist Party pressed energetically to build up the Partisan forces. In 1942, the Partisans already had begun to organize in *çetas*, or guerrilla units of fifty to sixty troops each. By 1943 the *çetas* were combined to form battalions, and in July of that year the General Council of the NLF met in Labinot, a village near Elbasan in central Albania, and proclaimed the founding (July 10) of the Albanian National Liberation Army (ANLA). Spiro Moisiu was appointed commander-in-chief, while Secretary-General of the ACP Enver Hoxha was chosen political commissar of the Army General Staff.

The next phase in the development of ANLA began in August 1943, when battalions were merged to form brigades. The first of these larger army units, known as the First Shock Brigade—the most celebrated of all Partisan detachments—was placed under the command of Mehmet Shehu, a veteran of the Spanish Civil War. Shehu proved to be the most daring and skillful commander in the Partisan army and is believed to have made the greatest single contribution to the military effort that brought the communists to power.

A further phase in ANLA's development occurred in May of 1944 at the meeting of the First Anti-Fascist National Liberation Congress, held in the town of Përmet in southern Albania. The Përmet congress introduced military ranks in the army, an action that converted the Partisan forces into a regular people's army. This move did much to raise the self-esteem of the guerrillas and strengthen their faith in final victory. By this time the Partisan army, according to communist sources, had grown to 35,000 fighting men and women. Consequently, shortly after the Përmet congress, the NLF leadership began to organize the Partisan forces into divisions and even "army corps." At the height of its strength, ANLA is said to have numbered 70,000 troops— including 6,000 women—organized in three army corps, consisting of eight divisions and twenty-six brigades.[18]

The preceding discussion of ANLA reveals the progressive, step-by-step growth of the Partisan army over the three-year period from 1942 through

1944. This was the military side of ANLA. But the more important factor was the political framework within ANLA's structure. For the Party in fact operated as a parallel organization within the army structure. Thus, at the head of each fighting unit stood a military officer and a representative of the Party—the political commissar. Together they coordinated and directed the activities of the troops and were jointly responsible for the troops' combat efficiency and ideological education.

Nor was it necessary to be a Party member in order to join the Partisans. Being a Partisan was not synonymous with being a communist. The great majority of the guerrillas were noncommunists. Indeed, Party directives specified that, while political commissars and their deputies had to be Party members, it was preferable that military commanders did not hold Party membership.[19] This policy was desirable, from the communist point of view, because it made the Party less visible in the eyes of rank-and-file Partisans and the public at large and helped to project the image of a broad-based nationalist liberation movement, as opposed to a strictly sectarian and ideological movement. At the same time such a policy enabled the Party to maintain firm control over the army.[20]

The Party leadership was anxious to develop and preserve correct relations with the armed forces and took care to assign only its best cadres to do political work in the army. Such work aimed above all at maintaining high morale among the troops, both on the battlefront and in their conduct toward the people. The story of the Partisans, like that of all guerrilla movements, is a saga of great adversity, trials and deprivations. But political indoctrination by Party cadres apparently had prepared them for such trials, imbuing them with a high degree of discipline and a remarkable capacity for endurance of suffering and pain and for self-sacrifice. This attitude and spirit is illustrated by the following passage, taken from the diary of a nineteen-year-old Partisan: "We have begun a fierce and grave struggle. But we know that this is no dead-end road. . . . [The Party] teaches us to fight for the people. We know what awaits us: suffering, trials, perhaps death; but we know also that at the end of this road . . . lies victory. . . . We will win!"[21]

The other facet of Partisan morale concerned relations with the people. Those relations had to be correct in every respect, for "any violations [of Party regulations] such as stealing, entering homes without permission, raping of women, killing without reason, and taking personal revenges" were punishable "on the spot"; that is, by death.[22] This draconian policy was in keeping with the policy that ANLA was "a true army of the people"; consequently, its conduct among the people had to be exemplary.

This account is a discussion of the Albanian communists' three-pronged drive for seizing power in the country. It was a strategy that called for a determined and energetic, yet disciplined struggle against their foes on the political, the diplomatic, and the military fronts.

On the Eve of the Civil War

The Partisans' first organized armed attacks, which began in 1942, were directed against the Italian army of occupation. In November 1942, however, Midhat Frashëri and other influential nationalists formed a new resistance group, the *Balli Kombëtar* organization (*BK*).[23] During the first half of 1943, both the Partisan and *Balli* guerrilla units carried out operations against the occupiers. Indeed, on occasion, ANLA and *Balli* commanders exchanged information and coordinated their attacks on the Italians. But localized military cooperation did not extend to the political plane. The communist leadership of the NLF and the top echelon of *Balli* nourished a deep distrust of each other's motives, programs, and goals. This distrust surfaced, among other ways, in bitter polemics between the two sides. The propaganda war escalated sharply in the spring of 1943. The nationalists accused the Partisans of being agents of the Soviet Union and fighting recklessly, without regard for enemy reprisals against civilians or destruction of property. The communists in turn accused *Balli* of sabotaging the war effort, collaborating with the Fascist enemy, and seeking to wreck the NLF by spreading lies about communist battle tactics, political aims, and the morals of female Partisans.[24] By summer of 1943 tensions between the two sides had risen greatly, and the country seemed to be on the verge of civil war.

At this point, the communists proposed to the *Balli* leaders that they hold a joint conference with a view to resolving their differences peacefully and furthering the cause of national liberation. The *Balli* leaders accepted the invitation, and delegations of the two resistance movements met in the village of Mukaj, not far from Tiranë, on August 1 and 2, 1943. It was a fateful conference, for on its outcome depended not merely the course that the struggle for national liberation would take but whether the question of political power in the nation would be resolved peacefully, by means of elections, or violently, by means of a destructive civil war. The two sides reached agreement just as the news of Mussolini's fall from power reached the delegates. The essentials of the Mukaj agreement were the formation of a common resistance front against the occupiers; the creation of an ethnic Albanian state, including the Kosovo region in Yugoslavia and the Çamëria region in Greece; and free postwar elections to determine the country's form of government. It appeared that the threat of a fratricidal war had been evaded.

Within a week, however, after the signing of the Mukaj agreement, Enver Hoxha said that the communist delegation had "capitulated completely" to the *Balli Kombëtar* and that the nationalists were planning to seize political power when Italy surrendered. He denounced the *Balli* organization and declared the agreement with the nationalists null and void.[25] It could be that Hoxha's action was influenced by the Yugoslav representatives in Albania, who very likely objected to the clause for an "ethnic Albania" that was to include Kosovo. As a result of Hoxha's action, the lines of communication with *Balli* were cut off. A point of no return had been reached. Henceforth, the differences between the Partisans and the nationalists were to be settled by force.

The Partisans Take Power

On September 8, 1943, Italy capitulated to the Allies, and some 15,000 Italian troops in Albania surrendered to the Partisans. Of these, 1,500 joined the Partisan formations, after organizing into a contingent called the "Antonio Gramsci" battalion. The Italians were quickly replaced by the German occupation army, which reportedly totaled 70,000 troops.[26]

In consequence of the new situation that had developed, the Partisan General Staff issued a call for the general mobilization and uprising of the Albanian people. At about the same time, the communist leaders made the decision to "crush" the *Balli* movement.[27] Shortly after, Partisan forces began to attack the *Balli* contingents, and the flames of civil war started to spread throughout southern Albania.[28] Unable to withstand the Partisan assault with its own forces and seeing that its survival was at stake, *Balli Kombëtar* turned increasingly to the Germans for support.[29]

During the winter of 1943-1944, the *Balli* forces, in close collaboration with the Germans and the gendarmerie of the puppet government of Tiranë, mounted a general offensive against the Partisans, with the aim of destroying the NLF completely. The anti-Partisan forces reportedly totaled 45,000 troops. Opposing them was a Partisan force of approximately 20,000 troops. Communist sources admit that the enemy offensive inflicted severe losses on some Partisan units and that the Partisan forces were "often encircled by the enemy." In fact, the General Staff of the Partisan army, including Enver

Hoxha, was surrounded by enemy troops in early December 1943 and did not break out of encirclement until March 1944.[30] Nevertheless, the *Balli* offensive failed. The Partisans survived, primarily by making a skillful withdrawal into the mountains. Mehmet Shehu has remarked that "Our mountains have always been the age-long allies of our people" and that "during the war for national liberation our mountains became the impregnable refuge of [the] partisans."[31]

The *Balli* leaders relied on the professional training, combat experience, and superior equipment and firepower of the German army to deal a mortal blow to their hated communist foe. But while they profited militarily by their alliance with the Germans, they lost heavily on the political front. For the communists made skillful use of *Balli*'s collaboration with the Nazis to turn the Albanian public against the nationalists and in favor of the Partisans. The Party's official history notes that it was the support of the masses of the people that saved the National Liberation Army from annihilation during the critical winter period of 1943-1944.

In June 1944, German and *Balli* troops, estimated by the communists at 50,000, made the last major effort to annihilate the Partisan movement, but again they failed. The communists responded by initiating a counterattack. On June 14, 1944, Hoxha ordered a general ANLA offensive against the German occupiers and "the traitors of the country," which did not halt until the *Balli Kombëtar* was completely destroyed. The end came in November 1944, when the *Balli* leaders fled Albania.

In the meantime, a new opponent had risen to challenge the communist bid for power. Abas Kupi had resigned from the General Council of the NLF and in September 1943 announced the formation of a new organization, the *Legaliteti*. Kupi was a member of the NLF delegation that negotiated the Mukaj agreement with *Balli*. His split with the Partisans, therefore, in the wake of Hoxha's denunciation of the Mukaj protocol, presumably was prompted by Hoxha's move against *Balli*. Kupi was an illiterate but respected Geg chieftain and the principal rallying figure for Zogist forces in northern Albania.

Following Kupi's defection from the NLF, the communists accused him of being a tool of the British mission in Albania and said that his movement, the *Legaliteti*, was founded "upon the initiative of the English . . . with the object of restoring Zog's regime in Albania."[32] Accordingly, the NLF leadership declared Kupi "an enemy of the Albanian people," and on June 26, 1944, Hoxha ordered the First ANLA Division "to attack and liquidate" the *Legaliteti* forces. The Partisans met little resistance from the loosely organized, poorly equipped, and weakly motivated Zogist bands. By early autumn, the Partisans were in effective control of nearly all of northern Albania.

Thus, within a year following the inception of the civil war, the communists had vanquished their class enemies, grouped in the *Balli Kombëtar*, their major rival, and *Legaliteti*. Beginning in September 1944, German occupation forces began to withdraw from Albania. On the twenty-ninth of November, as the last German troops left the country, the communists proclaimed the liberation of Albania from the Fascist forces and the domestic reaction. Partisan forces paraded in triumph through the boulevards of Tiranë. Within three years following the formation of the Party, the communists had reached their goal of seizing power through the sword, and the small semifeudal nation of Albania stood on the threshold of a new era—that of socialism and the dictatorship of the proletariat.

Concluding Remarks

In his study of revolutions, covering a period of several centuries, Chalmers Johnson found that they could be grouped into six types, the last of which he calls the "Militarized Mass Insurrection."[33] This is a type of guerrilla warfare that one commentator has described as "a new phenomenon of the twentieth century in that it is a deliberately planned mass revolutionary war, guided by a dedicated elite. The outcome of guerrilla warfare is determined by political attitudes, not military strategy or materiel, for the rebels are wholly dependent on broad popular support...."[34] Examples of this type of insurrection are said to be the Algerian revolution and the communist revolutions in Yugoslavia, China, and Vietnam.

To these may be added the communist revolution in Albania, for it, too, answers closely to the description given above. The manner in which the Partisan insurrection unfolded fits in also with the four-stage process described by Rex Hopper.[35] Springing from a generalized feeling of social malaise and uncoordinated mass unrest (stage 1), the revolutionary movement in Albania next crystallized into organized opposition led by the Communist Party (stage 2), fought a successful struggle against all rivals (stage 3), and finally installed itself in power in the name of the proletariat (stage 4).

Displaying keen political sense, the Partisans took advantage of the profound contradiction in the Albanian society between the old hierarchy of power and privilege—chiefly the landowning beys and the bairaktars—and an impoverished peasantry, plus a new generation of youth, imbued with a new mentality, new values, and eager for radical change in the direction of a modern, progressive society. They perceived that the time was ripe for the transformation of Albanian society, in response to popular pressures and aspirations.

The communists won the war in part because they waged a more effective struggle than the nationalists on the political, diplomatic, and military fronts. Many political opponents of the communists, now living in exile, agree that the Partisan army proved superior as a fighting force to the *Balli* irregulars. Compared with the oldish *Balli* forces, the Partisan army had the advantage of youth on its side, mobility, and control of the countryside. Then, too, the establishment by the Partisans of bases in secure mountain hideouts contributed greatly to their victory over the nationalist forces. Above all, the Partisans had the guidance of a disciplined and highly motivated corps of political cadres that was resolved to win, even at the cost of vast destruction of life and property.

Morale, of course, played an important part in the outcome of the struggle. In this respect also the Partisan forces excelled their nationalist enemies. Their faith in the ultimate victory of their cause was continually nourished by news of the victorious advance of the Red Army against the Germans on the eastern front and by the Allied propaganda media that hailed their struggle against the Axis occupation troops.

In retrospect, the fighting in Albania during World War II seems to have been mainly a struggle for political power between the communists and the nationalists and only secondarily a struggle against the Italian and German occupiers.[36] Both sides understood by 1943 that the Axis powers were going to lose the war and would inevitably withdraw from Albania, even if there were no resistance movement in the country. As a result of this evaluation, both resistance groups changed strategy, and instead of focusing on the Axis armies, each sought to gain supremacy over the other. Even so, the Partisans did most of the fighting against the occupiers, and it was for this reason that they received the greatest amount of aid from the Anglo-Americans, both material and moral. They used a large portion of that aid to prosecute the struggle against their rivals all the more effectively.

Summing up, then, the Partisans won the war as a result of a propitious conjunction of internal and external developments, aided by their own skillful strategy, fighting spirit, ruthlessness, and total determination to take power.

3
The Nature of the Albanian Communist Party

According to classic communist doctrine, of all the countries in Europe Albania was the least qualified candidate for communism. With a backward, semifeudal social and economic order, Albania in 1944 was the farthest removed of any European nation from the industrialized, capitalist society that Marx believed to be a prerequisite for transition to socialism and communism. Yet, for the past three decades Albania has been ruled by the most doctrinaire and orthodox of all the ruling communist parties in Europe.

The Dissenting Voice in European Communism

An examination of the current positions of the Albanian Community Party—known officially as the Albanian Party of Labor (APL)—reveals that on a surprising number of issues and developments, the Party stands apart from all the communist parties in Eastern Europe. Indeed, in some respects it stands out from all the other parties in the socialist world.

Unlike other East European parties which, in the wake of the Twentieth Congress of the Communist Party of the Soviet Union (CPSU) in 1956, abandoned Stalinist practices—to a greater or lesser degree—in their domestic and foreign policies, the Albanian Party successfully resisted all pressures to decentralize and liberalize its policies. Consequently, Albania at present has the distinction of being the last stronghold of Stalinism in Europe. The only Moslem country in the world to have adopted communism to date, Albania is currently the most isolated country in Europe ideologically, politically, and in most areas of her cultural life. She attained to this position as a result of the break between APL and CPSU in 1961 and the subsequently hostile foreign policy that the Albanian Party has pursued ever since, toward both East and West Europe. On the question of the Warsaw Pact as well, the Albanian Party stands apart from other East European parties.[1] Following the invasion of Czechoslovakia by members of the Warsaw Pact in 1968, Albania made history in East Europe when she formally withdrew from the pact in September of that year—the only East European country to sever ties with the Warsaw Pact. The leaders of the APL felt compelled to denounce the pact, in the conviction that the East European collective security system had become an instrument of aggression in the hands of the Soviet leaders, against the very member states it was designed to defend.

Contrary to all the socialist countries in East Europe, the Albanian Party leaders refused to take part in the European Security Conference that was held in Helsinki in July 1975. Their dramatic boycott of the conference underscored the Albanian Party's rejection of détente politics in Europe and all efforts to relax tensions between NATO and the Warsaw Pact.[2] Far from supporting the trend toward détente, the Albanian Party at the midpoint of the 1970s stood out among the East European communist parties as the lone defender and propagator of Cold War politics.

On the issue of Sino-Soviet relations, APL held the unique position among Europe's communist parties of being the "fiercest enemy" of the USSR and until recently the closest ally of China. A major reason for the Albanian Party's total hostility toward the Soviets was its position on the question of revolution versus peaceful coexistence with regard to relations between socialist and capitalist countries. Unlike other communist parties in Europe that had long ago accepted peaceful coexistence as the general line of the socialist camp in its relations with the capitalist West, the Albanian Party put its trust in revolution; that is, in armed struggle and the violent seizure of political power as the only reliable strategy for insuring the victory of socialism and communism over the capitalist world.

A striking fact about APL which is not generally known—even among some specialists in communist affairs—is that it was the only communist movement in East Europe that seized power without the direct aid of the Red Army. Albania achieved liberation from the Nazi-Fascist occupation armies by her own efforts, though she received considerable military materiel and moral support from the Anglo-American Allies.

Western tourists to Albania almost invariably comment on the fact that there are no churches or mosques open for public worship in that country. This has been a feature of Albanian society since 1967. In this respect also the Albanian Party stands alone in East Europe—and indeed in the entire socialist world—for it is the only communist party in existence to have institutionalized atheism. In the area of "manners and morals," too, the Albanian Party occupies an extreme position, compared with other East European parties. Tourists to Albania have reported that bearded and long-haired men, for example, were not allowed to enter the country unless they first groomed themselves in a "respectable" manner. That is another distinct feature of Albanian communism. For although the Albanian Party leaders abolished the religious establishment and proudly proclaimed Albania as "the first atheist country in the world," in their public attitude toward morality and personal habits and tastes they project an image that is closer to that of the Grand Inquisitor than to modern libertarians and advocates of the sexual revolution.

As a consequence, Albania stands out as the country with the most puritanical communism in East Europe.

Finally, visitors to Albania are fascinated by the virtual absence of automobile traffic in Tiranë and the rest of the country. It is a unique phenomenon among the countries of Eastern Europe, and a reflection of Albania's economic system. The absence of private cars in Albania is chiefly the result of the economic policy that has been practiced by the Party leaders in their efforts to industrialize the country. The Albanian leadership directs a highly centralized economic system in a relatively undeveloped country where priority has been given to the development of heavy industry, rather than to the production of consumer goods, least of all "luxuries" such as civilian cars.

In all of these respects, therefore, the Albanian Party of Labor stood out as the dissenting voice in European communism—a loner party that not only seemed convinced of the correctness of its lonely path but presented Albania as the model for the future social and political development of the nations of Europe.

Mainsprings of APL's Politics

It seems worthwhile at this point to determine as far as possible the mainsprings or primary motives that underlie the Party's activity.

Perhaps the most important factor in this regard is the nationalism of the Albanian Party leaders. The evidence for nationalism as a motive force in the policies and actions of the APL's leaders is incontestable. It is present in the homage they pay to Albania's national figures, above all to Skënderbeu—the medieval National Hero—and to the leading patriots of Albania's national movement for independence, such as Kristoforidhi and Naim Frashëri, writer-patriots; Abdyl Frashëri, statesman; Isa Boletini and Çerçiz Topulli, freedom fighters; and Ismail Qemal, the venerable patriot who in 1912 proclaimed Albania's independence from the Turks. It is apparent in the attention they have given to the observance of important anniversaries in the country's history, as, for example, the League of Prizren, 1878, which sparked the movement for independence; the Congress of Monastir (now Bitola in Macedonia), 1908, a milestone in the unification of the Albanian alphabet; and the Battle of Vlorë, 1920, which resulted in the expulsion of Italian occupation forces from Albanian territory they had seized during World War I. It is evident in the care taken by the regime to preserve national monuments, including castles, towns of unusual historical interest, such as Krujë, Berat, and

Gjirokastër—these have been officially declared "museum cities"—and even certain churches and mosques of rare architectural and artistic value. It manifests itself also in the Party's stress on preserving and enhancing the nation's cultural heritage—the folk costumes, folk songs and dances, and the treasury of national folklore. Truly, there is no lack of data to support the claim that nationalism is a dominant force in the politics of the Albanian Party.

It is perhaps not too difficult to understand why Albanian Party leaders value nationalism and use it to win popular support for their policies. Albanians have been fiercely proud of their country and are renowned for their spirit of independence. They have been conquered many times but never wholly subdued. Albania moreover was the last country in the Balkans to win her independence from the Ottoman Empire. Having emerged from nearly five centuries of Turkish dominion, the Albanian people are understandably jealous of their newly won national independence and sovereignty. The fact, too, that even after 1912 their nation was seriously threatened with partition by the neighboring countries has made them still more nationalistic, wary of foreigners, and extremely sensitive to threats—whether real or imagined—to their national existence and security. Such, it appears, is the background and the soil in which the nationalism of the Albanian Party leadership is rooted, takes its nourishment, and operates as a vital force in contemporary Albanian politics. Patriotic and national feelings and considerations played a major role in the efforts of Albanian Party leaders to resist Yugoslav encroachment on Albania's sovereignty in the 1940s and to weather successfully the unsettling effects of the split with the Soviet Union in the 1960s.

Another motive force that has helped to shape the politics of the Albanian Party is ideology. First Secretary of APL Enver Hoxha has always insisted that the break with Moscow in 1961 was due to ideological and political differences between the two former allies.[3] While that is an oversimplification of the matter, it is nonetheless true that ideology has been one of the more important mainsprings in APL's activity throughout its history. Albanian Party leaders seem convinced that ideology, or the mastery and practice of Marxism-Leninism, is indispensable for victory over the class enemy and for the successful construction of a socialist society. They are persuaded that only correct political ideas can lead to correct political action. Such orientation, they believe, is provided only by the principles of Marxism-Leninism, which are universally true at all times, inasmuch as they derive from the science of dialectical materialism. To be sure, these principles have to be adapted to the particular conditions of the country in which they re applied, but they must not under any circumstances be revised, as the "modern revisionists" have done, under the pretext that this or that principle or doctrine has been outdated by events. The Albanian Party insists that the Marxist-Leninist ideology is a powerful weapon in the hands of communists and an infallible guide to the inevitable triumph of socialism over capitalism. Accordingly, the Party has expended vast energy and resources in propagating its conception of Marxism-Leninism, both at home and abroad.[4]

The Albanian Party's interpretation of Marxist-Leninist ideology is exceptionally orthodox, with the emphasis being placed on the revolutionary aspects of that ideology. The revolutionary world outlook is thus another characteristic feature of the general line of APL. Albanian leaders have long maintained that "revolution is the main trend in the world at present." They claim that Marxism-Leninism is essentially a revolutionary ideology; it is a blueprint for the violent seizure of political power. Consequently, APL draws a clear demarcation line between the forces of revolution and progress on the one hand and the forces of reaction and revisionism which seek to stem the tide of revolutionary change in the world. In the true spirit of the Cold War era, the APL scenario divides the world rather neatly into two distinct, irreconcilable camps that are destined by historical forces to struggle against each other until the old order gives way to the new. The scenario rejects such "anti-Leninist" doctrines as "peaceful coexistence" in the ideological sphere, détente, negotiations, and collaboration between East and West and instead hails the politics of revolution: confrontation, open polemics, and relentless class struggle against the enemies of socialism. From the Albanian Party's viewpoint, the two opposing camps are engaged in a life-and-death struggle that embraces all fronts—political, economic, cultural, and military.

In looking further for an explanation of APL's passionate advocacy of revolutionary politics, one can find helpful clues in Albania's history and in APL's own past. First, the Albanian people are noted for their martial traditions, especially in northern Albania, where until very recently the rifle was a man's "best friend," so to speak. Second, Albania won her independence and defended her territorial integrity against foreign aggression in large part through the force of arms. This historical fact is reflected in Albania today in the oft-quoted slogan of Hoxha, "The Albanian people have hacked their way through history, sword in hand." Third, APL's great trust in arms springs also from the fact that the Party came to power by means of an armed struggle. Albanian leaders point to their successful guerrilla war as proof that only through revolutionary warfare can the working class, the peasantry, and all oppressed peoples of the earth seize political power from the hands of their oppressors.

The fourth mainspring of APL's politics is the commitment to the modernization of Albania. The motive to modernize stems mostly from historical and political factors. The leaders of the Albanian Party of Labor are anxious to overcome Albania's age-old poverty and backwardness—a bitter legacy of her semifeudal past and centuries of Ottoman misrule. They are painfully conscious of the public image of Albania abroad as "the most backward country in Europe" and of the phrase, "darkest Albania," that still circulates abroad.[5] They are eager, therefore, to bring Albania into the twentieth century, as it were, as rapidly as possible. APL ideologists often remark that there are two kinds of liberation, one political, the other socioeconomic. When Albania won her independence in 1912, they say, she achieved only political liberation, and as a result the country's internal conditions hardly changed in the following three decades. It was only in 1944, when the Partisans seized power, that Albania not only regained her political liberation but for the first time in her history embarked on the road of complete social and economic liberation for the Albanian masses.

APL's desire to modernize Albania is rooted also in communist dogma. Being highly doctrinaire communists, Albania's leaders are striving to carry out faithfully Lenin's thesis that "Communism is Soviet [or people's] power, plus electrification." Their objective, it appears, is to make "Marxist-Leninist" Albania a "showcase" of all-round progress in Europe and a concrete and inspiring example of the power of a genuine socialist state.

The method chosen by the Albanian Party for modernizing Albanian society is tight centralism. This is a system of central control that in terms of its severity and the extent of its reach into all aspects of Albanian life probably has no equal in East Europe. "Extremist centralism" thus emerges as another distinguishing character trait of the Albanian Party. Almost from the beginning of APL rule, Hoxha, Mehmet Shehu, and other Party leaders made centralism a guiding principle of their regime. They were convinced that strong centralized rule was indispensable for political stability and the modernization of the country. Centralism in the Albanian context means both centralized planning and direction of the economy and central control of the political, social, and cultural life of the country. It is a form of oligarchy that is intended to insure the Party's "leading role" in all phases of Albanian life. From APL's frame of reference, centralism not only is a valuable administrative technique but serves also a vital political end. It helps to guarantee the "dictatorship of the proletariat" in the Albanian state, a term Party spokesmen define as "rule by the working masses."

There are reasons, of course, why this extremist form of centralism became a dominant feature of the ideology and practice of the Albanian Party. As in so many other instances, these reasons are rooted for the most part in Albania's past. Tight, centralized political authority came rather naturally to a country that in the past had known almost nothing but conditions of near anarchy and autocratic rule. Two other social conditions that prepared the ground for strongly centralized communist rule were the factionalism of the clans and tribes of prewar Albania and the intense localism and provincialism of the population, which served to divide and weaken the country. In addition, the primitive and largely disorganized economic life of presocialist Albania generated strong popular sentiment in favor of a regulated, centralized economic system. Furthermore, in the old society, the average working man and peasant lacked the habits of discipline and industry. Hence, a tight, centralized economy, capable of mobilizing the nation's manpower into a unified labor force, seemed to be the logical solution to the problem of worker indiscipline and lethargy.

The sixth mainspring of APL's activity is its radicalism. The Albanian Party of Labor has gone farther, it appears, than any East European communist party in resorting to radical solutions in the building of socialism. In this regard, APL has lived "by the book," so to speak, for it has consistently sought to be faithful to the letter—if not always to the spirit—of the teachings of Marx and Lenin. In line with orthodox Marxist doctrine, the Albanian Party has nationalized all industry and commerce and collectivized all agriculture. In other words, it socialized the entire wealth of the country, thus completing the transition from private to public ownership of the means of production. The absence of ranks or gradations in the Albanian armed forces is further testimony to the Party's radical bent. The most dramatic and notorious example of the Party's radicalism is its abolition of the religious establishment in the country.[6] Albania's Ideological and Cultural Revolution—carried out over a four-year period (1966-1969)—also testifies to the Party's radical posture in grappling with social, economic, and other problems.

Classic communist ideology has been an important formative influence on APL's radical character. But an even more important influence, perhaps, is to be found in Albania's history. The extreme radicalism of APL is a measure, as well as a product, of the extreme conditions that prevailed in prewar Albania:

the crushing poverty, the overwhelming illiteracy, rampant superstition, blood feuds, and ravaging epidemics, above all malaria and syphilis.[7] To deal effectively with those conditions, Albanian Party leaders apparently found it both reasonable and necessary to take strong measures and develop a certain style of rule and those features that, taken together, make up what we today call Albanian Stalinism.[8]

In identifying the mainsprings of the politics of the Albanian Party of Labor, on both the domestic and foreign levels, we have tried to describe the main features of the Party's character: nationalism, ideology, revolutionary militancy, modernization, centralism, and radicalism. There are other features in APL's political makeup, such as utopianism, conspiracy, nepotism, ruthlessness, puritanism, and even elements of messianism. But these are probably not as important and need not be treated at length here. With the foregoing as a background, let us now examine in some detail the practical experience of APL, especially in relation to recent developments in Albania.

The Politics of APL in Practice

The road traveled by the Albanian Party of Labor since its founding may usefully be divided into three periods or stages. The first stage covered the war years and extended from the founding of the Party on November 8, 1941, to the seizure of power by the Party-controlled National Liberation Front on November 29, 1944. The essential character of this stage was political, since the main aim of the Party at this time was to liberate the country from the Nazi-Fascist occupiers and their Albanian collaborators, regain national independence, and install communist rule.

The second stage covered roughly the first two decades of communist rule in the country (1945-1965). It is the time frame that is commonly referred to by APL historians as the stage of the construction of the economic base of socialism in Albania. During this period the Party leadership was preoccupied chiefly with socioeconomic questions; above all, with programs designed to effect "the public ownership" of the nation's wealth, through the nationalization of industry and commerce and the collectivization of agriculture.

The third stage began in 1966 with the launching of the Ideological and Cultural Revolution and is currently in progress. This stage has been designated by Party ideologists as that of "the complete construction of socialism" in Albania. During this period APL has been and will continue to be concerned mostly with the solution of problems of an ideological and cultural character.

Table 3.1
Growth in Party Membership (1948-1976)

Number and Year of Party Congress	Full Members	Candidate Members	Total	Change over Preceding Congress
First, 1948	29,137	16,245	45,382	–
Second, 1952	–*	–*	44,418	–964
Third, 1956	41,372	7,272	48,644	+4,226
Fourth, 1961	50,802	2,857	53,659	+5,015
Fifth, 1966	63,013	3,314	66,327	+12,668
Sixth, 1971	68,858	18,127	86,985	+20,658
Seventh, 1976	88,000	13,500	101,500	+14,515

Source: Compiled from Hoxha's reports to the respective Party congresses.
*No breakdown of figures given.

The overall goal in this connection is to stamp out "bourgeois and revisionist ideas" from the consciousness of the Albanian masses and to imbue them instead with the communist world outlook and morality. The idea is to create the "new communist man," in preparation for entrance into the communist society that lies somewhere in the distant future.

It is understood that these stages interlink and overlap with one another, since the questions and problems dealt with in one stage have existed in some measure in the other two stages. Nevertheless, there has been a shift of emphasis from political to socioeconomic to ideological and cultural goals in the activity of the Party over the entire period.

As a monolithic political organization of a militant character, APL exercises a monopoly of power in the Albanian regime. Modeled on the 1936 constitution of the Soviet Union, the Party has a three-tier structure, starting with the base organization at the local level, the district organization at the regional level, and the all-Party organization at the national level. At its seventh and most recent congress (1976), the party numbered 101,500 members, a far cry from the 2,800 members it had in November 1944.[9] Table 3.1 shows the size and growth of the Party from the First to the Seventh Congress (1948-1976).

The figures in the table indicate that membership in the APL more than doubled over nearly three decades, rising from 45,382 in 1948 to 101,500 in 1976. Except for the Second Party Congress, which registered a drop of nearly

Table 3.2
Growth of the APL Central Committee (1948-1976)

Party Congress	Full Members	Candidate Members	Total	Change over Preceding Congress
First, 1948	21	10	31	–
Second, 1952	27	12	39	+8
Third, 1956	43	22	65	+26
Fourth, 1961	53	29	82	+17
Fifth, 1966	61	36	97	+15
Sixth, 1971	71	39	110	+13
Seventh, 1976	77	38	115	+5

Source: Compiled from Hoxha's reports to the respective Party congresses.

1,000 members compared with the First Congress, all succeeding congresses showed increases in membership. The increases ranged from a low of 4,226 in 1956 to a high of 20,658 in 1971. These increases apparently paralleled the increase in the country's total population. Thus, in 1948 Politburo member Tuk Jakova reported that communists made up 3.9 percent of Albania's population; while in November 1976 Hoxha reported that communists accounted for 4 percent of the population.[10] The ratio therefore of communists to the population as a whole has remained nearly stationary over the years, up to the present.

Between the rank-and-file membership and the top leadership of the Party stands the Central Committee. The 1976 Party Congress elected a Central Committee of 115 members—a figure nearly four times larger than the 31 members chosen at the First Congress. Table 3.2 shows the growth of the Central Committee since 1948.

At the head of the Party's Central Committee is the Politburo. This body numbered seventeen members in 1976, as against nine members in 1948. An examination of the data on the Politburo, as given in the appendix to this chapter (Table 3.4), shows that of the original nine Politburo members in the First Party Congress, only four remained at the close of the Seventh Congress: Hoxha, Shehu, Kapo, and Koleka. Four of the missing had been purged, while the fifth, Gogo Nushi, died in office. The rate of attrition reached a high point at the Seventh Congress, with the expulsion of six members, or over one-third of the Politburo membership.

Since the Politburo is the real seat of power in the Party hierarchy and the nation, the decisions taken by that body and approved by the Central Committee constitute "the line of the Party" and may not be questioned by Party members or the rest of the citizenry.[11] Party policies may be discussed by Party members, provided such discussions do not lead to decisions or actions that conflict with the line of the Party. The Albanian Party insists on compact ideological unity in its leadership and "steellike" political unity between the masses and the Party. It views such unity as a prerequisite for the effective implementation of its general line. It does not tolerate opposition to its policies, whether organized or merely vocal. It interprets such opposition as "factionalist activity" designed to break up the unity of the Party. Whenever it has detected or suspected tendencies to "factionalism," it has reacted with great severity against the alleged offenders. Hence its long record of purges against dissenters, as for example in 1946, when Sejfulla Malëshova, the leading Party ideologist, fell from power; in 1955, when Politburo members Tuk Jakova and Bedri Spahiu were dismissed; and the more recent shake-ups in 1973-1976.[12]

The Albanian Party of Labor represents itself as the "organized vanguard" of the working class and as a "detachment of the international communist movement." According to Albanian leaders, APL has been a revolutionary Party from the outset and is comprised of revolutionaries bent on advancing the process of the "uninterrupted revolution" in the country. Statutes regulating Party life say that the primary political, economic, and social tasks of APL on the domestic front are to "strengthen the dictatorship of the proletariat" in order to assure the political unity of the Party and the working masses, which is the indispensable condition for safeguarding the revolution and building socialism; to transform Albania from an agrarian-industrial society to an industrialized country with a modern agriculture; and to advance toward an egalitarian society by gradually narrowing the differences between the working class and the peasantry, between towns and villages, between theory and practice, and between mental and physical labor. On the foreign front, APL—true to its dogmatic interpretation of Marx and Lenin—is pledged to an irreconcilable struggle against imperialism, "headed by the United States," and modern revisionism, "headed by the Soviet Union"; support for all revolutionary Marxist-Leninist parties and groups; support for national liberation movements of oppressed peoples in the Third World; and solidarity with the workers in capitalist countries who are struggling to overthrow monopoly capitalism. The Albanian Party, in brief, is resolved to do its part, however minute, to advance the cause of world revolution in the interest of socialism.

The top leader of the Albanian Party of Labor, Enver Hoxha, has served as its first secretary since the formation of APL. Mehmet Shehu, the second-ranking member in the Party hierarchy, has held the post of prime minister of the Albanian government since 1954. In view of the fact that these two men are primarily responsible for charting APL's course and giving it its particular temper and character, it is instructive to consider briefly their background.

Hoxha, a skillful organizer and versatile politician with a flair for public speaking, has one of the best records for political longevity among leaders in the communist world. He was born in the town of Gjirokastër in southern Albania on October 16, 1908. In 1930 he graduated from the French lyceum in Korçë, reportedly with a brilliant record and a good foundation in the humanities. In 1931 he enrolled at the University of Montpellier in France on the strength of a scholarship granted him by the Albanian government. While in France, he wrote articles for the French Communist Party organ, *L'humanite*, denouncing King Zog's government, an action that led to the termination of his scholarship. He then moved to Brussels, where he took a job as a private secretary at the Albanian consulate. At the same time, he studied law and continued his anti-Zog activities, until he was detected and dismissed from his post.

In 1936, he returned to Albania, where he taught first at the Tiranë Gymnasium and later at the Korçë Lyceum. He lost his job again—shortly after the Italian invasion of Albania in 1939—on charges by the Fascist authorities that he had engaged in subversive procommunist activity among his students. Hoxha then moved to Tiranë where, behind the facade of a tobacco shop, he worked underground as a leader of the Tiranë communist group. When the Albanian Communist Party was formed in Tiranë in November 1941, Hoxha was chosen as head of a seven-member Provisional Central Committee.[13]

Hoxha is a nationalist, a doctrinaire communist, and an intellectual who admires both Stalin and the genius of men like Balzac, Montaigne, Shakespeare, and Molière. He combines in his person ruthlessness toward "enemies of Albania, socialism, and the Party," a certain fondness for conspiracy, messianic zeal for the propagation of the "communist faith" in the world, and great trust in the efficacy of radical measures for the modernization of Albania. With a background in Western education and his experience as a liberal arts college professor, Hoxha seems to be well informed about literature, the theater, and philosophy, particularly the philosophy of education.

He is fluent in French and has knowledge of Russian, English, Italian, and Serbo-Croatian. He might well be pictured as holding the sword of the dictatorship of the proletariat in one hand and the Western "lamp of learning" in the other.

Five years younger than Hoxha, Mehmet Shehu has a reputation as a brilliant army commander and as the most ruthless leader of the Albanian regime. He was born on January 10, 1913, in Çorrush, a village in the Mallakastër region in southern Albania. After graduating from the American Vocational School in Tiranë in 1932, he went to Italy where he enrolled at the Military Academy in Naples but was expelled four months later because of his procommunist sympathies and activities. When the Spanish Civil War broke out, he joined the "Garibaldi" International Brigade, and fought as commander of its Fourth Battalion. He spent three years (1939-1942) in a concentration camp in France, then returned to Albania, where he joined the newly founded Albanian Communist Party and the anti-Fascist resistance struggle.

He was the Man of the Hour for the Partisan cause. Owing to his professional military training, his battleground experience in Spain, his natural gifts as a commander, plus his fanatic zeal for communism and his ruthless disposition, he soon became the most renowned commander in the Partisan army and the scourge of the *Balli Kombëtar*—the Partisans' leading rival for power during the war. It is said by some *Balli Kombëtar* leaders that without Shehu the communists could not have won the war and come to power in Albania. Following the war, Shehu held a number of high military, Party, and government positions, such as army chief-of-staff, APL-CC secretary, and minister of the interior. At present he holds the posts of prime minister and minister of defense.[14]

Opinion varies concerning the relationship between Hoxha and Shehu, some saying that external fear—formerly of Yugoslavia and now of the Soviet Union—has been the basis of their cooperation, while others believe that they have managed to share power principally for internal reasons, above all the need to maintain the balance of power within the country. More likely, the main reason the two have ruled successfully together is that they are the strongest symbols of the National Liberation struggle, Hoxha in the political field and Shehu in the military arena. They appear to complement each other, in the sense of fulfilling each other's weak points, as the country's top leaders. Shehu's image as an uncompromising, authoritarian figure is probably as useful to Hoxha in maintaining control in the country as Hoxha's image as a man of broader sympathies and a skillful, versatile statesman is useful to Shehu.

Internal Life of the Party
In order to preserve its "ideological purity" and revolutionary orientation, as well as strengthen its working-class base, the Albanian Party—as is customary with militant, monolithic organizations—has been constantly preoccupied with the question of the quality of its members. The Party leadership has voiced frequent complaints over the petit bourgeois background of many of its members, their low level of education and culture, and recurring violations of Party regulations in the selection of candidates for Party membership. Apparently, candidates in many cases are selected not according to Party criteria—character, morals, spirit of sacrifice, and political and ideological maturity—but rather on the basis of "nepotism, family relations and friendship."[15] In order to deal with this situation, the Party has from time to time carried out purification-of-ranks campaigns, which have resulted in the expulsion of thousands of members and candidate members from the Party.[16]

Above all, the leadership sought to increase the percentage of workers in the Party, at the expense of intellectuals, students, and bureaucrats who are regarded as less reliable politically than members of the working class. As a result of strenuous efforts by the Party, and the swelling of the ranks of industrial workers with the gradual development of the nation's industry, the membership of workers in the Party increased from 15 percent in 1945 to 37 percent in 1976. The working-class representation in the Party became the dominant bloc or group in 1971. Commenting on that long-awaited event at the Sixth APL Congress, Enver Hoxha said: "It is a great joy and victory for the Party and all the people that now, for the first time in the history of our Party, the worker communists occupy the first place in party membership."[17] He added that "the evil" which befell many communist parties in revisionist East Europe stemmed from the fact that their ranks were "deproletarianized," for they were filled with technocrats, bureaucrats, and intellectuals. The implication was that the Albanian Party was now practically ensured against such a disaster.

Table 3.3 indicates the changing relationship between the working class and other strata of the population in the Party.

It will be recalled that the third stage of Albania's "uninterrupted revolution" has as its main goal the cleansing of the superstructure of Albanian society by uprooting "alien ideologies" from the consciousness of its citizens. It is a goal that involves every citizen in a continuous struggle against bourgeois and revisionist ideas, liberalism, and conservatism. The object of the Ideological and Cultural Revolution in 1966-1969 was essentially to make "a great leap forward" in this direction. At that time, the struggle focused on wiping out the harmful effect of bureaucracy—which threatened to alienate the Party from the masses—and its social roots in conservatism; that is, backward customs, patriarchy, superstition, and a host of feudal and Oriental remnants that stifled Albanian society.

These anachronistic concepts and practices, as well as "harmful alien influences" from West and East Europe, had become widespread among cadres in Party and state apparatuses, creating numerous problems of administration for the regime and causing great alarm among the Party leaders. One of the more persistent problems was that many party cadres confused the roles of the Party and the government, and instead of simply directing and supervising the work of government workers—as they were supposed to do—often took over the functions of the latter and ended by botching both their own job and that of the government worker. A more serious problem that developed in the mid-1960s was the gap between Party cadres of limited education and culture and the more advanced body of citizens they were expected to lead in the building of a modern, progressive society. Reacting to this situation, Enver Hoxha said in April 1966: ". . . how can one seriously believe that Party members in the villages, some of whom are illiterate, or with only a grade school education . . . can advise or direct the army of teachers, agronomists, doctors, veterinarians that dot the countryside?"[18] Ironically, this was a problem created by the very modernizing process that the communist regime had set in motion twenty years earlier.

Perhaps the best statement and summation of the major problems in APL's internal life were made by the Party's first secretary in a speech to the Polit-

Table 3.3
Social Composition of APL, 1945-1976 (In Percentages)

	1945	1956	1966	1976
Workers	15.3	19.7	32.9	37.5
Farmers	49.7	31.4	28.6	29.0
White-collar	21.1[1]	45.2[2]	37.1[2]	32.0[3]
Others	13.9	4.0	1.4	1.5[3]

Source: Compiled from Hoxha's reports to the Party congresses.
1. Includes civil servants and students.
2. Includes civil servants only.
3. Data not available; estimated figures.

buro in February 1966 at the beginning of the Cultural Revolution. While reaffirming the long-held position that "the line of the Party in all matters has been basically correct," Hoxha nonetheless was unusually frank in the discussion of the problems of bureaucracy that have plagued the Party since the late 1940s. He spoke of his frustration in trying to communicate with local and regional Party leaders concerning problems they faced. All too frequently their reticence, it turned out, was but a device to cover up their incompetence, ignorance, and violations of "Party norms" and "socialist legality." Some of the bureaucratic vices to which they had become addicted were thievery, favoritism, "bossism" toward subordinates, and indolence. Hoxha said that the cadres "had become captives of conservatism."[19]

He complained that too many communists preferred a desk job to working on the production line, because they had the mistaken antiegalitarian notion that office work is more "honorable" and more "worthy" than manual work. He labeled these people "petty tyrants," whose "sick psychology" leads them in the end to embrace antirevolutionary and even anti-Party positions. Another common failing of cadres was their reluctance or refusal to leave the city and work in the countryside, giving as a pretext that they were frail of health or that it would interrupt their children's education or that their expertise was such that they were irreplaceable, and similar "petit bourgeois" ideas.

A disturbing consequence of these bureaucratic practices was that the bureaus of the state and mass organizations, in both the cities and the countryside, had become overstaffed with Party cadres, thus hampering their efficient operation and threatening to negate the all-important political goal of the revolutionary transformation of Albanian society. Touching on this problem, Hoxha has on many occasions spoken with indignation about the disproportion between communists and noncommunists in various bueaus, including the ministries in Tiranë. In a major speech on April 26, 1972, he remarked that of the total number of cadres in the central organs of the ministries the communists accounted for 45.5 percent and that in some ministries the figures were even higher.[20] He asked: "Why on earth are so many communists needed [in these ministries]? Wouldn't it be better for many of the communists ... to go without delay to the grass roots, where the practical struggle is being waged to supply the people properly and to serve them better?"[21]

The first secretary of the Party also denounced repeatedly the enormous growth of the "paper bureaucracy," which paralleled the staffing of state organs, as well as organs of mass organizations, with superfluous personnel.

As a result, the administrative machinery of the regime groaned under the weight of myriad laws, decrees, rules, and regulations. An ever more refined government code for doing even the simplest job generated an endless stream of mostly meaningless figures and statistics. The condition provoked Hoxha to cry out, "We are obsessed with figures and statistics."[22] He condemned the judicial authorities for trying to codify everything under rules and regulations and creating along with other bureaucrats a potentially dangerous gulf between the Party and the people.

The rampant growth of the bureaucracy in the Albanian regime confronted APL with still another problem—the propensity of cadres to act in an arbitrary manner. Certain communists operated under the assumption that "the Party is infallible," or that "the Party has unlimited rights" and therefore can do anything it pleases, or that "the Party must not be criticized" because criticism impaired its authority.[23] In some cases, such arbitrary acts were due to wrong interpretations of Party regulations, while in other cases they were subterfuges to hide their mistakes and evade criticism of their conduct by using the Party's authority as a protective shield. Examining this issue, Hoxha informed Party cadres that "the Party has some rights, but it does not have unlimited rights over everything; it cannot act at will."[24]

As mentioned earlier, the official Party line is that the "dangerous disease" of "bureaucratism" is the offspring of "alien ideologies," principally conservatism and bourgeois and revisionist influences. However, in his speech to the APL Central Committee plenum of February 3-4, 1966, Hoxha took the extraordinary step of going beyond the official position and attributing most of the blame for "the evils" of bureaucratism to the Party leadership itself. He said: "It is important to understand that ... we, the leaders, are the biggest culprits for this condition. . . . We the leadership demanded to be ... consulted over almost everything; we insisted on giving guidance in everything. . . . No one could operate outside that framework."[25]

Albania's top leader noted that the policy of unrestricted "control by the leadership over everyone and everything" had proved to be wrong. He added that as long as the administrative apparatus is not under the complete control of the people, bureaucratism "with all its evils will surface again and again" in Albania. Hoxha, in effect, admitted that tight centralism as a guiding principle for governing Albania was at least open to question, if not totally discredited, by the mid-1960s, however useful or necessary it may have been in the early years of the regime.

Drawing the logical conclusions from his own analysis of the problem of bureaucracy and its corrosive effects on the Party and the country, Hoxha proposed a daring solution. He suggested that the Party open itself up to questioning and criticism by rank-and-file members. He said that no one should hesitate to criticize the distortions and the errors that may be made by the Central Committee, the Politburo, or any of their members.[26] Hoxha repeated this proposal six years later, in his February 16, 1972, speech, when he said—in language reminiscent of Mao's "Let one hundred flowers bloom" campaign: "Let everything seethe within the organization. Even if someone comes up in opposition to the line of the Party, let him oppose it...."[27] The fact, however, that he repeated the proposal means that nothing was done about his original proposal in 1966, which in itself is an indication of the difficulty of the problem or, as is more likely, that the Party leadership had no intention of making such a basic reform in its style of rule.

Other steps actually taken or proposed since 1966 as a means of overcoming the paralyzing effects of bureaucracy, and "perfecting" the internal life of the Party, included the reduction of personnel in state organs, requiring administration workers and intellectuals to do physical labor for one or more months a year, and increasing "workers' control" by giving the working masses greater power in the management of the economy and a wider role in the work of the state apparatus. All of these measures aimed ostensibly at bringing the regime closer to the people by making the government more responsive to their needs and aspirations and by strengthening the bonds between them and the Party. Another step along this line was the suggestion that more attention be given to electing "the best people" to office, people who are honest, courageous, hard workers, "revolutionaries ... who know the problems of the people, live and work with the people."[28] The suggestion implied that "right government" is a function—at least in part—of "right people" and not merely the result of an ideology or a particular economic system or social order.

Despite, however, the actual and potential value of these measures, the Party leadership viewed them more as stopgap, rather than as long-term solutions to the problem of bureaucratism. The long-term solution, in APL's view, was above all a question of education: of raising the ideological consciousness of the cadres, the workers, and the collectivized peasantry; of strengthening their revolutionary spirit so that they may shun the comfortable and easy life and choose instead the life of hardship and self-denial; and of putting politics ahead of everything, which meant judging all things from a political viewpoint. More specifically, "putting politics ahead" in this context meant asking whether a particular action, policy, or proposal was in the interest of the people, the country, and socialism or simply in one's personal interest. It meant giving politics priority over economic, technical, and pragmatic considerations in the performance of one's job and the solution of the nation's problems. These ideas motivated to a large extent the reform of the educational system in 1969 and the series of propaganda campaigns that were carried out in recent years. The Party leaders hoped through these efforts to "revolutionize the life of the country" and deal a crushing blow to the endemic problem of bureaucratism. They warned constantly that it was precisely "the worm of bureaucratism" that gnawed at the vitals of the CPSU and brought on the tragedy of revisionism in the Soviet Union. Hence, they were determined not to allow a recurrence of that tragedy in Albania.

In spite of the problems facing APL in the "third stage" of its path and development, namely, the ideological and cultural stage, Enver Hoxha was able to report to the Sixth Party Congress in November 1971 that during the period from the Fifth to the Sixth Congress (1966-1971) "not the least sign of hostile work, or of inconstancy in the [Party] line" had appeared "either in the Party as a whole, or within the ranks of the Central Committee."[29] It seems likely that the stability experienced by the Albanian Party during the late 1960s encouraged the Politburo to toy with the idea of relaxing APL's stand and moderating its rule to a degree. This notion is reflected in a number of speeches Hoxha made at Party meetings in 1972, in which he invited criticism of the Party line "from below" and advocated the abolition of "excessive secrecy" in the work of the Party.[30] On the question of secrecy he said the times had changed since the National Liberation War, the "antagonistic classes" had been smashed; therefore, there was no longer any reason for excessive secrecy. It was a potentially significant moment in the history of the Party's domestic policy, but it produced no fruits.

APL's hesitant steps toward relaxation and limited dialogue with the Albanian masses came to an end within a year. Alarmed by the liberal and reformist trends in the country, which by the end of 1972 had gathered much strength, the Party reverted to its customary Stalinist position. It fell back on the trusted mechanism of the purge, as it set out to curb the deviationists and dissenters and reestablish the familiar pattern of extremist centralism.

External Life of the Party

The term "external life of the Party" is used here to mean APL's relations with organizations and groups in Albanian society outside the Party organization. In the discussion that follows, we shall deal with APL's relations with one representative sector of Albanian society, namely, the youth of the country. The Party's relations with other major groups, such as the technocrats, women, the intelligentsia, and the army, are discussed in separate chapters.

In the early seventies, the APL leadership became acutely concerned over the attitudes of important segments of the youth population toward ideology, politics, education, and personal tastes. The Party's watchful guardians of communist manners and morals detected signs of dissent from the Party's official line among many youth. They attributed the dissent to the vice of "liberalism"—a term used to describe positions or inclinations of individuals or organizations that did not conform with "strict proletarian discipline" and the Party's position on art, literature, and cultural life in general.[31] To be sure, there was some justification for concern on the part of Albania's rulers over so-called "manifestations of liberalism" among youth. In 1972, for example, there was a sharp increase in youthful hooliganism and crime; in the rate of failures, repeats, and expulsions among students at the University of Tiranë; and in the spread of the more vulgar Western life-styles among young people. Antisocial attitudes of this sort had spread even among children of Party members, provoking Hoxha to say: "How can communists, whose children turn into hooligans, vagabonds, and purveyors of extravagant bourgeois fashions and tastes, be in the vanguard and set an example for others?"[32] Party leaders, however, moved to condemn not only such negative manifestations but the more legitimate and reasonable aspirations of youth and intellectuals for autonomy, experimentation, self-expression, and dialogue with the outside world, particularly the West.

The growing divergencies between the Party and the young generation became evident in a most revealing confrontation at a meeting of the APL Secretariat on February 23, 1973. The meeting was presided over by Enver Hoxha and was called to discuss a report by the leadership of the Labor Youth Union of Albania (LYUA).[33] The youth report complained that the Party leadership did not seem to understand "the concerns, requirements, interests and problems" of young people. The report was critical of the fact that Partisan war themes dominated the lives of youth, from history books in school to literature for the young, films, the theater, and so on. In an effort apparently to help redress the balance, the report called for more books by foreign authors in Albanian libraries and bookstores. More important still, the LYUA report seemed to question the validity of one of the Party's most cherished slogans; namely, that "Albania is building socialism under conditions of a fierce encirclement by imperialist and revisionist enemies." It is a slogan the Party has used with obsessive intensity to justify its hard-line centralist rule and militant ideology, fuel its vitriolic polemics against the Soviet bloc and the West, whip up revolutionary fervor among the masses, and accelerate the pace of modernization in the country. The report of the youth leaders left no doubt that the young people in Albania did not share the revolutionary fervor of Hoxha's generation and were restive over APL's isolationist politics. They were looking toward Europe and links with the Continent as an alternative to isolationism.

There were calls from the youth that the Party relinquish its close supervision of LYUA. The argument against Party tutelage and in favor of autonomy, made by the youth, had won support even from some Party members—a fact that caused much distress in the leadership of the Party.

In spearheading APL's drive to silence dissent among the intelligentsia and the youth, Hoxha said that the Party was "opposed to tutelage and to dictatorial methods," but at the same time it was "opposed to any weakening, however slight, of [its] leadership in the mass organizations."[34] He took issue with almost every point raised in the February 1973 report by the youth leaders. Contrary to the negative impression the report gave concerning young people, Hoxha said: "I am of the opinion that our youth are the happiest and most cheerful in the world," then went on to give a vivid description of the benefits enjoyed by youth in contemporary Albania.[35] He insisted that Partisan war themes were "the most suitable" of all themes for socialist Albania's youth, in order that they learn of the heroic sacrifices made by the makers of Albania's revolution. He said that the imperialist-revisionist encirclement was primarily ideological rather than geographical in nature. The encirclement was the sum total of myriad pressures exerted through literature, radio, TV, tourists, trade, fashions, and so on, and aimed at confusing the gullible, creating disorder in the country's economy, and causing political and ideological degeneration among the masses, above all among youth and intellectuals.

In brief, the enemy's goal was to destroy socialist rule in Albania by encouraging liberalism and introducing alien influences into the country. Hoxha denounced those who advocated that Albania "should follow ... the course of European development," saying: "No, comrades, we cannot and should not follow 'the European road'; on the contrary, it is Europe which should follow our road, because from the political standpoint, it is far behind us . . . far from that for which Marx, Engels, Lenin and Stalin fought. . . ."[36]

At the Fourth Plenum of the Party's Central Committee on June 26, 1973, Hoxha tried to show that the most serious international questions, such as détente and European security, cannot be divorced from seeming trifles as, for example, miniskirts, pickpocketing, and rock and roll music. In APL's vocabulary, détente means liberalism, and liberalism means degeneration and ruin for Albania's political system and social order. The Albanian Party was opposed to European bourgeois culture not only for ideological and political reasons but because of a certain puritanical element in its character. It was jealous of its socialist culture and feared that exposure to European cultural influences would impair its "purity" and destroy its usefulness in building a morally sound and vigorous society. After denouncing every aspect of the bourgeois way of life, Hoxha concluded: "We have nothing to learn from this culture; we have no reason to impart it to our masses and youth, but should discard it contemptuously and fight it with determination."[37]

The Fourth Party Plenum expelled Agim Mero from his post as first secretary of the youth organization on the ground that he had "slipped into liberalism." Other expulsions resulted in the decimation of the leadership of the League of Writers and Artists.

The purge of the leaders of the youth organization revealed a gap in the understanding of Albanian reality between the Hoxha-Shehu team on the one hand and the youth on the other hand. The divergence in views between the two sides brought into question many of the basic premises or mainsprings of the Party's general line: its militant ideology, its revolutionary orientation, its extremist centralism, even its conception of Albanian nationalism. The doubts expressed by youth about the reality of "enemy encirclement" of Albania were part of the attack on APL's ideology on such issues as isolationism, polemics, détente, and peaceful coexistence. Criticism of Partisan war themes implied rejection of the Party's class and revolution-oriented art and culture, the militancy of the "uninterrupted revolution," and the "war psychosis" that pervaded Albanian society. In short, it implied a rebellion against the perpetuation of the Cold War atmosphere in the nation. Finally, the desire of young people to reach out toward other nations in Europe and establish meaningful communications with them spoke of a different conception of Albanian nationalism from that of Party leaders. Compared with their idea of nationalism, Albania's rulers were guilty of "narrow nationalism," for they stood for a form of patriotism that seemed to be both politically unenlightened and a hindrance to the modernization of the country.

The sharp confrontation between the Party leadership and the LYUA leaders seemed motivated above all by the Party's concern for its authority and its determination to maintain and strengthen its directing role in Albanian society. The perception by APL leaders that the Party's authority was weakening and its teachings and directives were being ignored or resisted by various strata of the population led to a series of crises and purges between 1973 and 1976. They involved the artists and cultural intelligentsia (1973), the military (1974), and the economic elite (1975-1976). These crises and purges are discussed in the chapters on the intelligentsia, the armed forces, and the economy.

The New Constitution and the Party

Probably nothing illustrates better the nature of APL than the new Constitution of the Albanian state, which was adopted by the People's Assembly on December 28, 1976.[38] The new Constitution replaced socialist Albania's first Constitution, which was adopted in March 1946 and revised in 1950. The document is a vivid embodiment of the principles, experience, and latent dispositions that make up the character and nature of the Party. The following are some of the main points.

1. The document changed the official name of the country from the People's Republic of Albania to the People's Socialist Republic of Albania (Art. 1). The word "socialist" was added to the name in order to distinguish Albania from all other communist countries, which, in the opinion of the Hoxha leadership, are pseudosocialist or, more precisely, revisionist states that have nothing in common with Marxism-Leninism and genuine socialism. Albania thus set herself explicitly apart from all East European states, not only with respect to ideology and politics but in terms of the legal designation of the state.

2. The intense spirit of nationalism is evident in the new Fundamental Law of the state, particularly in the Preamble and in the section on national defense. The Preamble opens with Hoxha's celebrated slogan, "The Albanian people have hacked their way through history, sword in hand." The slogan is significant in that it sets the tone for the new Constitution, revealing in graphic imagery its Stalinist temper and character. The regime is acutely concerned about the defense of Albania's national security and independence. Through the instrument of the Constitution, the regime advises that the defense of the country is "the highest duty and the greatest honor" of Albanian citizens,

while treason to the country is "the greatest crime" (Art. 62). Indeed, the Hoxha-Shehu leadership has sought, by means of the new document, to assure Albania's sovereignty and independence indefinitely. A most unusual clause in the section on national defense states that "no one has the right to sign the surrender of Albania or to accept the occupation of the country" (Art. 90), no matter what the circumstances.

3. The new Constitution sanctions the Party's dedication to ideology by making Marxism-Leninism the official and sole ruling ideology in the country (Art. 3). This ideological monism implies the rejection of all other ideologies that might compete with Marxism-Leninism, such as capitalism, fascism, nonalignment, social democracy, and others. It implies, in addition, open and vigorous polemics against all other competing ideologies, in order to maintain the purity and efficacy of the ruling ideology. The Party's orthodox stand on communist ideology is evident also in the Preamble, which says that Albania "is guided by the great ideals of socialism and communism and struggles for their triumph throughout the world." APL's total rejection of ideological pluralism means in effect the prohibition of the free circulation of ideas, including unrestricted and uncontrolled tourism in Albania. It means limiting severely cultural exchanges with the outside world.

4. The Party's fervor for revolutionary politics is made plain in several places in the Constitution. The Preamble notes that Socialist Albania "is an active factor in the struggle for national and social liberation" of all peoples. Article 4 says that Albania develops the revolution unceasingly by adhering to the class struggle, for the purpose of "ensuring the final victory of the socialist road over the capitalist road. . . ." Elsewhere, the document states that in her foreign policy Albania "supports the revolutionary movement of the working class and the struggle of peoples for freedom . . ." (Art. 15). Despite the obvious discrepancy between Albania's violent anti-imperialist polemics and her actual power in the world scene, the APL retains its faith in revolutionary politics and is bent on promoting the cause of world revolution. The Party's stance on this question is amply reflected in the articles of the new Constitution.

5. The Party's continuous preoccupation with the problem of modernization is evident in the Constitution, above all in the Preamble. Several paragraphs in the Preamble enumerate—with much flourish and pride—the gains of the regime in the development of the country. Some of the gains, according to the document, are the nationalization of industry; agrarian reform, followed by the collectivization of agriculture; the emancipation of women; the devel-

opment of culture; the availability of education to all the people. The Preamble notes that as a consequence of the gains made so far "Albania has entered the stage of the complete construction of socialism." Modernization, as one of the mainsprings of the politics of APL, is an integral part of Albanian life, and this is evident in the new Constitution.

6. Tight centralism, another dominant feature of APL, is abundantly illustrated in the new document. It is evident in the observations on the dictatorship of the proletariat and the role of the Party in the Albanian state. We read in Article 2 that Albania is "a state of the dictatorship of the proletariat, which expresses and defends the interests of the working people." By giving this doctrine a prominent position in the document, the Hoxha-Shehu leadership signaled to the Albanian population and the outside world that it had no intention of liberalizing its rule or carrying out significant reforms of the country's economic system. APL leaders shall continue to view Albanian society as an arena of class struggle, as a dichotomy of antagonistic and non-antagonistic contradictions, as a battlefield of forces aiding the revolution and forces opposing it.

The new document declares the Party to be "the sole leading political force of the state and of the society" (Art. 3). The single-party system is thereby legally affirmed, and the supreme, oligarchic authority that APL has always enjoyed and exercised in Albania is openly acknowledged. The 1976 Constitution confirms the widely known fact that APL is the true and only source of political power in Albania. All other institutions, including the Council of Ministers, the courts, the armed forces, and the various organizations of the masses are only creations of the Party and exist to serve the ends of the Party. The Constitution authorizes APL not only to perform a didactic function but to play an active and directing role in Albanian society.

7. The radicalism of APL also finds expression in the articles of the new Constitution. We see it particularly in the sections on "the economic order" and on the "rights and duties of citizens." Accordingly, private property is officially liquidated, and the entire economy of the nation is proclaimed "a socialist economy" (Art. 16). The land belongs to the state, rather than to those who till it but is "granted" to the farmers and other groups for purposes of "social use" (Art. 19). The most radical social experiment carried out to date by APL is of course the abolition of religion. The wording in the Constitution on the ten-year-old experiment is as follows: "The state does not recognize any religion and supports and develops atheist propaganda" (Art. 37).

Albania's 1976 Constitution, reflecting as it does the nature of APL, apparently has no equal in the socialist world as a militant, authoritarian, and doctrinaire document. It was ostensibly designed to meet the present and future needs of Albania in the period of the total construction of the socialist society. Actually, it is an instrument intended above all to legitimize the dictatorial rule of the Party. The new Constitution is the distillation of three decades of Cold War politics in the Albanian nation, marked by a verbally aggressive foreign policy and recurrent purges on the domestic front. It is the end result of the theory and practice by APL of dogmatic communism, modeled on Stalin's precepts and style of rule. It is the best single document that expresses in compact form the experience, philosophy, and hopes of the Albanian Party of Labor—in short, its nature and character.

The Question of Succession

At present, Enver Hoxha and his erstwhile most hated enemy, Josip Broz Tito of Yugoslavia, as heads of state have held power longer than any other leader of a ruling communist party. Both have been in power since assuming the leadership of the resistance movements in their respective countries during World War II.

Although Hoxha is sixteen years younger than Tito, the question of succession to power in a post-Hoxha Albania is already being discussed. In a sense, the question of succession in Tiranë is surrounded by greater uncertainty, and therefore freer speculation, than in Belgrade. For, unlike Tito, Hoxha has made no constitutional provision regarding the manner in which he is to be succeeded. Too, recurring reports in the Western press that both Hoxha and Shehu are in ill health have heightened the interest of students of Albanian affairs in this question.

At present, most observers seem to agree that the top five men in the Albanian hierarchy of power are Enver Hoxha, Mehmet Shehu, Hysni Kapo, Ramiz Alia, and Kadri Hazbiu. Shehu is the most likely person to succeed Hoxha, especially since he now holds the posts of both premier and minister of defense. While the two men have much in common, Shehu's background, temperament, and style of rule are vastly different from Hoxha's. His rule therefore would very likely be a harsh military dictatorship; indeed, the first communist military dictatorship in the history of Europe. It would be a step backward, at least temporarily, rather than a step toward relaxation and de-Stalinization of Albanian politics. The more intriguing question, therefore, is what would happen when both Hoxha and Shehu leave the scene.

Their exit could precipitate a struggle for the vacant spot among Kapo, Alia, and Hazbiu. None of them is endowed with "charisma," and none has demonstrated exceptional leadership qualities. But all of them have their particular strengths and weaknesses.

Hysni Kapo, a southerner from the Vlorë region, is at sixty-two the oldest of the three, as well as the oldest in terms of his affiliation with APL. He joined the Party at its founding, became a member of the Central Committee in 1943 and a Politburo member in 1946. An often decorated man, Kapo is an "organization man" type at the highest level of power, whose expertise in fact has been, and still is, the Party organization. He has the advantage of seniority in the Party, the support presumably of the *apparatchiki*, and most of all a long record of harmonious relations with Hoxha. He is the only member of the wartime ACP Central Committee who has retained the confidence of Hoxha and survived all the crises and purges that mark the Party's thirty-six-year path. Kapo has a sense of the art and craft of politics and can appreciate the import of a political development.

Those are points in his favor with regard to the question of succession. On the other hand, his age would be a drawback in his bid for supreme power. Moreover, he projects the image of a plodder and a perpetually morose man, with little imagination or vision. He appears to be a retiring personality, who seems rather comfortable in his present niche of power and may be reluctant to exchange it for the ever-exposed and risky post of the secretary of the Party, unless pushed to it irresistibly by events.

Kadri Hazbiu is Albania's minister of the interior, a post he has occupied since 1954. At fifty-seven, he is five years younger than Kapo and five years older than Alia. Like Kapo he is a southerner from the Vlorë district. He joined the Party in 1945, gained admittance to the APL-CC in 1952, but did not attain full membership in the Politburo until 1971. Hazbiu's expertise has been in the area of internal security, almost from the beginning of his work in the Party. As head of the country's state security forces—the ubiquitous and much-feared *Sigurimi*—he wields a powerful weapon and in this sense enjoys an advantage over potential rivals for power.

It is obvious that possession of police power is not necessarily the same as possessing political power. Indeed, in a Stalinist state such as Albania, it will probably be a drawback to the drive for the top position of power in the post-Hoxha-Shehu period. As head of Sigurimi, Hazbiu has undoubtedly earned the hatred of many groups in Albania's society which have experienced the ruthless blows of his secret police. On balance, it seems that Hazbiu's strengths and weaknesses cancel themselves out and in effect leave him at ground zero, so to speak, in the race for supreme power. An unusual combination of political forces or circumstances, however, could propel the minister of the interior to the top spot in the APL hierarchy, at least in the short run.

The third high Party figure who might be Albania's next leader is Ramiz Alia. Born in 1925, he is the youngest of the three possible successors to Hoxha and Shehu discussed here. His age then is a point in his favor. But unlike Kapo and Hazbiu, Alia was born in Shkodër, the principal city in northern Albania—a fact which could harm to some extent his candidacy for power, since the south, rather than the north, has been the decisive source of political power in postwar Albania. Alia has been a member of APL since 1943, a member of the Party's Central Committee since 1948, and a full member of the Politburo since 1960. In terms of seniority, therefore, he is weaker than Kapo but considerably stronger than Hazbiu.

Alia built his political career on a foundation of successful work with the communist youth organization. Subsequently, he gained valuable experience in leadership posts in the Office of Propaganda, and in the Ministry of Education and Culture. He has occupied himself particularly with questions of ideology and the "cultural revolution" in Albania. And since problems of ideology and culture have been at the center of the Party's attention in the past decade, Alia's candidacy for power presumably would have considerable support among leaders and rank-and-file members of the Party. Alia is reported to be a man of keen intelligence and to enjoy the respect of Hoxha. The fact also that he has had considerable exposure in the Albanian press in recent years suggests that he exerts more than ordinary influence in the Party. On balance, then, Alia emerges as a stronger contender for Hoxha's or Shehu's place than either Kapo of Hazbiu—provided he can overcome the disadvantage of being a northerner.

In any case, the successor to Hoxha and Shehu is bound to alter the nature of the Albanian Party of Labor to a lesser or greater degree. The dream and hope of the Hoxha leadership is to perpetuate Stalinism on the shores of the Adriatic. But the "dialectical unfolding" of history, indifferent to the subjective wishes of men, may have in store a different verdict for Albania's political future.

Appendix

Table 3.4
Membership of the Politburo, 1948–1976 (F = full member; C = candidate member)

Member	Number, Year of Party Congress, and Total Membership						
	First, 1948 (9)	Second, 1952 (10)	Third, 1956 (15)	Fourth, 1961 (15)	Fifth, 1966 (16)	Sixth, 1971 (17)	Seventh, 1976 (17)
Hoxha, Enver	F	F	F	F	F	F	F
Shehu, Mehmet	F	F	F	F	F	F	F
Kapo, Hysni	F	F	F	F	F	F	F
Koleka, Spiro	F	F	F	F	F	F	F
Balluku, Beqir	F	F	F	F	F	F	dropped
Nushi, Gogo	F	F	F	F	F	died	—
Belishova, Liri	F	F	F	dropped	—	—	—
Jakova, Tuk	F	dropped	—	—	—	—	—
Spahiu, Bedri	F	dropped	—	—	—	—	—
Marko, Rita	—	C	F	F	F	F	F
Myftiu, Manush	—	C	F	F	F	F	F
Peristeri, Pilo	—	C	C	C	C	C	C
Çarçani, Adil	—	—	C	F	F	F	F
Alia, Ramiz	—	—	C	F	F	F	F
Toska, Haki	—	—	C	F	F	F	F
Theodhosi, Koço	—	—	C	C	C	F	dropped
Dervishi, Rrapo	—	—	C	dropped	—	—	—
Hazbiu, Kadri	—	—	—	C	C	F	F
Dume, Petrit	—	—	—	C	C	C	dropped
Këllezi, Abdyl	—	—	—	—	C	F	dropped
Dodbiba, Pirro	—	—	—	—	—	C	dropped

Spahiu, Xhafer	–	–	–	–	–	C	dropped
Miska, Pali	–	–	–	–	–	–	F
Isai, Hekuran	–	–	–	–	–	–	F
Gegprifti, Llambi	–	–	–	–	–	–	C
Mihali, Qirjako	–	–	–	–	–	–	C
Çuko, Lenka	–	–	–	–	–	–	C
Stefani, Simon	–	–	–	–	–	–	C

Sources: *Kongresi i Irë i Partisë Komuniste të Shqipërisë* (Tiranë: M. Duri Press, 1950), pp. 643–644; *Kongresi i IItë i Partisë së Punës të Shqipërisë* (Tiranë: M. Duri Press, 1952), pp. 423–424; *Bashkimi* [Unity] (Tiranë), June 4, 1956; Feb. 21, 1961; Nov. 9, 1966; *Zëri i popullit*, Nov. 8, 1971; Nov. 8, 1976.

4
The Socialization of the Economy

The nature of Albania's economy after the communist seizure of power in November 1944 and the manner in which it developed in the next three decades were determined inevitably by the prewar economic conditions in the country. Before World War II, Albania was a very backward agricultural country with practically no industry. Approximately 87.9 percent of the population was engaged in agriculture, but Albanian farmers were generally ignorant of chemical fertilizers, tractors, and other agricultural machinery. The irrigation of the soil was very limited and at a primitive level.[1]

Although the country was rich in mineral resources, such as oil, copper, chromium, and iron-nickel, they were largely undeveloped. There were no industries for oil refining or the processing of copper and chromium. Industrial units or enterprises were almost uniformly small. About 88 percent of them employed less than fifteen workers, and only 12 percent had more than fifteen. As a result, industrial production in 1938 accounted for only 9.8 percent of the total industrial and agricultural production in the country. Of the total national income in 1938, 92.4 percent derived from agriculture, and only 4.5 percent came from industry.[2]

Using classic communist terminology to explain conditions in prewar Albania, Albanian ideologists contend that the country's pronounced backwardness was due to the prevalence of semifeudal relations in the social order, the exploitation of the masses by the "feudal-bourgeois" ruling class, and the extensive penetration of the economy by foreign capital. This criticism, however, is somewhat distorted, since it makes no allowances for historical, cultural, and other factors that combined to produce such backwardness. It neglects or belittles, for example, the ruinous consequences of nearly five centuries of misrule of the country by the Ottoman Turks and the immense problem of laying the foundations of the new state that confronted King Zog's regime. To some extent, at least, Zog was a captive of the Ottoman legacy he inherited.[3]

A Radical Economic Policy

Communist governments that were established in postwar East Europe "made industrialization the principal aim of their economic policy, and state management the means."[4] Albania's economic policy fits this formula better perhaps than that of any other East European country. As soon as they seized power, Albania's communist leaders took steps to nationalize the basic means of production and establish central planning. Toward that end, they introduced a

Socialization of the Economy 53

"command"-type or centrally directed economic system. The "command economy" had almost irresistible appeal to the country's new rulers, because it seemed to offer the most promise toward the solution of the nation's urgent economic problems. Unlike the dispersed, small-market economy that prevailed before the war, the new system allowed them to concentrate the nation's resources on any sector, or sectors, of the economy and achieve results in a relatively short time.

Albania's first step in this direction was to nationalize all factories. This occurred in December of 1944. There followed in rapid order the nationalization of all industry, banks, the transportation system, foreign and wholesale trade, mineral resources, bodies of water, pastures, and forests. A distinguishing feature of Albania's policy of nationalization is that it was carried out "quickly and without compensation" to the expropriated parties.[5] It was a case, one might say, of "confiscation without compensation." By the end of 1946, 87 percent of the total industrial production in the country was due to the state, rather than the private sector of the economy. A year later, "capitalist industrial production" had been almost totally eliminated.

Albania's new leaders at this point seemed to have three main objectives in mind, in their drive to nationalize "the main means of production" and to industrialize the country as rapidly as possible. One objective was to extricate the country from the oppressive economic and technical backwardness of the past. Another was to "destroy the economic power of the bourgeoisie and foreign capital." The third aimed at consolidating the power of the Albanian Communist Party by placing the levers of the economy "into the hands" of the state. In brief, the economic policy of the new leaders was motivated by economic, political, and power considerations.

From 1945 onward, the overall goal of Albania's communists in the economic sphere was to transform the country from a backward agrarian society to an agrarian-industrial and finally to an industrial-agrarian one. This scheme gave priority to industry over agriculture within the total economy and to heavy as against light industry within the industrial sector. The new economic policy received strong endorsement at the First Party Congress in 1948, which drafted the main outlines "for the construction of the bases of socialism" and proclaimed "the socialist industrialization and electrification of the country" as the central task of the economy.[6]

The policy of nationalization and central control of the economy met with opposition from both within and without the country. Already in 1945, the nationalization of transportation prompted owners of motor vehicles to damage them or "hide them in various places," rather than turn them over to the state. The decisive confrontation between defenders of moderate-liberal economic policies and proponents of "anticapitalist," "anti-imperialist" economics came in February 1946 at the meeting of the Fifth Party Plenum. At that meeting, the Party's secretary-general, Enver Hoxha, clashed with Sejfulla Malëshova, a member of the Central Committee, leading communist theoretician, and advocate of an economic policy favoring the coexistence and simultaneous development of both socialist and capitalist economies. Malëshova was defeated and expelled from the Party's Central Committee. His defeat marked a turning point in Albania's economic orientation, signaling the abandonment of even a mild form of private enterprise and the zealous adoption of statist and socialist economics.

The sharp turn toward a radical collectivist economy fostered a polarization of procapitalist and prosocialist forces in the country, which in some instances led to acts of violence. Albanian officials and historians claim that the overthrown classes, landlords and capitalists, attempted to rise against the new communist government. "The characteristic feature of the birth of the socialist sector of our country," according to Albanian sources, "is that it was created and strengthened in the course of a sharp class struggle."[7] The domestic "class enemies" reportedly were incited to engage in sabotage of the people's economy by foreign imperialists, headed by the Americans and the English. Whether or not there was any truth to this accusation, it was obviously useful to the Hoxha leadership at the time, in order to discredit the opposition and mobilize popular support for the new radical economic policy. Indeed, this accusation—namely, the branding of domestic dissenters as agents of foreign powers—subsequently became a standard formula in the Party's propaganda arsenal and was liberally applied against the opposition, not only on questions of the economy but in relation to any phase of the Albanian society, be it in politics, literature, education, or the armed forces.

In a few years, as the state sector of the economy grew and the private sector diminished, Albania's economic system began to show the first symptoms of the malady of bureaucracy. By the early 1950s, Party spokesmen were already identifying bureaucracy as the chief obstacle to the healthy development of the economy, and from time to time they initiated a variety of programs to eradicate the malady. During this period, Albania, along with other East European countries (except Yugoslavia), copied faithfully the Soviet type of economy as it developed under Stalin in the 1930s. But whereas the economies of other East European countries underwent significant reforms in the 1960s, Albania never went that far. Kaser and Zielinski have correctly noted that Albania "has steadfastly preserved the directive [that is, the highly centralized economic] system it took from the USSR," despite a program of "workers' control" that was launched in 1968 with the aim of overcoming the numerous problems spawned by the new economic system.[8] While it is true that in 1966 Albania simplified her planning system somewhat, there has been no true economic reform there. Albania's economy continued to be characterized by her "highly centralized, rigid, authoritarian, and generally primitive planning system," leaving little leeway for "a transfer of certain decision-making powers to lower echelons" of the economic structure.[9]

The Development of Industry

As of 1976, Albania had completed five 5-YPs (Five-Year Plans), covering the twenty-five year period from 1950 through 1975. Throughout this period, the emphasis in the development of the economy was on industry, especially the extractive and processing branches of industry. This policy has been expressed by Hoxha as follows: "In its economic policy for the socialist industrialization of the country, the party . . . [was] always guided by the Leninist thesis that heavy industry is the basis of socialist industrialization, that in this process the production of the means of production must have higher rates of growth than the production of consumer articles."[10] As a result, throughout the process of economic modernization in Albania, priority was always given to the development of heavy industry.

One of the directives in the industrialization effort aimed at a "rational distribution of industry" in the country. This meant building enterprises close to the sources of raw materials—above all, electric power and mineral resources—and as evenly throughout the various districts and regions of the country as possible. Apart from the economic rationale of such a directive, there was also a political rationale; namely, to bring industry to the countryside and in the process break down the traditional social division of labor in the village, which held in check the modernization of rural society. As a consequence, Albania gradually began to develop a fledgling industry, including a number of totally new industries. New communities grew in time around the new industrial enterprises where oil, chromium, copper, and other natural resources were being exploited. Some of the new industrial centers are Cërrik, Bulqizë, Krabë, Memaliaj, Maliq, and Patos. The expansion of the industrial sector and the rise of new technologies brought into the hands of

Albania's rustic population a growing list of domestically produced industrial products, such as glass, paper, copper wire, generators, transformers, chemical fertilizers, and soil cultivators.

Albania made her first efforts at a planned economy as early as 1947, when she launched a program for "the development of industry and mines" as the basis for the development of other branches of the economy. The same basic idea became the cornerstone of the Two-Year Plan (1949-1950), which preceded the inauguration of the country's First 5-YP in the 1950s. The 2-YP envisioned the development above all of industry, especially the mineral industry, such as oil, bitumen, chromium, coal, and copper.

First 5-YP (1951-1955)
Following the pattern set by the Soviet Union, Albania adopted the principle of long-term economic planning as the most suitable model for the modernization of her productive forces. On September 21, 1951, the Eleventh Plenum of the Party's Central Committee announced the directives for the country's First 5-YP.[11] At the heart of the plan, like its less ambitious forerunners, lay the development of industry. The plan concentrated on the development of light industry, in order to resolve the most urgent tasks confronting the country, such as the food and clothing needs of the population. The overall objective of the plan was to transform Albania from a backward agrarian country to an "agricultural-industrial" country. The original production goals of the plan, however, proved to be overambitious. Following Stalin's death in 1953, the Party leadership was obliged to revise the plan downward and eliminate the construction of a number of projects, including a steel mill, a paper mill, and a plant for briquetting coal.

At the end of the plan in 1955, it was announced that a light industrial base had been built in the country and that Albania had now become an agricultural-industrial society. Some of the projects completed during the First 5-YP were the Nako Spiro lumber combine in Elbasan, the V. I. Lenin power plant and the Stalin textile combine in Tiranë, a cement factory in Vlorë, cotton gins in Rrogozhinë and Fier, and a tobacco fermentation plant in Shkodër.

Owing however to the government's obsessive preoccupation with industrial development, the development of agriculture lagged far behind industry. This gave rise to a discrepancy in the development of the two sectors which, in spite of efforts to eradicate it, remained substantially large by the end of the plan in 1955. It was an ominous sign that persisted through succeeding Five-Year Plans and became a blot on the Albanian economy.

Second 5-YP (1956-1960)

The major effort during this time frame was on the development of heavy industry—called the "heavy artillery" in the building of socialism in Albania. It was the time of China's Great Leap Forward (1958), and Albania, like two other Balkan countries, Bulgaria and Romania, came under the influence of that unorthodox Chinese economic concept. Being a largely agrarian country, Albania showed interest in the Chinese idea of a rapid transition to communism. She found merit in China's claim that the "great leap forward" technique made possible the most effective mobilization of a developing nation's economic resources.[12]

The flirtation with the Chinese model of economic development, however, did not last long, since at this time Albania was predominantly under the influence of the Soviet Union and East Europe. Responding to increased Soviet economic assistance in February 1958, Albania revised her Second 5-YP in favor of a more rapid development of the national economy, above all in the area of heavy industry. The result was that industry for the first time surpassed agriculture in the total industrial and agricultural production. Thus, in 1960, industrial production climbed over the 50 percent mark to 57.1, a remarkable advance from the 9.8 percent figure it registered in 1938.

At the end of the Second 5-YP, Albania's leaders announced the completion of "the construction of the economic basis of socialism," both in the cities and in the countryside. The results of the plan, therefore, were seen as a great historical victory for the Albanian people and Albanian socialism. During this period, the production of chromium made great strides, giving Albania first place in the world in per capita production of chromium ore.[13] Among projects completed during the second half of the 1950s were the Karl Marx hydroelectric plant on the Mati River, with a capacity of 120 million kwh per year; an oil refinery at Cërrik capable of refining 159,000 tons per year; the Dinamo sports stadium in Tiranë; tourist hotels in Durrës; and a number of hospitals, theaters, and cinema houses in Berat, Lushnjë, Korçë, and Shkodër.

The Second 5-YP marked the high point of economic cooperation between the Soviet Union and Albania. A special feature of this period was the long-range planning by Albanian and Soviet experts for the most rational development of Albania's economy. The planning involved a fifteen-year perspective (1961-1975), which was going to "change the face" of Albania. The idea was made known in a joint Soviet-Albanian declaration issued in Moscow on April 17, 1957. The declaration said: "... the government of the U.S.S.R. is extending to Albania scientific and technical assistance in working out the prospective plan for developing the national economy for 10-15 years, which will insure a balanced development of the country's economy by means of greater agricultural development."[14] As it turned out, Soviet economic cooperation with Albania soon foundered on the rocks of ideological and political conflict that destroyed the Soviet-Albanian alliance, and the fifteen-year-plan perspective worked out by experts of the two countries never materialized.

Third 5-YP (1961-1965)
Albania began her Third 5-YP in conditions of a major shift of political allies, from the Soviet Union to communist China. The shift of alliances had important consequences for Albania's economy. The directives of the new plan were announced by Premier Mehmet Shehu at the Party's Fourth Congress in February 1961. Like its predecessors, the new plan emphasized "the continuation of the industrialization" of the country. More significantly, perhaps, Shehu declared that Albania had now "entered a new historical stage—that of the complete construction of the socialist society."[15] He was prudent not to say how long the new stage would last.

The new feature of the plan was that, unlike any previous plan, it paid more attention to the development of agriculture. Possibly because of the influence of Chinese advisers, for the first time in a Five-Year Plan the growth rate for Albania's agricultural production was set at a higher figure than that of industry. The motive behind this decision was to move faster toward the closing of the gap in the development of industry and agriculture and thereby achieve a more balanced growth of the entire economy. The final results of the plan, however, showed that neither industry nor agriculture was able to fulfill the production goals envisaged for them.[16] The failure was due largely to the serious dislocations experienced by the economy in the wake of the halt by the Soviets in 1961 of all economic assistance to the intransigent Balkan country. Albanian sources admit that work on the construction of several major projects, such as the Mao Tse-tung textile combine at Berat and a fertilizer plant at Fier, was delayed almost three years because of the break with the USSR. Albania's leaders, moreover, have frequently said that the 1961-1965 period was "the most difficult period" since they took power in 1944.

Nevertheless, the economy proved resilient enough to withstand the strains created by the cut-off of Soviet aid and credits. Among the projects completed during the Third 5-YP were metallurgy plants in Elbasan and Gjegjan, a copper processing plant in Rubik, a caustic soda factory in Vlorë, several paper manufacturing plants, and the building of a considerable number of schools, hospitals, maternity houses, vacation resorts, and cultural centers. In addition, land reclamation projects were carried out in the districts of Durrës, Lezhë, Vurg, Thumanë, and Fier-Roskovec, resulting in an expansion of the total arable land in the country.

Fourth 5-YP (1966-1970)
By the beginning of the Fourth 5-YP Albania, with the help of her Chinese ally, had substantially recovered from the economic crisis of the early 1960s. Accordingly, the government raised the production targets for the new plan, in comparison with the production percentages attained in the preceding plan. The basis of the new plan again was "the continuation of the socialist industrialization of the country," in order to accelerate the complete construction of "the material and technical basis" of socialism.[17] The plan stressed above all the development of the processing sector of heavy industry. This view was in line with the policy of cutting down imports of manufactured goods, while increasing the export of finished and semifinished goods.

A characteristic of the Fourth 5-YP is that it coincided almost exactly with Albania's Ideological and Cultural Revolution (1966-1969). As such, it became the object of unprecedented campaigns by the Party leadership to stamp out stifling bureaucratic practices in the economy, stimulate production, equalize wages, and narrow the differences between the populations of the lowlands and the highlands, between urban and rural dwellers, and between white-collar and production workers. The plan thus became both a mirror and a test of the effectiveness of the cultural revolution. It was during this time frame that Albania eliminated direct taxation of her citizens (November 1969) and completed the electrification of all towns and villages in the country (October 25, 1970). Accordingly, the government decreed that October 25 be observed annually throughout the land as "The People's Festival of Light."

As part of the cultural revolution, Albania made special efforts during the Fourth 5-YP to enlarge the ranks of the working class and strengthen the role and authority of workers in the operation of the economy. Toward that end, the government began a campaign in 1968 to institute "working-class control" in the economy, with the object of encouraging initiative and greater industry among workers, developing their class consciousness, and making them the final arbiters in all matters of dispute with managers of enterprises. The government also promoted the movement of workers from the cities to the countryside, mostly it seems in order to further the dissemination of the Party line to rural areas. The idea was to carry the "working-class spirit" to the four corners of the land and to strengthen "the leading role" of the workers in the construction of the socialist economy. These efforts produced only minor results in curbing bureaucracy and advancing the process of modernizing the economy. However, the ranks of the workers did grow steadily with the development of industry and the economy as a whole, as table 4.1 shows.

From a mere 15,000 workers in the Albania of 1938, their number grew to 357,000 in 1973 and to 370,000 in 1976.[18] Albanian demographers confidently predicted that within twenty years the working class, which in 1971 represented one-third of the nation's population, would become the major segment of the population. It was a prospect the Albanian regime welcomed, since it looked upon the working class as the most reliable element for the building of socialism in the country.

As the economy became more industrialized and the program of farm collectivization moved forward, a change occurred also in the social composition of the population. Thus, between 1950 and 1973 the percentage of office workers increased from 10.1 to 14.4—a reflection in part of the swelling ranks of the state bureaucracy and the larger role of the social services sector in the economy. It was the industrial workers, however, who registered the biggest gains, advancing from 11.2 percent in 1950 to 36.2 percent in 1973. The gain of 25 percentage points by the industrial workers over a twenty-three year period spoke eloquently of the rapid strides that industrialization

Table 4.1
Growth of the Working Class

Year	Number of Workers	Increase since 1938 (in times)
1938	15,000	1
1950	55,000	4
1960	154,000	10
1970	307,000	20
1973	357,000	24

Source: *30 vjet Shqipëri socialiste* [30 years of Albanian socialism] (Tiranë: M. Duri Press, 1974), p. 41.

Socialization of the Economy

Table 4.2
The Social Composition of the Population (In Percentages)

	1950	1960	1969	1973
Office workers	10.1	11.3	11.3	14.4
Industrial workers	11.2	29.1	32.9	36.2
Farmers	74.3	58.7	55.7	49.4
Cooperative	1.7	41.6	55.4	49.4
Private	72.6	17.1	0.3	—
Tradesmen and storekeepers	4.4	0.9	0.1	—

Source: Compiled from a table in *30 vjet*, p. 28.

was making in the country. During the same period, the farming population fell below the 50 percent mark, while the sector of independent tradesmen and storekeepers disappeared altogether. These changes become manifest in table 4.2.

Fifth 5-YP (1971-1975)

Inaugurated in 1971, the Fifth 5-YP called for "the further development of industry," especially the heavy extracting and processing industries. The plan was designed primarily to expand Albania's capacity for processing her rich reserves of mineral ores, such as copper, chromium, and iron-nickel, as well as oil and bitumen. It was the belief of Party leaders that rapid progress in this area would make Albania progressively self-sufficient in the economic sphere and therefore more independent politically as well.

The plan revolved principally around three industrial projects—the most ambitious in the history of modern Albania. They were: the Fierzë hydroelectric power plant on the River Drin in northern Albania, with a capacity of 500,000 kwh and an annual capacity of 1.5 billion kwh—nearly equal to the total electric energy (1.6 billion kwh) produced by Albania in 1973; the metallurgy combine in Elbasan, central Albania, which was designed to produce 800,000 tons of iron-nickel a year—more than double the amount produced in the entire country in 1973 (384,000 tons); and the oil refining plant at Ballsh in the southwestern part of the country, with a capacity of 1,000,000 tons a year, a vast increase from the 624,000 tons of oil refined in 1973 throughout the nation.[19] The completion of these projects was expected to accelerate substantially the construction of the material base of socialism in the country. Accordingly, progress on these projects received great publicity in the media and was exploited to stimulate production, build up credit for the Party leadership, and create a favorable image of Albania abroad as a country well on the road to modernization.

Indeed, during the Fifth 5-YP Albania made a number of leaps forward into the twentieth century. In October 1970, an announcement noted the inauguration of a nuclear radiation research laboratory on the campus of the State University of Tiranë. The equipment for the laboratory came from China, in the form of a gift from the Chinese Academy of Sciences. The installation of Albania's first electronic computer center in 1971 was another indication of forward movement for the country's economy. This was also the year of the debut of Albania's first television station, not far from Tiranë. Two years later (December 1973), the news media reported the linkage of all towns and villages in the country by a national telephone communications system. These developments testified to the transformation that was taking place in Albania's economy since the war. They showed increasingly the impact of modern science and technology in Albanian society, and all of this in the face of an orthodox economic ideology, a dictatorial political system, and a stifling bureaucracy.

Table 4.3 illustrates more graphically the development of industry during successive five-year plans.

The table is revealing in a number of respects. It shows the rate of industrial growth falling as the economy becomes more industrialized. All items,

Table 4.3
Annual Average Growth Rates in Industrial Production for Selected Items, According to Five-Year Plans (In Percentages)

	First, 1951–55	Second, 1956–60	Third, 1961–65	Fourth, 1966–70	Fifth, 1971–75
All industry	22.6	16.9	6.8	12.9	8.7
Oil	7.4	33.1	4.7	15.2	4.3
Chromium	18.5	19.1	1.4	9.3	11.0
Coal	36.5	7.8	6.2	11.9	7.6
Copper	3.2	13.8	38.7	25.1	8.8
Food	14.9	15.4	6.1	5.8	—*

Source: For 5-YPs One through Four, *30 vjet*, p. 64. For Fifth 5-YP, *Albania today*, no. 5 (Sept.–Oct. 1976), p. 10.
* Data not available.

Table 4.4
Investments According to Five-Year Plans (In Percentages)

	First, 1951–55	Second, 1956–60	Third, 1961–65	Fourth, 1966–70	Fifth, 1971–75
Industry	52	44	49	46.6	65.7
Agriculture	12	18	15	16.0	11.7
Transportation and communication	13	13	11	11.4	5.7
Housing	8	8	8	6.9	4.9
Education, culture and health	6	5	4	5.4	3.6
Other	9	12	13	13.7	8.4

Sources: Besim Bardhoshi and Theodhor Kareco, *Zhvillimi ekonomiko-shoqëror në Shqipëri, 1944-1974* [Economic and social development in Albania, 1944-1974] (Tiranë: M. Duri Press, 1974), p. 131; (hereafter, *Zhvillimi ekonomiko-shoqëror*). M. Shehu, *Report on the 5th 5-Year Plan* (Tiranë, N. Frashëri Pub. Hse., 1971), p. 85.

except copper, show drops in growth rates, with the biggest decreases occurring in coal and food production. Even the copper industry suffered sharp reversals in production since the early sixties. The table reveals the negative effects on Albania's Third 5-YP that attended the break with the USSR. It also shows that the same general pattern of falling production occurred in the Fifth 5-YP, though to a lesser degree than that which occurred in the Third 5-YP. The reversal in the growth rates of the latest plan indicates that the economic tie between Albania and China began to weaken during this period.

The strong emphasis on industrial development, in accordance with classic communist doctrine and Soviet experience, becomes manifest in table 4.4.

It is obvious from the data that the overwhelming share in investment funds went into industry, followed by agriculture, while the least amount went into what might be called "social service" programs: education, culture, and health. More important, perhaps, is the great gap in allocations made to industry and agriculture, with the allocations to industry being from two to nearly six times as large as those to agriculture.

The Development of Agriculture

Agricultural productivity, especially the cultivation of grain crops, is dependent of course on many factors: climate, soil, technology, topography. In the

Table 4.5
Classification of Land Area, in Prewar Albania (In Thousand Hectares)

	1938	Percentage
Total area	2,875	100.0
Agricultural area	1,180	41.0
Arable	292	10.2
Pasture	888	30.8
Forests	1,308	45.5
Arid land	387	13.5

Source: Compiled from a table in *Zhvillimi ekonomiko-shoqëror*, p. 32.

case of Albania, topography is of particular importance, owing to the peculiar character of the Albanian terrain. Albania, as is generally known, is a very mountainous country, with 70.5 percent of her territory lying more than 300 m (about 1,000 ft) above sea level. This altitude is "twice the average altitude of Europe."[20] Of necessity, the development of agriculture in Albania is limited by the unusually rugged terrain of the country. Compared with the other Balkan countries, Albania has from 50 to 100 percent less arable land area per capita. An important consequence of this condition is the limitation it places on efforts to mechanize agriculture. A report on Albanian agriculture, published in 1957, said that about "40 percent of the sown area is made up of mountain slopes which are inaccessible to tractors."[21] The characteristics of the terrain, and their significance for agriculture, come into clearer focus in table 4.5.

As can be seen, only two-fifths (41.0%) of Albania's total land area was suitable for agricultural use. More importantly, only one-fourth (10.2%) of the agricultural area was utilized for crop cultivation and horticulture. Such are the facts of topography Albanian agriculture has had to contend with.

Before World War II, agriculture, like the rest of the economy, reflected the backward state of Albanian society. The wooden plow was an apt symbol for it. Extensive plains along the seacoast—potentially the most productive areas in the country—lay under marshy, malaria-infested waters. Almost no work had been done in irrigation and land reclamation. The average farmer had no familiarity with modern agricultural machinery and techniques, such as the use of tractors, chemical fertilizers, seed selection, and insecticides.

Following the war, the communist regime began to reorganize the agricultural economy in line with its program to weaken and destroy private ownership of the land and replace it with the collective system. Party leaders were convinced that the collectivization of agriculture was a prerequisite for modernization. Beyond that, the policy of collectivization had a political goal, namely, to place agriculture under the firm control of the state. There is evidence that the Party leadership considered the option of the "nationalization of the land" more or less simultaneously with the nationalization of industry, commerce, and banking, which was carried out soon after the war. The option was dropped, we are told, "because it did not answer to the relations of class forces in the countryside. The majority of the farmers were strongly attached to the land...."[22] In other words, the idea was abandoned because the leadership feared the social and political consequences of such a measure.

Instead, the government adopted a gradualist approach to the transformation of the agricultural economy, based on persuasion and education of the peasantry but, if need be, the employment also of "administrative measures"— a euphemism for the use of force to implement state policy. The first step in the process was the promulgation of the Law on Agrarian Reform in August 1945 on the principle that "the land belongs to the tiller." The reform, which Albanian sources have called "the most important" early postwar measure taken by the Albanian Communist Party, was completed in May 1946. Under the provisions of the agrarian reform act, the government confiscated the large landed estates without making any compensation to the owners. The land was then distributed among the peasants, with the stipulation that it could not be sold, bought, or rented. The reform act reportedly affected 4,720 big and small landlords, comprising 3 percent of the country's farming households. It resulted in the destruction of the landlord class, which in the view of Albanian communist leaders was the most reactionary class at the time in the country.

The Albanian leadership resorted to a subtle tactic in carrying out the agrarian reform. The preparatory step was "the creation of poor peasants' committees" which "demanded" agrarian reform. Albanian sources note that under these circumstances the reform "was presented as a measure that was carried out in response to demand from below, from the broad masses of the peasantry."[23] In other words, the land reform was not prompted by a spontaneous mass peasant movement; rather, it was engineered from above. This same tactic apparently was used in 1967 to close down the churches and mosques and to officially abolish the religious establishment in the country.

Party leaders, however, did not view agrarian reform as a completely adequate measure for bringing about more equitable social and economic relations in the countryside. They claimed that the only way to build socialism in the villages was to collectivize agriculture. "Any other road," Hoxha said in 1966, "leads only to the restoration of capitalism in the countryside."[24] The first step toward collectivization was taken in 1946, with the establishment of the first agricultural cooperatives in the country. This development marked the start of "the second and most radical revolution" in the socioeconomic relations in the countryside. The "revolution" proceeded slowly during the first decade, or until the end of the First 5-YP in 1955. In that year, Albanian agriculture was for the most part still dominated by independent farmers. Slightly over 87 percent of the total agricultural produce in 1955 was due to the private sector, and only about 13 percent came from the socialist sector.

The pace of collectivization accelerated with the beginning of the Second 5-YP in 1956. The change of pace was initiated at a meeting of the Party Plenum in December 1955, which concluded that "the necessary conditions were ripe" for speeding up the development of agriculture along "socialist lines."[25] By 1960, 86.9 percent of the country's agriculture was in the socialist sector (including both the state and cooperativist sectors), and only 13.1 percent—mostly the economies of the highlands—remained in the private sector. In general, then, the collectivization of Albanian agriculture was completed by the end of the Second 5-YP.

It was also during this period (in 1959) that the Albanian government—probably under the influence of China's "people's communes" program—initiated a policy of merging or unifying small cooperatives into larger units. Thereafter, the total number of farm cooperatives began to decrease from year to year; for example, from 1,915 in 1959, the number dropped to 819 in 1966. In 1967, the Party took the decision to extend the experiment of farm collectivization even to the remote hinterlands of the country. The Fourth 5-YP (1966-1970) thus stands out as the plan of the complete collectivization of Albanian agriculture. The road to collectivization is shown in tables 4.6 and 4.7.

Officially, Albania maintains that the collectivization of agriculture, like the agrarian reform, was a voluntary process. The data, however, from Albanian and other sources suggest that the process was not entirely voluntary but met with strong resistance on the part of at least a portion of the peasantry. This can be inferred from frequent statements in Albanian materials that collectivization was carried out "in the face of a sharp class struggle"—a synonym for popular resistance to unwanted government programs.

Table 4.6
Shift in Ownership of Land (In Percentages)

	1945	1950	1960	1973
Landlords	40	—	—	—
Peasants	60	91.6	12.9	—
Collectivized farms	—	8.4	87.1	100

Source: Compiled from a table in *30 vjet*, p. 103.

Table 4.7
The Development of Farm Collectivization

	1950	1960	1965	1970
No. of co-ops	90	1,484	868*	643*
No. of co-op families	4,500	114,500	130,500	98,800
Percentage of collectivized area	5.5	85.0	88.5	100.0

Source: Compiled from a table in *Zhrillimi ekonomiko-shoqëror*, p. 95.
Note: Does not include the state sector.

The government's radical farm policies also provoked the resistance of peasants in connection with livestock. According to Soviet sources—at a time when the Soviets were on friendly terms with the Albanians—during the first years following the war, the "kulaks" in Albania "started a mass slaughtering of cattle, as a result of the transfer of large herds of cattle to the state farms" as well as to the very poor peasants.[26] Another study shows that in 1957 the number of livestock per 1,000 inhabitants was lower than in 1938.[27] Even when allowance is made for the fact that a percentage of the cattle perished during the war, the lack of progress in the breeding of livestock in postwar Albania suggests that this was in large part due to the peasants' resistance to the government's policies on animal husbandry.

One government policy that had an inhibiting effect on livestock breeding was the emphasis given to the production of industrial crops, such as cotton, tobacco, and sugar beet, which cut down progressively the acreage of natural pastures. Whereas in 1938 pastures accounted for 30.8 percent of the total land surface in the country, in 1971 the percentage was down to 21.5.[28] In 1972, 13.8 percent of the arable land was utilized for the production of industrial plants, compared with only 1.3 percent in 1938. The government gave priority to the growth of industrial plants to meet both domestic needs—such as cotton and sugar beet for the developing textile and sugar industries—and export needs, especially tobacco, for which there was a great demand abroad, owing to its fine quality.

The major problem by far that Albania's leaders have had to face in agriculture has been the shortage of food production. It is not a new problem. Agriculture in prewar Albania was able reportedly to meet "only one-half of the country's requirements for bread."[29] As a consequence, King Zog's government had to import vast quantities of grain annually: 25,300 metric tons in 1936; 40,000 tons in 1937; and 34,600 tons in 1938.[30] The situation persisted in postwar Albania, becoming very serious by 1955. Owing largely to the Party's preoccupation with the development of industry, plus the rapid growth of the country's population, especially in urban centers, agriculture lagged behind and failed consistently to fulfill the plans for food production. Albanian sources admit that "normally tens of thousands of tons of wheat and corn" were imported "every year" during the first decade of communist rule.[31] According to Skendi, Albania imported from 50,000 to 60,000 tons of bread grains annually from the Soviet Union and East European countries.[32]

In 1956, Albania's leaders resolved to overcome the problem of food production. They confidently expected that by the year 1960 food cereals would no longer be imported, since domestic food production would meet all the food needs of the population. This was to be a historic achievement of the Second 5-YP, as decreed by the Third Party Congress in May 1956. The plan to become self-sufficient in food production had the strong support of the Soviets, who thought that the most important aspect of the development of Albania's economy was agriculture. The Soviets were interested above all in citrus fruits and did their best to encourage Albania's industry-oriented leaders to adopt the view that the cultivation of citrus fruits was "an obligation of Albania" within the context of the socialist division of labor in East Europe.[33]

But neither Soviet encouragement and material assistance nor the extra efforts made during the Second 5-YP in the development of agriculture were enough to achieve the grand goal of self-sufficiency in food production. Albania continued to import food as before. In 1959, for example, Albania produced 101,666 tons of wheat but had to import an additional 94,300 tons from the USSR to meet her food needs.[34] The experience of the Second 5-YP, namely, the drafting of plans to resolve the question of food production and the failure to realize the plans, became a ritual at every succeeding Five-Year Plan. It is a pattern of failure that no amount of planning, investment funds, organization of farm labor, or foreign aid for agricultural development was able to reverse during the Third, Fourth, and Fifth 5-YPs, covering the period 1960-1975.

Probably on the advice of the Chinese, Albania's economic planners for the first time set a higher growth rate, during the Third 5-YP (1961-1965), for agricultural production than for industrial production. At the end of the plan, food production increased 51 percent over the previous plan but failed nevertheless to achieve the goal of self-sufficiency. During the Fourth 5-YP, the food crops yield again showed an increase (60%), compared with the preceding period, but again fell short of the announced goal. The figures on the results of the Fifth 5-YP showed that agricultural production fell far short of the target set for it. Compared with the Fourth 5-YP, production grew only 33 percent instead of the projected 65-69 percent.[35] The annual growth rate during this period was 5.9 percent instead of the planned figure of 10.8 percent. Once again, the hopes of Albania's leadership to meet completely the food needs of the country through domestic production fell short of realization.

Albania's efforts to modernize her agriculture involved work in two major areas: expansion of arable acreage and the "intensification" of farming. Through extensive land reclamation programs in marshy areas and the conversion of hilly territory into arable land, Albania was able to increase the total area of arable land from 292,000 hectares in 1938 to 636,000 in 1973. Thus, by 1973 the total arable land had increased 2.2 times. This represents significant progress over a period of roughly three decades. Yet, owing to the mountainous terrain of the country, "extensive agriculture"—that is, expansion of the cultivable area—was necessarily limited.

Accordingly, Albania's planners focused their attention primarily on "intensive agriculture," which is to say, obtaining greater rates of productivity for a given area of land through wider and better irrigation, increased use of chemical fertilizers and insecticides, electrification of the countryside, and the mechanization of farm work. The irrigation program made much headway. In 1973, 56 percent of the arable area benefited from irrigation, as against 10.5 percent of the land in 1938. Use of chemical fertilizers is reported to have increased forty times between 1950 and 1973, or from 5,200 tons (1950) to 208,900 tons (1973). In the same period, the use of insecticides went up from 138 tons to 8,700, an increase of sixty-three times.[36]

The Albanian leaders attached great importance to the electrification of rural areas. They reasoned that electric power would play a big role in the "intensification" of agriculture by advancing the mechanization of farm

Table 4.8
Use of Motor and Animal Power

	1938		1972		
	In Thousand hp	In Percentage	In Thousand hp	In Percentage	Growth in Times (approx.)
Total power used	109.3	100.0	641	100.0	6
Motorized power	0.8	0.8	592	92.2	740
Draft animal power	108.5	99.2	50	7.8	—

Source: *Zhillimi ekonomiko-shoqëror*, p. 116.

Table 4.9
Utilization of Farm Machinery

	1938	1972	Growth in Times
Tractors (15 hp)	30	12,505	417
Threshing machines	75	1,300	17
Combines	—	988	
Reapers	—	885	

Source: *Zhvillimi ekonomiko-shoqëror*, p. 117.

work, lightening the work of farmers, and increasing farm output in all indexes. The increased use of motorized power in postwar Albania, as against animal power, becomes evident in table 4.8.

The increase of motorized power by 740 times between 1938 and 1972 is truly remarkable. It practically displaced the use of draft animals, on which Albanian peasants had depended for thousands of years in their efforts to eke out a living from a not too hospitable soil. Progress in mechanization is also indicated by statistics on the use of specific items of farm machinery, as shown in table 4.9.

Albanian economists claim that 75 percent of the increase in food crops production from 1938 to 1972 was due to the employment of the intensive rather than the extensive method in agriculture. During the same period, production per 100 hectares of arable land reportedly increased 3.8 times, a development that pointed to "a significant transition from the extensive to the intensive road in ... agriculture."[37]

In addition to the extensive and intensive methods, Albania relied heavily on yet another method for the modernization of agriculture, which may be designated as "political work." Activities relating to this method were generally pursued under the slogan of "putting politics ahead," which meant that political considerations had priority over practical, technical, and scientific questions in agriculture. In effect, political work involved the "class education" of farmers to make them politically mature and work harder; the reorganization of rural life along the socialist path so as to enable more people, especially women, to work on the farms; a more efficient organization of farm labor and procedures; and the periodic mingling of northern and southern farm populations for varying lengths of time, in order that they might profit from each other's knowledge and experience in farming, as well as in home economics, personal hygiene, and general cultural development. Albanian leaders believed that the exchange of personnel between north and south was both politically sound and economically productive.

The uppermost question by the midseventies remained, as before, the domestic production of food grains sufficient to meet the needs of the population. There was no evidence, at the end of a twenty-year effort, that the answer to that question had been found.

The Changing Face of the Economy

One of the more significant results of the development of the Albanian economy since 1938 has been the change in the urban-rural ratio of the population. The process of modernization brought about an increase of the urban population from 15 percent in 1938 to 34 percent in 1973 and a corresponding

Table 4.10
Urban-Rural Distribution of the Population (In Thousands)

Year	Total Population	Urban	Percentage	Rural	Percentage
1938	1,040	160	15	880	85
1950	1,198	245	20	953	80
1960	1,607	470	29	1,137	71
1970	2,135	719	34	1,416	66
1973	2,297	778	34	1,519	66

Source: *30 vjet*, p. 22.
Note: As of 1976, Albania's population was about 2.5 million.

Table 4.11
Sources of National Income: Industry vs. Agriculture (In Percentage)

	1938	1950	1960	1973*
Industry and agriculture	100.0	100.0	100.0	100.0
Industry (including construction, transportation, and commerce)	6.9	23.7	55.6	65.8
Agriculture	93.1	76.3	44.4	34.2

Source: *30 vjet*, p. 180.
*Estimated figures.

Table 4.12
Military, Education, and Health Expenditures in Albania and Neighboring Countries (Per Capita, in U.S. Dollars, 1973)

	Military	Education	Health
Albania	53	20	5
Greece	75	34	20
Yugoslavia	42	52	10
Italy	75	119	29

Source: Compiled from a table in the *New York Times*, Mar. 7, 1976.

decrease of the rural population from 85 to 66 percent. Compared with 1938, the urban population in 1973 was five times greater, while the rural population registered only a 58 percent increase. The statistical evidence for this shift is given in table 4.10.

With regard to national income, Albanian sources indicate that it grew nearly eleven times between 1938 and 1973. The per capita income in 1973 reportedly was 4.8 times as much as in 1938. As table 4.11 shows, there was a significant shift in the sources of national income, as between agriculture and industry. Already in 1960 agriculture had taken a subordinate position to industry in the generation of national income. It continued to weaken thereafter, so that by the midseventies it generated only half as much income as industry.

But although per capita income and expenditures in postwar Albania increased appreciably since 1938, a comparison of military, educational, and health expenditures in that country with neighboring nations in 1973 shows that Albania spent proportionately more for military purposes than her neighbors. The country's basically isolationist politics and economic policy had the effect of siphoning substantial sums of money from the social services sector, including education and health, for use in the military sector. The actual data appear in table 4.12.

The Dilemma of Foreign Trade

On October 3, 1974, Enver Hoxha said that Albania had diplomatic, trade, and cultural relations with sixty-five countries. By contrast, in 1950 Albania traded only with the seven countries of the Soviet bloc. The number trebled by 1958, when the list of trade partners increased to twenty-two and more than doubled by 1970 when it exceeded the fifty mark.

Moreover, as her economy became more industrialized, the number of items for export grew steadily, above all in the category of manufactured goods. Compared with 1938, when the list of exports totaled forty-eight articles, the number grew to eighty-five in 1960 and to over two hundred in 1973. Table 4.13 shows the growth of exports of leading articles in the mineral sector—Albania's greatest source of income in foreign trade.

In 1973, the list of export items also included ready-to-wear clothes, wine (57,000 hl), tobacco (7,894 tons), cigarettes (3,885 tons), vegetables (31,000 tons), and fruits (6,642 tons).[38] In turn, imports consisted of such items as industrial and farm machinery; electric equipment; spare parts; chemical products; medical supplies; construction materials; motor vehicles; glass, paper, and rubber products; and food shipments. The policy on foreign trade was to import producer goods for the purpose of building the country's heavy industry and to reduce progressively the importation of consumer goods. Conversely, this policy called for reducing the export of raw materials,

Table 4.13
Export of Leading Minerals (In Thousand Tons)

	1938	1950	1960	1970	1973
Oil	105	67	329	81	412
Bitumen	12	65	236	677	967
Iron	—	—	245	390	318
Chromium	7	21	249	452	466
Copper	—	723	761	1,354	2,016

Source: *30 vjet*, p. 180.

Table 4.14
Export of Processed and Unprocessed Goods (In Percentages)

	1950	1970	1973
Processed	37.3	58.7	64.4
Unprocessed	62.7	41.3	35.6

Source: *30 vjet*, p. 179.

including mineral ores and foodstuffs, and increasing the export of finished and semifinished products. The results of this policy are shown in table 4.14.

Yet, progress toward industrialization had not changed Albania's basic economic relationship to the outside world by the midseventies. Ever since she became an organized state in the 1920s, Albania has had to rely on a bigger and more industrialized country to maintain herself in an economically viable position. Since 1924, when King Zog came to power, the country's economic life has been dominated by four foreign powers. During Zog's reign (1924-1939), Italy received most of Albania's exports and, in turn, was the source of most of her imports. Following World War II, Italy's place was taken by Yugoslavia, then by the Soviet Union, and most recently by China.

In the 1950s, Albania traded heavily with the COMECON (Council for Mutual Economic Assistance) countries of East Europe, led by the Soviet Union. She joined COMECON in February 1949, a month after the founding of the organization.[39] For three years after the break with Yugoslavia in 1948, Albania traded exclusively with COMECON members. She thus became completely dependent on East Europe for her foreign trade needs. This relationship continued largely unchanged throughout the 1950s, even after Albania began to trade with a number of Western countries in the latter part of the decade, such as Italy, Finland, Switzerland, and West Germany.

During this period, the Soviet Union accounted for more than half of Albania's foreign trade, followed by Czechoslovakia and East Germany. For example, in 1951 the USSR led all other countries with an export-import exchange of goods amounting to 57 percent of Albania's total foreign trade. By the late 1950s, the Soviets were receiving 95 percent of Albania's oil exports, 76 percent of the tobacco, and 38 percent of the bitumen. More than any other country in East Europe, Albania confined her foreign trade to the socialist bloc. This is true both of the period of Soviet influence and of the post-Soviet years, when the focus of Albanian trade shifted from East Europe to the Far East. The actual figures are given in table 4.15.

Table 4.15
Albania's Foreign Trade within the Communist World (In Percentage of Total Trade)

	1958		1960		1962	
	Import	Export	Import	Export	Import	Export
Socialist bloc	97.3	97.9	94.9	98.8	95.5	93.6
East European bloc	94.5	92.1	85.9	93.0	26.9	60.9
Asian bloc	2.2	2.7	8.6	4.9	66.3	29.6

Source: Josef Korbel, *Détente in Europe: Real or Imaginary?* (Princeton, N.J.: Princeton University Press, 1972).

Albania's trade with the USSR ceased completely in 1963 and remained frozen thereafter. Subsequently, Albanian leaders accused the Soviets and their East European allies of imposing an economic blockade on their country. But, in fact, Albania continued to trade with East Europe even after 1961. For example, during 1962-1964, East Europe accounted for about 25 percent of her foreign trade.[40]

As long as Albania maintained close economic relations with East Europe, she defended the COMECON as a most valuable economic institution. The official position was that COMECON aimed "primarily at increasing collaboration among the [member] nations by an exchange of experience, technical aid ... raw materials, food, machinery, installations" and that this collaboration was "based on the principle of equal rights, mutual aid, and the respect of national independence."[41] Enver Hoxha himself acclaimed COMECON because of the "immense advantages" it afforded Albania for "developing all the branches" of her economy.[42] The enthusiasm of Albania's leadership for COMECON diminished progressively as Soviet-Albanian relations deteriorated in the 1960s. Although formally Albania has remained a member of COMECON, in effect she withdrew from the organization in 1962. The Albanians failed to attend COMECON meetings after 1961—allegedly because they had not been invited to "some" of the meetings in 1962—and their membership in the organization technically expired in March 1962, over the failure to meet their subscription obligations.

Albania's trade with Western Europe remained minimal by comparison with the socialist bloc, even though it began to climb gradually after the mid-fifties. It amounted to 5 percent in 1961 and 12 percent in 1968. Italy remained consistently Albania's major trading partner in the West, followed by

Table 4.16
Albania's Trade with Major Western Powers (1960–1969)

	Imports from Albania (In Millions of $ c.i.f.)	Exports to Albania (In Millions of $ f.o.b.)
Italy	20.7	49.3
France	3.5	11.5
West Germany	2.8	9.6
United Kingdom	0.7	3.1
Total	27.7	63.5

Source: Korbel, *Détente*, compiled from data in table 10.

France, West Germany, and the United Kingdom, in that order. The volume of this trade for the decade of the sixties is given in table 4.16.

As can be seen from these figures, Albania's trade with the major West European powers suffered from a heavy imbalance. Such imbalance has been a peculiar characteristic of Albania's foreign trade both before and after World War II. Figures show that the value of exports before the war ranged from 50 to 60 percent of the value of imports. The resulting deficit was covered by aid and credits from Italy. After the war, Albania ran large deficits in trade with the Soviet Union and China. One study has revealed that during the 1950s as little as one-fourth of the country's imports were covered by exports, while in the early 1960s the proportions were one to three of favor of imports.[43] Another study has shown that her balance of trade for the ten-year period from 1955 to 1964 resulted in an annual deficit of $31.5 million.[44] R. H. Osborne correctly observes that "in spite of a useful range of primary products for export, Albania has [had] a chronically adverse balance of trade which has [had] to be covered by foreign aid or credits. . . ."[45]

In sum, the Albanian economy has been dependent on foreign aid ever since the country became an independent state. This was true of heavily agrarian, prewar Albania and has been true also of the postwar period, in spite of the considerable expansion and modernization of the economy since the war. Being still a relatively undeveloped country, Albania has been obliged to enter into close economic association with a larger and more advanced trading partner. In each case, she has paid for her economic weakness with political subordination to her economic benefactor. Economic dependency in effect reduced Albania to a semicolony of Italy before the war and to a satellite of

Yugoslavia and the Soviet Union since the war. It was largely the need to escape the intolerable consequences of deepening political subordination that drove the Hoxha leadership to break first with Tito, then with Khrushchev. Essentially the same problem occurred in Albania's relations with China in the current decade, leading to a rift between the two countries in 1977.

The need for economic assistance versus the price of political allegiance, and at worst political submergence to a foreign power, has posed a persistent dilemma for Albania. How to obtain economic aid without compromising political independence is a problem for which her leaders have yet to find a solution.

Economic Relations with Yugoslavia, USSR, and China

Yugoslavia

Albania's economic cooperation with Yugoslavia after 1944 was the natural extension of the wartime collaboration between the Partisan movements of the two countries. According to Yugoslav historians, Yugoslavia helped Albania's economy in a variety of ways, in a spirit of proletarian internationalism rather than for political gain. Such aid included the advance of credits in 1947 and 1948 amounting to 5 billion Albanian leks (about $100 million),[46] shipments of 20,000 tons of corn and wheat in 1946 to relieve famine in the country, and a grant in October 1946 of 57 million dinars ($1,140,000)[47] to be used as first aid for flood victims. Other forms of aid involved the sending of 597 Yugoslav experts to help build Albania's industry, plus installations for the construction of a number of projects, including a sugar factory at Korçë, a fruit and vegetable processing plant at Elbasan, a fish cannery at Vlorë, a hemp and flax factory at Rrogozhinë, and a printing press, an automatic telephone exchange, and a textile plant at Tiranë.[48] Moreover, the joint-stock Albanian-Yugoslav companies allegedly were established at Albania's request and benefited the Albanians.[49]

The Albanians, however, far from acknowledging that they benefited from their close economic ties with the Yugoslavs, have charged instead that the Yugoslav government pursued an economic policy of "colonial exploitation" in their country. They claim that the Yugoslavs tried to persuade them to produce "raw industrial and agrarian materials to meet the needs of Yugoslav industry; that is, turn [the] country into a supply base for the processing industry of Yugoslavia."[50]

Despite denials by Belgrade officials, the consensus among scholars is that Tito aimed at the incorporation of Albania into Yugoslavia, and the Albanian-Yugoslav economic agreements support this thesis. In particular, the Economic Treaty of July 1946 had the effect of making Albania's economy "part and parcel of the Yugoslav economy," until the break in 1948.[51] It is not without significance that Albania was the first communist nation to break her trade agreements with Yugoslavia, following Tito's expulsion from the Cominform.

The Soviet Union
Albania's split with Yugoslavia and alliance with the Soviet Union in 1948 were fortunate developments for at least two reasons. Politically, they prevented Albania's absorption into Yugoslavia and ended the dangerous division within the Albanian Communist Party. Economically, they opened up new and wider channels of aid for the country, since Moscow's potential for furthering Albania's economic development was far greater than that of Belgrade.

The Soviet Union's aid to the Albanians during the thirteen-year period of the Albanian-Soviet alliance (1948-1961) was vital and decisive in Albania's pioneering efforts at modernization. It was huge in size, vast in scope—encompassing financial, material, and technical assistance—and affected profoundly the development of the country's industry, agriculture, and, indeed, every aspect of Albanian society, including art and literature, education, and the military.[52]

To turn to the record, on January 1, 1957, the USSR advanced Albania $18.5 million in credit. On April 17, 1957, she canceled previous Albanian debts totaling $105 million. On November 22, 1957, the Soviets signed an agreement with Albania providing $40 million in credit. In January of 1959, they agreed to advance $75 million in developmental credit to finance Albania's Third 5-YP and also committed themselves to a loan of $8.75 million for the development of Albania's oil industry. Some 4,500 Albanian students studied in the Soviet Union and East Europe during the 1950s and 1960-1961, in a variety of disciplines relating to industry, agriculture, the arts, and military science. In turn, Soviet specialists in oil drilling, mining, geology, agronomy, construction, and other fields worked in Albania and trained Albanian cadres. In the area of trade, Albania's chronic trade deficit was covered with credit extended largely by the Soviet Union.

The evidence demonstrates that the USSR provided the basis for Albania's economic advancement up to 1959. To be sure, in giving such aid the Soviets did not dismiss altogether expectations of benefits to themselves. Apart from political loyalty from Albania, they expected also a small economic return for their costly investment. They hoped to derive some gain from the development of Albanian agriculture, including horticulture. Their calculations, however, came into conflict with the thinking of their Albanian allies, who were practically obsessed with the vision of an Albania with a heavy industry. It was a vision the Soviets tried in vain to relegate to a subordinate position in Albania's economy. According to Tyagunenko, the establishment of heavy industry in Albania was considered to be "unfeasible and economically disadvantageous," since Albania could receive "all the necessary machinery" from other socialist countries.[53]

The Soviets stressed rather the development of Albania's agriculture. Presumably, Khrushchev himself argued this point of view when he visited Albania in May 1959.[54] Hoxha alluded to the position of the Soviet leadership on this question when he said: "We rejected Tito's nonsensical idea to plant only sunflowers, on the pretext that he would supply us with wheat from the Vojvodina; likewise, we rejected Khrushchev's 'advice' that we should cultivate only fruit trees and vineyards, since he would supply us with wheat grown on his virgin lands...."[55]

Hoxha's attack was part of the violent polemics against the Soviets, which Albania began in 1961. Subsequently, Albania charged that Soviet experts tried to sabotage her industrialization program by concealing geological data, in order to argue that the country lacked raw materials for the development of industry. After accusing the Soviet leadership of restoring capitalism in the USSR, Albania's leaders began to belittle progressively the aid received previously from the Soviets. Speaking on the occasion of the sixtieth anniversary of Albania's independence (November 28, 1972), Enver Hoxha described Soviet economic aid as consisting merely of "some painted-over machines from old workshops."[56]

But that is not what he, and other Albanian leaders, had said before. In 1956, for example, the Party's theoretical journal wrote as follows on Soviet aid. "Without this aid, without the economic might of the Soviet Union, we could never begin socialist industrialization."[57] Two months later, Hoxha expressed a similar view at the convocation of the Party's Third Congress. He said:

The very great moral and material support that the Soviet Union has given to our people is incalculable. The political and economic aid of the Soviet Union has enabled our backward country to progress with great strides....

> The most modern machines have come to us from the Soviet Union. We had no cadres whatever. Hundreds of Soviet cadres came here and with care and affection trained our cadres.[58]

Premier Mehmet Shehu acknowledged Albania's indebtedness to the USSR in the economic field as early as 1954 when he said: "We have created a light industry with modern equipment granted us by the Soviet Union and the People's Democracies."[59] Albania's leaders found it politically expedient after 1961 to disparage the contribution of the Soviet Union to the economic development of their country. But the record cannot be concealed; their own statements give validity to that record.

China

Short of adopting the economic policy on trade and foreign aid of her then archenemy, Yugoslavia, and turning to the West, Albania probably had no alternative in 1960-1961 but to face eastward and forge close economic ties with communist China. Political and ideological differences in the Soviet leadership played a large, if not primary, role in the shattering of the Albanian-Soviet alliance. Since the Chinese had similar grievances with the Soviets, they and the Albanians found it mutually advantageous to strengthen their ties and maintain a common front against the Soviets, whom they now accused of ideological, economic, and cultural revisionism. China needed Albania's political support at this time, and Albania in turn needed China's economic support.

Chinese economic assistance began in 1954 with a grant of $2.5 million and a loan of $12.5 million. In January 1959, China advanced a $13.75 million loan to Albania. On April 23, 1961, it was announced that the two countries had signed an agreement on February 2, 1961, which committed the Chinese to a loan of $125 million to cover payment for the construction of twenty-five large industrial projects for Albania's Third 5-YP (1961-1965). This loan was, of course, critical for Albania, considering that Soviet and East European loans, designated for the plan and totaling $118.75 million, were canceled in 1961. Had Albania not received such aid from Peking, the Soviet economic "blockade" of the largely isolated Balkan country would have probably succeeded and led to the downfall of the Hoxha leadership.

In June 1965 and October 1970, the Albanians negotiated new agreements with the Chinese for loans in connection with the Fourth and Fifth 5-YPs. Exact figures for these loans are not known, but it is estimated that they totaled about $344 million ($214 million and $130 million, respectively).

Table 4.17
Chinese Food Shipments to Albania, 1960-1963 (In Tons)

Year	Wheat	Corn
1960	60,000	—
1961	121,400	28,500
1962	89,100	—
1963	109,800	20,400
Total	380,300	49,900

Source: *Vjetari statistikor i R.P.SH.* [Statistical yearbook of APR, 1964] (Tiranë: Directory of Statistics, 1964), p. 339.

The grand total, then, for Chinese loans to Albania over a roughly twenty-year period (1954-1975) comes to approximately $500 million.[60]

Apart from loans and grants, China assisted Albania with shipments of vast quantities of wheat and corn. These shipments totaled 430,200 tons over the critical four-year period from 1960 to 1963, as table 4.17 indicates.[61]

Despite her own relatively meager resources, China presumably continued to ship food grains to Albania annually after 1963. This is hinted in a speech by Hoxha in 1965, when he said, "China is making sacrifices in order to assure us the food items we need."[62] That such shipments were a strain on China can be inferred from Hoxha's warning to his countrymen that Albania could not afford to "import continually grains, rice, oils, etc." He urged them to make greater efforts to increase the production of foodstuffs.

Following the switch from the Soviet Union to China, there was a reversal in Albania's trade with respect to those two countries. Whereas in 1961 the USSR accounted for 54 percent of the trade, as against 7 percent for China, in 1964 trade with China climbed to 55 percent and dropped down to zero with respect to the Soviet Union.[63] It is estimated that since the midsixties, between 60 and 70 percent of Albania's foreign trade was with China.[64]

There is no doubt that Chinese trade and specialists enabled Albania to weather the crisis of the Third 5-YP (1961-1965), occasioned by the rupture of relations with Moscow. But the quality of the goods China supplied Albania, the scope of her aid, and the level of competence of her specialists could not match those of the Soviet Union. Because of China's relative backwardness with respect to the USSR and the urgent need to develop her own economy, the probability of a drop in her aid to Albania in later years could not be dismissed. It was always present in the background of Sino-Albanian relations and could be expected to come to the foreground under a variety of circumstances, especially if the political tie between Tiranë and Peking were to weaken.

As of 1977, at any rate, China continued to be Albania's main economic support. The two countries were bound by a number of short and long-term agreements. In November 1974, a weekly airline service was inaugurated between Tiranë and Peking, via Bucharest and Teheran. The Albanian Academy of Sciences and its Chinese counterpart collaborated regularly on technical and scientific projects. The Joint Chinese-Albanian Maritime Association, which regulated the shipment of surface goods between the two countries, represented another aspect of the economic bond between Tiranë and Peking.

In June 1975, an Albanian economic delegation headed by Adil Çarçani, first deputy chairman of the Council of Ministers, traveled to Peking and on July 3, 1975, signed a five-year pact (1976-1980) with the Chinese, corresponding to the time frame of Albania's Sixth 5-YP. The pact said that China was to provide long-term credit without interest to Albania and "complete sets of equipment for projects" but did not specify any figures.[65] The five-year pact seemed to reaffirm the stability of the Albanian-Chinese alliance and assure its continuation through the decade of the seventies. But there were signs that the amount of aid stipulated in the pact was below the expectations of the Albanians and less than what was considered necessary to assure balanced growth rates for Albania's economy in the next five years. Contrary to previous practice, there was little reportage on the signing of the pact and an absence of warm praise for it by high Albanian Party officials. Moreover, the dominant theme in the propaganda media in 1975-1976 was to impress upon the population the urgent need to economize and to depend on itself for its economic well-being.

Note on Economic Relations with Balkan Neighbors
Beginning with 1970, Albania broadened her economic relations with Yugoslavia and Greece. She signed long-term agreements with both nations, as well as with Italy. In May 1976, a high-level Greek government economic delegation, headed by the minister of trade, Ioanis Varvitsiotis, arrived in Albania and was given unusual prominence in the Albanian press. On May 22 the delegation signed an important economic pact in Tiranë, covering a "long-term agreement" on the exchange of goods, payments, a veterinary convention, and a trade protocol for 1976. The pact was a milestone in the development of postwar economic relations between Albania and Greece and seemed to

indicate an interest on the part of Albanian leaders in exploiting new channels of trade closer to home. The pact could also be taken as an indirect confirmation of the drop in Chinese economic assistance to Tiranë.

On the other hand, Albania's refusal to attend the Balkan Regional Economic Cooperation Conference in Athens (January 26-February 5, 1976) served to underscore her continuing isolationism and wide differences with the other Balkan nations over ideology, politics, and national minority questions. According to reports from Tiranë, Albanian leaders were persuaded that at present only bilateral, rather than multilateral, cooperation in the Balkans could serve a useful function.[66]

State of the Economy in the Seventies

Eye-witness accounts of many Western travelers to Albania and official Albanian statistical data support the view that the economy has made significant progress since the war. The breadth of the achievements to date has impressed Western observers and even exiled political opponents of Albania's regime. Perhaps only under the discipline of a centralized state authority could Albania have made such strides in the modernization of her economy. There is speculation that socialism was probably the only model of development possible for a very backward country like Albania.[67]

At the same time, there is broad agreement among observers of communist Albania that by the early 1970s her economy had reached a crossroads and could no longer afford to proceed as before. The rigid controls on planning by the Party leadership, the weight of a stifling bureaucracy, and the restrictions placed on free inquiry in the educational system, including scientific and technical research on economic problems, put a heavy burden on the economy. They hampered its efficient operation, productivity, and capacity to adapt itself to technological advances. Albanian officials and academicians were not unaware of this condition. In 1971 Hoxha granted that scientific research on agriculture, for example, required that Albanian scholars "be familiar with the achievements of world science."[68] More recently, a scholar at the University of Tiranë argued that the development of the "technological and scientific revolution" in Albania made it necessary for Albanian specialists to "know and exploit the advances of world science, and be familiar with the new developments in science and technics."[69]

But the need to keep abreast of developments in world science and technology was only a part of the problem. The more important aspects of the problem related to the question of the diffusion of the decision-making power to the lower levels of the economic structure, and the question of the diversification of foreign trade. On such questions, however, the Hoxha-Shehu leadership seemed unwilling to make basic reforms. This became abundantly evident in the draft of the new state Constitution which was made public in late January 1976. In a commentary on "the economic order" of the draft Constitution, Albanian academician Foto Çami said that the Constitution

... mirrors broadly the activity of the state ... which organizes, directs, and develops the entire economic and social life of the country on the basis of a unitary and general plan, protects socialist property ..., exercises control over consumption, maintains a monopoly over foreign trade, sets prices for industrial and agricultural goods, ... strives to narrow the differences between town and country, etc.[70]

Çami's discourse and other commentaries on the economic order reaffirmed the centralist, command-type character of the economy and served notice that the government did not contemplate making significant economic reforms. This hard-line, dogmatic position by the Hoxha leadership, plus a slowdown in economic growth during the Fifth 5-YP, apparently provoked bitter controversy within the top levels of the Party hierarchy regarding economic policy and administration. The resulting atmosphere of crisis in the economy was reflected in the nation's press in the spring of 1975 and continued strong in 1976.

An unusually revealing article on the subject of self-reliance suggested that opponents of Hoxha and Shehu had argued in favor of broadening economic relations with the outside world by "granting concessions" to Western and East European investors. Furthermore, they had a rather negative view, it seems, of the principle of self-reliance—a leading slogan of the Hoxha leadership—arguing that it was largely a subjective concept which tended to foster "narrow nationalism" and a "closed economy." In answering the first point of criticism, the author of the article said: "In the last analysis, no country can ever build itself up by granting concessions to the imperialists and revisionists. ... Such a road would lead to the economic subordination of the country. It would also pave the way for ... saboteurs and diversionists who, under the garb of 'specialists,' would in fact wreck socialism."[71]

Turning to the second point of criticism, he remarked: "Reliance on one's own forces and ... the strengthening of economic independence is neither a subjective wish nor an all-embracing political slogan, just as it is not, nor can it be, a disposition toward autarchy, 'narrow nationalism,' or the so-called 'closed economy.'"[72] The article stressed that the economic tasks facing the nation took on "special importance" because, apart from their economic significance, they had important ideological and political implications.

The evidence indicates that the fall from power in 1975 of the top leaders of the Albanian economy was linked to this controversy. The main figures in the purge were Abdyl Këllezi, chairman of the State Planning Commission; Koço Theodhosi, minister of industry and mining; and Kiço Ngjela, minister of trade.[73] Their attempt to diversify Albania's economic relations apparently followed a review by the Chinese of their economic ties with the Albanians and the decision to reduce the amount of aid to Albania.

In late April 1976, Albania announced the dismissal of two more cabinet ministers, on the grounds that they were guilty of "grave faults with regard to the Party line." One of them was Minister of Agriculture Pirro Dodbiba, a candidate Politburo member. The other was Thoma Deliana, minister of education and culture.[74] The purge of the minister of agriculture served to reinforce reports that agriculture, and indeed the entire economy, was in turmoil.

Equally revealing of the troubled state of the economy was the report on the state budget and the economic plan for 1976 by Petro Dode, deputy chairman of the Council of Ministers and chairman of the State Planning Commission. Dode's report showed that while industrial production in 1975 registered a slight growth (4%) over 1974, the major indexes for agriculture fell short of the plan. As a result, "the state had to import tens of thousands of tons of grains to meet the food needs of the population."[75] His discussion of the plan for 1976 conveyed a sense of alarm and included a strong appeal to the Albanian people to make special efforts to overcome the economic crisis facing the country. Speaking of agriculture, Dode said that the Council of Ministers had redrafted the 1976 plan for food crops production, "since not enough attention was paid to the difficulties that have arisen and the situations that have been created. . ."[76] The production of food crops, he noted, "must take precedence over other economic tasks."

Touching on other areas of the economy, Dode called for greater efforts to save electrical energy, announced a governmental cutback by 40 percent on orders for imports of spare parts in 1977 and a cutback of 30 to 40 percent in the allocation of funds for "nonproductive projects" in 1976, as compared with 1975. The dominant note in his report was the need to economize on energy, raw materials, and spare parts. The whole tenor of his remarks suggested unusual difficulties for the economy.

Among other measures taken by the government to cope with the problems of the economy were: (1) an initiative in the spring of 1976 for a mass movement to the countryside to spur agricultural production, involving close to 14,000 persons, most of them students and "working youth"; (2) promulgation of a governmental decree on April 1, 1976, to lower high wages by as much as 25 percent in order to narrow the gap between office workers and manual workers from the previous ratio of 1 to 2.5 to a new ratio of 1 to 2.[77] The decree provided certain benefits for farm workers, such as higher wages and pensions and greater state investments in irrigation projects and land reclamation in the highland regions. Indeed, the thrust of the decree was to stimulate the agricultural sector at the expense of the "nonproductive" sectors of the economy, such as the intelligentsia, education and research, management, and the armed forces. Albanian officials defended the new decree on political grounds, saying that it would bring to a halt careerism, yearnings for office work, and many other evils that lead to bourgeois-revisionist degeneration. But probably the more compelling reason was the reduction of Chinese aid and credits.

The deep concern of Albanian Party leaders over the state of the economy in the mid-1970s surfaced especially in discussions of the draft of the Sixth 5-YP (1976-1980). The communications media pointed out repeatedly during 1975-1976 that the drafting of the plan was "an action of great political and ideological import" and that the question of food production was not merely an economic question but "a struggle for socialism and the defense of the fatherland."[78] The state of the economy was thus tied to the political stability of the regime, the survival of socialism in Albania, and even the security of the nation.

The proceedings of the Seventh Party Congress in November 1976 included some positive reports on the economy, but the general picture of the state of the economy was negative. Both Hoxha and Shehu reported that Albania had made further progress along the road of modernization since the beginning of the Fifth 5-YP in 1971. The progress was evident in both industry and agriculture and was highlighted in 1976 by two interesting and rather dramatic developments. In that year socialist Albania began for the first time to produce her own steel, at the Elbasan metallurgical complex. It was also the year that she managed for the first time to fulfill the plan for food production; in other words, the country produced enough food grains to meet the needs of the population.

However, other data presented at the congress indicated that the Fifth 5-YP was a failure in both industry and agriculture. While industrial production in 1975 was 52 percent greater than in 1970, the figure was below the target of 61 to 66 percent envisioned by the plan. And instead of attaining an average annual growth rate of about 10.3 percent in industrial production, as called for by the plan, the actual growth rate was 8.7 percent. Hoxha confessed that production quotas had not been met in such critical sectors of the economy as oil, chrome, copper, and coal or in the construction of "certain industrial works." Among these were the three major projects of the plan, namely, the hydroelectric power plant at Fierzë, the metallurgical complex at Elbasan, and the oil refinery system at Ballsh. Hoxha added, however, that these projects would be completed during the current 5-YP. Agricultural production also fell considerably below the target, registering an increase of only 33 percent over 1970, rather than the 65 to 69 percent projected by the plan, and an annual growth rate of 5.9 percent instead of the expected 10.8 percent. It was not surprising therefore that production goals for the Sixth 5-YP were uniformly smaller than the goals of the previous plan. Thus, the goal for industrial production was set at 41–44 percent, as against the figure of 61–66 of the previous plan. The goal for agricultural production was 38–41 percent, a notable drop from the 65–69 percent aimed at by the Fifth 5-YP.

These facts pointed to an imbalance in the economy—the result apparently of long-standing defects and weaknesses in the country's economic system. In particular, the failure of the Fifth economic plan called for a thoroughgoing review of the policy on the economy by the country's leaders. But instead of questioning the policy, structure, and organization of Albania's tightly centralized economic system and considering the possibility of reforming it, the Party's leadership sought to blame the malfunctioning of the system and the failures of the Fifth 5-YP on the managers of the economy and the technocratic intelligentsia. Indeed, the top administrators of the economy became targets for attack precisely because they had dared to question some of the cherished economic dogmas of Hoxha and Shehu. The proceedings of the Seventh Party Congress and other reports from Albania revealed that the directors of planning, industry, and agriculture had called into question certain basic principles of the country's economic system. It was said, for example, that Këllezi, Theodhosi, Ngjela, and Dodbiba had "renounced the principles of centralized direction" and had attempted to introduce instead "the forms and methods of self-management" into Albania's economic system. The term "self-management" has long been anathema to Albanian Party leaders, since for them it symbolizes Yugoslavia's economic system, which they have consistently condemned as antisocialist, capitalistic, and chaotic. Këllezi, therefore, and the other purged leaders of the economy, were accused of seeking to "depoliticize planning" and abandoning the "principle of class struggle" in planning and production.[79] Their bold initiative to introduce rationalism and pragmatism into the system and reshape it to conform to the current needs of Albania's economy evidently proved to be premature and led not only to their dismissal from office but probably also to the physical liquidation of some of them.

Concluding Remarks

By late 1977, Albania's orthodox, oligarchic, and uniformly Stalinist social order continued to remain in force. At the same time, the pressures for reform continued to make themselves felt in various areas of society. The state of Albania's economy took on special importance owing to her ideological differences with China and the adverse effects of those differences on the economic tie between Tiranë and Peking. In spite of repeated denials by Party leaders that the unusual strains in the economy signaled difficulties for the Sino-Albanian alliance, the fact remained that the language used by Albanian leaders in 1975-1976 in talking about the economy was strikingly similar to the language used in 1961 when the Albanian-Soviet alliance was undergoing a fateful transition. In 1975-1976, as in 1961, Party leaders called on the Albanian people to make extraordinary efforts to economize, to cut down on imports of goods, to rely on their own forces instead of depending on outside support, and to grasp the political significance of economic matters.

Conclusive evidence of the weakening of Albanian-Chinese economic relations appeared in Premier Shehu's economic report to the Party's Seventh Congress in November 1976. There was a marked contrast in his remarks on China between that report and the report he delivered at the Party's Sixth Congress in 1971. At that time he made repeated references to the Chinese and devoted nearly five pages to praise, expressions of solidarity with China, and gratitude for her "important aid" to the Albanians. He noted that in the Fifth 5-YP the Albanians were "relying as before on the generous, powerful, and internationalist aid of the People's Republic of China," and he expressed "deep gratitude" to the Chinese for the aid given to Albania.[80] In contrast, Shehu's November 1976 report contained only a single short paragraph on

China. It made no mention of the "unbreakable friendship" with China, and no expressions of gratitude to Peking for aid given to Albania. The report said merely that in the drafting of the Sixth 5-YP "account has been taken" of China's aid and credits but gave no details.[81]

Referring to the purge of the directors of the economy, Shehu called them "conspirators and putschists who tried to undermine our economy and overthrow the dictatorship of the proletariat."[82] He said moreover that the conspirators had been "inspired by foreign revisionist enemies," and it cannot be excluded that this was an esoteric reference to the Chinese, just as in their pre-1961 polemics the Albanians used the term "modern revisionists" to make indirect attacks on their Soviet allies.

By 1975, it was evident that Albania's economic relations with China had reached a turning point. The change came about as a result presumably of Mao's decision not to continue to subsidize indefinitely Albania's economy. It may be surmised that Mao made such a decision in the early seventies, following China's reassessment and revision of her political priorities. An important consequence of Mao's decision is that Albania became politically expendable to her Far Eastern ally. This in turn was bound to affect the economic relationship between the two allies. The fruits of China's changed attitude toward the Albanians became known with the signing of the five-year (1976-1980) Albanian-Chinese economic pact in July 1975. Although in 1977 China was still Albania's main trading partner, the amount of economic aid Albania was receiving from Peking was substantially less than in former years. Moreover, because of the developing political rift between them, Albania was faced with the possibility of a total cutoff of Chinese economic aid and technical assistance.

It could be expected therefore that the progressive decrease in Chinese economic assistance would force Albania's leaders to seek new trade arrangements, most likely with nations "closer to home," as in the Balkans and in East and West Europe. The May 1976 economic pact with Greece appeared to point in that direction. Such an orientation on the part of Albania seemed almost inevitable, in the long run, in order to fill the vacuum left by dwindling Chinese aid, credits, and shipments of grain. Thanks to Peking's decision to revise the economic relationship with its Balkan ally, Albania in the mid-seventies seemed to have no choice but to formulate and implement a more pragmatic and rational economic policy than before.

5
The Movement for Women's Emancipation

Albanian Women in History

Viewed historically, the qualities for which Albanian women are most often admired are those of a martial type: heroism in battle, the spirit of self-sacrifice, loyalty to menfolk fighting for freedom, and devotion to country. Teuta, queen of the Illyrians, ancestors of the Albanians who defied the might of the Roman Empire in the third century B.C., is much admired, as are also the Illyrian women who hurled themselves from towers to destruction to avoid falling into the hands of the enemy.[1] Voisava, mother of Albania's national hero, Gjergj Kastrioti Skënderbeu (1405-1468), emerges as a long-suffering but unbowed woman, while her warrior daughter, Mamica, is described by Marin Barleti, Skënderbeu's most noted biographer, as "an astute and able leader" who excelled many male chieftains in battle. Another heroine is Nora of Kelmend—a town in northern Albania—who in the 1630s sacrificed her life for the people of her community when she assassinated the Turkish army commander, Vuçe Pasha, whose garrison had laid siege to the town.[2]

Apart from valor in battle and uncompromising opposition to the enemy, Albanian women displayed other patriotic virtues during the nearly five-centuries-long occupation of Albania by the Ottoman Turks, following Skënderbeu's death. According to Prof. Alex Buda of the University of Tiranë, throughout this period "it was mainly the womenfolk who persevered and carried on the cultural traditions, the language, and customs [of the country]."[3] The closing decades of Turkish occupation brought into public prominence two women nationalists, the sisters Sevasti and Parashqevi Qiriazi, who in 1891 opened the first Albanian school for women in Korçë in southern Albania. It was in Korce also where the first society of Albanian women, known as *Ylli i Mëngjezit* (The morning star), was founded in 1909 by Parashqevi Qiriazi. The chief aim of the society, which lasted until World War I, was the "education of women." Another woman, the teacher and poet Marigo Pozio of the city of Vlorë, gained national fame for having reportedly "embroidered the first Albanian flag which Ismail Qemal raised in Vlorë on the 28th of November, 1912,"[4] to proclaim Albania's independence. In recognition of their services to the nation, the Albanian government awarded decorations to the Qiriazi sisters and Mrs. Pozio in March 1960, on the occasion of the fiftieth anniversary of International Women's Day.[5]

The shining record of these and other women did not, however, alter the fact that by and large the lot of Albanian women during the Turkish occupation and the early decades following the country's independence was deplorable and ripe for significant change. Centuries of oppressive Ottoman rule, the weight of medieval customs and traditions, superstition, and widespread poverty made many of them receptive to the call of the Albanian communist Partisans to join the resistance movement and support their program for revolutionary change.

The Condition of Women in Albania Prior to World War II

An idea of the popular Albanian conception of women before World War II can be gathered from such sayings as "A woman is a beast of burden" or "A woman must work harder than a donkey, for a donkey feeds on grass, while a woman lives on bread" or "Women are long of hair and short of brains."[6] A sharp distinction was made between men and women with respect to their physical aptitudes, moral qualities, and natural intelligence. Thus men were strong, brave, and intelligent, while women were weak, timid, and stupid. Men were thought to be naturally superior to women, and this notion was reflected in the relations between husband and wife, in the attitude of parents toward sons and daughters, at work, and in numerous areas of private and public life. It followed from this that the husband was the master of the wife, whose duty was to obey him.

Parents favored boys over girls, for the boy was "the pillar of the house" while the girl was "destined for another home." This preference for sons over daughters revealed itself even at birth, as can be seen from the old Albanian saying: "Even the beams of the house shed tears when a girl is born." Thus, antagonism between the sexes started in the cradle and was nourished by the parents and society throughout life. As children grew up, boys were generally given preferential treatment in matters of dress, food, education, work, and leisure. At the same time, society forbade girls from associating with boys upon reaching adolescence, since a girl could not be trusted "to guard her own virtue."

Marriage for love was considered immoral and was practically unheard of in the rural areas. Matchmaking was the common practice, and in the northern part of the country girls were often engaged in infancy, or even before they were born. Nor was it rare for teenage girls to be married to men forty years of age or older, as it was common practice—particularly in the highlands of the north—to buy and sell girls into marriage. Marrying off a daughter was at best a time-consuming affair, involving long preparations for her dowry and watchful care for her morals. More often the wedding ceremony, while colorful and memorable, was a crushing financial burden on the parents, forcing them sometimes to toil for years to pay off the marriage debts. In marriage, the lot of the average Albanian woman was even harder than before marriage. Her function within the family was for the most part limited to giving birth to children and doing exhausting work at home or in the fields, including the carrying of loads on her back like a beast of burden.

Contemporary foreign observers appear to corroborate the above account of women's position in presocialist Albania. In the words of one observer: "A man's blood [life] was safe when with a guest or a woman. The blood of women is of no account so women are always safe."[7] Continuing, the same observer notes: "Women had no choice [in the matter] of husbands. They were betrothed by their fathers in infancy and sometimes before birth, their price often a heavy one, for they were the drudges, the breeding stock, the beasts of burden. Their lot ... is the household toil."[8]

Another writer of foreign origin remarks that the women thought of themselves as being "stupid," presumably because of the generally accepted social view that women were indeed stupid. Upon becoming a bride, this writer says, the Albanian woman goes about the household "obeying the commands of the elders, always standing until they tell her to sit, and for six months not speaking unless they address her.... Usually she has not seen her husband until she comes to his house."[9]

Her lot was particularly severe in northern Albania, where the entire social and economic structure was governed by the Law of the Lek, a set of unwritten laws, based on patriarchy, that was handed down from the Middle Ages.[10] In this region a woman was in effect the servant of her husband, the elders in the house, and the males in the family, even little boys, for the Law of Lek granted unquestioned authority to males over females. A male had "the moral right to give orders to a female, regardless of her age."[11] She was submerged in families having many couples, sometimes as many as ten, and numbering as many as fifty, sixty, or seventy members. This arrangement was part of the clan system, which comprised all families sharing a common name—handed down through countless generations—at the head of which stood the *bajraktar* or clan chieftain. Under this system, the husband made the decisions in the family and held the family purse, regardless of the feelings or opinions of his wife. As a northern woman from the Lezh district explained: "The wife [in prewar Albania] was practically a nonentity. We had to wash our husband's feet . . . and everything. There was no difference between us and the animals. We were not even permitted to open our mouths. . . ."[12]

The wife did not dare contradict her husband, for the unwritten law specified: "The husband is entitled to beat his wife and to bind her in chains if she defies his word and orders."[13] Nor could she eat at the same table with men, for the custom was for the men to eat first, then the women and children. When guests came to the house, the women had to retire from view, except in cases where it was the custom to wash the guests' feet. Outside the home, she went about veiled and dressed in picturesque but heavy and unwieldy clothing and limited her travels to her own district or locality. In short, under the patriarchal system of the Law of Lek, women scarcely enjoyed any private or civic rights but were in effect servants and a commodity in the hands of the males.

Margaret Hasluck, an authority on the social order in northern prewar Albania, appears to support this view of women in the highlands. She writes: "Society in the Albanian mountains was patrilineal, and took so little account of women that whereas the names of ancestors in the male line might be known for as many as twenty generations, those in the female line were forgotten after two or three."[14] She goes on to say that all property and civic rights were vested in men only and that the wife, not infrequently, "led a life of almost unrelieved hardship." The customs of the highlands forbade her from having "any dealings with the outside world," for that was the prerogative of the husband. Nor, according to Hasluck, could she criticize her husband's conduct or lack of industry, for "the Unwritten Law said that the husband was the head of the wife and might punish her for indiscipline. . . ."[15]

Foreign observers generally agree that women were confined at home, kept separate quarters from the males, and could not eat at the same table with the men.

The despotism of the male was reinforced by the religious establishment, which sanctified the submission of the wife to the husband and tended, moreover, to perpetuate the backward condition of woman by attributing misfortune and poverty to the will of God. Commenting on the superstitious practices of Albanian women, Swire remarks that they believed that "The Vampire Spirit went forth at night . . . and sucked the infant's blood till it died, because its mother forgot to hang a charm round its tiny unwashed neck."[16] An illuminating account on these points is given in a testimonial in 1967 by a group of women from the Shkodër district in northern Albania.

[We used to live] like animals. We had no houses, but only straw-covered huts blackened with soot and smoke. We shared quarters with the pig, the oxen, and the cow. Every month the priest would come to bless our huts, but nothing changed as a result of the blessings of "God." We remained poor and destitute, with no bread to eat.... Our children died from hunger, froze from the bitter cold, and neither the priest nor "God" could help us. The only thing the priest would say to us was: "Such is the will of God."[17]

The general and chronic poverty in the country added to a woman's woes, increasing her dependency on the husband and reducing almost to zero her ability to control her own life. This condition affected especially the women in southern Albania, for it forced the men to quit home and go abroad in search of work and a livelihood. A graphic description of this situation was given in a letter addressed to Hoxha by 200 women from the Sarandë district in February 1968. The letter read in part: "What were we like before? Servants and slaves of the existing order and of the men; in effect, widows whose husbands lived abroad in far-away lands, while our children grew up like orphans and ragged beggars.... What a miserable life we led!"

After noting that marriage in those days was ruinous because of enormous expenses and money given to the groom, the letter continued:

Some of us were married after seeing only the photograph of our [future] husband, and some of us lived with our husband for only a month or two. We cried rivers of tears and grew old from grief.
Many of our husbands [who] took the cursed path of migration abroad ... left their bones on foreign soil. We were human beings but lived like animals or worse.[18]

Patriarchy, religious obscurantism, and poverty conspired, so to speak, to subordinate Albanian women to men and to deprive them of any meaningful personal rights and freedom of action. Confined within the four walls of the house, they lacked also the right of divorce. This right was accorded by society only to the husband, who used it sometimes to divorce his wife on the sole ground that she did not bear him sons but only daughters, who, as noted earlier, were hardly welcome in the family. Such was the condition of the Albanian woman the Party leadership was confronted with, as it set out to implement its vision of the new Albanian woman, freed from the debilitating remnants of the past.

Albania's Conception of Women's Liberation

There are important differences between the women's movement in highly industrialized and affluent countries, such as the United States, and in underdeveloped, authoritarian, and ideologically militant Albania. The leaders of the Albanian Party of Labor (APL) denounce the "feminist," "illuminist," and "allegedly apolitical" women's liberation movements, "which are so fashionable in the capitalist world, and which have been so fervently embraced by the modern Khrushchevian and Titoist revisionists."[19] Unlike these, they see the women's movement in Albania as a struggle for the triumph of revolutionary ideology over the bourgeois, feudal, and patriarchal ideology.

The Albanian leaders go a step further. They look upon the organized activity of women in their country as a model for the women of "the Third World." According to Enver Hoxha, the Party's first secretary: "The activity of the Union of Albanian Women is a shining example for many women's organizations in newly independent countries."[20]

In Albania the "struggle for the emancipation of woman" began even before the communists seized power in the country in November of 1944. As early as February 1942, while the Partisans were still organizing and building up their forces, Enver Hoxha, their leader, said: "The Albanian woman is oppressed by fascism, by bourgeois and feudal traditions and laws; she is more conscious than anyone else of our struggle [to gain power], for she sees in it her own salvation...."[21] From the beginning of the communist rule in Albania, the Party leadership has attached major importance to the problem of women, regarding it as an "exceptionally great social problem" and linking it with the very destiny of the Albanian people, socialism, and communism. The attitude of APL on this question was perhaps best expressed in a statement issued by the Party's Central Committee and the Albanian Council of Ministers on April 29, 1967: "The freedom of the people and of each individual, the progress of the country and fulfillment of our aims cannot be conceived without the complete emancipation of women."

To buttress their argument on women, and add a historical dimension to the question, the Albanians have appealed to the classics of communism, drawing on the authoritative pronouncements on women by Marx, Engels, and Lenin, as well as by Stalin and Mao. In fact, a brochure of some sixty pages entitled *On Woman* was published in Tiranë in 1967, containing citations on this subject from their writings. In an important speech devoted entirely to women, delivered in June 1967, Hoxha said that Marx, Engels,

Lenin, and Stalin gave serious attention to the liberation of women from exploiters, their emancipation from male domination, and the fullest development of their personality. He quoted Marx to the effect that the progress of any period in history can be measured by the degree of progress made by women in gaining freedom, particularly from male domination, for "the victories of human nature are best manifested in the relations between husband and wife."[22]

The Albanian Communist Party's position on women, and its general line on the social and economic development of the country, won the support and loyalty of many Albanian women soon after the Party was organized in November 1941. Some 6,000 of them reportedly took up arms and became a part of the 70,000-strong Partisan army during the War of National Liberation in the early 1940's. A number of them, including Zonja Çurre, Bule Naipi, Persefoni Kokëdhima, Margarita Tutalani, Mrike Lokja, and others, are honored in Albania today as martyrs to the cause of national liberation, socialist construction, and women's emancipation.

Indeed, participation in the war marked the first step in the Albanian women's struggle for emancipation and provided the initial momentum for the later stages of their struggle for equality with men. Fighting alongside the Partisans not only taught women to be independent and to develop initiative; most of all, it helped them to alter their psychological outlook, to revise their self-image and their image of the Albanian society, especially the role of women in it. As an Albanian writer put it in a short story about a woman Partisan: "With her father's old rifle ... she wanted to kill her past, to gain freedom, and to open the way to a new life."[23]

The Party's Program for Emancipating Women

The condition of women in pre-World War II Albania defined the problem facing the APL and determined the nature of the solution to it. The problem had several facets: male supremacy, that is, men's underestimation of women's intelligence, ability, volition, and moral responsibility; women's image of themselves, their deep sense of inferiority to men, their timidity, and lack of confidence in their own ability and creative powers; backward customs of engagement and marriage and unequal husband-wife relations; women's low level of education and culture; their traditional confinement at home and their consequent economic dependency on men; and the powerful influence of the Law of the Lek and of religion in preserving the women's status quo.

The solution proposed by Albania's leaders likewise had many facets, although these are all integrated around one central idea—the Marxist-Leninist theory of society. The emancipation of Albanian women, they believe, should be guided by the Marxist-Leninist theory of the economic development of society. This means above all that women must break out of their confinement at home and participate in the productive process of society. Along with Marx, the Albanian leaders believe that women's emancipation involves two phases: deliverance from "capitalist exploitation" and participation in production. Speaking at the Second Congress of the women's organization in July 1946, Hoxha spelled out the meaning of emancipation as related to production: "What does it mean to say that woman must win her independence? It means that she must become master of herself, that she enters production, work in factories, in hospitals, and offices ... wherever men work."[24]

Augmenting the labor force of the country through the enlistment of women; collectivized social work in place of private, domestic work; the development of the economy—all with a view to achieving the most rapid construction of socialism—thus emerged as a primary if not the fundamental motive of the country's leadership for the emancipation of women. Indeed, building socialism has been described by Ramiz Alia, APL's chief ideologist in the social and cultural field, as the very "mission of women as members of society."[25]

The goal of emancipation, by way of productive social work, will be reached through class struggle against all the forces in society that underestimate women and deny them the enjoyment of equal rights with men. According to Vito Kapo, president of the Union of Albanian Women, the struggle for the emancipation of her sex is a "struggle for the triumph of the revolutionary ideology of the working class, and the destruction of the reactionary bourgeois and petit bourgeois ideology."[26] This struggle, she added, has its economic, social, and ideological sides, but the most important of the three is its ideological side.

The Albanian leaders moved early to implement their program for women. Already in November 1944, before the termination of armed hostilities in the country, the National Liberation Council issued a declaration granting to women "equal rights with men, and the right to participate in the political and social life of the country."[27] Their legal rights are enumerated more fully in the new (1976) Constitution of the Albanian People's Socialist Republic, Article 41 of which says: "The woman enjoys equal rights with man ... in the entire social and political spectrum and in the family."

But de jure equality does not mean de facto equality. Hence there was a need to conduct a broad, intensive, and persistent campaign to break down all barriers to women's emancipation. In an attempt to divest men of their notions of inherent superiority over women and to bolster the latter's self-respect and self-confidence, Hoxha has over the years spoken in rather glowing terms about women. The composite picture of woman's nature and personality that emerges from Hoxha's remarks is highly complimentary to the female. For example, woman has more refined feelings and a cleaner conscience than man. She is distinguished by the "care, affection, and honesty" she shows at work and tends to be more economical and less roguish than man. She is usually more patient than man and more attentive to people. Nor is woman less intelligent than man. "Science has proved," Hoxha has said, "that woman has as much brains as man. There are women geniuses, just as there are men geniuses."[28]

The Party's first secretary has sought constantly to impress the idea of sexual equality upon the minds of Albanian men. Speaking at a conference of the Labor Youth Union of Albania in April 1965, he advised:

Consider them [the young women] as your companions in life and at work. Behave as comrades and brothers with them, and see to it that your relations with them are friendly, open, sincere, and honorable. Encourage young women to take part in discussions at meetings, and to criticize you when you are wrong. Do not be angry with them when they criticize you.[29]

At the same time, it was pointed out that a significant part of the task of emancipation falls on the women themselves. Accordingly, appeals were made to women to "cleanse their own conscience" of everything that hampers their progress and to oppose those who, either by their speech or actions, trample on women's rights. Women must reject the feudal and bourgeois idea that circumscribes a woman's world to the kitchen, the church, and the raising of children.[30] An article in *Zëri i popullit*, October 31, 1970, said that "it is the duty of women to stand on the front line of the struggle for their emancipation" and to "eradicate their sense of interiority and slave mentality which has been bred into them and transmitted through the centuries." Only then will they be able to demonstrate the full range of their abilities, aptitudes, and creative powers at work, at home, and in the social and political life of the country.

Women and girls are encouraged, moreover, to take advantage of the new educational and cultural opportunities available to them, in order to raise the level of their culture and attain positions of responsibility and leadership in the economy and society in general. This is seen as a vital part of the program for women, inasmuch as 90 percent of them were illiterate at the end of the war and their sense of inadequacy had reached the point where many of them accepted—and still accept—their inequality to men as a just condition and as a part of the natural order of things. Women are also taught to defy conservative tradition and to associate freely with men prior to engagement, to marry only for love, and to reject the backward and economically unsound custom of elaborate and expensive weddings in favor of simple civil ceremonies. Nor should they fear divorce any longer. The government has granted them the right of divorce and urges them to use it, if need be, without hesitation, knowing that the husband can no longer hold divorce as a sword of Damocles over the wife's head, now that women have the chance to earn their own livelihood and become economically independent.

To help women achieve equality within the family, efforts were made to eliminate the "bourgeois concept" of the family that, according to the Albanian leadership, is based on private property and empowers man to treat woman like a household commodity. Such efforts aimed at establishing new relations between husband and wife. Accordingly, husbands were called upon to "respect their life companions" and assist them with household chores, without feeling a sense of shame or loss of manhood. Hoxha even suggested that husbands turn over their wages to their wives and allow them to administer the family budget. Such an arrangement, he said, will teach Albanian men to "pay closer attention" to their wives and induce them to break the time-wasting "coffeehouse habit."

The government took steps to establish in every village and community, as soon as possible, a network of public facilities, such as day-care centers, kindergartens, bakeries, public bathhouses, laundries, and dining halls. The use of such facilities was expected to free the hands of women from much of the household drudgery, enable them to put more time in productive social work, and permit them to raise their own level of education and culture.

In order to put this program into effect, the Albanian leaders have found it necessary to combat not only the prejudiced views and practices of individual men and women but also the pervasive influence of powerful institutions, the most prominent of which are patriarchy, religion, and the Law of the Lek. They have attacked these institutions in the most forceful terms. Addressing the Fourth Congress of Women in October 1955, Hoxha, the first secretary of APL observed that "Religion [has] intervened at every moment to keep woman in the miserable state of slavery . . . by means of its savage tenets, which crushed her spiritually, kept her in the most profound darkness, terrified her by putting in her the imaginary fear of God, of sin, etc."[31]

Attacks on the system of patriarchy, especially in its feudal form, as found in northern Albania, have been severe and relentless. Ramiz Alia, for example, has said of the Law of the Lek that "as concerns [its] attitudes towards women, it contains the most enthralling, most humiliating and most ruthless norms that can be imagined. . . ."[32] Is it not time, he asked, to uproot once and for all this "savage and barbarous" system? The Party has assured the women of Albania that it stands by them as they strive forward on the path of emancipation. Simultaneously, it has appealed to mass organizations, including trade unions, the Labor Youth Union of Albania, the Democratic Front, and local state and party organizations to support the struggle of women in all its forms and thus push Albania toward the goal of a more productive and egalitarian society.[33]

The Union of Albanian Women

The main institutional force organized by the Party to translate its program for women into action has been the national women's organization, known as BGSH (*Bashkimi i Grave të Shquipërisë*) or the Union of Albanian Women (UAW). Established on September 23, 2943, under the name of the Union of Anti-Fascist Women of Albania, it took "a definite form . . . at its first congress, held in Berat in November 1944."[34] The congress elected Ollga Plumbi, a noncommunist, as president of the organization and communist Liri Gega as secretary-general. The second congress, held in July of 1946, changed the name of the organization to its present form and chose Nexhmije Hoxha as president, a post she held until the Fourth UAW Congress in October 1955, when she was replaced by Vito Kapo. The latter has been head of the organization from 1955 to the present.[35]

In addition to its preoccupation with domestic matters, the UAW has also concerned itself with international affairs, mainly to give backing to the Party line on foreign affairs but also to break down the provincialism of Albanian women by forging ties with women in the socialist countries and "progressive women" throughout the world. To this end, UAW commemorates the International Women's Day on March 8 and has participated in various meetings the International Democratic Federation of Women (IDFW), including the 1956 IDFW meeting in Peking. The organization also exchanges visits with women's delegations from various countries, particularly in the Middle East, Africa, and Asia.

Prominent Albanian Women

Efforts to establish full equality between Albanian men and women by activating the women into production and the social and political life of the country have thrust into prominence a number of women. The oldest leading figures at present are Vito Kapo, UAW president; Nexhmije Hoxha, director of the Institute of Marxist-Leninist Studies; and Fiqret Shehu, director of the V. I. Lenin Party School. All three are long-time members of the APL Central Committee and the wives respectively of Hysni Kapo, Enver Hoxha, and Prime Minister Shehu, the top three members of the Albanian hierarchy.

Lately, there have been new faces among the women who have risen to positions of power and prestige. The influential position of first secretary of the Central Committee of the Labor Youth Union of Albania is held by a woman, Lumturi Rexha. In April 1976, two women filled the vacancies left by the dismissal of two members of the cabinet, thus breaking the male monopoly of that governmental body. Themie Thomai was appointed minister of agriculture, replacing Pirro Dodbiba, who was expelled on charges of committing "grave errors" with regard to the Party line. Thomai made her way to the top "from the fields," where she worked first as a common laborer, then as a work brigade leader, and still later as head of a model agricultural cooperative at Këmishtaj. In addition to her practical experience, she brought to her cabinet post the credentials of an economist and agronomist.[36] The other woman, Tefta Cami, was appointed minister of education and culture. She replaced Thoma Deliana who had held that post since March 1966. Cami is a university graduate and has a background that includes work as a teacher, school director, and secretary of the Party organization at the district level.

The appointment of the two women to cabinet-level positions could be taken as evidence of continued vitality and strength of the movement for women's emancipation in Albania and growing professionalism and expertise among the female population. It can also be interpreted as a subtle move on the part of APL leaders to strengthen women's self-confidence, enhance their public image, and hopefully increase their participation and industry on the economic front, in order to stimulate a sluggish economy and deflate dissent concerning the Party's general line.

In November 1976, Lenka Çuko, heretofore an unknown figure, emerged as a candidate member of the powerful Party Politburo. It was the greatest success in the field of politics achieved by an Albanian woman since 1960.[37]

Two other prominent but ill-fated women have been Liri Gega and Liri Belishova, both members of the Party's Central Committee and both purged as traitors and enemies of the Party and the people. Gega was executed in 1956 on charges of being a Titoist agent, following her capture "while attempting to cross the [Albanian-Yugoslav] border."[38] Belishova's downfall came in September 1960, allegedly for being involved in a plot of the Communist Party of the Soviet Union to overthrow the APL leadership. The indictment against Belishova was articulated by Enver Hoxha in his speech at the Moscow Meeting of 81 Communist and Workers' Parties in November 1960.[39]

The importance of Gega and Belishova is illustrated by the fact that they became a source of open polemics between Albania, the Soviet Union, and China. At the Twenty-second CPSU Congress in October 1961, Khrushchev rose to the defense of the two unfortunate women and accused the APL leadership of executing Liri Gega while she was pregnant.[40] He also commended Belishova for her "courage" in taking a stand for "Albanian solidarity with the Soviet Union." On the other hand, the Chinese communists, in a letter to the CPSU dated February 27, 1964, denounced Belishova for allegedly conspiring with the Soviet Union against the Albanian leaders.[41]

Sino-Soviet polemics over Belishova are understandable in view of her position in Albania politics. She had been elected to the powerful Party Politburo in 1948, at the age of twenty-two, and at the height of her power she was the sixth-ranking member in the Albanian hierarchy.[42]

However, the less spectacular but more important developments in the world of Albanian women relate to the masses of inconspicuous women, as they moved to shape a new life for themselves, within the context of a socialist society. To these we shall now turn.

Implementing the Party's Program

Over a period of three decades following the war, Albania has made valiant and determined efforts to implement her program for the emancipation of women. These efforts began to show results, as women started to work in agricultural cooperatives, factories, and various construction projects; attend school and enter the professions; and alter their relations within the family and in society. Hundreds of women, for example, began to work in the Stalin textile combine in Tiranë and on the Durrës-Elbasan railroad construction project in the late 1940s and early 1950s. Those who distinguished themselves on the production front were awarded the title of "Heroine of Socialist Labor."

Women began to make inroads, for the first time in the history of the country, in such fields as engineering, architecture, agronomy, and to participate more and more in various government bodies, such as the courts and the People's Assembly. Women began also to assume positions of leadership in various economic, cultural, and educational enterprises.

However, the successes women achieved during this period were below expectations, a fact which caused the Party leadership to grow increasingly irritable as time went on. Age-old prejudices were working against them. As they challenged the privileges, status, and authority of men, they ran into stiff opposition from men, including in many cases communists. Curiously, they also met opposition from members of their own sex, generally elderly women. Hoxha reported in 1947 that on occasion women were beaten up or killed by their husbands, fathers, or brothers for wanting to work on construction projects away from home.[43] On several occasions Party leaders warned communists that they would be expelled from the Party if they continued to violate the rights of women. The problem nevertheless continued, and by 1966, the year marking the start of Albania's cultural revolution, Hoxha was forced to admit that "Man dominates over woman everywhere among us."[44] He vowed that the Party would not tolerate the situation.

1967: The Year of the Albanian Woman

Hoxha's Speech of February 6, 1967

As the cultural revolution intensified, it became clear that Albania's leaders were not satisfied with the pace of progress in the struggle for the emancipation of women. The chief offenders were reported to be the communists themselves. Accordingly, the Party embarked on a campaign against its own bureaucracy. In an impassioned and now famous speech on February 6, 1967, at a meeting of "certain basic party organizations of Tiranë," Hoxha said:

How can the Party organization of the Lezhë district be on a revolutionary course, when the base custom of selling girls into marriage has silently assumed the force of law? The entire Party and country should rise up and smash backward customs, and break the head of anyone who violates the Party's sacred law for the defense of the rights of women....[45]

Hoxha's speech reportedly set off an immediate reaction throughout the country. In the weeks and months that followed, numerous mass meetings were held in towns and villages by women, girls, workers, students, youth, old people, and other groups. They expressed wholehearted support for Hoxha's speech and pledged to sweep away all backward customs and superstitious beliefs and practices that were holding women in chains.

These mass meetings were significant because, first, they made the cause of women an urgent public issue; second, they seemed to generate vast popular support for the women's movement; third, they afforded women an excellent platform for expressing their own ideas and pent-up emotions with regard to their subjection; fourth, they served notice to offenders, particularly to the Party cadres, to rectify their behavior toward women; and lastly, the meetings resulted in an open and at times most revealing dialogue, through the press, between Hoxha and the people.

In order to further impress the campaign for women's emancipation on the public mind, the APL leaders held a plenum in June of 1967, devoted mainly to the problem of women. Entitled "On Some Aspects of the Problem of the Albanian Woman," the Second APL-CC Plenum convened on June 15 and 16 and heard speeches by Hoxha and Ramiz Alia, the Party's cultural and ideological czar.

The June 1967 Central Committee Plenum on Women

In his report to the plenum, Alia noted that, of all the revolutionary movements that had occurred in Albania until then, "that of achieving the complete emancipation of women [was] of foremost importance."[46] He said that the women's movement had made a "qualitative leap forward" during the preceding months, by virtue of its unprecedented massiveness and the ideological awakening it had fostered in the country. The plenum learned that the women's organization numbered 300,000 members in its ranks (out of a total population in the country of about two million) and that women constituted 42 percent of Albania's total labor force. About 250,000 women were taking part in production, and in some areas of the economy, as in health and the textile and food industries, they outnumbered men workers by 69 percent, 73 percent, and 52 percent, respectively.

Alia pointed out, however, that only 8,280 women (12.4%) were members of the Party and that the great majority of women in production were engaged in simple, unskilled labor. In an attempt to get at the heart of the problem, Alia observed: "The root of all evil and main obstacle to the emancipation of women in our society lies in the alien concepts about women which are deep-rooted in the mentality of men and, to a large extent, in that of women themselves ... [namely], that women are inferior beings destined to serve men."[47] He appealed to Party cadres and mass organizations to mobilize their energies and do a more satisfactory job with women.

Hoxha's remarks to the plenum put the problem of Albanian women in a broad historical and philosophical perspective. He observed:

Women have been the first slaves ... in the history of mankind. Whether in the period of the Hellenic civilization or of the Roman epoch, whether in the Middle Ages ... or the "refined civilization" of the contemporary bourgeoisie, women have been and are the most downtrodden, exploited and spurned human beings in all respects. Laws, customs, religion, the masculine sex have kept them oppressed ... underfoot.[48]

Hoxha quoted Engels to the effect that the first class oppression in history was the enslavement of the female by the male and that the abolition of private property would transform the relations between the sexes, since the "two main props" of the property-oriented bourgeois marriages are the "submission of the wife to the husband and that of children to their parents."[49] Turning his attention to philosophy, Hoxha made strong attacks on Saint Thomas Aquinas and Saint John Chrysostom for their negative philosophy on women and on Napoleon Bonaparte for his alleged remark that "Mother Nature made women to be our slaves." He also hit Nietzsche and Freud for upholding the theory that "the male is active, while the female is passive," a theory which "leads to Nazism in politics, and to sadism in sex."

In conclusion, the Party's first secretary painted a glowing picture of the emancipated Albanian women of the future and called on all Albanians to help them in this struggle. "Open up all the portals of work, of learning, production, management to women," he said, "and help them to fashion their own personality on sound foundations, [and] to acquire self-reliance and courage ... in life, work and study."[50]

The June conference on women was the culmination of the Albanian leaders' efforts over a period of twenty-five years in behalf of women. Its significance, moreover, was heightened by the fact that it took place at the zenith of Albania's cultural revolution, and the conjunction of the two events very likely contributed to the immediate impact of the conference and its later repercussions.

The Sixth Congress of UAW
The third important event in the women's movement in Albania during 1967 took place on the last week of October, when the UAW convened its Sixth

Congress. Vito Kapo, UAW president, presided. Between Hoxha's speech in February and the UAW Congress in October, Albania witnessed a period of intense revolutionary enthusiasm and activity. The impact of this eight-month interval was apparent in Kapo's report to the congress.

During this period, she said, thousands of engagements of minors or infants, and between old men and teenage girls, had been broken. Women in many parts of the country had thrown away the veil, cut their hair, put on work pants, and abandoned the custom of carrying loads on their backs. Numerous other women, especially from the northern districts of Tropojë, Mirditë, and Mat—strongholds of patriarchy—defied age-old tradition and left home and town to work on construction projects such as roads, railways, and hydroelectric plants. Furthermore, peasant girls by the hundreds had come to live in the cities, among families, for periods of one to several months in order to learn home economics or some useful craft. At the same time, volunteer brigades of women and youth from the cities swarmed over the countryside to teach peasant women and children reading and writing, personal hygiene, dressmaking, and so on—in short, to raise their level of education and culture and to narrow the gap between cities and villages and between the highlands and the coastal regions.

"Our people," said Vito Kapo with satisfaction, "are uprooting in a few decades, years and months a world . . . which it took the ruling classes centuries to build."[51] She concluded her report to the congress with a strong pledge of loyalty to the APL. "We Albanian women," she said, "are . . . an armada of the Party," ready at any moment to respond to the Party's call, in defense of the country and the revolution.

Shkurte Pal Vata

In early November 1967, Shkurte Pal Vata, a fifteen-year-old girl from the Dukagjin region in northern Albania, died accidentally while working with a volunteer girls' brigade on the Rrogozhinë-Fier railroad construction project in central Albania.[52] Her death was widely publicized and she was made a symbol of the new, emancipated Albanian women and a heroine of the women's movement and the youth of the country. Soon afterward, the Party Central Committee granted her membership, posthumously, in the Party—an unprecedented action. A monument was also erected in her honor on the site where she fell.[53] Shkurte's tragic death furnished a dramatic ending to 1967, the most momentous year in the Albanian women's struggle for emancipation.

The eulogy of Shkurte was closely linked to a new revolutionary ferment that swept over the country at this time. Perhaps the most significant consequence of the new revolutionary upsurge was a remarkable increase in communication and cooperation between southern and northern Albanians, two groups of somewhat different backgrounds, which traditionally have tended to mistrust and to compete with each other for power and influence in the country. The experience is described by a group of women from the north who had traveled to the coastal region of Myzeqe in the south.

Just think of it, sister. . . . We are traveling all by ourselves in another part of the country. Can you believe it? Because you know a woman's place in the highlands has always been at home. . . . By seeing how our sisters work in Myzeqe, by getting to know them, we see Albania united as one . . . without the old distinctions between Geg and Tosk [the traditional identification labels of northern and southern Albanians, respectively]. . . . In this manner the sense of separation and isolation which has reigned for centuries in our highlands will break down, and our love for each other and for the Fatherland will increase.[54]

It was pointed out that the visit to the south would help the highlanders to live like the people in Myzeqe, "with beds and mattresses, to eat each one out of his own plate. . . ," and so on.

Balance Sheet of Gains and Losses

Considering the unusually difficult obstacles they have had to face in their "struggle for emancipation," Albanian women have scored some impressive gains over the past thirty years. They constitute 46 percent of the nation's labor force and over one-half (52%) of all workers in the cooperative sector of agriculture.

These and other data were given by Vito Kapo in her report to the Seventh UAW Congress, which was held on June 11-14, 1973, in the city of Shkodër, the main metropolis in northern Albania. The congress coincided with the thirtieth anniversary of the women's organization and was attended by Enver Hoxha, Shehu, and other Party leaders. The congress also drew twenty-five women's delegations from foreign countries—including a so-called delegation from the U.S.A.—somewhat less than the total present at the Sixth Congress in 1967, which was thirty-four.[55]

Premier Mehmet Shehu brought to the congress the greetings of the Party. He praised the women of Albania who "are struggling . . . for the complete construction of the socialist society," urged men to conquer their atavistic desire to dominate women, and took pride in the fact that Albania is "the first country in the world without religious rites."[56]

In her lengthy report to the congress, UAW President Kapo thanked the Party profusely for its support and admitted that the women's organization is "the offspring" or creation of APL.[57] She said that UAW had affiliations with eighty "progressive and revolutionary" women's organizations and groups in the world, thus implying that Albanian women, like the Albanian regime, were not isolated but enjoyed wide recognition and support abroad. Kapo then enumerated the gains achieved by Albanian women under socialism, especially in the three main areas of government and politics, the economy, and education and culture.

She noted that women comprised 24 percent of the total membership in the Party, compared with 12 percent at the Sixth Women's Congress, an impressive rise of 100 percent. In the Albanian People's Assembly, they accounted for 27 percent of the deputies, as against 16 percent at the time of the last UAW Congress. At the Seventh APL Congress in 1976, it was announced that women accounted for 27 percent of the rank-and-file members of the Party, an increase of five points since the Sixth Party Congress in 1971. In 1976 they also comprised 33 percent of the deputies to the People's Assembly, a gain of 6 percent since 1973.[58]

In the field of the economy, more women than ever before worked outside the home, thus further accentuating the change in women's traditional role from that of housewife to that of a jobholder in all sectors of the economy. Indeed, in 1976 women outnumbered men workers in some areas of the economy. For example, in the food industry women made up 65 percent of all workers; in health 70 percent; and in commerce 53 percent.[59] In the textile industry, they have had for many years a commanding lead over the men. However, women's representation in managerial and executive positions was far less than their numbers in the labor force warranted. This lopsided situation aggravated women's sense of inferiority to a point where some of them refused to accept promotions or appointments to positions of responsibility, even when they were highly qualified for such positions.

In the domain of education, women registered new successes even in institutes of higher learning where previously their numbers were low. Thus, in 1976, women accounted for 40 percent of the students in secondary schools and colleges. They also made up 43 percent of the middle-rank specialists and 25 percent of the specialists with advanced education and training.

In the cultural sector, men in general were enjoying the benefits of culture, including reading and recreation, to a greater extent than women; and a considerable number of women were ignorant about personal hygiene, home economics, and child raising. In the creative arts, women lagged behind men in all genres. It is remarkable, for example, that out of 117 prizes for outstanding achievement awarded by the Albanian government in 1970 to artists and writers, only two went to women.[60]

In the more complex area of social relations, the pace of progress has been slower and marked by lapses into the old patterns of culture. For example, in the fall of 1969 a boy and a girl in the Tepelenë district in southern Albania committed suicide as a result apparently of vicious gossip concerning their relations with each other. Both of them were leaders of the youth organization in the district. Their death was called "political murder" by Hysni Kapo, third-ranking member of APL. The tragedy, said Kapo, was "incited by the class enemy to damage the party. . . ."[61] The incident prompted Hoxha to make a speech to the Party Secretariat on October 18, 1969, dealing with "the rights of women and youth," which has since become one of the classic statements in defense of Albanian women. More recently, a conference of the Women's Union for the district of Tiranë complained that there were women who were still under the influence of backward customs, religious ideas and beliefs, and the stubborn custom of spending lavishly for the engagement and wedding of their sons and daughters. The conference further noted that some women manifested alien life styles in their family and social relations.[62]

In sum, the women of Albania have made important gains on the production front, in education, professional advancement, and participation in politics. In other areas, as in family and personal affairs and in their efforts to rise to positions of leadership and authority in the economic and cultural life of the country, they have been much less successful. While striving to achieve equality with men and gain control over their lives, Albanian women have at the same time sought to exert their influence beyond the borders of their mountain-locked country.

UAW and International Relations

In her report to the Sixth UAW Congress, held in October 1967, Vito Kapo remarked: "The experience gained by the Party in the struggle for the full emancipation of the Albanian woman has a value and importance which transcends the borders of our country and enriches the revolutionary Marxist-Leninist theory and practice in this field."[63] The position of the women's organization on international affairs was a reflection of APL's foreign policy. As a result, the UAW agitated faithfully for the Albanian Party line in meetings of various international bodies. Prior to Albania's break with Moscow in the fall of 1961, the UAW was strongly oriented to the USSR and looked upon Soviet women as models of emancipated females who "by their example [were lighting] the path of millions of women in the world."[64] Following the Soviet lead, UAW supported the position of the International Democratic Federation of Women (IDFW) on peaceful coexistence and world disarmament.

Yet, even at that time, Albanian women showed growing sympathy for China and in opposition to the Soviet line praised the Chinese experiment with communes, which were "playing an important role in the construction of socialism in China" and relieved women "of the main burdens of household chores."[65] At the Fifth UAW Congress in October 1961, Vito Kapo officially upgraded the role of Chinese women when she declared that the path of the Chinese sisters had become "a beacon of light for the peoples and women of the oppressed countries of Asia, Africa, and Latin America."[66] The leader of the Chinese women's delegation to the congress in turn praised the "revolutionary heroism" of the Albanian women and pledged to always stand by them. The alliance with Chinese women became formalized and was further strengthened when Kapo led a delegation of Albanian women to Peking in April of 1964. Such activities on the part of the Albanian and Chinese women's organizations were useful as a measure of the actual relations between the APL and the Chinese Communist Party.

Three years later, on the occasion of the Sixth UAW Congress, both Albanian and Chinese women delegates to the congress were attacking the USSR as revisionist and calling on Soviet women to revolt.[67]

At the recent Seventh congress, held in June 1973, Kapo praised Mao's China of 800 million and the Chinese sisters to whom Albanian women were bound by "a great militant friendship," attacked IDFW for its "demogogic and capitulatory stand" concerning Soviet policy on Europe, denounced the Vatican and the pope who, "together with imperialists and revisionists . . . organize plots and subversive activities against Albania,"[68] and welcomed the "growth of efforts by progressive women throughout the world for freedom and equality." Here again, the UAW positions mirrored the Party's international stance.

Conclusions

Toward the end of his talk at the June 1967 conference on women, Enver Hoxha described his conception of the fully emancipated Albanian woman in language befitting a visionary or a poet. Such a woman, he said, freed from economic dependence on the male, educated, cultured, and occupying her rightful place on the production front and in the social and political life of the nation, "will contribute to a large extent to the perfection of a new world . . . in which the material and spiritual life will flourish as never before."[69] Being a realist, however, he added that it will take "whole generations" to achieve the full emancipation of Albanian women.

Current Albanian reality bears out Hoxha's view. A survey of the recent literature on Albanian women shows that the problems and obstacles they are facing at present are essentially the same as those of the past. The main problems seem to be (1) male supremacy within the family, resulting in despotic behavior on the part of the husband toward the wife; (2) patriarchy, especially in the north, which denies individuality to woman and seeks to control every aspect of her personal and social life; (3) parental authoritarianism, or the stubborn tendency of many parents to demand absolute obedience from their children, and especially from their daughters, an attitude which all too often prevents the children from expressing themselves and developing their personality; (4) a curious puritanism with regard to love and sex, which induces members of the older generation to frown on romance among young people and to pin the label of "harlot" on single girls who associate with boys. To these may be added the conservatism of males on the production front, with the result that women are frequently prevented from advancing at work in accordance with their abilities.

In brief, the Albanian women's struggle for emancipation up to now has been, and still is, a determined attempt to emerge from the darkness and poverty to the past and catch up with the twentieth century. These efforts are likely to continue for many years before the heavy legacy of the past is overcome. This fact, incidentally, illustrates one major difference between the women's movement in Albania and women's liberation in the United States today which, by comparison, is affluent, educated, and socially advanced. A more important difference between the two, perhaps, is that the movement of Albanian women is a single, well-organized, and centrally directed effort with clearly defined goals, in contrast to the movement of American women which is fragmented, amorphous, and without a common program of action or shared objectives for which to strive. Moreover, Albanian women are a part of the Establishment, as it were, and enjoy the deliberate and powerful support of the state, while in the United States activists in the women's movement tend to feel alienated from the Establishment, and the more radical among them would overthrow the entire system.

Indeed, the organization of Albanian women, like other mass organizations in Albania, was conceived and created by the Albanian Party of Labor in order to carry out more effectively its program for the revolutionary transformation of the country's economy and society, in line with the Marxist-Leninist ideology, as interpreted by Tiranë. After moving to collectivize first the industry and next agriculture, the highly doctrinaire Albanian leaders are now embarked on collectivizing family and social life, which they describe as the "last stronghold of feudalism and bourgeois individualism and ideology." That is, they are striving to change the foundations and structure of family life in order, it seems, ultimately to socialize all family relations so that the husband and wife, male and female members of the family, may share equally in decision making, housework, and the management of the home, while at the same time each one reserves the right and the freedom to order his or her personal life in accordance with natural inclinations.[70]

The Union of Albanian Women is working closely with the Party to realize this goal. But neither the APL nor the UAW has any illusions about the difficulty of the task. To achieve the goal of full emancipation, Albanian women have to overcome the deeply rooted male supremacy in Albanian society, and Albanian men—proud, rugged individuals who in the past defended their rights with rifle in hand—are not about to give up their privileges or their belief that they are superior to women.

In April of 1965, Enver Hoxha remarked, "It will take the Albanian male a long time to realize that he is not superior to woman." That is certain. But the leaders of Albania and Albanian women seem determined to succeed in the struggle for the full emancipation of women.

6
The Evolution of the Arts

Following World War II, Albania embarked on an ambitious program to explore her ethnic origins, trace the roots of the Albanian language, exploit her national folklore; in short, to find her identity as a nation and people. This deep yearning for self-affirmation is understandable, coming after nearly five centuries of national oblivion under Turkish rule and several attempts by Albania's neighbors to partition her or annex portions of her territory. It accounts in part for the strong, sometime xenophobic nationalism of communist Albania and her conscious and persistent efforts to cultivate her martial and folk traditions, as well as to develop as rapidly as possible the potential for culture and cultural institutions.

The regime had several motives for wanting to develop culture. Culture was to be a means for indoctrinating the people with the communist ideology and enlisting them in the construction of socialism. By popularizing national folklore and the "progressive" traditions of the country, culture would promote patriotism and national pride among the people. Culture was to be exploited as an ideological weapon in the class struggle against the former ruling classes and the imperialist powers with their "decadent" way of life. Moreover, by raising the cultural level of the masses, particularly in the countryside, Albania would overcome her heavy legacy of cultural backwardness and refute the notion abroad that it was a primitive country, still languishing in the grip of feudal and Ottoman habits and institutions. In general, the Party leaders wanted to demonstrate that only under "the people's power" could Albanian culture attain full maturity and a level of achievement unparalleled in the country's history.[1]

In Search of the Nation's Cultural Heritage

Growing national interest and steady progress in the field of folklore culminated in 1960 in the establishment of the Albanian Institute of Folklore. By 1972, the institute had collected some 10,000 folk songs from all parts of the country and published 40 works on various aspects of folklore. This was reported by Zihni Sako, director of the institute, at the First National Conference on Albanian Folklore, held in Tiranë on May 26-27. 1972.[2] The conference was attended by folklore scholars, musicologists, writers, and educators, plus guest scholars from Kosovo, Macedonia, Montenegro, Romania, Austria, and Denmark. Some of the works published by the Institute of Folklore are:

Pralla popullore (Popular fables), *Valle popullore* (Folk dances), *Këngë dashurie* (Love songs), *Fjalë të urta të popullit shqiptar* (Albanian popular sayings), and *Folklori shqipëtar* (Albanian folklore).

Part of the effort to bring the benefits of culture to the people related to the past rather than the present or the future. These efforts resulted in the establishment of a network of local and national museums, the exploitation of the country's archaeological wealth, restoration work on art objects and buildings of historical value, and the popularization of little-known or unknown Albanian artists of the past. It was expected that progress in these areas would enlighten the people more fully about the nation's cultural heritage, increase their knowledge of local and regional history, and generate feelings of pride and patriotism.

At the end of nearly three decades of labor, much had been accomplished along these lines. Archaeologists carried out excavations of some scope on the sites of ancient Illyrian centers at Durrës, Pojan, and Butrint, Albania's main points of archaeological interest. By 1972 restoration work was completed on the old Church of Saint Triadha and the Church of Saint Nikolla in the "museum city" of Berat in central Albania.[3] Work continued toward the full restoration of the monastery of the Helvetii sect of Islam, also in Berat. Work on these religious edifices included the restoration to their original freshness and beauty of many damaged or neglected frescoes and icons.

In this connection, Albania did much to publicize the art of two sixteenth-century masters, Onufri and his son Nikolla, the country's greatest medieval painters. Although trained in the highly stylized Byzantine tradition of religious painting, they transcended that tradition and introduced elements of Renaissance art in their work, thus effecting a fusion of the ethereal and the mundane, the divine and the human in their work. Another one of these old masters is David Selenica, an eighteenth-century painter whose frescoes decorate the Church of Saint Nikolla in Voskopojë, southern Albania. Selenica, too, sought to "humanize" his saints by giving each figure its own individuality.[4]

Two major publications that aim to throw light on art treasures of the past are *Monumentet* and *Shqipëria arkeologjike*. The latter reportedly was "received with interest by archeologists and scholars in various countries," among them I. I. Russu, head of the Romanian Institute of History and Archaeology; Alfonso de Francisci, curator of antiquities in Naples; plus scholars from Yugoslavia, France, Belgium, England, and Iceland.[5]

The task of coordinating and furthering research work on cultural treasures, and protecting them from possible harm, was delegated to the Institute for the Preservation of the Monuments of Culture. Albanian leaders and scholars attached much importance to the institute. As they saw it, the work of the institute and, indeed, its very existence bolstered the argument that Albania had now become the center of research on Albanian studies. They claim that this is a historical reversal of the prewar situation, when the most serious studies on Albania were carried out in some West European country, such as Germany, Austria, or Italy.

A by-product of Albania's attention to her past has been the "resurrection" and popularization of the cultural achievements of Albanians who attained prominence abroad—in some cases, centuries ago—but who were little known to the contemporary Albanian public. Foremost in this group are Andrea Aleksi, Sadefqar Mehmeti, Elena Gjika, Aleksander Moisiu, and Viktor Efthimiu.

Andrea Aleksi, a fifteenth-century sculptor from Durrës, is said to have won renown for his contributions to secular and nonsecular architecture in towns along the Dalmatian coast and in Italy.[6] Sadefqar Mehmeti reportedly was a celebrated architect from Elbasan, born in 1562, who is credited with the building of the Blue Mosque in Istanbul, reputed to be one of the best examples of religious architecture in the world.[7]

Much has been written in Albania about Elena Gjika (1822-1888), known in Europe as Dora d'Istria and acclaimed as a poet and fiery defender of the national rights of the Albanian people. Although she was born in Constantsa, Romania, her family origins apparently were in the locality of Përmet in southern Albania. Gjika knew Albania well and maintained contacts with many Albanian nationalists of her day, including Jeronim de Rada, Zef Jubani, Dhimitër Kamarda, and Thimi Mitko.[8]

Aleksander Moisiu (1880-1935), perhaps the most prominent figure in the list of resurrected Albanian artists, came from a family that traced its beginnings to the Kavajë-Durrës region in central Albania. Moisiu was a character actor who won fame throughout Europe for his interpretations of leading roles in plays by Shakespeare, Schiller, Ibsen, Chekhov, Shaw, and Pirandello. He performed in the foremost theaters of Berlin, Vienna, Paris, Moscow, New York, and Chicago and won high praise from such celebrities as Hugo von Hofmannsthal, the Austrian poet and dramatist; Stanislavski; Max Reinhardt, director of the famed Berlin Theater; and authors Gerhart Hauptmann and Ferenc Molnár. In recognition of his outstanding artistic achievements, the

Albanian government in 1962 awarded Moisiu, posthumously, the title of Artist of the People, the highest award in art given in communist Albania.[9]

The most recent of these Albanian nationals who rose to a position of prominence in the world of art and culture, beyond the shores of Albania, is the late Viktor Efthimiu (1905-1972), distinguished Romanian writer and member of the Romanian Academy of Sciences. In the summer of 1971, Efthimiu took a trip to the land of his origin and visited the village of his birth, Boboshticë in southern Albania. While in Albania, the People's Assembly awarded him the Order of Naim Frashëri—named after socialist Albania's National Poet—for "his special contribution to the strengthening of friendly relations between the Romanian and Albanian peoples." He also accepted an honorary membership in the League of Albanian Writers and Artists.[10]

The Festival

Festivals and commemorative conferences and programs have become standard forms of cultural expression in Albania. Examples of such festivals are the Theater Olympiad of Tiranë and the Radio-TV Song Festival, both of them annual events of wide popular appeal, which last for as long as ten days. The biggest popular festival held to date was the National Festival of Folklore, which took place in Gjirokastër, October 6-12, 1968. A total of 1,500 singers, dancers, and instrumentalists, chosen from among 15,000 aspiring amateurs, participated in that cultural event. The Gjirokastër festival was repeated five years later in autumn 1973. The event was filmed in color and was subsequently shown to audiences abroad, including Western Europe and the United States. The film was titled *Burim i pashtershëm* (Inexhaustible fountain).

Festivals were also organized to commemorate special national and Party anniversaries or to honor particular groups in society such as the working class, women, and the armed forces. Contests were held, in connection with these festivals, among professional artists—writers, painters, sculptors, composers—and prizes were awarded to the winners. In recent years, festivals of this kind were held to commemorate the five hundredth anniversary of the death of Skënderbeu (1968), the twenty-fifth anniversary of liberation (1969), the thirtieth anniversary of the Party (1971), the thirtieth anniversary of the People's Army (1973), and the thirtieth anniversary of Albania's liberation from the Fascist occupation (1974).[11]

The Skënderbeu festival, in particular, was an impressive and memorable event. It lasted for one week, from January 11 through 17, but preparations for it had begun one year earlier. During that time, Albanian artists worked on projects in honor of the National Hero, while scholars compiled extensive studies of his life and times. The results of this immense outpouring of creative energy became apparent during the commemorative week. Thus, a new monument to Skënderbeu was inaugurated in the principal square in Tiranë, displacing the monument of Stalin, which was relocated elsewhere in the capital.[12] There were art and book exhibits on Skënderbeu, and a new opera, *Gjergj Kastrioti-Skënderbeu* by Prenk Jakova, had its premiere in the Theater of Opera and Ballet. At the same time, scholars of Albanian studies, from within and without the country, gathered in Tiranë for the Second Conference on Albanian Studies, the central theme of which was Skënderbeu and his era.

Other milestones in the nation's history that were celebrated in recent years with considerable fanfare, including "solemn meetings" by government officials, and supplemented by a host of cultural activities were the ninetieth anniversary of the League of Prizren (1878-1968), starting point for Albania's national awakening;[13] the sixtieth anniversary of the Congress of Monastir (1908-1968), which laid the foundations for the alphabet currently in use in Albania;[14] the fiftieth anniversary of the Congress of Lushnjë (1920-1970), convened to save the country from being partitioned by its neighbors;[15] the fiftieth anniversary of the Battle of Vlorë (1920-1970), which resulted in the expulsion of Italian occupation forces from Albania following World War I;[16] and the fiftieth anniversary of the June 1924 "revolution," which brought to power Bishop Fan S. Noli.[17] Noli's "bourgeois-democratic" government—as Albanian communists call it—is viewed in Albania today as a significant political development, owing to its "progressive" and "anti-imperialist" character and orientation.

The League of Albanian Writers and Artists invariably played a part on such occasions by holding conferences and discussions and publishing materials relevant to the occasion. Similarly, the league paid tribute to patriots like Sami Frashëri, Mihal Grameno, Luigj Gurakuqi, Isa Boletini, and others by observing the anniversaries of their birth or death and by highlighting their services to the nation. The league also hailed the outstanding figures of the Albanian communist movement—pioneers like Vasil Shanto, Qemal Stafa, Margarita Tutulani, Zonja Curre, Misto Mane, and Mihal Duri. Writers and artists extolled their lives and through their creative works sought to imprint the memory of their martyrdom on the consciousness of the people and integrate them into the cultural heritage of the nation. They showed the same regard for heroes of socialist labor like Adem Reka, Shkurte Pal Vata, and Ismet

Sali Bruçaj. It seemed as if Albania wanted to elevate these martyrs and heroes to sainthood, communist-style, to be dutifully praised and emulated by the people, as they toiled and marched ahead in the hope of reaching that distant day when the communist utopia would become a reality for all Albanians.

The Growth of Cultural Institutions

Along with efforts to enhance the country's cultural heritage and affirm its cultural identity, the Albanian regime invested much energy in programs aiming at the development of art and culture. Such programs provided for the growth, on the one hand, of cultural institutions and the training of a growing body of creative artists and workers in the field of culture.

Education
An important step in this direction was taken in 1947, when the Institute of Science was founded in Tiranë. The institute became the nucleus for research activities that later led to the establishment of the first university in Albania's history.

Albania's highest institution of learning, *Universiteti shtetëror i Tiranës* (the State University of Tiranë), was founded in 1957. It offers instruction in seven faculties or departments, including history and philology; the social, political, and juridical sciences; economics; engineering; the natural sciences; agriculture; and medicine. At its founding, the university had an enrollment of 3,600 students and a faculty and research staff of 200. By 1976, enrollment had grown to 17,000 students, while the staff numbered about 800.[18] Currently the university is headed by rector Petrit Radovicka.

On June 20, 1972, fifteen years after the establishment of the State University of Tiranë, Albania proclaimed "the founding of the Academy of Sciences of the Albanian People's Republic." The announcement said that the fundamental duty of the academy would be "the development of research and studies based on scientific cirteria and the Marxist-Leninist methodology.[19] The announcement prompted messages of greetings from UNESCO and from a number of scholars of Albanian studies in East and West Europe. Among them were Prof. V. Dimitrescu of the University of Bucharest; Prof. G. Kastelan, director of the Center for Southeast European Studies in Paris; Prof. N. G. Hammond of the University of Bristol in England; academician J. Irmscher of East Germany; Prof. H. Olberg of the University of Innsbruck, Austria; Prof. V. Georgiev of the University of Sofia, Bulgaria; Prof. R. Katičić and Prof. A. Stipčević of the University of Zagreb, plus many Albanian scholars from Kosovo and Macedonia in Yugoslavia.[20]

Six months after the founding of the academy, a group of twenty-five scholars, presumably the top intellectuals of Albania, was chosen to staff it. The list of these "charter member" academicians—all of whom held the title of professor—included historians Aleks Buda and Androkli Kostallari; Dhimitër Shuteriqi, writer and former president of the League of Albanian Writers and Artists; Eqrem Çabej, philologist; Bedri Dedja, writer and deputy minister of education and culture; and Zija Këlliçi, formerly rector of Tiranë University.[21] Buda also became president of the academy.

The academy functioned as an umbrella organization that comprised over half a dozen institutions of higher learning. These were the Institute of History, the Institute of Language and Literature, the Institute of Economic Studies, the Institute of Nuclear Physics, the Institute of Hydrology and Meteorology, the Institute of Folklore, the Center for Computer Mathematics, the Laboratory for Hydraulic Research, and the Seismological Center.[22] Other centers of education were the Institute of Agriculture, the Teachers' Training Institute, and the Institute of Arts, also known as the Academy of Phonetic and Plastic Arts. This is a cultural complex which includes the Institute of the Figurative Arts (painting, sculpture), the State Conservatory of Music, and the Actors' Academy. The various divisions of the institute train students to develop skill in painting, sculpture, music, and the dramatic theater.

By the midseventies, over 700,000 persons were reported to be attending school in Albania, compared with about 300,000 in 1960 and 56,000 in 1938. According to Albanian statisticians, only one out of eighteen people attended school in 1938. This figure was reduced to one out of five in 1960, while by 1970 one-third of the population reportedly was enrolled in a formal study program.[23] The progress achieved in education since the war can be seen in tables 6.1 and 6.2.

It is true that Albania has made rapid strides in the area of education. However, the statistics of growth shown in the two tables can be misleading if one does not take into account the growth also of the country's population over the same period of time (from 1,000,000 in 1938 to 2,300,000 in 1973). For example, if allowance is made for the increase in population, the growth in the number of students in 1973 is five times, rather than twelve, compared with 1938. Even so, the growth in all categories of education has been impressive, a fact in which the regime takes rightful pride.

Table 6.1
Expansion of the Educational System (1938-1973)

	1938	1950	1960	1970	1973
8-grade schools	–	193	557	1,374	1,470
Middle schools[a]	11	23	69	131	155
Higher schools[b]	–	1	6	5	8

Source: *30 vjet Shqipëri socialiste* [30 years of socialist Albania] (Tiranë, 1974), p. 205.
[a]Roughly equivalent to high school in the U.S.
[b]Roughly equivalent to college in the U.S.

Table 6.2
Growth in the Number of Students (1938-1973)

	1938	1950	1960	1970	1973
Total number of students	56,300	177,900	311,500	661,200	700,900
In 8-grade schools	54,600	170,800	274,900	555,300	569,600
In middle schools	1,700	6,800	29,900	80,400	102,600
In higher schools	–	300	6,700	25,500	28,600
Growth in number of students since 1938 (in times)	1	3	6	12	12

Source: *30 vjet*, p. 206.

The Theater

Socialist Albania has taken a keen interest in the theater. One evidence of this is the vast amount of literature that has been published on the problems, themes, achievements, and failures of the drama. This is understandable in view of the immediacy of this art form and its direct impact on public opinion. Contemporary Albanian drama has its roots in the Partisan war, where it emerged as guerrilla theater for the purpose of aiding the war effort. Already in May 1944 the Partisans had created the People's Theater—as distinguished from the "bourgeois theater"—dedicated to achieving victory for the people's revolution. The nature of the new theater was described by Hoxha in a message to the "theater workers" on the twentieth anniversary of the People's Theater in May of 1964. He said that the theater in Albania was nationalist and socialist in character and called on actors, stage directors, and playwrights to develop the revolutionary conscience of the masses and imbue them with communist morality and loyalty to the Party line.[24]

A survey of the drama in Albania over the past twenty-five years shows that it has been dominated by two major themes: the War of National Liberation and the construction of socialism. At all times, the theater was subordinated to politics and utilized to achieve definite ends prescribed by the state.

In view, then, of the subservience of the theater to the state, it is rather surprising to find that much of the drama in contemporary Albania is competent and some of it good, even excellent. The "classic" dramas of postwar Albania are such pieces as *Shtatë shaljanët* (The seven men of Shala) by Ndrekë Luca; *Familja e peshkatarit* (The fisherman's family) and *Trimi i mirë me shokë shumë* (Valiant leader, loyal followers) by Sulejman Pitarka; *Toka jonë* (Our land) and *Halili e Hajrija* (proper names) by Kolë Jakova; and *Cuca e maleve* (The mountain lassie) by Loni Papa. However, in the light of the increasingly dogmatic literary and dramatic criticism that appeared in the 1960s, many of the "classic" plays were found to suffer from ideological errors and weaknesses. They were criticized, above all, for allegedly harboring fuedal concepts and romantic notions.[25]

In general, plays about the Partisan struggle, while informative as social documents, have been failures as works of art, owing mainly to lack of insight into character and to stereotype plot development. The more successful dramas are those dealing with family conflict, the evils of bureaucracy, the breakdown of personal ethics and ideals, backward traditions, women's emancipation, and social satire. Among the best known works in these categories are Ibrahim Uruçi's *Doktor Aleksi*, which tells of the rectification of erring intellectuals, and his *Shëmbja* (The collapse), a powerful attack on the custom of infant engagements, still practiced in the Albanian highlands. Fadil Paçrami, a prolific and, until his fall from grace in 1973, widely influential dramatist, is the author of what was regarded as the classic play on the nationalization of industry, *Mbi gërmadha* (Over ruins). He is also the author of *Shtëpia në bulevard* (The house on the boulevard), a thought-provoking piece about a young woman who is abandoned by her lover in her pregnancy. Paçrami used the plight of the heroine to make an indignant, yet reasoned attack on the double standard system of morality and called on women to develop self-respect and become masters of their own lives, even at the cost of a degree of cynicism.[26]

Possibly the best drama on the emancipation of women is *Lina "e urta"* ("Quiet" Lina) by Arsinoi Bino, one of the top female authors in the country. Bino's play is an incisive study of the life of a young, submissive wife and her successful rebellion against her patriarchal and elitist husband, for whom she was but a sex object and an embellishment to his life, rather than an equal and respected marriage partner. In the course of the resolution of the basic conflict, the play makes some interesting statements on the clash between old and new concepts of love, work, amusement, and the search for self-fulfillment.[27]

A part of the new drama in Albania is "documentary" in nature and aims at eulogizing heroes of socialist labor, in order that others may emulate them. One such play is *Ditari i një mësuesi* (Diary of a teacher) by Fadil Kraja. This is a play written in memory of Ismet Sali Bruçaj, a teenage teacher who died in 1968 in a blizzard while on the way to the village where he taught grade school. In the play, Bruçaj emerges as the model of the "new Albanian man," who is thoroughly imbued with the ethics of socialism and who sacrifices his own interests, even his life, for the common good of society. As Kraja develops this thesis, he comments vividly on the backwardness of hinterland Albania and denounces such practices as husbands' exploitation of their wives— for example, keeping them pregnant in the hope of having a male offspring; superstition, an instance of which is the wearing of a wolf's tooth to ward off illness; ignorance of elementary hygiene; and the almost total absence of home furnishings and decor.[28]

Comedy in the theater of socialist Albania is, strictly speaking, social satire. Its primary object is not to titillate the audience but through laughter to cause it to think seriously about the problems and contradictions confronting the emerging Albanian society, as revealed by the foibles, arrogance, selfishness, and greed of the "enemies of socialism," as well as its "unenlightened" supporters in the ranks of the masses.

D. Bubani and O. Grillo achieved a measure of success as comic playwrights with their *Parimori* (The man of principle), a piece about a pseudoatheist professor. But the master of satirical drama in Albania, who stood fairly alone in the field, was Sprio Çomora (1918-1973), author of two outstanding works, *Karnavalet e Korcës* (The carnival of Korçë) and *Dy me zero* (Two to nothing). For the latter play, Comora shared the top prize awarded for the best comedy in the 1969 Festival of Literature and the Arts, held in commemoration of the twenty-fifth anniversary of liberation.[29]

Çomora's play is a thoughtful exposition of the socialist world view with its collectivist ethics; and its rival, the "bourgeois" world view, with its individualist and egocentric ethics. The central character in the drama is Enrieta, a teacher, who is married to an engineer, Viktori. A severe crisis, however, threatens their marriage when Viktori is transferred from Tiranë to a small and distant town, while his wife—under the influence of her "petit bourgeois" mother—remains behind. The mother cannot conceive of her daughter living happily in an insignificant town. The separation is a nerve-wracking experience for Enrieta, who is torn between her desire to be with her husband and her reluctance to oppose her mother. In the end she quits Tiranë and rejoins her husband. The play thus deals with a timely and, indeed, endemic problem of socialist Albania—the reluctance of educated young people to live and work in the countryside, away from the cultural and social excitement of the nation's capital.

As the play unfolds, the author makes forceful comments on such questions as careerism, big-town snobbism, momism, and the role of work in the achievement of personal happiness and the goals of a socialist society. *Dy me zero* stands out as a play of excellent characterization, intelligent dialogue, and sharp wit interspersed with striking poetic imagery. The author shows unusual insight into his characters and develops their relationships with natural ease and clarity. They are believable human beings, who seem to function naturally, without any visible constraints, even though they live in a centrally directed society that is saturated with ideological slogans and official decrees.[30] The death of Çomora is a loss for Albanian drama.

Another dramatist of note is Minush Jero, who unfortunately has lost favor with the regime, owing to his challenging dramatic protrayals of Albanian reality.

In addition to plays by local dramatists, the Albanian public has seen performances of works by Shakespeare (*Hamlet, Othello*), Molière (*Tartuffe, Le bourgeois gentilhomme*), Carlo Goldoni (*The Mistress of the Inn*), Gogol (*The Inspector General*), Brecht (*Arturo Ui*), Arthur Miller (*The View from the Bridge*), and others.

A number of actors and actresses distinguished themselves on the dramatic stage. Among the more prominent names are Sandër Prosi and Marie Logoreci, holders of the title, Artist of the People; Tinka Kurti, honored with the Actress of Merit award; Kadri Roshi, Lazar Filipi, Roza Xhuxha, and Margarita Xhepa.

In June 1950, a new form of the dramatic art appeared, when the first Albanian puppet theater for children was created in Tiranë. The content of the shows, like all art in contemporary Albania, had a heavy ideological flavor and dealt with such themes as the National Liberation War, patriotic education, struggle against exploitation by the class enemy, and vigilance against saboteurs and counterrevolutionary agents. "The ideological content of our shows [for the children's theater]," Albanian ideologists claimed, "inspires the children with sound revolutionary, patriotic, and human sentiments."[31] The shows also treated of love of school and learning, good behavior, respect for the family, and devotion to work and the welfare of society, all within the context of Marxist-Leninist ideology.

The Opera and Ballet

A milestone in the development of Albania's cultural life was reached on November 29, 1953. On that day, the ninth anniversary of liberation from the German occupiers, the National Theater of the Opera and Ballet opened in Tiranë. The new cultural institution, the first of its kind in the country's history, was greeted with understandable enthusiasm and pride by Albanians, both within and outside the country. The debut of opera and ballet, in all their lavish splendor, in a country which to large numbers of people in the world was best known for its primitiveness and age-old blood feuds, gave to Albanians the feeling that they had reached the highest levels of cultural sophistication. They felt that now they need no longer apologize for the condition of their culture.

The prestigious opera and ballet troupe performed works from the classic operatic repertoire, as well as operas, operettas, and ballets by Albanian composers. The list of classic operas included Bizet's *Carmen*, Puccini's *Madame Butterfly* and *La bohème*—which has since become the most popular opera on the Albanian concert stage—Mascagni's *Cavalleria rusticana*, and several of Verdi's works, among them *La traviata* and *Rigoletto*.

The pioneer work in the operatic genre by an Albanian composer was *Agimi* (The dawn), an operetta that had its premiere in 1954. It was composed by Kristo Kono, who is thought to be Albania's best known musician and who holds the title of Artist of the People, the highest award given to an artist by the Albanian government.[32]

Operatic history was made in Albania in 1959, when *Mrika* (proper name), the first Albanian grand opera, was performed in Tiranë. Composed by Prenk Jakova, this musical drama is about a girl, Mrika, who arms herself with the teachings of the Party and goes forth among the highlanders of the Mirditë region in northern Albania to fight the legacy of the Law of the Lek and replace it with the new socialist order. Another opera, *Pranvera* (The spring) by Tish Daija, one of the most gifted and prolific composers in the country, made its debut in 1960. Its theme is the National War of Liberation.

Lulja e kujtimit (The flower of remembrance), another opera by Kristo Kono, is based on the immensely popular 1924 novel of the same title by Foqion Postoli. The setting of this deeply nationalistic work is the town of Korçë in the period immediately preceding the independence of Albania. The main protagonists are two patriotic young people, Dhimitri and Olimbia, who love each other but whose love is thwarted by the girl's pro-Greek father, Kristo, a very successful merchant. Subsequently, Dhimitri is driven into exile in Serbia, where he joins a *çetë* (a band of Albanian freedom fighters). In the end, he returns to Korçë with the çetë, as the Turks and pro-Greeks are routed and Albania wins her independence. Dhimitri and Olimbia are reunited, and their love blossoms again, this time under the bright skies of a free and sovereign Albania.

Other Albanian operas are *Skënderbeu* by Jakova; *Prometheu* (Prometheus), another work by Kono; and *Minatorët*, a work by Pjetër Gaci, which sings the praises of mine workers and the virtues of socialist labor. Recent work in the operatic field includes *Komisari* by Nikolla Zoraqi, with libretto by Dritëro Agolli, which had its premiere in 1975; *Dhëndëri u transferua* (The bridegroom was transferred), with music by Agim Prodani and the libretto by Sprio Çomora; and *Mulliri i Kostë Bardhit* (The flour mill of Kostë Bardhi), a product of composer Tonin Harapi and librettist Mirash Markaj. The last work is based on a play of the same title by Naum Prifti.[33]

In the field of ballet, the two most successful original Albanian productions seem to be *Halili e Hajrija* by Tish Daija; and *Cuca e maleve*, a work by Nikolla Zoraqi, based on Loni Papa's drama of the same name.

Daija's ballet is an adaptation of a famous folktale about a brother and sister, Halili and Hajrija, in the time of Ottoman rule in Albania.[34] As the story unfolds, we learn that Halili has taken to the mountains to resist the rule of the Turk by force of arms. His sister is married and is living with her husband and their son in the town of Shkodër in northern Albania. Knowing that a price is on Halili's head, the husband cunningly persuades Hajrija to invite her brother for dinner. Halili, who loves and trusts his sister, accepts the invitation and comes to town to dine with her and her husband. His brother-in-law then betrays him to the Turkish pasha of Shkodër and he is taken away to prison, where he is to be executed. Believing that it was his sister who betrayed him, Halili curses her and her offspring. Shocked by her husband's treachery and remorseful over her brother's accusation, Hajrija vows to revenge. Within a week, she shoots her husband dead, takes the life of their son, then flees to the mountains to take her brother's place in the resistance movement. Meditating over the tragic events, she says that killing her husband was like saving her beloved brother's life but that slaying her child was like putting out her own eyes.

There are, of course, various interpretations of Hajrija's motives and morality. The most extreme unsympathetic view is that her behavior symbolizes the savagery and barbarism of the Albanian people, who are known for their martial spirit and traditions. But in the eyes of socialist Albania, Hajrija apparently emerges as a heroine who will spare neither husband nor child to avenge an act of double treachery: that against kin and that against country. Certainly her hard, merciless attitude toward her husband's pecuniary greed and collaboration with the enemy agrees well with the regime's militant and uncompromising stand toward its enemies.[35]

Zoraqi's ballet, *The Mountain Lassie*, is a musical dramatization of the true story of a young woman of the highlands who in 1949 was kidnapped by anticommunists and killed. The young woman, who was known simply as Cuca (girl, lassie), defied time-honored conventions and challenged the male-dominated social and economic order in her region. Instead of bowing to the patriarchal system of the Law of the Lek and the powerful Catholic Church—the two mainstays of the old order in the highlands—Cuca rebelled and began to agitate for change among the women in her community. She taught them to read and write and encouraged them to lead independent lives, even to work away from home—a heretical notion in her region. Her attempts to spread such "unnatural and immoral" ideas among women in the highlands aroused deep hostility among defenders of the status quo and cost Cuca her life.

A noted name in Albanian ballet is Çesk Zadeja, composer of the ballet *Delina* (proper name), which had its premiere in 1968 as part of the festivities commemorating the 500th anniversary of the death of Skënderbeu. Some other Albanian ballets are *Partizani* (The partisan) by Kozma Lara; *Zanusha* (proper name), another work by Zadeja; and *Bijtë e peshkatarit* (Sons of the fisherman), a recent composition by the talented Tish Daija.

Among artists who have attained prominence as singers and dancers in the opera and ballet are Zoica Haxho and Ganimet Vendresha, ballerinas; Avni

Mula, baritone; and Stavri Rafael, tenor. Nina Mula and Leonora Pejo, sopranos, both have played leading roles in Puccini's *La bohème*; and Gaqo Çako, a popular tenor, is a holder of the Artist of Merit award for high achievement in his field. Avni Mula holds the title, Artist of the People.

A big step in music was taken at the beginning of 1972 with the formation of the Philharmonic Society in Tiranë. The new musical ensemble gave its first concert on January 11, 1972, on the occasion of the twenty-sixth anniversary of the Albanian People's Republic. In addition to the Philharmonic Society, there were symphonic orchestras in the cities of Durrës, Shkodër, Elbasan, and Korçë. They performed music by native Albanian composers and classical works by Mozart, Haydn, Beethoven, Chopin, Dvořák, Tchaikovsky, Smetana, and others.

Painting and Sculpture
In 1954, a new cultural institution, the Gallery of Fine Arts, opened in Tiranë. It housed the best work in painting and sculpture produced in Albania, past and present. The gallery held annual expositions of new paintings, sculpture, and graphic art. The gallery also sponsored expositions of its holdings abroad in the socialist countries, the Middle East, and a number of West European and other countries.[36]

Painting in socialist Albania tended to be conventional by current Western art standards. Painters were expected to produce works that reflected optimism and communicated clearly and easily with the public. Art critics frowned on paintings that were done in somber colors or attempted to convey their message in allegory, symbolism, and other abstract terms.

Among Albania's best painters are Vilson Kilica, Nexhmedin Zajmi, Agim Faja, Sadik Kaceli, Vangjush Mio, and Zef Shoshi. One of Zajmi's works, *Grua labe* (Lab woman), is a sensitive portrait of an elderly woman in Albania's rural south. The artist has captured her mood and spirit; he reveals her suffering and her strength. Her features are a mingling of compassion and hardiness and suggest a life of self-denial, adversity, quiet pride, and dignity.[37]

Agim Faja's *Luftë kundër thatësirës* (Battling the drought) is a strikingly beautiful tableau of a rural scene, rich in colors that contrast sharply, yet form a harmonious whole. The figures in the painting are enhanced by clean lines enclosing bright, solid masses. It is a pleasant work, reminiscent in some ways of Paul Gauguin.[38]

Vilson Kilica, a master of technique, has done some interesting work in a semi-impressionistic style that is at once soothing to the eye and compelling to the mind. He invites the spectator not only to savor the surface beauty of his paintings but to search beneath the surface for meanings and nuances that are not readily apparent to the eye. In this sense, his work has a spiritual, even mystical quality that is rare in contemporary Albanian painting. Two of Kilica's works are *Portret i një puntori* (Portrait of a worker) and a group portrait of Skënderbeu and his warriors that is essentially static, yet pulsates with latent energy and power.[39]

Aksionistja (Woman of action) by Zef Shoshi is a painting of an endearing young woman on her way to work. She is a lively specimen, self-confident and purposeful. She creates the impression that work is a healthy and ennobling activity. Indeed, glorification of work in the interest of socialist construction was a top priority item, in terms of propaganda, in socialist Albania. Accordingly, artists were expected to employ the tools of art to make work attractive and morally rewarding to the masses, quite apart from any material gains they might derive from it.[40]

Safo Marko is easily the best graphic artist in the country. Marko has done most of her work as an illustrator of books, pamphlets, magazine stories, and as a designer of posters to commemorate or publicize various anniversaries and events. But regardless of the genre in which she has worked, she has displayed considerable talent, characterized by imagination, versatility, and a graceful, almost effortless touch. Marko's work is tender, playful, or austere as the situation may demand and is nearly always revealing of the inner world of her subjects, whether they are children romping in a playground or revolutionaries about to be shot. She is one of few artists in Stalinist Albania who, by the force of her creative power, has risen above ideology and speaks to the public in the common language of humanity.[41]

Two women who have gained recognition as painters are Liljana Çefa and Lumturi Dhrami. Dhrami was one of two women (among 115 men) who in 1970 won the Prize of the Republic for her engraving *Rruga jonë* (Our path), which depicted the role of Albanian women in the struggle for liberation and the construction of socialism.[42]

Among the talented new arrivals in the world of Albanian painting are Selim Bilali, whose mural *Our Land* pays homage to agricultural work and life; Hiqmet Agolli, whose skill is well manifested in his portrait of a sensitive, yet confident young woman worker entitled *Girl on a Project*; and Guljelm Kraja, one of whose works, *In the Cooperative Fields*, is an attempt to show the quiet beauty of the countryside and the harmonious relationship between men and nature.[43]

One aspect of culture that received growing attention from Albania's leadership and the artistic intelligentsia was the creation of public monuments and other works of sculpture. Such art was designed to express and symbolize in metal, stone, plaster, and wood the nation's revolutionary and patriotic traditions, the "epic" of the Partisan struggle, and the inspiring work and ideals of the "new heroes" of the country who were daily building socialism.

Apart from the two equestrian statues of Skënderbeu in Krujë and the main square in Tiranë, the most ambitious sculptural creations in the country were the monument to the martyrs of the War of National Liberation, known as Mother Albania and located just outside the nation's capital; and the Monument of Independence in Vlorë, which was unveiled in November 1972 on the occasion of Albania's sixtieth anniversary of independence. The Vlorë monument was designed to express "the struggles and centuries-old efforts" of the Albanian people for liberty and independence and the continuity of the revolution from the past to the present. The monument took three years to build. Cast in bronze, it stands 17 m (about 55 ft) high and is the product of the combined labors of three of Albania's top sculptors: Kristaq Rama, Mumtaz Dhrami, and Shaban Hadëri.[44] The central figure in the monument is that of Ismail Qemal, the old patriot of Vlorë who proclaimed Albania's independence. He is flanked by several other figures representing Gegs and Tosks, highlanders and plainsmen who fought in unison with passion and ideas, with rifle and pen, to make possible the country's independence. Hektor Dule, an Albanian sculptor, described the monument as "a powerful synthesis of the strength, nobility, wisdom, and valor of [the Albanian] people."[45]

There are many less ambitious sculptural works, some of which are resourceful in conception and stimulating. *Malet tona* (Our mountains) by Andrea Mana seems to be misnamed, for the piece is actually a bronze bust of an armed highlander of noble, yet severe expression. The intent of the sculptor apparently is to suggest that Albania's highlanders are identical with the country's mountains, and just as reliable and tough as they.[46] *Filizat e rinj* (The new shoots) by Kristina Hoshi is a somewhat sentimental, yet honest sculpture of a boy and a girl planting a sapling. Hoshi, along with Valentina Balli, is probably the best known woman sculptor in Albania.[47]

Janaq Paço, creator of the bronze equestrian statue of Skënderbeu in the Hero City of Krujë, is also the author of less heroic works, as for example, *Portret pioniereje* (Portrait of a pioneer girl). This is a lovely bust of a young woman—the counterpart, more or less, of an American Girl Scout—whose face, like many girls her age, is a mirror of innocence and the delicacy of youth. At the same time, she has a serious air about her, making her seem mature beyond her years, as if she symbolized in some way the magnitude of the problems facing a developing society.[48]

Mësues i popullit Ndrec Ndue Gjoka (Teacher of the people Ndrec Ndue Gjoka) is the work of Kristaq Rama. The sculpture portrays a handsome, thinly mustached man, holding a book in one hand and a rifle in the other. The work apparently suggests that the advancement of knowledge goes hand in hand with armed vigilance and that national defense must be an integral part of a sound education in a socialist society, as long as the gains of the revolution "are threatened by the class enemy."[49]

The Film

A cultural first in the country's history occurred on July 10, 1952, with the inauguration of the New Albania Film Studio (Kinostudio "Shqipëria e Re"). The studio was an outgrowth of a decision taken in April 1947 by the popular assembly to set up the Albanian State Film Enterprise.[50]

The first memorable cinematic event in socialist Albania was the filming of the life and deeds of Albania's national hero, Gjergj Kastrioti Skënderbeu. Released in 1953, the film was a joint Albanian-Soviet enterprise that depicted in vivid color the epic twenty-five-year-long struggle of the Albanian people against the Ottoman Turks.[51] In addition to portraying Skënderbeu as an intrepid and brilliant commander, the film attempted to recreate the hero's family life and reveal something of his personal characteristics. The film thus emerged as a patriotic as well as a human document. It made a great impact on Albanian audiences both in Albania and abroad, including America, where it was shown in Boston, New York, Philadelphia, Detroit, and Los Angeles. To see their national hero in the flesh, so to speak, across the span of five long centuries and watch him fall upon the enemy with the swiftness of an eagle, hear his booming voice and merry laughter reverberate across Albania's rugged mountains, and see him eat and drink heartily with his warriors under open skies was more than a memorable cinematic event. It was a stirring cultural experience that satisfied deep national feelings.

New Albania Studio's first feature film dealing with contemporary Albanian society was *Tana* (proper name), a semihumorous story of farm collectivization, based on a novelette of the same name by Fatmir Gjata. The ideological message of the film was interwoven with such elements as rustic simplicity and charm, romance, village gossip, and kinship ties and loyalties. The film was also shown in the United States to Albanian-American audiences and was well received, not so much perhaps for its intrinsic artistic merits as for its rustic humor and the nostalgia it evoked among the older generation for the homeland, with its still slow-paced and relatively uncomplicated life.

In 1971, the studio produced five feature-length films, plus forty-one documentaries and news shorts. By 1975, it doubled the production of feature films. The message of the films was invariably political, patriotic, and didactic and aimed primarily at indoctrinating audiences, rather than entertaining them or diverting them into a world of fantasy and escapism. Some of the better known releases of the studio were *Furtuna* (The storm), *Ngadhnjim mbi vdekjen* (Victory over death), *Toka jonë* (Our land), *Vitet e para* (The first years), *Komisari i dritës* (The commissar of light), *Plagë të vjetra* (Old wounds), and *Beni ecën vetë* (Beni walks all by himself).[52]

Albania also showed films imported from the socialist countries, including China, and from the West and nonaligned countries. Such films, however, were supposed to be ideologically correct in order not to impair Albania's Marxist-Leninist culture. Yet, there were complaints from the guardians of "cultural purity" that most of the foreign films shown in the country did not meet the required standards.[53]

Television

In November 1971, Albanians greeted the debut of the country's first television station, located in Tiranë. It was a major achievement for a country where, a scant thirty years before, radio, electicity, the newspaper, and the cinema were unknown quantities to the majority of the population. In 1976 Albania's TV station was transmitting for a limited time, about four and a half hours in the evening, but it attempted to offer its viewers a varied fare of news, music, and comments on books and other items of cultural and educational interest. Along with the inauguration of her TV station, Albania began to manufacture her own TV sets. It was reported that in 1972 a total of 15,000 sets had been produced locally, at a plant in the seaport of Durrës. However, no figures were given on the total number of TV sets in use throughout the country in 1972.[54] In the field of radio broadcasting, it is known that Radio Tiranë is one of the most active and powerful transmitting systems in the world. Its signal girdles the globe and carries the line of the Albanian regime and news of Albania daily in eighteen foreign languages, including English.

By 1976, there were twenty-five newspapers in the country, with a total annual circulation of about 47 million copies. This figure marked a fourfold increase over the total of six newspapers published in prewar Albania. The striking increase in the circulation of the government-controlled press can be gathered from the fact that *Zëri i popullit*—the Party daily—has a circulation of 105,000, compared with the 4,000 copies of *Drita*, the largest daily in prewar Albania.[55]

This account of the cultural development in Albania is in large measure an account of the cultural life of Tiranë. The nation's capital has undergone a great transformation since the prewar period, when it played a secondary role to towns like Shkodër and Korçë in matters of art, education, literature, and culture in general. Today it is the nerve center of the country's cultural life. In addition to the institutions mentioned previously, it is the home of the League of Writers and Artists Club, the State Variety Theater, the Museum of Ethnology, the National Library, the People's Dramatic Theater, the State Ensemble of Popular Songs and Dances, the People's Army Ensemble, and the Palace of Culture.

The hub of cultural activity in Tiranë, and the preeminent example of modern Albanian architecture, is the Palace of Culture. Built over a period of six years and inaugurated on September 17, 1966, the palace houses the Theater of Opera and Ballet and the National Library. It is also the locale for

Table 6.3
Growth of Cultural Institutions in Albania (1950–1973)

Type of Institution	1950	1960	1973
Theaters	4	18	27
Cinemas	35	72	105
Houses of Culture			
In cities	11	29	45
In villages	–	135	446
Libraries	12	16	40
No. of volumes	202,000	736,000	2,516,000
Museums	7	13	1,570*
Museum houses (national or historical shrines)	2	12	44

Source: *30 vjet*, pp. 216, 219.
*The precipitous increase in the number of museums from 1960 to 1973 was due to a governmental decision to establish museums at the local or village level.

Evolution of the Arts 133

Albania's major expositions, scholarly conventions, and Party congresses. The National Library, oldest among the country's leading cultural institutions, was founded in 1922 and contains documents dating from the fourteenth century. Its holdings in 1972, the year of its fiftieth anniversary, numbered 630,000, a vast increase from the 12,000 volumes it had before the war.[56] The largest city in Albania, Tiranë has currently a population of 190,000, an increase of nearly eight times over its prewar population of 25,000.

Albania's agenda for cultural development called for the growth of culture in the countryside as well. One of the objectives of this program was to reduce the enormous cultural differences between town and country, between the intelligentsia and the peasantry. It was not unusual, therefore, to find in rural communities a "house of culture," a reading room, a modest museum, a cinema or film showings, an amateur theater, a musical ensemble, and cultural exhibits of local interest.

One can perhaps obtain a clearer idea of the cultural transformation of postwar Albania by referring to table 6.3.

Literature

One index of Albania's cultural development was the rapid growth of the book-publishing industry. Albanian sources note with justifiable pride that more books were published in the country within the first twelve years following the war (1945-1957) than had been published during the 400-year period from the publication of the first book in the Albanian language in 1555 until 1944.[57] In the fifteen-year period from 1945 to 1960, Albania published more than 3,000 titles, totaling nearly 30 million copies. These publications covered works by Albanian and foreign authors, including translations of world classics.

Translations of classic literature encompassed works by Gorki—the most popular Russian author in Albania—Pushkin, Tolstoi, Chekhov, Gogol, Dostoevski, and writings of contemporary Soviet authors, such as Mikhail Sholokhov (*The Quiet Don, The Fate of Man*), Vladimir Mayakovsky, Ilia Ehrenburg, Aleksander Tvardovski, and Konstantin Paustovski. Translations of classics other than Russian included books by the world's greatest writers. Among these were Goethe's *Faust*, fables by Hans Christian Andersen, Balzac's *Père Goriot* and *Euénie Grandet*, several Greek plays including *Medea* of Euripides and *Prometheus Bound* of Aeschylus, *Tartuffe* and *Don Juan* of Molière, de Maupassant's *Bel ami*, Swift's *Gulliver's Travels*, Friedrich Schiller's dramas in prose, Stendhal's *The Red and the Black*, and works by Voltaire, Heine, Lope de Vega, Emile Zola, Carlo Goldoni, Pablo Neruda, and Tagore. Translations of American authors included Mark Twain's *Adventures of Tom Sawyer* and *The Prince and the Pauper*, Dreiser's *An American Tragedy*, stories by Jack London, and selections from Walt Whitman's *Leaves of Grass.*[58]

Side by side with publications of world classics, there was a steady rise in the literary output of Albanian authors, whose numbers kept growing with the emergence of new, postwar writers from the younger generation. In October 1965, Ramiz Alia, member of APL's Politburo, made an analysis of the twenty-year history of socialist literature in Albania and named the writers who, in the opinion of the Party leadership, were the best and most deserving of praise. About a dozen made Alia's "honor list." They were Shevqet Musaraj, Dhimitër Shuteriqi, Fatmir Gjata, Kolë Jakova, Ali Abdihoxha, Petro Marko, Sterjo Spasse, Zihni Sako, Llazar Siliqi, Ismail Kadare, and Dritëro Agolli.[59] Literary critics made frequent and favorable mention also of other authors such as Jakov Xoxa, Loni Papa, Spiro Çomora, Gjergj Zheji, Dhimitër Xhuvani, and Naum Prifti.

Albania made a conscious effort to link the literature of Socialist Realism with the "realistic" literature of writer-patriots of the National Awakening in the nineteenth century and early twentieth century. This was made clear by an editorial in *Nëndori* in 1965. "Our new literature," the editorial said, "developed further those realistic tendencies that characterized [Albanian] literature in the past, especially the realism of A. Z. Cajupi, N. Mjeda, F. S. Noli . . . and Migjeni."[60] The new literature seized upon the patriotic, revolutionary, and progressive elements of prewar Albanian literature and identified with it, while dismissing those elements of that literature that have an affinity to romanticism, pacifism, idealism, and individualism.

Traditionally, Albanian literature has been highly politicized, owing to the enmeshing of literary and national interests and the subordination of the former to the latter for the purpose of achieving vital national goals—above all, independence and security. Following the war, a new demand was made on the nation's literature; namely, that it should serve an international ideology, for the purpose of achieving the goals of world revolution in the interest of the world's proletariat and the national liberation movement. Literature thus became the handmaiden of both traditional Albanian nationalism and contemporary communist internationalism. It is a literature that is politicized and ideologed to a great degree.[61]

Among the novels most often cited by Albanian critics as the best examples of socialist literature are *Përmbysja* (The collapse) and *Këneta* (The swamp) by Fatmir Gjata; *Çlirimtarët* (The liberators) by Dhimitër Shuteriqi; *Afërdita* (Aphrodite) and *Ata nuk ishin vetëm* (They were not alone) by Sterjo Spasse; *Para agimit* (Before dawn) by Shevqet Musaraj; and *Hasta la vista* by Petro Marko, a veteran of the Spanish Civil War. Other novels that have won high critical praise are Jakov Xoxa's *Lumi i vdekur* (The dead river), a vivid portrayal of the miserable lives of peasants in the malaria-infested lowlands of Myzeqe in central Albania prior to the war; Dhimitër Xhuvani's *Përsëri në këmbë* (Standing up again), whose hero, Din Hyka, is said to be the most successful model of "the positive hero" in recent Albanian literature; and Elena Kadare's *Një lindje e vështirë* (A difficult birth), a book on the emancipation of women as seen by a woman.[62]

Most critics in Albania and Albanian communities abroad agree, however, that the outstanding author in socialist Albania, both in prose and poetry, is Ismail Kadare, a member of the younger generation. Born in Gjirokastër in 1936, Kadare studied literature in Moscow prior to the Soviet-Albanian break in 1961 and was also in New York for two weeks in July 1970 as a member of the Albanian delegation to the UN's World Youth Conference.[63]

Kadare first attracted national attention as a poet, with works like *Përse mendohen këta male* (What are these mountains thinking of?), *Endër industriale* (Industrial dream), *Shekulli XX* (The twentieth century), and *Shënime për brezin tim* (Notes for my generation).[64] These poems revealed Kadare as an original artist, with a broad sweep of ideas and rare skill in the use of vigorous language, marked by striking imagery and metaphor. Arshi Pipa, a poet in his own right as well as a critic, has called Kadare "a lonely star" on the Albanian literary horizon and "a highly original and personal poet," some of whose poems "shatter to pieces the narrow framework of socialist realism."[65]

In the early 1960s, Kadare turned to prose and wrote the now celebrated *Gjenerali i ushtrisë së vdekur* (The general of the dead army), a novel about an Italian general who is commissioned by his government to go to Albania and collect the remains of Italian soldiers who fell there during World War II. Published in 1963, the book was extensively reviewed by Albania's foremost literary critics, such as Dalan Shapllo, Razi Brahimi, Kudret Velça, and Koço Bihiku. In 1970, a French version of the book was published in France by the Albin Michel house. By 1975, it had been translated into twenty languages and became available to readers in England, the United States, Sweden, Finland, West Germany, Holland, Spain, and other countries.[66] One of Kadare's more recent novels is *Dimri i vetmisë së madhe* (Winter of the great isolation), a work in which he attempted to recreate the crisis in Albanian-Soviet relations during 1960-1961. It is a work in which Enver Hoxha emerges as the hero, but certain critics complained that the author had slighted the masses and was tainted by modernist literary currents, such as irrationalism and symbolism.[67]

Like the novel, poetry in contemporary Albania has been converted into an ideological weapon to give expression to the teachings of the Party. It is a poetry that is permeated by an air of militancy, the phraseology of war, and a system of absolute rather than relative values. In general, this poetry extolled struggle, confrontation, the Spartan virtues, and the ethics of hard work, rather than accommodation and the peaceful pursuit of happiness. For all that, one could find in this poetry an occasional poem, or portions of a poem, of undoubted beauty and power. This happened when a writer of unusual talent expressed himself or herself with obvious sincerity and devotion to the professed humanistic goals of socialism.

Apart from Kadare, three authors whom one critic has described as "innovating poets" are Fatos Arapi, Dritëro Agolli, and Llazar Siliqi.[68] However, the first poets to attract attention, either during the war or soon after, were Aleks Çaçi, author of *Ashtu Myzeqe!* (Ah so, Myzeqe!); Sejfulla Malëshova, known as "the poet of the communist revolution in Albania"; Shevqet Musarj, whose poem *Epopeja e Ballit Kombëtar* (The epic of the National Front) heaps scorn on the main political rivals of the Partisans during the war; and Kolë Jakova, author of *Herojt e Vigut* (The heroes of Vig), another poem about the war. Among women, Klara Kodra, Adelina Mamaqi, Xhuljana Jorganxhi, and Beatriçe Balliçi have published much poetry in recent years in *Nëndori*, *Drita*, and other organs.

In the short-story genre, the best writers are said to be Naum Prifti, Sotir Andoni, Teodor Laço, and Dhimitër Xhuvani. Since the mid-1950s, Prifti has published over half a dozen books of short stories, among them *Çezma e floririt* (The golden fountain) and *Duar të fuqishme* (Powerful hands), for which he won first prize in the 1969 National Festival of Literature and the Arts.[69]

Some of Prifti's work has been published in Kosovo, under the auspices of the Rilindja Publishing Enterprise in Priština. Reviewing his volume of collected stories, *Një pushkë më shumë* (An extra rifle), the Priština daily, *Rilindja* (Rebirth), wrote: "[Prifti's] style . . . is very simple, and captures the reader precisely because of its masterly simplicity. These stories unfold naturally, and a short dialogue, even a single word, suffices to illuminate the soul of the protagonist. The author's heroes are basically positive, life-oriented, optimistic.... [The stories] are moving and profoundly human."[70]

Not much can be said for humor and satire in contemporary Albanian literature. Apart from the writings of a few people like Miço Kallamata and Dionis Bubani, the field of humor and satire is fairly dry. An exception is Qamil Buxheli.

Born in the district of Sarandë, southern Albania, in 1925, Buxheli at first studied at the Gjirokastër Gymnasium. Later he pursued his studies in Moscow, at the Gorki High Institute of Literature. Returning to Albania, Buxheli matured into a skilled craftsman, well equipped to exploit his unusual gift for seeing the comical in the commonplace. Among his better known works are two volumes of collected stories: *Një ndodhi në plazh* (An incident on the beach) and *Njeriu që ndal kohën* (The man who stops time). His satirical novel *Kariera e zotit Maksut* (The career of Mister Maksut) is a hilarious account of the adventures of an ambitious but bumbling bureaucrat in King Zog's regime that is reminiscent—at least in spirit and flavor—of Gogol's *The Inspector General*. Buxheli's biting satire has probably done more to discredit Zog's regime than volumes of speeches and declarations by Party leaders.[71]

Cultural Relations with the Outside World

In addition to developing culture at home, Albania cultivated cultural relations with other countries. The responsibility for this task fell primarily to the Committee for Cultural Relations with the Outside World, headed until recently by Misto Treska. Relations in this area covered the exchange of artists, writers, and scholars; exhibits of fine arts and handicrafts; expositions on Albanian history, ethnology, and archaeology; sports, film showings, and tourism. Usually these exchanges were carried out under the auspices of "friendship societies" organized in the host countries, ostensibly for the purpose of promoting friendship and cooperation with Albania.

Cultural relations mirrored more or less the status of Albania's political relations with other socialist countries: the more intense the cultural ties, the closer, in general, the political ties. This was true especially with regard to relations with the Soviet Union, and later with China. With regard to capitalist countries in the West, or nonaligned states like Egypt and Algeria, Albania tended to exploit cultural ties for ideological purposes. Cultural exchanges served to "demonstrate" to the advanced West the great progress that a formerly backward nation had made in the various fields of culture. Thus, there was much elation in the country when the Albanian Ensemble of Popular Songs and Dances won first prize—the Golden Garland award—in competition with thirty other groups at the 1970 International Fall Festival in Dijon.[72] To the leaders and peoples of poor, nonaligned nations, Albania paraded her cultural achievements to demonstrate the superiority of socialist over bourgeois culture, and by extension the superiority of the socialist system over the capitalist system.

There were two broad aspects to Albania's policy on culture with the outside world. One was to create an image of herself as a progressive society, in respect to the nations with which she had cultural agreements or connections. The other was to make scathing attacks on the arts and culture of "modern revisionism"—which in recent years meant the USSR and Eastern Europe—and the bourgeois way of life of "Western imperialism," principally the United States.

Yet, the foundations for the growth of culture in socialist Albania were laid largely in the decade of the fifties, during the period of closest ties with the Soviet Union. By the end of the 1950s, Albania's cultural relations with Moscow had intensified in all directions, and numerous delegations of Soviet scholars, women, sport teams, and artists, including members of the Bolshoi Ballet, visited Albania.[73] The scope and intensity of Soviet influence on Albania's cultural development can best be gauged, perhaps, from the following citation from an Albanian source.

The cultural revolution in Albania cannot be clearly understood without stressing the liberal aid and support which the Soviet Union has given our country to develop education, culture, art, and the sciences. It is not possible to estimate all that the Soviet Union has done for us. . . . A proof of the fraternal aid which the Soviet Union is giving our people is the decision of the Soviet Government to build in Tiranë a great palace of culture.[74]

Soviet influence was evident also in Albanian translations of works on politics, literature, social studies, and technology. A survey of the literature on social studies published over a fourteen-year period (1944–1958) showed a preponderance of titles by Soviet authors. Soviet titles also led in the field of literature. Thus, out of approximately 400 literary works translated into Albanian during the same period, over two-thirds (approximately 270) were authored by Soviet writers, while only eight were of Chinese origin. Sixty-four titles were translations of Western classics, fourteen of them by American authors.[75]

After the break with the Soviet Union in 1961, Moscow's cultural influence in Albania began to wane, while that of Peking began to rise. Albania's cultural relations with China encompassed the entire gamut of activities in that area, all the way from expositions of paintings and sculpture to song and dance concerts, translations of literature, film showings, and exchanges of students and sport teams. Among the more prestigious Chinese art troupes to visit Albania was the China Ballet, which in February 1972 performed "The Red Detachment of Women" ballet in honor of President Nixon and his entourage during his visit to Peking. The China Ballet toured Albania in September 1971 and was acclaimed by Hoxha, Shehu, and other top Party leaders for its performance of the Red Detachment ballet in Tiranë. In October 1975, another troupe of Chinese artists, the Liaonin Song and Dance Ensemble, toured Albania. Its concerts were hailed as a "powerful manifestation" of China's cultural revolution and militant art.[76]

Yet, unlike the Soviet Union and the West, China made practically no impact on Albania's cultural life. In spite of the breadth and variety of Sino-Albanian relations in this area, Chinese influence on Albanian art, literature, and culture remained peripheral and superficial. It was not possible, apparently, to overcome the differences of race, language, history, and tradition between China and Albania, in spite of the best efforts made by Albanian and Chinese leaders to ignore those differences and to stress instead their ideological and political bonds, such as their common struggle against revisionism, imperialism, and reaction.

Cultural Polemics
The struggle against revisionist culture took the form of violent polemics against the Soviet Union, as well as East Europe. Albanian polemicists charged that the first symptoms of revisionism in Soviet art and culture appeared even before the death of Stalin and that the cause of this unfortunate development was "a strata of the intelligentsia that had become bourgeois, bureaucratic, and degenerate."[77] Following the death of Stalin, the Khrushchev revisionists, according to Albanian critics, removed all barriers to the spread of Western culture in Soviet society, on the pretext that Soviet culture had been sectarian and isolated from world culture. The trend in the USSR toward cultural revisionism accelerated in the wake of the fateful Twentieth CPSU Congress in 1956, which led to calls by "so-called liberals" for the rehabilitation of "counterrevolutionary artists" like Pasternak and the surfacing of decadent art currents, such as imagism and expressionism. In addition to Pasternak, the

Albanians made fierce attacks on a number of noted Soviet authors, including Yevtushenko ("the devoted servant of imperalism"), Solzhenitsyn ("a falsifier of history"), and Sholokhov, who sought to "discredit" the Great Patriotic War (WWII) of the Soviet Union.[78] Other writers who came under fire were Ehrenburg, Dudintsev, and Paustovsky, whose works had been published and praised in Albania during the era of friendly Soviet-Albanian relations.

The Albanian position was that the post-Stalin leadership in the Soviet Union had abandoned the revolutionary tradition of Soviet art and culture and had replaced it with the decadent bourgeois culture of the West, which is vitiated by Christian humanism, pacifism, the spirit of pessimism, nihilism, and intellectualism. A major purpose of this cultural revisionism, according to Tiranë, was to deaden the conscience of the working masses and create sweet illusions of philistine happiness: a life of comfort, luxury, diversion, and moral chaos.[79] Albania further charged that the Soviets were trying to effect a synthesis of the Marxist view of art and culture, which respects reason and is rooted in objective phenomena, and Freudian psychoanalysis, which seeks to explain creativity and culture in terms of irrational drives rooted in the subconscious. Such an attempt, according to the Albanians, was preposterous, since Marxist materialism and Freudian idealism are irreconcilable.

Western art and culture and some leading Western artists and social philosophers also came under heavy attack. Albanian guardians of culture viewed the Western way of life as decadent, believing that it is destructive of man's potentiality for self-sacrifice, collective effort, and heroism. They heaped scorn on James Joyce, Marcel Proust, and Franz Kafka and called them "merchants of decadence."[80] Similarly, they attacked such celebrated Western painters as Dali, Rouault, Jackson Pollock, and Picasso, on the ground that they distort reality and the figure of man, making them seem ugly and evil. Looking at the theater, Albanian critics were revolted by the avant-garde dramas of Ionescu and Beckett and by Julian Beck's Living Theater, which, they claimed, were "inundated by mysticism and pornography."[81]

Apart from psychoanalysis—a favorite target of vilification—Albanian polemicists preoccupied themselves with surrealism and existentialism, presumably because these two schools of thought are closely associated with art, literature, and questions of culture. They said that the aesthetic and social premises of these philosophies were false and inimical to society. Accordingly, they denounced André Breton and his Surrealist Manifesto (1924), as well as such leaders of the existentialist movement as Sartre, Camus, Kafka, and Simone de Beauvoir. They claimed that existentialism separates men from society and from one another and accused both Sartre and Camus of being anti-Marxists, for despite their criticism of capitalism, the effect of their aesthetics and social philosophy is to demoralize the masses and perpetuate the decadence of capitalism and the Western way of life.[82]

Concluding Remarks

A survey of the development of culture and cultural institutions in socialist Albania shows that there has been a qualitative leap forward in this area of Albanian life. Considering that culture—in the sense of aesthetic and intellectual enrichment—was almost totally absent in the lives of most of the population prior to the war, the achievements of Albania in this area have been remarkable.

The country had strong motives for developing her artistic, literary, and cultural life. The unusually heavy legacy of cultural backwardness, inherited from medieval times and reinforced mainfold by centuries of despotic Ottoman rule, was in itself a powerful motive for energetic measures to correct the imbalance. In ancient times Albania, then known as Illyria, reflected the crosscurrents of Greek and Roman cultures, most strongly perhaps in architecture and sculpture. Seen from that angle, the nation had a built-in inclination, so to speak, to work for cultural renewal.

Beyond these incentives, it was the deliberate policy of the doctrinaire Albanian leadership to stimulate activity in the fine arts and other areas of culture, as a means toward achieving its overall political and ideological goal: the construction of a socialist society on the Stalinist model. Accordingly, the development of culture was not a matter of spontaneity or the product of numerous individuals giving expression to their creative drive according to their fancy; rather, it was an organized effort, directed by the government for the attainment of predetermined ends. Art and culture thus took on a militant character and had a definite didactic role to play in society, namely, to educate, inspire, and serve the masses.

With regard to foreign influences on the growth and flowering of culture in postwar Albania, the most significant have been Western and Soviet, in that order. The roots and technique of this cultural resurgence issue from the West; its social character and basic ideological orientation were derived from the Soviet Union—by virtue of her being the first socialist state in history. Yet, much of the content, too, of contemporary Albanian art and culture is Western. This is seen in the repertoire of Albanian opera and symphonic music, in the theater, and above all in literature. The zealous translation of Western classics into Albanian put into the hands of the public books that opened a new window on the Western world and brought the average Albanian into contact with a wide range of Western literary tastes, cultural traditions, manners, and morals. The evidence indicates that this exposure increased the taste and appetite of the intelligentsia and the masses for Western culture and styles of life.

With the launching of the cultural revolution in the midsixties, Albania tried to limit drastically Western cultural influence in the country. At the same time, she tried to minimize the contributions of the Soviets to the development of Albanian culture and prevent by all means the penetration of Soviet "revisionist" culture. In this connection, Albania's polemics against the USSR were significant on at least two counts. They revealed, first, that Soviet-Albanian differences—contrary to Tiranë's official explanation—were not solely ideological in nature but involved cultural matters as well; and second, that the differences did not begin in June 1960—at the Bucharest Conference—but had their origin in the early 1950s, shortly before Stalin's death.

At one level, Albania's quarrel with Western and Soviet culture seems to be motivated by ideological and political factors. But at a deeper level, the effort to "shut out" both East and West Europe in this respect springs from Albanian nationalism; which is to say, from the powerful yearning for cultural affirmation that had been bottled up for centuries. The Albanians are anxious, it seems, to "show their mettle" in matters of culture by "relying on their own efforts," just as their forefathers proved their worth in the field of battle in earlier and rougher times.

The past three decades show that culture in Albania has made rapid strides, in spite of the ideological encumbrances placed on the path of its development. Very likely this cultural resurgence will continue in the years to come. But it is doubtful that Albania can proceed along this path for long in defiance of the mainstream of Western culture, for the record shows that Albanian arts and culture are predominantly Western in origin, inspiration, and character.

7
The Cultural Revolution (1966–1969)

The future and fate of socialist construction in Albania, considered a closed question in 1961, was an open one in 1966; and the tone of confidence and optimism so evident in 1961 had given way five years later to uncertainty and an attitude of watchful caution against alien ideologies that would subvert socialism.

The ideological distance traveled by Albania in the span of five years—indeed, the impact of China's cultural revolution on the thinking of the Albanian leadership—becomes evident from the difference in content and tone of certain statements made by Enver Hoxha and Mehmet Shehu in 1961 and 1966 respectively.

For example, in his report to the Fourth Congress of APL, held in February 1961, the Party's first secretary, Enver Hoxha, said:

On the basis of the magnificent successes and profound revolutionary transformations that have occurred in all countries of the world socialist system, the complete and final victory of socialism has now been assured not only in the Soviet Union but also within the framework of the entire socialist system. The internal economic and social conditions for the restoration of capitalism have now been eliminated. . . .[1]

At the Party's Fifth Congress, held nearly six years later, in November 1966, Hoxha had modified his enthusiasm. He said:

As long as the complete victory of the socialist revolution in the fields of ideology and culture has not been assured, neither can there be any security or guarantee of the gains of the socialist revolution in the political and economic fields. That is why the struggle on the ideological front, for the complete destruction of the bourgeois and revisionist ideology, at bottom concerns the question: can socialism and communism be constructed and the restoration of capitalism be evaded? . . .[2]

Albania's prime minister, Mehmet Shehu, for his part, triumphantly told the 1961 APL Congress that the question "Who shall win?" in Albania, as between socialism and capitalism, had been "irrevocably resolved in favor of socialism,"[3] while at the Fifth Party Congress he warned that "the class struggle will continue not one or five years but throughout the entire historical epoch of the construction of socialism.[4]

In the period between the Fourth and Fifth Congresses of APL, Albania broke with the Soviet Union, openly allied herself with the Chinese People's Republic—becoming almost totally dependent on Peking for her economic needs—isolated herself from Eastern Europe, and for all practical purposes withdrew both from the Warsaw Pact and COMECON (Council for Mutual Economic Assistance).[5] In the meantime, China's split with the Soviet Union widened, and as of November 1965, fully a year before Albania's Fifth Party Congress, China embarked on the Great Proletarian Cultural Revolution, with the avowed aim of preventing the tragedy of Soviet revisionism from overtaking socialist China; that is, to block the restoration of capitalism.

Albania's cultural revolution took place almost concurrently with the cultural revolution in China. That such a revolution should have taken place in Albania is perhaps not surprising in view of the background of China and Albania, their history, their experiences with the USSR, and Albania's special relationship to communist China.

Both China and Albania have known great poverty—a factor which possibly accounts, to a degree, for their impatience to industrialize and their willingness to try radical measures to achieve industrialization. Both have a keen memory of the exploitation and humiliation they have suffered at the hands of foreigners. Both felt betrayed by the "revisionist Khrushchevian leadership" of the CPSU. Both perceived themselves as encircled and threatened by enemies—Albania by the "capitalist-revisionist-fascist encirclement" of Yugoslavia, Greece, the U.S. Sixth Fleet, and Italy; and China by the "Ring of Fire" forged allegedly by the U.S., USSR, India, and Japan. Both have great respect for Stalin, and both are intensely nationalistic.

This is not to suggest that the cultural revolution in Albania was a spontaneous and independent development. Albania's special relationship to China—that is to say, her dependency, first of all, on China for economic and technical aid,[6] the strong political and ideological support she received from Peking, as well as implicit Chinese pledges of military assistance should she come under attack[7]—made it almost inevitable for Albania to react more or less positively to Mao's cultural revolution. Indeed, the Chinese leaders could ill afford an attitude of indifference on the part of their closest ally to the greatest event taking place in their country, especially in view of the series of diplomatic setbacks China had suffered in the course of her cultural revolution. Even if there were no pressure from the Chinese, Hoxha may have concluded that it was in the general interest of the Albanian-Chinese alliance, and useful also in terms of Albania's own internal needs, to launch a cultural revolution concurrently with that of China.

An examination of China's and Albania's cultural revolutions seems to show that the differences between them were greater, and probably more meaningful, than the similarities. One difference is to be found in the terminology used in connection with the two revolutions, for while the Chinese called their movement the Great Proletarian Cultural Revolution, the Albanians called theirs "revolutionization," though sometimes they used the term "cultural and ideological revolution." Furthermore, while the Chinese spoke of the "permanent revolution" to describe the nature of their movement, the Albanians referred to their movement as the "uninterrupted revolution," thus implying that their evolution was not the direct offspring of Mao's but a continuation and deepening of policies, programs, and efforts undertaken by Albania over a period of some twenty years.

A main feature of the Chinese revolution was the constant, noisy, and indeed hysterical preoccupation with Mao, his thinking, and his "unique" position in the world communist movement. In the case of Albania, Enver Hoxha did not become the main focus of attention. He was neither an object of adulation nor an object of scorn. Unlike the attitude of the Chinese toward Mao, personal devotion to Hoxha did not become a yardstick of the true Albanian communist and revolutionary. To be sure, as the cultural revolution gathered momentum in 1967, there were increasing references in the Albanian press to "Hoxha's teachings" and to his speeches and writing.[8] But the fact remains that Hoxha never attained the symbolic and mystical stature in the Albanian revolution that Mao Tse-tung enjoyed in China.

This attitude of restraint was evident also in the references of the Albanian leadership and press to Chairman Mao. They were generally guarded and moderate, compared with the enthusiastic and exalted terms employed by the Chinese press and party leaders in connection with Mao. The Chinese hailed Mao as a creative genius in the realm of communist theory and ideology. He was "the reddest Sun" in the hearts of revolutionaries and "the Lenin of our time," whose thought was of "epoch-making significance." He was lauded for having lifted Marxism "to a completely new stage, the stage of Mao Tse-tung's thought."

Hoxha, Shehu, and other Albanian leaders, however, were more uninhibited in their praise of the Chinese cultural revolution than of Mao personally. Shehu, for example, called Mao's revolution "the most important historical event of our time" and the "broadest, most profound and most gigantic revolutionary mass movement history has ever known." But in speaking of Mao himself, the Albanian leaders confined themselves to such terms as "distinguished," "outstanding," or "great Marxist-Leninist" and were reluctant to raise Mao's thinking to the level of Marxism-Leninism. They spoke of "the

Marxist-Leninist teachings" of Mao, or "the great Marxist-Leninist ideas of Comrade Mao Tse-tung," but did not acknowledge that the Chinese leader's thinking constituted "a new stage" in the history of Marxist thought; nor did they rank Mao alongside Marx and Lenin and Stalin.

Apart from differences in the attitudes toward the leaders of China and Albania, there were notable differences in the roles played by the Chinese and Albanian communist parties in the cultural revolutions of the two countries. In China the cultural revolution was preeminently "a struggle within the Party"[9] and therefore a struggle for power, involving a number of very powerful figures, including members of the Politburo, such as Peng Chen, Lu Ting-yi, Teng Hsiao-ping, and, above all, Liu Shao-chi. Such a thing did not happen in Albania. Hoxha was at all times in firm command of the Party and government, and outwardly at least the top Party leaders were united and worked in harmony. Had a similar upheaval taken place within the Albanian Party, it would have meant, for example, that Mehmet Shehu, the number two man in Albania, and Ramiz Alia, the czar of culture and the arts, would have fallen from power and been labeled "revisionists" and persons of authority within the Party "taking the capitalist road." But neither the structure nor the line and authority of the Albanian Party were appreciably affected by the revolutionary events that occurred in the country through the four-year period of the cultural revolution.

One also searches in vain in the Albanian press for pictures showing Albania's minister of defense standing or sitting to the right of Comrade Hoxha, as was the case with Chairman Mao and Marshal Lin Piao, whom the Chinese leader called his "close comrade-in-arms." Unlike the People's Liberation Army, which played an unusual and indeed dominant role in both the inception and evolution of the Chinese cultural revolution, the Albanian People's Army remained distinctly in the background and was more of an object than a catalyst of the reforms that occurred in the country in the course of the revolution. The army endorsed the reform measures decreed by the Sixteenth Plenum of the APL Central Committee in March of 1966, two of which stipulated the abolition of military ranks and the reappointment of political commissars in military units.[10] By comparison with the Chinese army, the role of the Albanian army in the unfolding of the "uninterrupted revolution" was passive and relatively unimportant.

Many other events in China, generated by the cultural revolution, did not have their counterparts in Albania. There were no Albanian Red Guards,[11] no campaigns of terror against bourgeois and revisionist elements, no violent clashes with opponents of reforms, no influx of supporters of the revolution from the provinces to Tiranë, and no massive parades in the streets of the capital, involving thousands of youth, all shouting slogans in praise of Hoxha, the revolution, and socialism. There were no public purges, no turmoil in the State University of Tiranë or dislocations of the school system, and no damaging blow to the economy as a result of changes brought on by the revolution. The psychological excesses engendered by the revolution in China, the irrationslism, the feverish emotionalism, the fanaticism and hysteria, especially since the rise of the Red Guard movement, were generally absent from the Albanian scene. One notable exception to this was the abolition in Albania of public religious worship and religious institutions. This development, which took place in early summer of 1967, marked the most novel and striking event in the unfolding of Albania's cultural revolution. There were reports that this sudden blow against religion caused considerable distress among the older population.

In other areas, the two revolutions had much in common. Both the Chinese and Albanian leadership showed a deep and abiding distrust of intellectuals, whom they regarded as an unreliable element, easily influenced by alien ideology and propaganda. As early as 1964, Mao openly expressed fear of the formation of a Chinese Petöfi Club,[12] and Enver Hoxha, although an intellectual himself, has been deeply suspicious of writers and intellectuals. Presumably such motives of distrust and fear of intellectuals were a chief factor in Hoxha's decision early in 1966 to dispatch several dozen Albanian writers and artists to the countryside, to work and live there and draw close to the laboring masses.[13] The fact that this step was taken at the very beginning of the drive for the "revolutionization" of the country is an indication of the Albanian leaders' preoccupation with the problem of intellectuals and their interest in finding a solution to it.

As in China, the communist leadership of Albania views literature and the arts as an ideological weapon for the construction of socialism, and in particular for the formation of "the new communist man," who places the collective interest above his personal interest. Albania's propaganda arsenal made great efforts during the cultural revolution to strengthen and develop this didactic, strictly partisan conception of the arts, but the results of the effort were far from enviable.

A chief target of the cultural revolution in China and Albania was the educational system, its place and function in the socialist society, and its role in the development and transformation of students into reliable revolutionaries.

Like China, Albania instituted a part-work, part-study program for its students, designed to eliminate the gap between theory and practice, mental and physical labor. The results of this and other educational reforms were not entirely satisfactory, and in March 1968 Hoxha initiated a new movement to revolutionize the educational system, advising educators not to accept uncritically the Soviet educational system—upon which the Albanian system was modeled—and calling for a purge of all textbooks containing idealistic and theological ideas.[14] Unlike China, however, where the school system collapsed beneath the shock of the cultural revolution, the Albanian educational system continued to function more or less normally—another sign of the comparatively mild and nontraumatic character of the Albanian experiment.

The wall poster, which was the chief means of communication and criticism in the hands of pro- and anti-Mao factions in China, made its appearance in Allbania as well. But whereas in China the wall poster was used for political and ideological ends, in Albania it was used mostly for economic ends; namely, to stimulate agricultural production, improve the organization and methods of work in industry, and so on. Furthermore, in China the poster was used freely by both pro- and anti-Mao factions, while in Albania it was exploited only by pro-Party elements, to serve clearly defined Party goals and objectives. Three such objectives were "the struggle against bureaucracy, the struggle for the full emancipation of women, and the struggle against backward customs and religious beliefs." In the eyes of Party leaders, these were the three great stumbling blocks on the path of Albania's economic and social development.

In both countries the communist leadership sought to arouse and involve the masses in the revolutionary process. Here again an important difference emerged in the type of appeal made to the masses in China and Albania and the correspondent response of the masses to those appeals. Speaking at a rally of the Red Guards on November 3, 1966, Lin Piao said that the masses must be encouraged "to criticize and supervise the party and government leaders . . . at all levels." The Red Guards, according to reports, responded to such suggestions by criticizing every major governmental and Party figure, save Chairman Mao and Marshal Lin. No such phenomenon occurred in the Albanian People's Republic. True, the Albanian Party encouraged the masses and cadres to practice criticism and to fear no reprisals, but this criticism was not political in nature and in general came within the framework of the Albanian slogan to "build faster, better, and cheaper." Such criticism at times reached as far as the ministries of government, but where the Party was concerned it did not go beyond the level of the district Party committee.[15]

In sum, although the emphasis and methods of the Albanian Ideological and Cultural Revolution differed in several respects from those of the Chinese revolution, the basic premises of the two revolutions were identical. One such premise was that human nature is plastic and that by means of political and ideological indoctrination a new man, the Communist Man, could be forged, who placed the good of society above his personal good and shunned no sacrifice in the effort to build the socialist and eventually the communist society.[16] A minor premise was the concept of the class struggle as an integral part of life in the socialist society—a struggle that had to be waged relentlessly against internal and external enemies of socialism for generations and even centuries to come, until the final triumph of communism in the world. On a pracitcal level, the two premises apparently derived their motive power in part from fear—the obsessive fear of revisionism and the restoration of capitalism, which the Chinese and Albanian leaders seemed bent on instilling into the consciousness of their peoples—and in part out of an almost religious fervor to maintain and transmit intact to future generations the revolutionary purity of "genuine" Marxism-Leninism.

8
The Abolition of Religion

In September 1967, the Albanian literary monthly *Nëndori* announced that all religious edifices in Albania, including 2,169 churches, mosques, monasteries, and other religious institutions, had been closed and that Albania had thus become "the first atheist state in the world."[1] A fatal blow had been dealt to religion in a corner of Europe, midway between Rome and Athens, the centers of world Catholicism and Eastern rites Orthodoxy, respectively, yet it hardly attracted the attention of the world press. The event, however, did not come as a surprise to those familiar with domestic affairs in Albania and was in a way foreshadowed by an incident at the United Nations two years earlier. When Pope Paul VI delivered his historic address to the UN General Assembly in New York on October 5, 1965, the Albanian delegation, alone of all delegations to the UN, boycotted the address. The action of the Albanians was a dramatic revelation of the hostile attitude of Albania's communist leaders toward the Vatican and of their mood and thinking about religion in general. It was an illustration, moreover, of the fact that the religious establishment in socialist Albania was weak and its future uncertain.

Speaking at the Sixth Congress of the Albanian Party of Labor in November of 1971, Enver Hoxha, the Party's first secretary, described the abolition of the religious establishment as "a decisive victory" that prepared the ground for the "complete emancipation [of the people] from religious beliefs."[2] What were the forces and contradictions within the Albanian society that led to so radical a development in the life of the Albanian people?

Albania is a nation of two and a half million people and the only country in Europe with a majority Moslem population. According to the religious census taken in 1945, 72.8 percent of the population was Moslem, 17.1 percent Orthodox Christians, and 10.1 percent Catholic.[3] The Moslem percentage included also the Bektashi sect, which at that time was estimated to be about 20 percent of the country's population. Following Albania's independence in 1921, the three religious groups, while not entirely independent of the state, enjoyed a large measure of autonomy. The situation changed drastically after the communists seized power in November 1944.

Indeed, the conflict between church and state in socialist Albania began during the Partisan struggle for power in World War II. Albanian communists charge that in the course of the civil war traitorous clergymen called on the faithful to oppose the Partisans, who were leading the struggle for national liberation against the Italian and German occupiers.[4] Following the war, they say, reactionary clergymen engaged in counterrevolutionary activity against the Party and the "people's power," by distributing antigovernment tracts; forming opposition groups such as Albanian Unity and Catholic Action; sheltering criminals in churches and mosques; opposing the agrarian reform; and seeking to incite the people with slogans such as, "We must not trust those who do not believe in God."[5] In fact, the agrarian reform law of August 29, 145, deprived the religious institutions of nearly all their property and met with resistance on the part of "the clerical caste" which, like all propertied classes, "had no intention of renouncing its privileges without a struggle."[6]

The tensions between the Albanian leadership and the Church,[7] which surfaced during the war, were aggravated in the postwar period. The communists now began to characterize dissenting clergymen as class enemies and to view the religious establishment as an antagonistic contradiction within the Albanian society. Accordingly, they took steps to combat and neutralize, at least, the threat that, in their view, religion and religious bodies presented to their power and authority as well as to their program for building a socialist society. Their larger design, in strict accord with their Marxist-Leninist outlook, was to eliminate religion as a feature of Albanian life. But since "the conditions were not ripe" for such a move, the Party resorted to interim methods in dealing with the Church—methods intended to render the Church impotent as an institutional force but viable enough to be used whenever possible, for furthering communist ends.

The Church and state confrontation during 1945-1950 was sharp and often violent. Albanian sources claim that the policy of the Party toward religion at this time had a two fold aim: (1) to separate the Church completely from the state; and (2) to end the church-school relationship, that is, to separate education from religion. The intention was to make religion a purely private affair in contrast to its role in former times, when the Church served as an "official instrument of politics" in the hands of the ruling classes. This policy was subsequently described as "an important political step toward totally divorcing men from the spiritual shackles ... of religion."[8]

Such was the theory and the justification put forth by the Party, as it moved to apply pressure on the religious establishment in order to make it conform to its demands. In the course of about five years, from 1945 to 1950, the government proceeded to limit severely the Church's autonomy and freedom of action. Its sources of revenue were curtailed. Religious instruction was forbidden, and the education of youth became the responsibility of the state alone; that is, all education was secularized. All religious publications and communications such as sermons, pastoral letters, and memoranda had to be approved by the government before being made public. The state exercised control over the election and appointment of personnel to all religious posts. Religious communities were enjoined from maintaining and operating hospitals and other charitable institutions. Lastly, the land reform of 1945 deprived the Church of considerable property, including monasteries, libraries, and seminaries.[9] The implementation of these measures curbed the influence of religion and in turn provoked much resistance on the part of the Church leadership. The Party responded by indicting, arresting, trying, and sentencing recalcitrant clergymen.

In the case of the Orthodox Church, this confrontation resulted in the virtual elimination of the church leadership. Among those purged were Bishop Agathangjel of Berat; Bishop Irenei, deputy metropolitan of Korçë and Gjirokastër; and Archbishop Kristofor Kisi, primate of the Albanian Orthodox Church. Kisi was deposed on August 28, 1949, for the crime of "plotting to detach the Church from the Eastern Orthodox faith and surrender it to the Vatican."[10] All three reportedly were interned. Subsequently Kisi was succeeded by Archbishop Paisi (Pashko) Vodica, who had given strong support to the communists during the war.

Similar purges occurred in the Moslem community, many of whose clergymen were charged with aiding the Fascist and Nazi cause. The list of those who were executed or imprisoned included Mustafa effendi Varoshi, mufti of Durrës; Hafëz Ibrahim Dibra, former grand mufti of Albania; Baba Zylfo; Sheh Xhemal Pazari of Tiranë; Bexhet Shpati; Hafëz Tahir Kolgjini; and Qerim Shehu.[11] Two prominent figures of the Bektashi sect, Baba Fajo of Martanesh and Baba Fejzo, both of whom supported the communists, reportedly died violently in March 1947 under circumstances that are not entirely clear.

Communist pressure was particularly strong against the Catholic hierarchy. The regime justified this stance on the ground that the Catholic clergy was "the most organized and most active" religious body in the country and moreover was allied, through its link with the Vatican, with the "imperialist and aggressive West." Almost from the time they seized power, the communists began to attack the Catholic clergy as being the willing servants of foreign interests and powers. They complained that certain high members of the Catholic hierarchy in Shkodër—a city in northern Albania and main center of Catholic power in the country—considered themselves citizens of the Vatican rather than of Albania and operated as a "fifth column of Italian Fascism" prior to Mussolini's invasion of Albania in April of 1939. Father Gjergj Fishta (1871-1940), a Franciscan monk who is widely recognized as Albania's greatest epic poet,[12] came under attack for allegedly proposing that Albania become an Italian mandate.[13] Party spokesmen claim that Catholic clergymen helped organize terrorist bands against the people's power and that on September 9, 1946, several such bands converged from different directions for a concerted attack on Shkodër but were beaten back by the people's forces.[14] The incident led to the arrest, trial, and execution of a number of prominent Catholic clergymen. Among those who reportedly perished were Msgr. Vinçenc Prenushi, archbishop and metropolitan of Durrës; Msgr. Gjergj Volaj, bishop of Sappa; Msgr. Gasper Thaçi, archbishop of Shkodër; Father Bernardin Palaj; and Father Ndre Zadeja. Some of the victims had attained distinction in Albanian letters and academic circles as poets, novelists, and scholars.[15] One of these was Father Anton Harapi, who became a special target for communist attacks. Harapi was condemned as "an agent of the Vatican" and a Nazi collaborator, owing to his membership in the High Regency, the ruling body which the Germans set up in Albania during the war.[16]

The Party's drive against the clergy resulted in the virtual decimation of the Catholic, Moslem, and Orthodox leadership. According to a report of the Free Albania Committee in New York, by 1968 some 200 clergymen had been executed or sent to labor camps in Albania. It was a grim and major Church and state confrontation, in which the state apparently gained decisive supremacy. The communists seemed now to be in a position to deal a crushing blow to the religious establishment, yet for tactical reasons they did not press their advantage. For the moment they were content with the gains they had achieved, and these were considerable. They had eliminated the dissident and recalcitrant clergy and greatly weakened the capacity of the Church to function effectively. Moreover, by portraying opposing ecclesiastics as reactionaries, subversives, and antinationalists, it is possible that they inspired doubts in the public mind concerning the role and position of the Church in Albanian society.

In brief, by the late 1940s, the Albanian communists had succeeded in bringing the Church almost entirely under their control. Aware of its strength, the regime now set out to reorganize the religious establishment and to channel the expression of religious life in such a manner as to be consistent with, rather in opposition to, the Party's domestic and foreign policies. On November 26, 1949, the government issued a decree entitled, "On Religious Communities," which made it mandatory for all religious bodies to profess loyalty to the Party and the People's Republic of Albania. On May 4, 1950, new statutes were approved for governing the Moslem community and the Orthodox Church, based on Article 18, chapter 3, of the Albanian Constitution, which said: "Freedom of conscience and religion is guaranteed to all citizens."[17] Similarly, on July 30, 1951, the government approved new statutes for the Catholic Church on the basis of decisions taken by a "general assembly" of Catholic ecclesiastics in Shkodër the previous month. In the meantime, the Party "approved" the appointment, as heads of the various church bodies, of clergymen who were cooperative or sympathetic to the communists. In theory, the new governing statutes were sufficiently liberal and flexible to accomodate the church-going public. In practice, the Church as an institution had been nationalized.

Missionaries of Materialism

Throughout this period, and in the years that followed, the Albanian leadership carried out a vigorous propaganda campaign against religion and in favor of atheism. As early as April 1947, the Party recommended the introduction of antireligious propaganda in the schools and other sectors of society.[18] In April of 1955, a meeting of the Party Plenum on the question of ideological work stressed the need to "strengthen the materialist and scientific world outlook among the workers" and to combat religious beliefs and backward customs that were hindering "the spread of ... socialist culture among the masses."[19] The ideological drive to denigrate religious belief and promote atheism was based on the principle—as Hoxha put it—that "the religious world outlook and the communist world outlook are irreconcilable, [inasmuch as] they express and uphold interests of antagonistic classes,"[20] that is, the working class and the capitalist class. Hoxha was further quoted as saying that the religious ideology, being idealistic and mystical, distorts one's thinking and leads to the commission of serious political errors. Party ideologists and propagandists drew on the writings of Lenin and other communist classics to propagate the view that belief in God is enslaving and that all contemporary religions are organs of bourgeois reaction, which deceive, stupefy, and exploit the masses.

Albanian communists took note of the fact that religion was not an isolated phenomenon in the people's lives but that it had penetrated deeply into their lives and was intertwined with their customs, moral values, education, work ethic, family and social relations. Consequently, the offensive against religion had to be a prolonged and many-sided one, if it was to be effective. In mounting their offensive, the advocates of atheism relied not only on communist doctrine but on such disciplines as history, science, cultural anthropology, biology, medicine, and philosophy. In their zeal and industry, if not in originality, they proved themselves worthy heirs of Holbach, de la Mettrie, Cabanis, and other renowned figures of the French Enlightenment, as they set about to dethrone God and replace him with the trinity of materialism, science, and reason.

The arguments marshaled by the Party in its campaign against religion went beyond straightforward repetition of Marxist rhetoric. Presumably they were intended, for the most part, for a fairly sophisticated audience and above all, perhaps, for the cadres on whom the Party leadership relied heavily for the success of its drive against the Church.

Albanian missionaries of materialism argued that scientific Marxist materialism and religious idealism are diametrically opposed to each other.[21] The former, they said, explains the world, life on earth, and society on the basis of empirical evidence and the causal principle of natural law, while the latter relies on fanciful and infantile notions contained in revelation—notions that have been thoroughly discredited by science. It is no accident, they contended, that organized Christianity has traditionally opposed science and vilified or persecuted great men like Galileo, Giordano Bruno, Darwin, and others, for "every new discovery, every new success of science, is a blow to the teachings of the Bible, which to this day . . . remains the basis of [Christian] theology."[22] Darwin's theory of evolution dealt religion a particularly heavy blow, for it proved the oneness and continuity of life forms, that man is not a passive and obedient creature of "God," a mere plaything in his hands, but an active agent, a creator who is able to alter his environment and, indeed, create new breeds of plants and animals.[23]

As for reports of miraculous cures and other miraculous events that religion attributes to saints, shrines, and prayer and uses to build up its credit with the public, Albanian Marxists answered that all such "miracles" can be explained scientifically, except in cases of hoax that crafty priests perpetrate on innocent and superstitious people.[24] Moreover, prayer is in itself a vain attempt to defy nature. In the words of one Albanian writer: "At the foundation of every prayer stands the belief that God can change the course of nature [i.e., contravene natural law] and grant what is asked of him,"[25] which is absurd. To believe in prayer is to believe in word magic. In this connection, an Arab who toured Albania in 1968 reported that his Albanian guide said to him: "Why do you insist on seeing the mosque [in Tiranë]? . . . The six-Day War did not teach you anything. The Arabs lost precious time praying to Allah,"[26] thus implying that the war was lost because of the Arabs' reliance on Allah instead of on themselves.

In their spirited drive to demolish the philosophical, moral, and psychological foundations of religion, Albanian atheists wrestled with the question of the origin of religion and religious belief and claimed that the entire history of the development of human society demonstrates that man himself created religion and the idea of God according to his image and fancy. This came about not because man has a religious instinct but because our primitive ancestors, being weak and ignorant, trembled before the powerful forces of nature and sought to placate them by means of ritual and sacrifice.[27] In fact, fear, ignorance, and class oppression created the first gods. Science and history prove that all religions "emerged under definite historical conditions, have changed in accordance with changing economic, social, and political [conditions]," and will disappear from the earth when new conditions make the institution of religion an unbearable anachronism.[28]

The disciples of Marxist atheism in Albania also polemicized against religion over the doctrine of original sin, which, they said, views men as "inherently corrupt and evil" and which is utilized by the clergy to justify the misery and oppression of the working people, with the explanation that they are being "punished by 'God' for their sinful nature." In opposition to this view, they argued that man is not predestined from birth to become either good or evil. He is born morally neutral, and what he becomes in life depends on the conditions under which he grows up. In brief, human nature is not unchangeable; man can change his nature and become a better being by changing the circumstances of his life.[29] Nor is religion essential to morality. According to Albanian materialists, those who ground morality in religion or, more precisely, in doing the "will of God" are but apologists for the ruling classes, "for the 'will' of God is none other than the will of the class which holds power over the workers."[30] Moral conduct among men antedates religion by many millennia and shall exist long after religion makes its exit from the human scene.

Such was the theoretical attack on religion by Albanian advocates of atheism. This was, of course, a one-sided debate against the religious world view, and Albanian ideologists were not insensitive to the fact. They argued, however, that in a socialist society freedom of expression and freedom of conscience cannot be granted to advocates of theism, since "religion, by virtue of its substance, activity, and very existence is an affront to the human conscience, and . . . stifles reason" and the free development of the human spirit.[31] The task of communists is not to allow religion equal time, as it were, to defend itself and expand its noxious influence but to press the attack on it, so as to constantly weaken its foundations and decrease its hold on the people.

In addition to the theoretical attack on religion, Albanian atheists utilized a more practical approach.

Religion and the Albanian Reality

Focusing on the concrete experience of the Albanian nation, Albanian atheists found additional arguments to use against religion and the religious establishment. They contended that the history and culture of the Albanian people and their struggle for national independence show that religion has not been a strong force in their lives. According to Zihni Sako, Albania's leading spokesman on cultural history and folklore, the culture of the Albanian people is "in its core atheist" and pagan. He observes that to this day one hears people in Albania swear "by this earth" or by the sun or the bread they eat. "Our people," Hoxha has remarked, "have never been . . . [much] attached to religion."[32] This view is widely shared by Albanians and is supported by the research of Prof. Stavro Skendi, noted Albanian scholar in America. According to Skendi:

. . . the Albanians, owing to historical conditions, have never been a religious people. During the Late Middle Ages, their country had become the battlefield between the Catholic West and the Orthodox East. Whenever the West was advancing, the Albanian feudal lords—often followed by their populations—espoused Catholicism; whenever Byzantium was the victor and the West retreated, they embraced Orthodoxy. They lived, one might say, a religiously amphibious life.[33]

Indicative of this lighthearted approach to religion is the fact that the priest in the Albanian village was often the butt of jokes and anecdotes. Indeed, the favorite comic character in Albanian folklore is none other than Nastradin Hoxha, a bungling, often roguish, and rather irreverent Moslem priest.

The Hosha-Shehu leadership maintains that religion is alien to the Albanian people, since all three faiths in contemporary Albanian society were brought into the country by alien powers. In Hoxha's view:

All the religious sects existing in our country were brought into Albania by foreign invaders, and served them and the ruling classes of the country. Under the cloak of religion, god, and the prophets, there operated the brutal law of the invaders and their domestic lackeys. The history of our people demonstrates . . . how [religion] engendered discord and fratricide in order to oppress us more cruelly, enslave us more easily, and suck our blood. . . .[34]

This citation shows the emotional intensity and bitterness of the Albanian leadership toward the Church. It is an attitude, moreover, that to a large degree was shaped by the religious experience of the Albanian people over many decades, especially during the movement for national independence. Prior to Albania's independence from the Turks in 1912, religious services were conducted in three different languages: Arabic for Moslem Albanians, Greek for the Orthodox, and Latin for the Catholics. Furthermore, since the Turks identified nationality with religion, Moslem Albanians came to be called Turks, the Orthodox were called Greeks, while the Catholics were regarded as Latins. Religion thus became a source of discord and division within the Albanian society and a great obstacle to national unity and the struggle for independence. Since religion was used by enemies of Albanian nationalism against the national interests of the Albanian people, enlightened leaders of the country could not be expected to have much sympathy for the Church. Unlike other Balkan countries, where the Church championed the cause of independence from the Turks during the nineteenth century, in Albania the religious establishment did not play such a role. The result was that the nationalist movement there assumed a nonreligious character and in fact prompted leaders of the Albanian national movement to downgrade religion in order to upgrade nationalism. A celebrated slogan of the time was: "The religion of the Albanian people is Albanianism."[35] Thus, the poet Pashko Vase Shkodrani (1825-1892), addressing himself to the Albanian people, wrote:

Christian and Moslem priests have benumbed you,
To divide you, and impoverish you!
Look not to churches and to mosques,
For the religion of the Albanian is Albanianism![36]

Here we have one of the basic contradictions between religion and the Albanian reality, between the Church and the state, which made possible the abolition of religion in Albania. In the words of Hoxha, the road to Albania's independence was "watered with the blood of the martyrs of Albania's Renaissance, such as Papa Kristo Negovani [1875-1905] and Petro Nini Luarasi [1865-1911]. . . ."[37] Negovani was a priest of the Orthodox Church; Luarasi was a pioneer educator. Both men were victims of Greek fanaticism, which could not reconcile itself to their devoted efforts to teach the Albanian language in school and introduce it into the liturgy of the Orthodox Church.

Albanian nationalism thus provided the Albanian regime with a powerful base from which to mount an attack on the various religious bodies in the country. As Albanian Marxist-Leninists saw it, the Church had lost its raison d'être. It had no valid philosophical or rational basis. It had lost all credit with Albanian nationalism—although they granted that there had been a few patriotic clergymen, like Negovani and Fan S. Noli. Lastly, they were convinced that the Church had become a serious obstacle to the social, economic, and political development of the country.

Albanian materialists argued that the Church had a medieval outlook on life and expounded a pernicious social philosophy, including fatalism, inequality between men and women, and submission and passivity in the face of evil and injustice. In grappling with the pronounced backwardness of Albanian society, the Albanian leadership inevitably linked the Church with the backward customs and traditions that cluttered and plagued Albanian social life. The relentless struggle against the heavy legacy of backwardness thus became a struggle against the Church as well. Indeed, the Church was seen not only as an accomplice, so to speak, of a pervasive social evil but as the ideological basis for the evil.

A major aspect of this evil was the inferior and restricted position of women in Albanian society, for which religion was severely blamed. Speaking at the Fourth Congress of the Union of Albanian Women in October 1955, Enver Hoxha said that religion "intervened at every moment to keep woman in a miserable state of slavery" to her husband, family, and society.[38] Albanian atheists pointed out, for example, that the Koran calls woman "a submissive creature who lacks the perfection of man"[39] and grants the husband the right to beat his wife, divorce her at will, and even kill her.[40]

The economy, too, became an issue in the relations between Church and state. From Tiranë's viewpoint, the religious establishment was an obstacle to the full utilization of the labor potential in the country and the rapid development of the economy. Party propagandists complained that "religious festivals and holidays did great harm to the economy, since on such days believers would not go to work."[41] They further accused the clergy of perpetuating harmful superstitions among the people, claimed that many religious practices such as the kissing of icons and circumcision of Moslem boys were unhygienic and potentially deadly, and derided ecclesiastics as parasites who lived by fraud and guile.[42]

In addition to the internal pressures that brought the Church and state in Albania into a fateful confrontation, there were external pressures that heightened the confrontation and influenced its final outcome. The Albanian leadership saw the Church not only as an internal handicap but as an ideological "fifth column" of the imperialists, the revisionists, and the Vatican. From Albania's standpoint, Washington, the Kremlin, and the Vatican comprised a Holy Trinity, bent on suppressing national liberation movements and carrying out counterrevolution against Marxist-Leninist countries like China and Albania. Party polemicists denounced Pope Paul's visit to the UN in 1965 as a maneuver to help Washington achieve its imperialist objectives in Vietnam. Worse still, they charged that during the Italian occupation of Albania, the Vatican sought to turn Orthodox Albanians into Uniates—that is, to have them recognize the pope as their spiritual leader—and even "set up a special office, under Cardinal Tisserant, to deal with [this] question."[43]

Turning to Moscow's policy on the Vatican, the defenders of the communist faith in Tiranë were bitterly critical of Gromyko's audience with Pope Paul VI in 1966[44] and subsequent contacts between Soviet leaders and the pope. They reminded the Kremlin of the many sins committed by the Vatican against communism, including attempts by the Catholic Church to mobilize "crusades" against the USSR, following the October Revolution, and the part played by Cardinal Mindszenty in "organizing" the Hungarian counterrevolution. They further charged that the "traitorous Soviet revisionists" were fostering the revival of religion in "the first socialist state," in order to "numb the revolutionary will of the Soviet people,"[45] and attacked the Soviet religious monthly, *Nauka i religia*, as an organ for the propagation of religious ideology. Analyzing the Vatican's relations with Moscow and Washington, Albanian Stalinists concluded that the cross of religion and the sword of the military remain, as ever in the past, natural allies, the arms of tyrants and reaction.

1967: The "Dethronement" of God

The struggle of the Party to eliminate the Church as a social institution intensified in the years immediately following the war and reached the breaking point by the mid-1960s. Early in 1966, the Albanian Party of Labor began its Ideological and Cultural Revolution, with the avowed goal of preventing the restoration of capitalism and bourgeois ideology in Albania. A major aim of the revolution was to rid Albania of backward customs and "futile beliefs." In February 1967, at the height of the Ideological and Cultural Revolution, students at the Naim Frashëri High School in Durrës, Albania's major seaport, initiated a movement to close down the churches and mosques in the country. The movement spread, and by May 1967 all places of public worship—described by Hoxha as "centers of obscuratism and mysticism"—had been eliminated. God had finally been dethroned in socialist Albania. The regime's theoreticians now asserted that the "last and most parasitical form of exploitation" of the masses had been swept away[46] and that the Albanian people were freed not only from economic and social exploitation but from spiritual enslavement as well.

During this period and throughout 1967 numerous mass meetings were held in towns and villages, at which the Church was "hailed before the popular courts of reason" and condemend for its sins. At these meetings old men and women, students, workers, farmers, and party cadres denounced the churches as spiders' webs; renounced all belief in God and saints; reviled the clergy as parasites, exploiters, and frauds; and pledged never again to engage in religious worship or to observe religious holidays. Some vowed to give up religious expressions in social greetings and toasts and to refrain from naming their children after the saints, as was the custom.[47] In certain cases children denounced their clergymen fathers as fakers. "Thunder sheets" (*fletë-rrufe*) appeared in the streets attacking parents who had given religious names to their children.[48] At the same time, the Party presses turned out a spate of pamphlets and books satirizing religion and "exposing" the Church and the clergy. One such publication, a book of poems about clergymen entitled *Religion Stripped Naked*, contains the following lines:

Forever the people swept away,
These pillars of fanaticism,
And rid themselves of clericalism,
Which for many centuries past,
Using Christ and Mohamet,
Holy men, saint and prophet—
Made of life a sorry mess.[49]

The Party put the official seal on the presumed death of the Church on November 13, 1967, when the People's Assembly of Albania approved a decree annulling the religious statutes of November 1949, May 1950, and July 1951, which affirmed the right of believers to worship freely within the framework of the Moslem, Orthodox, and Catholic churches. The obituary notice appeared in *Gazeta zyrtare* (The official gazette) on November 22, 1967.

Addressing the Sixth Congress of the Albanian Party of Labor in November 1971, the Party's first secretary explained that there was no alternative to the abolition of religion in Albania. "As a Marxist-Leninist Party," he said, "[the APL] is clearly aware that . . . the socialist revolution cannot but cut off and uproot, when all objective and subjective conditions are ripe, all the strands that link the masses with the old world and hinder them from marching forward."[50]

Following the abolition of the Church, the Party advised that new festivals must replace the old religious ceremonies and holidays, in order to prevent the creation of a void in the people's lives. Accordingly, a new calendar of secular festivals began to emerge, including national holidays, such as Albanian Independence Day (November 28) and Liberation Anniversary (November 29); days for honoring the workers, such as Builders' Day, Miners' Day, Printers' Day; agricultural festivals in connection with the harvesting of grapes, olives, and so on; and celebration of local martyrs or heroes of labor, as well as events of historical significance to a particular community or region. Albanian sources complained, however, that many people—especially the old, but sometimes even communist youth—continued to believe in God and to practice religion, either privately or in some indirect way as, for example, observing one's name day on one's birthday. Religious influence was most evident in the countryside. A publication of the Labor Youth Union observed that "religious beliefs are the most durable of all remnants of capitalism"[51] —an open admission of the persistence of popular resistance to institutionalized atheism in the nation.

Aware of the enormity of the task before them, Albanian leaders resigned themselves to a long struggle and cautioned that missionary work with the religious should be marked by patience and care, like that of "a good physician who makes every effort to cure the sick."[52] The attitude, apparently, was to look upon believers as sick people, like drug addicts and the mentally disturbed, and to treat them accordingly.

The abolition of the Church in Albania passed almost without notice abroad and aroused little protest. *Osservatore romano* of the Vatican noted on July 11, 1967, that "churches in Albania had been closed or damaged in a wave of antireligious violence." Among the Albanians of America, the Albanian Orthodox Church wired a telegram to Haxhi Lleshi, president of the People's Republic of Albania, pleading "for the restoration of religious freedoms" in the country.[53] The message was drafted on July 4, 1970, some three years after the closing of the churches and mosques in Albania. The belatedness of the message was primarily due to the fact that the Albanian Church in America had been badly split for four years following the death of its founder, Bishop Noli, in March 1965. The mildness of the telegram could be attributed in part to the desire of members of the Church not to stir the embers of the post-Noli dispute within the diocese, since the dispute was partly political in nature and involved the question of what attitude the Church should take toward the atheistic regime in Albania. The mildness of the rebuke, therefore, reflected the reluctance of many Albanian Orthodox in America to become involved in Albanian politics. It could also be taken as an illustration of the Albanians' traditionally mild interest in the institution of religion. However, Rexhep Krasniqi, president of the Free Albania Committee located in New York, made a strong protest to the UN secretary-general against the abolition of religion in Albania and urged that steps be taken "to stop immediately the savage religious persecution" in that country.[54]

Since the late sixties, there have been many reports from Albania about the practice of religion by believers in more or less camouflaged ways. Vestiges of religion are seen in icons that believers keep at home, crosses worn around the neck, refusal to work on Easter and other holidays, pilgrimages to religious shrines, and the practice of having former priests perform religious services within the privacy of one's home.[55] Apparently, religious observances at home are not banned by law. But such practices are open to denunciation in the "thunder sheets" by anyone who is opposed to religion for personal, political, or other reasons. "Exposure" in such a medium of communication is a form of social pressure on believers and evidently has proved useful to the regime as a means of combating religious manifestations in the country.

Until 1973, the religious situation in Albania in general developed without attracting much attention from the outside world. The situation changed suddenly when on March 28, 1973, the *New York Times* published a dispatch from Vienna which said that a Catholic priest, Father Shtjefën Kurti, had been executed in Albania for secretly baptizing a child at the request of its mother. The news received wide publicity in the West, creating a most unfavorable image of the Albanian regime.[56] Incensed by Western reports about Father Kurti, Albania responded with characteristic violence through her news media. Reports from Tiranë acknowledged the execution of the Catholic priest, reportedly at the age of seventy-four, but denied Western allegations that he was shot for baptizing a child. The Albanian version is that Kurti was shot in 1970 for the crime of collaborating with the Italian and German invaders during the war, spying for English and American intelligence services, and working as a subversive agent of the Vatican.[57] The Kurti incident unleashed a torrent of invective by the Albanian press against the Vatican, going so far as to accuse the center of Catholicism of seeking to "place under its talons the Albanian Orthodox Church in the United States,"[58] a rather farfetched hypothesis.

Another three years passed before the question of religion in Albania—a seemingly dormant but ever delicate issue in the country—again made news abroad. Early in 1976 reports circulated in the Western press that Albania had ordered all of her citizens whose names were considered objectionable by the Party leadership to change them by the end of the year.[59] The reports were based on fact. They were inspired by a decree dated September 23, 1975, and published in *Gazeta zyrtare* in Tiranë on November 11, 1975, which said: "Citizens who have inappropriate names and offensive surnames from a political, ideological, and moral viewpoint are obliged to change them." The decree added that persons affected by the edict were expected to comply with it voluntarily and that those who did not comply would be given "appropriate names" by social organizations in their locality. It was not specified what constituted an unsuitable name. But it was generally assumed by Western diplomats and media commentators that the decree was aimed at Albanians having religious names, especially Orthodox Christians and Roman Catholics. The decree was thus interpreted as another effort by the Albanian government to wipe out the remaining traces of religion in the country.

Religious considerations probably played a part in the thinking of the drafters of the decree. It seems likely, however, that the regime issued the decree more for nationalistic than religious reasons; namely, to eliminate "alien influences" in the names of persons, as well as places, and replace them with what the regime regards as purely Albanian names. The regime responded to the adverse publicity abroad mostly by publishing testimonials by members of the Greek minority in the southern part of the country to the effect that they were living happy lives in Albania.

The barrage of negative publicity in the West regarding the question of religion in Albania presumably worried the Party leaders and caused them to adopt a policy of largely ignoring the issue for the time being. This became evident in the fact that in his lengthy report to the Seventh Party Congress in November 1976 Enver Hoxha made no reference to religion—a departure from his report to the previous Party Congress in 1971, when he devoted two pages to the struggle to "smash the influence of religion" in Albanian society.

The year 1976 closed with the adoption of the new Constitution by the People's Assembly, which officially banishes religion from the Albanian state. The document comments initially that the "foundations of religious obscurantism" have been smashed in Albania. Article 37 says unequivocally that "The state recognizes no religion whatever and supports atheist propaganda for the purpose of inculcating the scientific-materialist world-outlook in [the Albanian] people."[60]

There were signs however of renewed active opposition abroad to Albanian state atheism, on both an individual and organized level. The publication of John Sinishta's book, *The Fulfilled Promise* (1976), dealing with "religious persecution in Albania," is an example of such opposition. More significantly perhaps, a report in the Boston-based Albanian-American newspaper *Dielli* (The Sun) dated August 10, 1977, told of the convocation in Philadelphia, Pennsylvania, of an international conference of Muslim Organizations in the United States and Canada that adopted a proposal aimed at the restoration of religious freedom in Albania. The proposal was submitted by Imam Vehbi Ismail of Detroit, Michigan, who attended the conference as a member of the Council of Imams of North America. Imam Vehbi is also head of the influential Albanian-American Moslem Society that has headquarters in Detroit.

Concluding Note

It is now a decade since Albania proclaimed herself "the first atheist state in the world." After a twenty-year struggle for survival, the Church in Albania succumbed to the state—a victim of the Ideological and Cultural Revolution. More precisely, however, the Church fell victim to a combination of forces and contradictions within Albanian society, chief among which was the Party's inveterate animosity toward religion and its relentless drive for hegemony over every phase of Albanian life, including the material and the spiritual. As long as God and the Church lived in Albania, there existed an alternate center for the people's loyalty, affection, and support, and the Party had no intention of tolerating such competition. In this attack, the Stalinist leaders in Tiranë were apparently helped by a number of circumstances, more or less peculiar to Albania, including the historical friction between religion and Albanian nationalism, a largely uneducated clergy, the identification of religion with the backwardness of the country, and the fact that Albanians have never been a deeply religious people.

It is ironic that the downfall of the Church in Albania should have occurred at a time when religion was experiencing a revival of sorts in other countries in Eastern Europe and the Soviet Union.[61] The Albanian experiment ran counter to the seeming religious revival in Eastern Europe. One might therefore ask: Was the "dethronement" of God in Albania the result of a strange but temporary aberration of the human mind and spirit? Or is it perhaps a "sign of things to come," an experiment in social extremism that presages the eventual disappearance of organized religion as we know it today?

The answer would seem to depend primarily on the evolution of political and economic life within Albania and the Party's ability to guide or control such evolution. More exactly, it depends on whether the Party can truly substitute itself for the Church, whether the Marxist faith can replace traditional theology, and whether secular holidays and festivals can effectively displace religious ritual and myth. It depends on whether the Albanian leadership succeeds in its struggle to eliminate the pervasive backwardness of Albanian society and raise the economic level of the country to such a degree that the people will identify their own welfare—and the good of the country—with that of the Party. The answer depends also on the fortunes of religion in East Europe and in the world in general.

The determination of the Albanian leaders to change almost completely the face of Albanian society is a remarkable example of the faith of a revolutionary elite, with regard to remaking society in accordance with a preconceived model—in this case, the Marxist-Leninist model of society, as envisioned by Hoxha and Shehu. At this point, it is an open question whether this radical social experiment will succeed. For their part, this disciples of "scientific atheism" in Albania remain confident that the day will surely come when *Requiem eternam* shall be sung to religion, along with the Vatican, revisionism, and imperialism.

9
The Party *vs.* the Intelligentsia

The Party vs. the Intelligentsia

The overall attitude of the Albanian Party of Labor (APL) toward the intelligentsia seems to have been molded by two considerations: on the one hand, the awareness of its vital need for the intelligentsia's unique services in building a socialist society, and on the other its uneasiness over the "political instability" of this particular social element. Accordingly, the Party adopted from the start of its rule a dual strategy in dealing with members of this group, consisting of reward and punishment, praise and intimidation, aimed at winning their assent to its authority, their cooperation, and their loyalty.[1]

The method decreed by the Party in the development of art and culture in general was that of Socialist Realism. Of necessity, the adoption of this method meant the rejection of a long list of "isms," such as idealism, impressionism, abstractionism, mysticism, subjectivism, expressionism, surrealism, cubism, existentialism, and naturalism—this last one taken in the sense of a photographic, rather than selective, presentation of reality.

Running like a thread in the relations between the Albanian leadership and the intelligentsia was a strong element of mistrust and fear of the latter by the former. There is much evidence to support this hypothesis. In March 1968, five months before the invasion of Czechoslovakia by Warsaw Pact countries, a major statement in *Zëri i popullit*, organ of APL, ascribed the ferment and unrest then current in Czechoslovakia primarily to the intelligentsia. The statement said that Czechoslovakia was degenerating into capitalism and that the process of degeneration "started with the writers and students."[2] The statement went on to say that in Poland "the reactionary intelligentsia and the students" were seeking to overthrow Gomulka and that "the Hungarian counterrevolution was initiated by some intellectuals and students."[3] It sought to explain the attitude and position of the intelligentsia in the body politic by saying that members of this group comprise a wavering stratum that becomes an easy prey of the bourgeoisie and other reactionary forces, when it is not under the firm influence and guidance of a genuine Marxist-Leninist party.

These remarks in the Party's daily are not merely an illustration of the theoretical position of the Albanian leadership on the intelligentsia, developed over the years in reaction to events in the socialist countries. They testify also to the practical experience of the leadership with Albanian intellectuals, dating as far back as 1941, the year when the Albanian Communist Party was organized. The resolution adopted upon the formation of the Party on November 8, 1941, accused intellectuals of standing on liberal and opportunistic positions that harmed the movement of the masses and urged Party cadres to struggle against "sick intellectualism."[4] Subsequent Party documents and press articles drew a dividing line between intellectuals described as genuine, honorable, and dedicated to the service of the masses and others who were labeled, either openly or by implication, as dishonorable, egotistic pseudo intellectuals who despised the masses and nourished remnants of bourgeois and revisionist ideology in their conscience.[5] "In general," Enver Hoxha, APL secretary, once said, intellectuals "have a tendency to daydream" and "a marked penchant to become infatuated with themselves."[6]

The results of APL's policy toward the intelligentsia over a period of three decades have been a mixture of successes and failures, of confrontation and accommodation, highlighted by a series of crises or near crises occurring at intervals of about ten years. The first and by far the most serious of these took place in 1945-1947; another, much less visible, occurred in 1956-1957; the third in 1965-1966; and the latest in 1972-1973.

The Confrontation of the Forties

The events of 1945-1947 revolved largely around the person of Sejfulla Malëshova, APL Politburo member, minister of culture and propaganda, leading Party ideologist, and the outstanding poet of the Albanian Partisan struggle. In October 1945, Malëshova organized a meeting in Tiranë for the purpose of uniting Albanian writers into an association of their own. In his remarks to the meeting, Malëshova took a middle-of-the-road course between extreme liberals, who advocated an "art for art's sake" position, and the radicals who demanded the purging from educational texts and literature of the writings of certain Albanian authors they considered objectionable. On October 7, 1945, the Union of Albanian Writers was formed, with a total of seventy-four members, including both communist and noncommunist writers. Malëshova was elected president of the union, and a publication called *Bota e re* (The new world) was adopted as the union's official organ.[7]

In line with this moderate, conciliatory policy on culture and the arts, Malëshova permitted the publication in *Bota e re* of the writings of communists, such as Dhimitër Shuteriqi, Fatmir Gjata, Kolë Jakova, and Andrea Varfi; and noncommunists, such as Dhimitër Pasko and Arshi Pipa. With regard to old, established authors of the precommunist period, as, for example, Gjergj Fishta, Andon Çajupi, Fan S. Noli, Faik Konitza, and Kristoforidhi, he advocated a critical, selective approach to their writings, with the aim of "discarding what was 'reactionary' and retaining only what was 'progressive.'"[8] Malëshova's attempt to effect a compromise between communist and noncommunist writers, and between traditional and socialist literature, did not work. He came increasingly under the suspicion of top Party leaders like Hoxha and Koci Xoxe, vice-premier of Albania, who were alarmed not only by his position on culture and the arts but by his views on a whole range of domestic and foreign issues, including the economy, the Catholic Church, and relations with the West.[9]

The fact that in October 1945 the newly formed Albanian Writers' Union appealed to President Truman and Prime Minister Clement Attlee of Great Britain for recognition of Albania only strengthened the suspicions of the Party leadership concerning the soundness of Malëshova's politics. The blow came five months later. At a Party Central Committee meeting on February 21, 1946, Malëshova was accused of opportunism and Right deviationism and was expelled from the Politburo and the Central Committee.[10]

The fall of Malëshova in early 1946 was a decisive event in the history of postwar Albanian literature and a turning point in the fortunes of the intelligentsia. This became apparent at the Second Writers' Conference, held in June 1946. Hoxha was pleased with the conclusions of the conference. He said that the work of the Writers' Union took "a good direction" following the June conference.[11] These developments in fact "marked the triumph of the extremist policy in literature"[12] and led to the banishment from literature textbooks of writers like Fishta, Konitza, the Albanian-Italian poet Zef Schiro, Vincenc Prenushi, and others whom the radicals identified with political parties and movements they regarded as reactionary, Fascist, or imperialist.

The dismissal of Malëshova as minister of culture and president of the Writers' Union—he was replaced in the latter post by Dhimitër Shuteriqi, a prewar communist writer—signaled the beginning of a new period in Albanian literature and cultural life. Henceforth, there was no middle ground left for the noncommunist writer. He had to accept the Party line on art and culture "or be declared an opponent, and as such pay the consequences."[13]

Since at that time the majority of the writers reportedly opposed communism, a crisis situation developed in which the Party and opposing writers became locked in a grim power struggle that brought personal tragedy to many of the writers and altered significantly the role and standing of the intelligentsia in Albanian social and cultural life. The confrontation was particularly severe in 1946-1947, but it continued with varying degrees of intensity until the early 1950s. Hardest hit by the waves of repression that marked those years were the writers and intellectuals of Shkodër, the main city in northern Albania, a prominent center of literary activity, and the stronghold of Catholic power and tradition in the country.

The harsh administrative measures taken by the Party against unsubmissive members of the intelligentsia wrecked the lives of a number of intellectuals, including several Catholic clergymen active in the field of letters. Among those arrested and imprisoned were Mitrush Kuteli (Dhimitër Pasko), Albania's foremost lyric poet; Prof. Selman Riza, philologist; Andon Frashëri and Arkile Tasi, both former editors of *Dielli* (The sun), Boston-based organ of the Pan-Albanian Federation of America (VATRA); Musine Kokalari, perhaps the best known Albanian woman writer;[14] Dionis Miçaço and Kudret Kokoshi, jurists; and Etëhem Haxhiademi, a dramatist noted for his plays in the classic tradition. A number of others were killed or died in prison. This group included among others Kol Prela, professor of Albanian; Lazër Shanto, noted translator of German classics; Vinçenc Prenushi, a Franciscan Catholic clergyman, poet, and folklorist; and Anton Harapi, another Franciscan and a leading member of the Catholic hierarchy. Harapi was executed as a Nazi collaborator.[15]

Altogether, some ten intellectuals were executed, and over three dozen others were imprisoned during this period. Such was the ferocity of the Party's reaction against confirmed or suspected opponents in the ranks of the intelligentsia that in a few cases even communist writers fell victim to it. Thus, Andrea Varfi and Petro Marko, whose sympathies for communism predated the founding of the Albanian Communist Party, were imprisoned for a while, then released.[16]

What were the forces or causal factors that produced so sharp and violent a confrontation between the Party leadership and a small but vital segment of the Albanian society, the intelligentsia? Apparently, the clash was due in part to Hoxha's mistrust of intellectuals, and Koci Xoxe's personal dislike of Malëshova[17] and his neutralist policy toward communist and noncommunist writers and patriots. Albania's lack of ties with the West facilitated the confrontation, since it tended to inhibit the growth of liberal forces and the expression of noncommunist viewpoints in arts and letters, while it encouraged extermist forces to become more vocal and to take the offensive against the opposition.[18] The situation of the liberals was made more acute by the fact that Yugoslavia supported and encouraged Albania's isolation from the West, in order to cultivate her own influence in Albania, free of competition from the Western powers.[19]

But perhaps more important still was the fact that Albania at this time was undergoing a vast and rapid process of radicalization, characterized by a shift away from rational dialogue and liberalism toward strict partisanship and centralization of power and authority in the Party. For example, in agriculture the government instituted an agrarian reform, which caused much upheaval in the countryside; and in the religious sector, it proceeded to limit drastically the autonomy and influence of the religious bodies in the country. The radicalization process affected the intelligentsia as well. The Party leadership was determined to bring the intellectuals under its control and to transform the intelligentsia into a transmission belt for the implementation of its line and program. To reach that goal it had to suppress dissident writers, artists, and intellectuals and create a new intelligentsia, loyal to Marxism-Leninism, committed to the new social order, and obedient to the Party's authority.[20] By the early 1950s, the Albanian communist leaders had largely succeeded in this aim.

The Party viewed the confrontation with a largely liberal, pro-Western, and independent-minded intelligentsia—as well as with recalcitrant forces among the peasantry, the religious establishment, and other institutions—as a merciless, life-and-death class struggle between socialism and its assorted enemies: the feudal reactionaries and capitalists, idealists, liberals, and various petit bourgeois elements. Although the pro-Party forces won these initial battles, the Party was nonetheless concerned over the class composition of its membership, which in the 1940s and early 1950s had a weak working-class representation. Accordingly, it took steps to bring more workers into the Party and at the same time reduce the percentage of the "less reliable" social classes, including the intelligentsia. Other steps taken by the leadership in the wake of the confrontation with the intelligentsia were the launching of an ideological struggle aimed at educating writers and artists in the principles and goals of Socialist Realism in literature, art, and culture; and the orientation of literature and the arts toward the Soviet Union. The regime's policy was to subordinate art to politics; that is, to resolve questions of literature and culture in terms of the positive or negative impact they were likely to have on the political process. In the context of such a policy, authors like Fishta were judged to be reactionary,[21] and that in turn made their literary work unacceptable to the regime.

New Direction for the Arts

With the defeat of liberal and moderate intellectuals, led by Malëshova, and the banning of the writings of "reactionary authors," the Party set out to eliminate all remnants of bourgeois influence in culture and the arts and to educate the intelligentsia on the basis of Marxism-Leninism. Enver Hoxha set the tone and direction of the new cultural policy in a speech he made in October 1946, a few months after Malëshova's fall. "Our schools and culture," he said, "must . . . be cleansed of all reactionary ideologies, for they are in flagrant opposition to the great principles which emerged from the National Liberation Movement and guide our . . . People's Republic."[22] Henceforth, Albanian culture was to be "socialist in content and national in form." It would become the wealth of the masses instead of a luxury of the wealthy few and "serve the people, educate the people in a spirit of proletarian internationalism, [and] strengthen the people's power."[23]

The role and function of the new intelligentsia were now clear. The regrouped and reeducated intellectuals were to serve the people by serving the Party; that is, by faithfully implementing the Party's directives for bringing culture to the people. The Union of Albanian Writers thus became a forum for airing the Party's doctrines and decrees on questions of culture and an organizational vechicle for carrying them out in practice. In this regard, the function of the Writers' Union was similar to that of mass organizations such as the Albanian Trade Unions, the Union of Albanian Women, the Democratic Front, and the Labor Youth Union of Albania—all of which were looked upon by the Albanian leadership as transmission belts for the Party's ideology and programs in their respective fields.

Accordingly, writers and artists were urged to popularize the War of National Liberation, promote patriotism among the people, and make manifest the struggle of the people for the construction of socialism.[24] They were asked also to strengthen the people's understanding and appreciation of the nation's cultural heritage by creating appropriate works of art on such subjects as Albanian history, language, folklore, and music.[25] In dealing with current Albanian reality, they were to give prominence especially to the new heroes of the land: the worker, the peasant, the cadre, the soldier, and the new Albanian man and woman who were building socialism in the face of opposition from remnants of the former ruling classes within the country and the pressures of the class enemy without.

These prescriptions amounted, in effect, to a working definition of Socialist Realism in literature and the arts, as the Albanian communists conceived of that celebrated but elusive term. More specifically, Socialist Realism meant an art born of the revolution and designed to carry that revolution forward on several planes. On the economic plane, the new art would point out the fruits of socialist construction and the virtues of socialist labor, especially the readiness to forego personal gain and comfort in favor of the collective good. On the psychological plane, it would reveal the great transformations taking place in the minds and conscience of the Albanian people and the process by which they were developing a thoroughly socialist world outlook. On a third plane, that of politics, the method of Socialist Realism would cultivate a militant spirit and revolutionary vigilance among the masses, to the end that they might better defend the gains of the revolution, including national sovereignty, collectivization of the economy, and increasing material benefits. Lastly, Socialist Realism meant exploiting the nation's cultural heritage with the aim of creating a truly original and enduring national art—an art that would bear the distinct imprint of the Albanian character, with all its unique features.[26]

Such in sum was the conception of Socialist Realism as an art method. But in practice the new method presented many problems, of which four seemed perennial: how to write knowingly and credibly about life and the inner world of the people; how to avoid dry, stereotyped plots and characters; how to deal with the negative aspects of Albanian society; and whether the "positive hero" in socialist literature has any vices or human weaknesses.[27]

The radicalization of Albanian literature and culture that followed the Second Writers' Conference in June 1946 did not occur in a vacuum. It was influenced to some extent by Yugoslavia, but the primary and decisive source of influence was the USSR. After Stalin's break with Tito in June 1948, Albania oriented itself toward the Soviet Union. The First APL Congress in November 1948 decreed that Albanian "education, culture, and art must be oriented toward Soviet education, culture, and art [which are] the most progressive in the world. . . ."[28] The decree of the Party congress was implemented at the Third Writers' Conference in October 1949. Thereafter, the Soviet experiment in socialist construction and the Soviet world view in general—on art, culture, religion, the family, education—became models for Albanian writers, artists, and cultural workers in the practice and development of their profesions.

The decade of the fifties saw a rapid development in Albania's relations with the USSR and its allies in Eastern Europe. There was a corresponding expansion in Albania's cultural and intellectual life. By 1950, the writers' first organ, *Bota e re*, had been replaced by *Letërsia jonë* (Our literature). In 1952, Albanian artists other than writers—composers, painters, sculptors, and engravers—formed their own organization, the Union of Albanian Artists. By 1954, *Letërsia jonë* was in turn replaced by *Nëndori* (November) as the new organ of the Writers' Union.[29]

The First Congress of the League of Albanian Writers and Artists

After continuing as a separate organization for twelve years, the Albanian Writers' Union in 1957 joined with the Albanian Artists' Union to form the League of Albanian Writers and Artists (LAWA). The merger occurred at the convocation of the First Congress, held jointly in that year by the members of the two organizations. The new organization had a Presidency, headed by Dhimitër Shuteriqi, a larger body known as the Directing Committee, and a Committee of Revision, whose main function apparently was to keep records on membership and related matters. The total membership of the league was 150.

The congress marked the culmination of another confrontation between the Party and the intelligentsia that had begun in 1956, shortly after the holding of the Twentieth CPSU Congress in February of that year. The de-Stalinization waves that swept East Europe following Khrushchev's attack on Stalin reached the Albanian shores as well but were much too weak to cause a storm in the country. A hint of the aborted storm appeared in an article by Razi Brahimi—perhaps the leading literary critic in Albania—in which he discussed some problems of Albanian literature. In a departure from Marxist dogma with respect to the relation of individuls and social classes, Brahimi said that people cannot be explained merely in terms of classes. He said "class characteristics make up the skeleton of the personality," but his "individual traits" give him flesh and blood. The conditioning factors "are not determined entirely by his economic situation, although this is the basic factor; they are also determined by his environment and his individual traits."[30]

A further hint of the underlying and potentially explosive intellectual ferment of 1956-1957 is revealed by the following quote from a speech by Shuteriqi:

Anti-socialist manifestations on the eve of our first Congress were characterized by attempts to deny the creation in Albania of a literature of socialist realism. There were calls for a "return" to the old methods of romanticism and bourgeois realism. This "return to the past" meant, above all, a return to the literature of the reactionary Catholic clergy and its followers.[31]

Shuteriqi added that a characteristic of that literature was the "idealization of the patriarchal life," especially that of the highlands.

The First Congress of LAWA was attended also by Soviet and Chinese representatives. Their comments at the congress reflected the simmering tensions between the APL and the Albanian intelligentsia and revealed interesting differences between Moscow's and Peking's appraisal of the situation of the arts in Albania.

The Soviet delegate, V. V. Jermilov, a representative of the Union of Soviet Writers, seemed to give indirect support to liberal Albanian intellectuals and to criticize implicitly the regime's concept of Socialist Realism, particularly its stress on the creation of an Albanian national art form. He said that "One of the traditions of Soviet letters . . . [is] to develop the idea of unity, brotherhood and friendship of all the people living in the socialist camp" and that this idea was "fundamentally opposed to the so-called concept of 'national communism.'"[32] By attacking "national communism," Jermilov was, in effect, attacking its corollary, "national art." In support of the liberal position on literature that more attention should be given to the individual as against his social class or background, Jermilov said:

Sometimes, certain writers neglect to delve deeply into the particulars of their characters, and bring out their individual qualities. Such neglect of the individual's psychology and behavior can only result in a vulgarization of the method of Socialist Realism. . . . Socialist Realism is not a dogma or a stereotype, but a generalization of experience which is the living stuff of literature. Socialist Realism includes a variety of styles, and a variety of methods by different artists.[33]

The greetings to the congress by the Chinese representative, Ko Pao Chuan, contrasted sharply with the remarks of Jermilov in terms of substance, tone, and most of all, perhaps, latent political implications for the developing Albanian-Soviet-Chinese relations. Unlike Jermilov, Chuan spoke of the similarities between Albanian and Chinese writers and artists—they "have walked the same revolutionary path"—and noted that "the art and literature of the Albanian people have a gloriously militant tradition."[34] He told the congress that the Chinese were becoming ever more familiar with Albanian art and literature, which they "understood and enjoyed." He remarked:

The ties of art and literature between us have been strengthened, alongside the development of friendly and cultural relations between our two countries.

In 1955, a cultural delegation and your People's Army Ensemble came to visit China, and were accorded a warm reception. The visit afforded the Chinese people, for the first time, the chance to become familiar with Albanian art. In recent years, our artists and our people have welcomed a number of artists and writers from your land.[35]

Among Albanian writers and artists who visited China during this period were Sterjo Spasse, Fatmir Gjata, and Aleks Çaçi (writers); Nexhmedin Zajmi (painter); Gaqo Avrazi (musician); Stavri Rafael (tenor); and Avni Mula (baritone). Chuan added that a number of Albanian literary works, both classic and contemporary, had been translated into Chinese. Among Albanian writers whose works were available to Chinese readers, he mentioned Naim Frashëri, Çajupi, Migjeni, Sterjo Spasse, Dhimitër Shuteriqi, Zihni Sako, Fatmir Gjata, and Luan Qafëzezi. The Chinese people, he said, were also familiar with a number of Albanian songs and popular dances. One of the songs mentioned by Chuan was a popular tune called "Tiranë-Peking."

In retrospect, it is evident that the First LAWA Congress brought out incipient differences between Soviet and Chinese positions on Albanian art and culture. For while Jermilov sought apparently to promote liberalism and individualism among the Albanian intelligentsia—in other words, the forces of revisionism—the Chinese representative sided with the militants who backed APL's uncompromising revolutionary line. Albania's leaning toward Peking on questions of art and culture at this time was another sign of her growing differences with the Soviet Union, which four years later burst out into the open.

Revival of Dissent in the Midsixties

The Albanian-Soviet split in 1961 was a jarring experience for Albania, leading to her political isolation from East Europe and severe dislocation of her economy. The split had repercussions on the intelligentsia and the arts as well. Some writers apparently questioned the Party's hard line on the arts and tried to "humanize" literature by orienting it in a less politicized and a more liberal direction. According to Razi Brahimi—who by this time had ostensibly abandoned his proliberal, 1956 viewpoints on art—they attempted to deemphasize the revolutionary element in Socialist Realism "under the pretext of drawing closer to 'the ordinary man,' 'ordinary life' and the 'day-to-day cares of the individual.'"[36] As a result, a number of works appeared in prose, poetry, the theater, and music "which lacked revolutionary inspiration."

An article published in the January 1965 issue of *Nëndori* attacked by name several works of literature and their authors, charging them with deviation from the principles of Socialist Realism, as a result of having come under revisionist and petit bourgeois influences. The first on the list, *Simfoni e pambaruar* (Unfinished symphony), a novel by veteran communist writer Sterjo Spasse, was attacked on the ground that the heroine of the work was "unreal" and an offense to the socialist concept of the heroine. *Dueli* (The duel), a play by Qamil Buxheli, Albania's noted humorist, about the German occupiers in Albania was found to be ideologically mistaken and historically inaccurate.

The article attacked two other plays: Naum Prifti's *Rrethimi i bardhë* (White encirclement), which dealt with a workers' collective isolated by a blizzard; and Minush Jero's *Historia e një nate* (The history of one night), a drama of family conflict and tragedy. Prifti's play was criticized for allegedly focusing on the selfishness of the characters in a crisis situation, instead of demonstrating their revolutionary heroism; while Jero was taken to task for resolving a family conflict between parents and children in an antagonistic fashion, instead of through persuasion and education. The same article also criticized poets Dritëro Agolli and Ismail Kadare for authoring works that distorted Albanian reality.[37] At the same time, these authors were praised for other works they had produced—the bulk of their creative output—that were consistent with the Party's conception of genuine socialist art. A few months later, another article in *Nëndori* made a strong attack on Fatos Arapi's play, *Drama e partizanit të paemër* (Drama of the unknown partisan), on the ground that it distorted the truth of the War of National Liberation and denigrated the figure of the Partisan.[38]

One feature of this confrontation between the intelligentsia and the Albanian leadership was that the writers who came under attack were nearly all members of the younger generation, thus showing that a "generation gap" had developed between the leadership and the intelligentsia. These were writers who were too young to fight in the Partisan war and had much less vivid impressions and memories of wartime hostilities and class hatreds than did Hoxha's generation. Consequently, they were inclined to see reality, the Partisan war, and the ideological struggle in less than absolute, black-and-white terms. The attacks on erring writers by the Party's literary overseers were intended to pressure them into conforming to the Party line on the arts and to warn other writers and artists not to fall into positions of deviationism. But the Party's struggle against manifestations of liberalism, individualism, and "bourgeois humanism" among writers had become more complicated now, as a result of the developing generation gap between the ruling hierarchy and youthful elements of the intelligentsia.

By mid-1965 it was clear that the threat of deviationism and revisionism in the arts persisted and that a more determined effort was called for to deal with the problem. Thus, on the twentieth anniversary of LAWA in October 1965, the Fifteenth Plenum of the Party's Central Committee convened in Tiranë for the purpose of discussing "the role of literature and the arts" in Albanian society. It was the first time that a Party plenum was called to deal specifically with the problem of the arts—an indication of the importance assigned to this problem by the Party leaders and of their resolve to take action to stabilize the situation before it reached crisis proportions. Ramiz Alia, the Party's leading theoretician on cultural questions, delivered the main report— a lengthy document that reviewed the development of the arts in socialist Albania, warned of the ever-present danger of cultural revisionism, and stressed the need for intelligentsia to draw closer to the masses.

"Our literature and arts," Alia said, "have become a strong support for the Party in the mobilization of the working masses for the construction of socialism . . . [and] for the defense of the purity of our Marxist-Leninist ideology and the independence and sovereignty of [our] socialist fatherland.[39] Alia sought to deglamorize cosmopolitan art, in order to better encourage the development of a more purely national Albanian art. He insisted that "the art which lacks national character" lacks true originality and true value. He also tried to dispel the sense of inferiority to non-Albanian art, felt by some Albanian artists, by pointing out the virtues and benefits of a wider Albanian art repertoire. On the relations between the artists and the masses, Alia said that the main requirement here was for writers and artists to portray in the broadest and clearest manner "the struggle, life, work, ideals and aspirations" of the people. He suggested that in order to do this more effectively they would have to mingle with the people in the factories and machine shops, in mines and farm cooperatives, in schools, military installations, towns, and villages.

In sum, by focusing attention on literature and the arts, the Fifteenth Party Plenum made them an issue of vital national concern. Alia's report to the plenum implied a number of things: (1) The intelligentsia must henceforth submit more thoroughly to the Party's authority. (2) Albania must weaken her cultural ties with the outside world and turn inward in the search for themes and resources for cultural exploitation. (3) The Party would not tolerate experimentation on the part of writers and artists but would insist on strict conformity to its line on art and culture. (4) Cultural centralism—as opposed to cultural polycentrism, liberalism, and humanism—would remain in force as a policy for regulating the cultural life of the country. Finally, Alia's remarks about the need for a closer rapport between creative artists and the masses hinted at a possible rectification program for intellectuals to overcome their alleged alienation from manual laborers.

The Fifteenth Party Plenum was held on the eve of Albania's cultural revolution and was followed by a number of developments that changed in some ways the character of the arts and the lives of many artists. On December 3 and 4, 1965, LAWA held a meeting in Tiranë to discuss the conclusions of the Fifteenth Party Plenum—in effect, to approve, publicize, and underscore their urgency.[40] The meeting was attended by Manush Myftiu, APL Politburo member, and Fadil Paçrami, minister of culture and the arts. Myftiu presented LAWA with the Order of the Red Flag of Labor, in testimony to "the high appreciation by the Party . . . of the great work done by [the] League in organizing, mobilizing and educating writers and artists" and in furthering the communist education of the masses.[41] The league in turn expressed its "boundless gratitude" to the Party for its constant support and aid and assured it of its loyalty.

The Cultural Revolution and the Arts

In early 1966, Albania began her cultural revolution, almost simultaneously with the launching in China of the Great Proletarian Cultural Revolution. The first step in Albania's "great leap forward" in the intensified struggle against alien ideologies and domestic bureaucracy was ostensibly taken by the artistic intelligentsia. On January 27, 1966, ninety-one writers and artists signed a letter—subsequently published in *Zëri i popullit*—in which they pledged to go out to the countryside and work and live among the people "in order to be inspired" by them. Presently, forty of them moved out to various rural areas along the coast and the hinterland.[42] Some of them spent as long as two to three years in the countryside before returning to urban life. The Party's program for the Rectification of Intellectuals had begun.

The fact that the intelligentsia became the first concern of the cultural revolution illustrated once again the Party's uneasiness over this social segment. The dispersal of writers and artists to the countryside was seen by the Party as a step toward breaking down the barriers between the city and the countryside, between mental and physical labor, and in this manner accelerating the advance toward a more egalitarian society. Perphas, too, this was a calculated move by the Party leadership designed to break up the heavy concentration of the intelligentsia in Tiranë, possibly out of fear that their presence there might pose a threat to the Party's control of the cultural revolution which, after all, was a novel enterprise, pregnant with uncertainties.

It seems likely, also, that the bitter attack on Dhimitër Xhuvani in mid-1966—unparalleled for its invective since the onslaught on the anticommunist intelligentsia in the mid-1940s—was intended to intimidate the intellectuals, in order to further discourage dissent and stifle possible turmoil in the course of the cultural revolution. The attack on Xhuvani took the form of an article in the Party's daily on his novel, *Tuneli* (The tunnel), a work about the construction of the Bistricë hydroelectric power station in southern Albania.[43] The article said that Xhuvani had become "a captive of bourgeois and revisionist literary currents." It added: "In this novel we are not dealing with partial errors, or slips, but with a work which is completely negative, which contains grave political and ideological distortions, and where we see clearly foreign bourgeois-revisionist esthetic concepts, the decadent spirit, the bleak and scornful portrayal of our socialist reality and working people." Startled by the sharp attack, Xhuvani responded by making self-criticism, and with that tensions subsided and the incident was closed. The assault on Xhuvani was the high point in the confrontation between the Hoxha leadership and the intelligentsia during the cultural revolution.

At APL's Fifth Congress in November 1966, the atmosphere was charged by the militant and somewhat feverish climate generated by the cultural revolution. In his report to the congress, Enver Hoxha called for a further radicalization of literature and the arts, demanding that they "become a powerful weapon in the Party's hands for educating the workers in the spirit of socialism and communism. . . ."[44] He asked for similar submission and allegiance on the part of all artistic and cultural institutions; they, too, "must be guided by the ideopolitical demands of the party." Hoxha also defended the policy of sending writers and artists back to the countryside. He said that "mental laborers and especially the creative, artistic, and academic intelligentsia [are] particularly divorced from physical labor" and as a result "provide a fertile terrain for the spread of individualism and careerism, arrogance and conceit . . . intellectualism and scorn of the masses."[45] The implication was that by mingling with the working people, intellectuals would be better able to ward off such dangers to their ideological and moral health and growth.

As the cultural revolution entered its second year in 1967, it achieved its greatest and most dramatic "victory" when the Party brought down the religious establishment of the country. The artistic intelligentsia was called upon to make its own contribution to the abolition of the condemned institution, and it responded by producing a spate of books, essays, poems, and plays attacking religion as anachronistic, alien to Albanian culture, and damaging to the social and economic fabric of the country. In September 1967, *Nëndori* wrote that Albania had become the first atheist nation in the world.[46]

The development of the cultural revolution accentuated the isolation of the art community from the world at large. Thus, in a reversal of previous policy, Albania scaled down her cultural exchanges with other countries. Similarly, there was a notable reduction in the publication of foreign works of literature. This trend reached an extreme in 1968 when *Nëndori*, contrary to its custom, failed to publish any works by non-Albanian authors in its issues for that year.

The Party in Albania presented itself to the intelligentsia and the masses as a nearly infallible teacher and guide. It exercised control over writers and artists through the Ministry of Education and Culture and the League of Albanian Writers and Artists—two institutions that served as direct links between the Party and LAWA members. Finances served as another means of Party control over the art community, since writers and artists, like other members of the Albanian society, are paid by the government. The Party thus exercised nearly total control over their work and livelihood.

Such conditions fostered the development of a cult of the Party and its leadership. The following poem about the Party is a sample of the literary pieces that both reflected and fomented the cultist attitude.

The Party—it is my first and last love,
The red rose of peace over the graves of the fallen,
The golden promise of future triumphs....
The Party—it is the loaf of bread on the breakfast table of everyone.
The Party—it is the warmth of our handshake,
The fire in our heart beating within the heart of the world,
Every good thing I have or ever shall have.
The Party—it is my first and last song.[47]

Enver Hoxha, leader of the Party since its formation in 1941, has been eulogized in recent years in every art form, above all in poetry, painting, and sculpture. He became the subject of a "personality cult" in Albania, as can be seen, for example, in the following lines, taken from a poem entitled "Enver."

I first heard those five dear letters at the dawn of my life.
Ever since, your name became as dear to me as my paternal home,
As precious as socialism,
As lofty as the mountains,
As vital as light. . . .
We shout ENVER!
   And the sky seems to us loftier than ever,
   The space around us vaster,
   The sun bigger,
   And our perspectives ever more magnificent.
We shout ENVER!
   And our days take on color and meaning
   As they fall in like soldiers
   Into the great ranks of the revolution.[48]

The Hoxha leadership has always denied the existence of a personality cult in Albania. Yet the evidence of such a cult seems irrefutable. The Party's claim of being nearly infallible, its strict authoritarian rule, the suppression of criticism of its basic policies, and its practice of calling attention constantly to its accomplishments created a fertile soil for the birth and growth of a cult around Hoxha and the Party.

The Second LAWA Congress (1969)

Twelve years after the holding of its founding congress, the League of Albanian Writers and Artists convened its Second Congress in Tiranë in April 1969. The two-day congress, held from April 24 to 26, occurred almost simultaneously with the convocation of the Ninth Congress of the Chinese Communist Party, which signaled the end of the Chinese cultural revolution. The Second Congress may thus be said to mark the end, at least, of the most intense and dramatic period of Albania's own cultural revolution and its reversion to a more normal or conventional pattern, a condition described by the regime as "the uninterrupted revolution."

The Second LAWA Congress did not have any dramatic high points. In his greetings to the congress, APL's Politburo representative, Ramiz Alia, again reaffirmed that literature and the arts must serve as "weapons . . . of the Party for the communist education of the masses" and that the artistic intelligentsia must be on guard against bourgeois and revisionist aesthetics.[49]

As usual, the main report to the congress was presented by Dhimitër Shuteriqi, president of LAWA.[50] Shuteriqi reported that since the First Congress the membership of the league had grown from 150 to 400. In his remarks on the struggle to preserve the method of Socialist Realism in the arts, he made reference to the condemned works of Arapi, Buxheli, Prifti, and Xhuvani. In addition, he criticized certain other works, including Kadare's novel *Gjenerali i ushtrisë së vdekur* (General of the dead army), first edition; Petro Marko's novel, *Qyteti i fundit* (The last city); some short stories by Dritëro Agolli, which Shuteriqi described as "antirealist and almost mystical" in character. Shuteriqi also attacked such manifestations in the arts as patriarchalism; sentimentalism; folklorism, or the preference for archaic songs and especially music that evokes arcadian scenes; and ethnographism, or the tendency to emphasize the material aspects of culture rather than its ideological aspects, including the psychology and behavior of the characters in a particular work of art.

Since 1957, the ranks of the intelligentsia had grown steadily, as the arts and cultural institutions in the country continued to expand. Accordingly, a proposal was made and adopted by the Second LAWA Congress to extend membership in the League to stage and film actors, dancers, and architects. By October 1970, when the League celebrated its twenty-fifth anniversary, its membership had grown to 490.[51] Party membership, however, was not a condition for admission to LAWA. In fact, most writers and artists were not Party members. Thus, of the 400 writers and artists residing in Tiranë in early 1973, only a little over 100 were communists.[52] The low percentage was the result apparently of a rare coincidence of interests on the part of the artistic intelligentsia, which preferred not to have formal ties to the Party; and the Hoxha leadership, which was reluctant to grant membership to intellectuals for fear of weakening and destabilizing Party ranks.

A Revealing Incident

The Albanian leaders have made much of the principle that the judgment of the people must be respected and that the masses are the best critics of a work of art. An incident, however, that occurred in 1969, in connection with Albania's twenty-fifth anniversary of liberation, reveals that the Party violated its professed principle and ignored the collective judgment of the people.

In late October 1969, the Fourth National Festival of the Dramatic Theater was held in Tiranë, as part of the preliminary festivities for the twenty-fifth anniversary jubilee. Prizes were awarded for the best plays, with the first prize going to Minush Jero for his drama *Njolla të murme* (Gray stains), a play about the class struggle against the bourgeois mentality of certain elements in contemporary Albanian society. Kudret Velça, a leading drama critic, wrote a very favorable review of the play, noting along the way its "enthusiastic reception by the public."[53] Jero's prize-winning drama aroused the interest of the Party's first secretary, who went to see it, accompanied by a majority of the members of the Politburo.[54] Apparently the APL leadership did not like what it saw, for shortly after, *Zëri i popullit* came out with a stinging editorial attack on Jero's play, assailing it as a "misleading portrayal" of Albanian reality and accusing its author of "inability to see phenomena from a Marxist-Leninist viewpoint."[55] The editorial went on to attack the A. Z. Çajupi theater troupe of Korçë that staged the play, the panel of judges that awarded it the first prize, and the Ministry of Education and Culture for including the play in the drama festival program.

As a result, the first prize was taken away from Jero and was given instead to Loni Papa for his play *Marga* (proper name), a decidedly inferior piece and probably the least worthy of all his plays.[56] In it Papa attempted to show that the poor masses are the moving force of society, but the piece suffers from amateurish dialogue, lacks a sense of the theater and coherence of thought, and is peopled with characters that are mere caricatures of human beings.

The Jero incident showed the Party's arbitrary position in evaluating a work of art and its indifference to the judgment of the public in matters of artistic taste. It showed that a serious gap existed between the Party's perception of cultural reality in Albania and the perception of that reality by the artistic intelligentsia and the public. Furthermore, the incident revealed that the Party leadership was isolated in its policy on the theater, and probably on the entire spectrum of art and culture.

Subsequently, Jero wrote another play, *Të pamposhturit* (The indomitable ones), which the critics called "a good work," thus enabling its author to restore to some extent his reputation as an "ideologically mature" artist.[57] By 1973 Jero seemed thoroughly vindicated as a playwright of merit—not, however, by the overseers of culture but by the people themselves. His play, *The History of One Night*, which was condemned in 1965, was being staged in Gjirokastër—Hoxha's birthplace—and in other communities, including Tiranë, in spite of continuing attacks on it by Party spokesmen.

Jero's victory over the cultural bureaucracy was not only a personal triumph; it was also a small victory for free expression in the arts and free choice for the art-consuming public. It revealed that the public was resisting the Party's attempts to define cultural and artistic values for it, regulate public taste, and—in this instance, at least—censor a work of art that had broad popular appeal.

Apart from the Minush Jero incident, the twenty-fifth liberation anniversary jubilee was interesting for the other prizes that were given to winners in the national contest for the best works in literature and the arts. The top prizes in literature went to Xhuvani, Arapi, Prifti, and Buxheli—writers who in 1965 and 1966 were attacked for allegedly straying off the path of Socialist Realism.[58] Undoubtedly, the works of these writers had exceptional artistic merit, for Xhuvani and the other top prize winners are among the best and most influential authors in contemporary Albania. Yet it is likely that political considerations as well influenced the decision of the judges. This seemed to be the Party's way of reaffirming its confidence in those particular writers and "rehabilitating" them, as it were, following their partial and momentary lapse into "bourgeois and revisionist error." It was one of the techniques used by the Hoxha leadership for controlling the intelligentsia: to assail artists and writers when they committed ideological errors but to be ready to reward them when they showed by their subsequent work that they had overcome their errors.[59]

New Rectification Program

As the decade of the 1970s opened, rumblings among the artistic intelligentsia about the limitations of Socialist Realism in the arts and culture continued. The Party, as usual, responded with a new propaganda campaign to stamp out, or at least to neutralize, the dissenting voices. At first, the propaganda effort focused on the evils of conservatism, or that which was archaic and patriarchal and therefore a stumbling block to the development of progressive forces in culture and other spheres of Albanian life. In 1972-1973, however, the focus of attacks shifted toward liberalism, or modernist trends in the arts and culture, including literature, fashions, music, radio, the theater, television, and the dance.

One of the means adopted for combating the harmful effects of both conservatism and liberalism, and for stimulating the growth of the arts in accordance with the prescriptions of Socialist Realism, was the creation in 1971 of Committees of Culture and the Arts in all districts of the country. Yet, after two years complaints were heard that many committees, including that of Tiranë, had all but ceased to operate.[60]

In February 1972, at a LAWA meeting called to discuss the implications for the arts of the conclusions of the Sixth Party Congress—held in November 1971—Ramiz Alia warned that "there are young men and women [in Albania] who read books by Camus or Sartre and dicusss existentialism."[61] Five months later, Alia found it necessary to address himself again to the problem of literature and culture. Speaking at a gathering of the Party's Central Committee on July 7, he noted that existentialist as well as Freudian authors were being read in Albania and complained also that the public was exposed to harmful alien influences through the media of television and the cinema.[62]

Alia's cue was picked up by the propaganda media, as the Party launched a new and massive campaign against liberalism. Writers, intellectuals, and cultural workers were mobilized in the campaign and spoke out forcefully against alien influences in the arts and culture, going so far as to criticize parents who gave their children non-Albanian names.[63] Meetings were held by Party organizations, the Ministry of Education and Culture, and LAWA to analyze problems of culture in the light of liberal manifestations and discover solutions to them. A report on the Fifth Tiranë Party Conference, published in the Party daily on April 20, 1973, noted that alien influences in the area of culture "were not peripheral, but central," and that "notable concessions" in the direction of liberalism had been made by the Tiranë Radio and TV, the Theater of Opera and Ballet, and the People's Theater. The report warned that "there must be no place for concepts according to which problems of art and culture . . . are best dealt with by the creative artists and specialists [in the arts] themselves," since such ideas "lower the leading role" of the Party.

As the campaign against liberalism developed, there were attacks on the literature of recent years, particularly on the novel and poetry. Writers were admonished for showing little interest in epic and heroic themes—such as class, nation, society, history, struggle—and concentrating instead on individualism; that is, their own feelings, attitudes, visions, and intuitions. Writing on "modernistic" poetry, Koço Bihiku, well-known art critic, found such poetry to be pantheistic, illogical, hermetic, and obscure. "Some poets," he siad, "did not care whether the masses of the people understood their works."[64] He complained that some recent poems pictured man as "a weak being, impotent, a toy of blind world forces," a concept that was "not far from the thesis of the existentialists" that in this absurd world man is an abandoned being, impotent and alone. Bihiku also assailed "certain editors of literary organs [namely, *Nëndori* and *Drita*] who thought that civic-minded and patriotic poetry is passé, that it sounds too much like agitation."[65] Dritëro

Agolli, a poet, charged that many of the younger poets were identifying themselves with natural phenomena and inorganic objects—the sea, earth, mountains, trees, rocks—instead of with the working masses and their problems.[66]

There were attacks on artists of the Theater of Opera and Ballet for their fondness for bourgeois stage settings and on foreign TV programs, especially Italian television which, according to the regime, was addicted to "the reactionary politics" of the Vatican and the decadent American way of life with its "cult of crime."[67] Individual tastes in matters of culture that ran counter to Marxist-Leninist standards of aesthetics and morality became a favorite target of attack, as did also those artists and critics who advocated or defended enthusiasm and spontaneity in artistic expression, as opposed to control and discipline. In rejecting the notion that taste is a purely personal matter, Party ideologists argued that one's tastes can influence society and therefore society has a right to criticize and mold the individual's tastes. One critic, for example, argued that outward appearances were ideologically and politically significant.

. . . to accept the extravagant bourgeois and revisionist mode of dress is to create an appropriate terrain for undermining socialist attitudes, behavior, and convictions. To think that long hair and narrow pants or miniskirts have nothing to do with one's world outlook, one's ideology, is as naive as it is dangerous. Not to fight alien fashions means to give up the fight against the penetration of the degenerate bourgeois and revisionist ideology.[68]

Albanian communists maintained that, unless checked in time, liberal attitudes in the arts translate into liberal manifestations in morals, and liberalism in morals translates into liberalism in ideology and politics, ending finally in the overthrow of the dictatorship of the proletariat.[69] Yet, despite the intense campaign against liberalism, or the penetration of Soviet and Western cultural influences, influential segments of the artistic intelligentsia persisted in their dissent from Party directives on art and culture. This became evident from remarks by Mantho Bala, a vice-minister of education and culture. Writing about dissent in the theater, Bala acknowledged that many artists of the dramatic theater had been afflicted by such liberal concepts as: "We must learn from others," "We must keep in step with the times," and "We are in Europe."[70]

"We are in Europe"—a revealing and significant remark. The phrase was a reaffirmation of Albania's historical links with European culture. It indicated that Albanian artists and youth in general identified with the Continent. The remark amounted to a rejection of the Party's militant and separatist ideology on art and culture.

Apparently disturbed by these manifestations of liberalism, the Party resurrected a policy it first instituted in January 1966, at the inception of the cultural revolution. It embarked on a new Rectification Campaign for the artistic intelligentsia. Thus, in mid-April 1973, the writers and artists of Tiranë ostensibly took the initiative and addressed a letter to Enver Hoxha, saying that forty-eight of them were leaving the capital and going to construction centers, factory locales, and cooperatives throughout the country in order to "live side by side with the people" and be inspired by them.[71] A month later, it was announced that eighty more writers and artists were leaving for the countryside and various industrial sites, to live there for periods of two to six months.[72]

The fact that Party officials reverted to the rectification technique to deal with the latest wave of dissent indicated that the Party did not intend to review its policy on the arts or to make any concessions to the aspirations of dissident writers and artists. If there were any doubts on this point, they were dispelled the following month, when the Fourth Party Plenum convened in Tiranë on June 26 to hear a report by Hoxha on "the struggle against alien influences and liberal attitudes."[73] Hoxha said that Albania would continue on a revolutionary course and insisted that art and culture must remain loyal to proletarian partisanship; that is, they must continue to serve as instruments of the Party, instead of seeking to be independent and experimenting with liberal forms of expressions. He defended the maintenance of a militant posture for the country on the ground that the struggle against alien influences was a life-and-death confrontation, on the outcome of which depended the fate of socialism in Albania and the very existence of the Party itself.

The Party's first secretary buttressed his argument on the need for vigilance and militancy by pointing to the old specter of the "capitalist-revisionist encirclement" of the country. But the general impression created by the secretary's report was that the Party felt besieged, not so much by its enemies abroad as by a restive population, particularly the intelligentsia, which questioned increasingly the rationale of the Party's highly doctrinaire and puritanical stand on the arts.

On July 24 and 25, 1973, a plenum was held by LAWA, attended by Politburo member Ramiz Alia. The plenum resulted in a shake-up of the entire LAWA leadership. Shuteriqi, president of LAWA since 1946, fell from power and was replaced by poet Dritëro Agolli, who also delivered the main report to the plenum.[74] Vilson Kilica was replaced as general secretary of the league by Xhemal Dini, and Hamide Stringa and Ksenofon Dilo were replaced as secretaries of the league by Anastas Kondo and Kujtim Buza.

A lengthy report on the LAWA plenum, published in *Zëri i popullit*, July 28, 1973, revealed that a purge of "anti-Party" elements had been carried out. The purge led to the ousting from their posts of two high-ranking Party officials: Fadil Paçrami, a leading playwright, member of the APL Central Committee, and Secretary of the Tiranë Party Committee; and Todi Lubonja, APL-CC member, former secretary of the Korçë district Party Committee, and former president of the Albanian Labor Youth Union, who was closely associated with the Tiranë radio and television stations. Paçrami was attacked as an "enemy of the party and the people" who nourished "counterrevolutionary aims," while Lubonja was accused as "a Right deviationist ... who supported liberal-opportunist viewpoints and had modernist aesthetic tastes...."[75]

From all indications, the central motive for the campaign against liberalism in the arts was not so much to combat alien influences as to maintain the Party's Stalinist control over the intelligentsia, as a means of preserving state power. To stifle the rising voices of dissent, the Party went so far as to invade the privacy of individuals and dictate to the citizenry on matters of manners and morals. The Hoxha leadership thus created a climate of intolerance and persecution of the intelligentsia reminiscent of Calvin's theocracy in the Switzerland of the sixteenth century and that of the Italian monk Savonarola in the fifteenth century. An ironic twist, indeed, for an atheist state.

After the Purge

In the three-year period from 1973 through 1976, there were no notable manifestations of dissent in the area of the arts and culture. In 1974, the Party made energetic efforts to mobilize the artistic community in the preparations for the observance of the thirtieth anniversary of Albania's liberation from the Italian-German occupation armies. Writers and artists were invited to participate in a "literary-artistic contest" to honor the jubilee. Over 2,200 works were entered in the contest. The winners were announced on November 27, 1974. A total of 261 prizes were awarded in sixty-six categories of competition, ranging from literature, painting, and sculpture to radio scripts, popular songs, drawings, and photography.[76] Also in November the Council of Ministers announced the winners of the prestigious Prize of the Republic, which is given in recognition of "distinguished works" in the fields of science, invention, literature, and art. Of the forty-four prizes given for such works, twelve went to artists, among them: Dritëro Agolli and Nasho Jorgaqi (writers); Kristaq Rama, Mumtaz Dhrami, and Shaban Hadëri (sculptors); Nikolla Zoraqi (composer); and Zoica Haxho (ballerina).[77]

On December 20, 1974, Enver Hoxha gave a speech at a meeting of the Secretariat of the Party's Central Committee on the subject of literature and the arts.[78] The speech was intended as a review of the situation in the arts since the holding of the Fourth Party Plenum in June 1973. In general, the Party's first secretary repeated the themes presented at the June plenum, urging writers and artists to follow closely the guidelines of Socialist Realism in their creative work, struggle against the penetration of bourgeois and revisionist influences in their work and life, and strive to imbue the working masses with sound communist virtues. He expressed the hope that LAWA would not become a "bureaucratic organ" but rather a center for spirited discussion of philosophical, artistic, and aesthetic ideas. The notion was reminiscent of Mao's celebrated slogan to "Let one hundred thoughts contend," but the Albanian intelligentsia had probably learned by this time not to take such pronouncements at face value.

Hoxha was rather harsh on Albanian art critics, warning them not to imitate modern bourgeois critics whose work is vitiated by "obscure, confusing and disorienting" ideas. He complained that Albanian cinemas were showing harmful capitalist and revisionist films, imported from such countries as Czechoslovakia, Romania, and Hungary, and urged the production of more Albanian films, which "are marvelous compared to films from abroad peopled with bandits and cowboys."[79] Furthermore, he was disturbed over the "disinterest" of writers in producing manuscripts for the theater, as well as libretti and film scripts. At the same time, Hoxha was unusually generous in praising by name a good number of artists, especially actors, composers, and popular singers. Finally, several times in the course of his speech, he made favorable references to classic Western art, including music, literature, and drama. He spoke well of the music of Liszt, Chopin, and Bizet and lauded classic French prose and poetry and "the immortal comedies" of Molière. In general, Hoxha's speech revealed his pride in Albania's cultural heritage and the basic contradiction between his ruthlessly authoritarian political philosophy and his fondness for the great art of Western civilization.

Responding to Hoxha's programmatic speech on the arts, the Directing Committee of LAWA met in Tiranë in late February 1975 and heard a report by Dritëro Agolli, president of the organization. Agolli's remarks gave the impression that the artistic intelligentsia was entirely loyal to the Party leadership and accepted without reservations the role assigned to it by the Party; namely, to use artistic talent to further the cause of socialism in Albania. In a revealing comment about Fadil Paçrami, Agolli noted that the fallen cultural leader and his followers had agitated for "an apolitical art," arguing that a work of art that was "deeply political in content" reduced itself to propaganda. Paçrami, he said, had argued in favor of the "free theme" in art; that is, that artists should not be restricted in the choice of subject matter for their work.[80] It proved to be a risky position, which led eventually to his downfall.

An event of major cultural interest was the announcement in Tiranë on March 5, 1975, of the latest winners of the coveted Artist of the People award. A total of nine artists, seven men and two women, were honored with the title. Among the winners were Avni Mula, singer; Çesk Zadeja, composer; and Marie Logoreci, a veteran actress. In addition, seventeen other artists, nine of them women, were given the title Artist of Merit, the second most prestigious title for high artistic achievement given by the Albanian Republic. The ritual of awarding prizes and titles to artists served a double purpose: from the Party's viewpoint, it was a politically useful exercise, insofar as it helped the leadership win the cooperation and loyalty of the intelligentsia; while from the viewpoint of the individual artist, it satisfied the longing for recognition of one's creative ability by others.

As with the celebration of the thirtieth anniversary of the country's liberation in 1974, so in 1976 the regime expected the artistic intelligentsia to make its contribution to the commemoration of the thirty-fifth anniversary of the founding of the Party. All the more so, in fact, since the anniversary coincided with the holding of the Seventh Party Congress. Thus, throughout 1976 the dominant tone of the press on art and culture was pride in the gains achieved in the cultural sector, especially since 1973, and optimism concerning prospects for continuing progress in the future. In a comment on the Seventh Party Congress (November 1-7), the *Nëntori* review called on all workers in the field of culture to mobilize all their resources in order to fulfill the tasks set forth by the congress for the further development of the country's cultural life. The review expressed confidence that by fulfilling their duties, the intelligentsia of Albania would render not only a great service to the fatherland but would become "an example to all revolutionaries throughout the world."[81]

In sum, it seemed that by the end of 1976 all dissent among members of the intelligentsia in Albania had largely disappeared, or at any rate had been brought under effective control by the Hoxha-Shehu leadership. But if the past history of the Albanian intelligentsia is a guide, the official picture of contentment and tranquility in the arts was probably more apparent than real, and the simmering tensions underneath could be expected to surface again before long.

Closing Remarks

Relations between the Albanian Party of Labor and the artistic intelligentsia evolved, over some thirty years, in an uneasy fashion, moving from periods of tension and sharp confrontation to relative calm and cooperation. The relationship was apparently marred from the start, owing to the Hoxha leadership's deep-seated mistrust of intellectuals on the issue of political loyalty and political stability.

It was a curious attitude that gave rise to a rather awkward situation. Curious, because the intellectuals in Albania, men such as Kristoforidhi (1830-1895), Naim Frashëri (1846-1900), Petro Nini Luarasi (1865-1911), and Mihal Grameno (1872-1931), were the moving force of the Albanian national awakening that led to the country's independence from Turkish rule in 1912—a fact, moreover, that Party leaders acknowledged with a sense of pride and gratitude. Awkward, because the resulting tension between the Party and the intelligentsia placed the latter in a state of limbo, as it were, in the Albanian society—somewhere between the workers and the kulaks, neither fully accepted and catered to, like the working class, nor entirely damned and crushed like the former ruling classes. There is an element of irony here, too, for Hoxha himself is an intellectual; indeed, the only communist leader in East Europe with an intellectual background of any significance.

The Party was obviously fearful that dissent and liberal manifestations among the intelligentsia might reach the masses and "endanger the dictatorship of the proletariat"; which is to say, the very existence of the Party. One of the principal aims of the cultural revolution (1966-1969) was to eradicate—or at least reduce to impotence for a long time to come—bourgeois and revisionist influences in the arts and thus remove the causes of unrest in the spheres of art and culture and in other domains of society. But the fact that in the spring of 1973 such influences were very much in evidence in all aspects of culture was proof of the failure of the cultural revolution on this point. The latest wave of unrest among the intelligentsia not only affected individual artists but had reached even the editorial staffs of the leading literary organs in the country. That was a sign, surely, that the alienation of writers and artists from the Party was widespread, and perhaps irreversible.

One of the paradoxes of the latest confrontation between the Party and the intelligentsia was that it stemmed in part from the very technological progress achieved in Albania under communist rule. I am referring here to the Party's violent attacks on foreign TV, whose transmissions were being received by a growing number of private Albanian TV owners. It was a case of technology "undermining" the Party's ideology or, more correctly stated, a case of ideology lagging behind technology.

Another paradox was the "boomerang effect" of the Party's polemics against alien ideologies. For in the very act of attacking those ideologies—as, for example, the theories of Freud and Sartre, existentialism, surrealism, and abstractionism—Albanian polemicists imparted much information to their readers about those forbidden philosophies that they did not know before, thus whetting their appetites for more of the same. It was a bit like the story of the mother who tells her child to keep away from the cookie jar.

The unrest of intellectuals in communist Albania was to a large extent due to the Party's continuing efforts to isolate the members of the intelligentsia ideologically as well as geographically. As writers and artists, they were forbidden to overstep the boundaries of Socialist Realism, and as citizens they were forbidden to travel abroad, except as members of official delegations or as students. Such restrictions understandably generated frustration and resentment among members of the intelligentsia.

But, while it was easy for the Party to isolate the intelligentsia geographically, it could not realistically hope for similar success in the ideological realm. Albanian intellectuals were naturally drawn to Europe, particularly the West, for Albania is, after all, a part of Europe physically, spiritually, and culturally. They admired the West's superb achievements in art and culture and had high respect for Western technology, which gave birth to the Industrial Revolution, whose fruits Albania was just now beginning to enjoy.

The Party's policy therefore to insulate the intelligentsia from their colleagues in Europe, and from contemporary cultural and literary currents abroad, seemed unrealistic and self-defeating. Such a policy was successful when Albania was a part of the East European bloc and the Cold War had split the Continent neatly in two parts. But in an atmosphere of developing détente between East and West, and above all between the United States and China, communist Tiranë's separatist policy on the arts seemed strange, unreasonable, anachronistic, and provocative to the alert body of Albanian writers and artists.

"We must keep in step with the times." Such appeared to be the general sentiment of writers and artists. The remark suggested that, in their view, the Party's policy on the arts was sterile, stagnant, and ultimately regressive. It implied that a change of policy was needed if the arts and culture were to progress and keep more or less abreast of art developments abroad.

In December 1968, Enver Hoxha, in a rare but certainly commendable mood of modesty, said: "Who among us can say that he has not erred in his work?"

The evidence concerning the state of the arts in Albania in recent years suggested that the Party's position on this question was in error. Unless the Hoxha leadership were perceptive enough, and objective enough, to admit the error and correct it, the restlessness among the intelligentsia seemed almost certain to persist and to grow, perhaps to the point of becoming uncontrollable and dangerous to the social and political stability of the country.

10
The Developments in the Armed Forces

The postwar leadership of both the government and the armed forces of socialist Albania was the product of the Partisan struggle, which resulted in the destruction of the largely patriarchal prewar society and the triumph of the communist-led National Liberation Front. The shared wartime experience, with all the trials and hardships peculiar to guerrilla warfare, followed by the exhilaration of the victory that came in November 1944, served initially as a strong bond between the Party and army leaders in the period immediately following the war.[1] This bond was strengthened by their quasi religious commitment to the communist ideology and the sense of mission they felt with regard to establishing a new order in Albania.

At the same time, Party and army leaders alike were keenly aware that they faced great challenges and risks in the years immediately ahead. They knew that the Partisan victory did not guarantee the survival of communism in peacetime Albania. On the one hand, they were faced with the problem of reconstructing the war-ravaged country, which meant grappling with serious economic, social, and political challenges. On the other hand, they felt threatened by remnants of the fallen classes within the country and by powerful capitalist powers such as Italy, Greece, England, and the United States from without. The result was that they did not feel altogether secure in their new positions of power and responsibility. In such an unsettled situation, army and Party leaders had great need of each other if they were to rule successfully, or even to survive. It was necessary—even indispensable, under the circumstances—for them to cultivate unity and close cooperation with each other.

These were some of the factors that apparently made for stability and relative harmony in Party-Army relations in Albania in the early postwar period. This working relationship derived support also from the close ties the new leaders had developed with the Albanian masses, especially the impoverished peasantry, which had been the backbone of the Partisan army and which tended to perceive an identity of interests with the country's new political and military leaders. The solidarity between the political and military sectors was expressed by the Resolution of the First Congress of the Albanian Communist Party (1948), which said: "Our army is strong and loyal because our officers and army cadres have sprung from the fire of battle . . . [and] because it was created and grew in a spirit of loyalty to the people, to the Party. . . ."[2]
In 1952, Gen. Beqir Balluku, then army chief-of-staff, reaffirmed the close bond between the Party and the army, at a time when Albania had become a

focal point of Cold War tensions in the Balkans. Addressing the Second Party Congress, Balluku said: "Our people's army, which was created by the party in the fire of sharp struggles against foreign and domestic enemies . . . will always be ready . . . to fight [our] enemies, whenever the party and comrade Enver give the word."[3]

These citations are typical of the tone and attitude of the Army leadership toward the Party and the first secretary, Enver Hoxha, through three decades of socialist rule in Albania. The evidence shows, however, that the past three decades were not entirely free of tension and incidents between the Army and Party establishments. In fact, friction and high-level splits within the Party invariably had repercussions within the nation's armed forces, threatening time and again army-Party unity and stability. Crises of this sort led to charges of betrayal of the Party, socialism, and the country; and to arrests, trials, and purges of a number of powerful figures within the Party and the armed forces. The Albanian leadership has attributed these incidents primarily to outside forces, centering in "bourgeois, fascist, and revisionist" countries, above all Yugoslavia, the United States, and the USSR. In order therefore to better understand the course of events in army-Party relations in Albania and their consequences, one has to examine Albania's relations with the outside world and their effect on her military establishment and posture.

Relations with Yugoslavia

At the end of World War II, Yugoslavia emerged as Albania's closest ally, just as Tito's Partisans had been the closest collaborators of Albania's Partisans during the war. The growth of Belgrade's influence in postwar Albania was thus a logical and almost inevitable extension of the wartime collaboration between the Albanian and Yugoslav resistance fronts, led by Enver Hoxha and Tito, respectively. Yugoslav influences now spread to practically all areas of Albanian life, including the military. Indeed, Albania's military forces in the immediate postwar period "were equipped, trained and modeled after Yugoslavia's."[4] Still, beneath the surface of overt unity, cooperation, and friendship between Albania and her northern neighbor, there was a strong undercurrent of tension, which threatened to derail the alliance. According to Albanian sources, these tensions had their origin early in the war. In his speech at the November 1960 Moxcow Conference of 81 Communist Parties, Hoxha said:

As far back as 1942 . . . the Belgrade Trotskyite group . . . tried their utmost to hinder the development of our armed struggle, to hamper the creation of powerful Albanian partisan fighting detachments and . . . to put them under their direct political and military control. They attempted to make everything dependent on Belgrade and our Party and partisan army mere appendages of the Yugoslav Communist Party and the Yugoslav National-liberation Army.[5]

Hoxha further charged that in 1942 Tito tried to found a Balkan Federation and "place the partisan armies of the Balkan peoples under the Yugoslav Titoite staff."[6]

One area of Albanian-Yugoslav disagreement concerned the role of Albanian Partisans in Kosovo, the largely Albanian-populated province in Yugoslavia. Albanians allege that in autumn of 1943 Svetozar Vukmanović-Tempo, a member of the Central Committee of the Yugoslav CP, opposed the dispatch of Albanian Partisans to Kosovo for the purpose of aiding the war effort of the Albanian minority in that region. His reason reportedly was that Albanian CP leaders were chauvinistic and nourished "Great Albania" aspirations, meaning that they aimed at "annexing" Kosovo to Albania.[7] Rejecting the allegations of Vukmanović, the Hoxha leadership has claimed that Albanian Partisans were sent to Kosovo with the knowledge and full approval of Tito's hierarchy. They went there "at the request of the CP of Yugoslavia . . . to organize the Party and the struggle against the fascist invaders. . . ."[8] Albanian Party and military historians ignore the contributions to the buildup of Albanian Partisan forces, which Yugoslav sources say were made by Bllazho Jovanović and Vojo Todorović, two members of the Yugoslav military mission in Albania. They have denounced the role of two other Tito envoys in wartime Albania, Dušan Mugoša and Velimir Stojnić, but have praised Miladin Popović as an "internationalist communist" who "always upheld" the stand of the Albanian Party.

Another point of disagreement between the Yugoslavs and Albanians was the question of Albania's active military aid to Yugoslavia's National Liberation struggle. Albanian historians note that two brigades of the Partisan army, the Third and the Fifth, crossed the Yugoslav border on October 5, 1944, "at the request of the General Command of the Yuguslav National-liberation Army . . . to take part in operations against the German Nazis in Kosovo."[9] After the liberation of Albania in November 1944, the Fifth and Sixth Divisions of Albania's resistance forces pursued the German forces into Yugoslavia and fought against them side by side with Yugoslav Partisans. Over 15,000 Albanian Partisans are said to have fought in Yugoslavia for a period of nearly five months (October 1944-February 1945). They carried the struggle deep into Yugoslav territory and helped to liberate Kosovo, western Macedonia, Montenegro, part of Serbia, and the southern part of Bosnia-Herzegovina. Some of the towns they helped liberate were Priština, capital of Kosovo province; Novi Pazar, about forty-five miles from Albania; and Višegrad in Bosnia—the farthest point of penetration by Albanian forces—which lies nearly eighty miles away, or better than one-third of the way across Yugoslavia to Hungary from Albania's border.[10] At least 350 Albanian troops are reported to have lost their lives fighting in Yugoslavia "for the liberation of the peoples of Yugoslavia and the fraternal Albanians of Kosovo."[11]

For over two decades following the break with Albania in 1948, Belgrade maintained official silence on the question of Albanian participation in Yugoslavia's war of liberation, an attitude that caused much bitterness and indignation among the Albanians.

But the weight of the evidence offered by Albania in support of her argument in this controversy was such that in recent years Yugoslav sources began to acknowledge that Albanian Partisans did indeed participate in Yugoslavia's war of liberation. Appropriately enough, the acknowledgment came initially in the form of an article in the Yugoslav military journal, *Front*. The article was reprinted by the Albanian-language daily in Kosovo, *Rilindja* (Rebirth), in a series of reports published on September 19, 20, and 21, 1972. The series affirmed that in late November 1944 the Third and Fifth Albanian Partisan Brigades participated, "with Yugoslav permission," in the liberation of the towns of Prizren and Peć in Kosovo and that in late 1944 and early 1945 the Fifth and Sixth Divisions of the Albanian army took part in the final phase of the fighting in Montenegro and Sandzak (Bosnia). *Front* noted also that Albania was the only socialist country in Europe that was liberated without the help of foreign troops.[12]

In spring 1975, confirmation of Albanian claims on this issue came from the highest levels of the Yugoslav hierarchy. Stane Dolanć, a member of the LCY (League of Communists of Yugoslavia) Presidium, was reported to have said that Albanian Partisans had fought side by side with Yugoslav Partisans.[13] President Tito himself elaborated on this point during a television interview, when he said, "I would like to recall the part played by a number of units of the Albanian National Liberation Army in the struggle on our own territory. By mutual agreement they joined our forces in opposing the Germans, the *Ballists*, and the Chetniks in Western Macedonia, Kosovo, Montenegro and Bosnia."[14]

The remarks of Tito and Dolanć followed an announcement in March 1975 that a pact had been signed in Belgrade by Albanian and Yugoslav representatives for the transfer to Albania of the remains of Albanian Partisans who fell in Yugoslavia during World War II. The agreement was implemented in early December of 1975. A solemn ceremony was held in the Palace of Culture in Tiranë in memory of the fallen Partisans, whose remains had just arrived from Yugoslavia. Their coffins were interred in the Cemetery of the Martyrs of the Homeland in the suburbs of the capital.[15] It was the final, irrefutable confirmation of a little known historical fact in the wartime relations between Albania and her northern neighbor. The memorial ceremony—widely publicized by the Albanian press media—presumably put an end to the long-standing controversy between the Albanians and the Yugoslavs regarding Albania's contribution to the liberation of Yugoslaiva.

It has already been noted that Albanian-Yugoslav military relations during the war, especially with regard to Kosovo, had a dual character; that is, both a positive and negative side. Apparently this reflected, on the one hand, the strongly nationalist anti-Slav attitudes of large numbers of Albanians, above all Kosovo Albanians; and on the other hand, the internationalist, class outlook of the communist Albanian leadership which sought to work closely with Tito's Partisans, on the basis of a common political ideology. While the war lasted, the urgent needs of the struggle against the common Nazi-Fascist foes impelled Albanian and Yugoslav Partisans to make every effort to avoid friction between them. But actually there was a strong undercurrent of tension between the two resistance groups, stemming in part from the harsh treatment of the Albanian minority in Kosovo by the Yugoslavs. The Albanian communist leadership maintained official silence on the matter during the period of Albania's alliance with Yugoslavia (1944-1948). Subsequently, however, the injustices committed by the Yugoslavs against the Albanians in Kosovo, both during and after the war, became the subject of a vitriolic campaign by Albania against Yugoslavia.[16] Indeed, Belgrade officials later admitted that Kosovo Albanians had been persecuted, to a certain extent, but blamed the incidents of persecution to the policies pursued by the former vice-president of Yugoslavia, Aleksandar Ranković, who was purged in 1966.

Following the war, Belgrade's persistent efforts to expand its influence in Albania by using all available means, including a variety of pressure tactics, produced a profound split within the Albanian CP, which had significant repercussions on the army as well. Indeed, this has been the characteristic pattern in the development of postwar Party-army relations in Albania. Conflicts and purges within the armed forces invariably paralleled the crises within the Party leadership. The first major incident of this sort occurred at the Eighth Party Plenum in February-March 1948. Albanian sources assert that Yugoslavia sought to subvert the Albanian army at that plenum. Thus:

Under the influence of the Yugoslav Trotskyites, the Army's Political Directorate aimed at . . . [forcing] the withdrawal of Soviet advisers . . . and the extinction of our Army's and country's independence. . . . The men chiefly responsible for these serious errors . . . [were] Kristo Themelko, a member of the Politburo and Chief of the Political Directorate, and comrade Pullumb Dishnica, Deputy Director of the Political Directorate.[17]

These sources further contend that the Eighth Plenum went so far as to "accept [a proposal for] the unification of Albanian and Yugoslav armies."[18] The unification did not occur, owing to the Stalin-Tito break in June 1948. The break led to the collapse of the Albanian-Yugoslav alliance, the reorganization of the Albanian Party, and the dismissal from their posts of Themelko and Dishnica. This brought to an end Albania's first close alliance with a communist country and ushered in an era of bitter ideological polemics between Tiranë and Belgrade that have never been equaled in the history of communist interparty feuds.

Albania's leaders subsequently maintained that Belgrade's attempt to gain control of the Albanian army was part of a grand scheme to take complete control of the country. The Yugoslavs in fact achieved a large measure of success in manipulating the Albanian Party but made practically no headway in controlling the army hierarchy. No significant shifts in the top personnel of the armed forces occurred as a result of the Albanian-Yugoslav split. The Resolution of the Eleventh APL Plenum, held in September 1948, notes that "The Political Directorate of our Army collided with the General Staff of the Armed Forces, which had a correct orientation on political-military questions, and defended the correct line of the Party in the military sector."[19]

It is likely that the presence of Soviet military advisers in Albania at the time tended to discourage high-ranking military personnel from supporting the pro-Yugoslav faction in the Albanian Party Politburo. The history of friction between Albanian and Yugoslav leadership during the war, plus the residue of traditional anti-Yugoslav public sentiment in the country, may also have contributed to the same result. Furthermore, the fact that the top two leaders in the Partisan struggle, Enver Hoxha, Supreme Commander of the Armed Forces; and Mehmet Shehu, the most skillful and respected Partisan commander, were reportedly the leading opponnets of Yugoslavia's policy on Albania could not be easily ignored by the military hierarchy at the time.

Relations with the Soviet Union

Even while Albania was practically a satellite of Yugoslavia during 1944-1948, the Albanian Party and army leadership looked to Moscow as a counterweight to Belgrade and began prudently to cultivate relations with the Soviets. In his 1947 report on the Partisan war and the development of the army, Shehu made frequent references to the Red Army of the USSR. In effect, Shehu rejected the Yugoslav army as a model for the Albanian army and at the same time appeared to signal Moscow to give its support to the Hoxha-Shehu faction, within the Albanian Party, as against the pro-Belgrade faction of Koci Xoxe.[20]

Freed from Yugoslav tutelage and pressures and the resultant tensions and divisions within the Party and the Political Directorate of the army, the Albanian leadership achieved a measure of unity and sense of direction such as it had not known since the wartime period. Albania's leaders then moved quickly to forge an alliance with the Soviet Union, which they praised as the savior of their country from the Italo-German Fascists, and now from the "Yugoslav revisionists." The USSR became the model for Albania in building socialism, including her military establishment, while in the eyes of Albania's leaders Stalin became practically a demigod. Thus, the First Party Congress, held in 1948, decreed that the army must modernize on the basis of the military art of Stalin. The congress noted in addition that the liberation of Albania was due "above all to the heroic struggle of the peoples of the Soviet Union, to the glorious Soviet Army led by the Bolshevik Party . . . and the greatest genius of all times, Joseph Visarianovich Stalin."[21]

The regime's pro-Moscow orientation led to a rapid and steady increase in Red Army influence in Albania. Army instruction manuals, training programs, military tactics, defense policy, even military uniforms were patterend after the Red Army. Contacts and exchanges of army personnel between Albania and the Soviet Union grew steadily. Soviet military instructors and technicians came to Albania to help modernize the country's armed forces, while thousands of Albanians went to the Soviet Union to receive both military and political training. Gen. Beqir Balluku, until 1974 Albania's minister of defense, was one of those who studied at the Voroshilov Military Academy (1952-1953).[22] For a period of twelve years (1948-1960), Albania's army was trained, equipped, and supplied by Moscow. By 1960, Albania's defense arsenal bristled with an impressive array of arms, including tanks, modern artillery, MIG planes, a number of small naval craft, a dozen submarines, plus several Soviet missile batteries. When Albania joined the Warsaw Pact in 1955, she became a part of an international defense system. The country now felt less vulnerable to the threats of her "aggressive" neighbors: the Italian "imperialists," the Yugoslav "revisionists," and the Greek "monarcho-fascists."

However, as happened with Yugoslavia earlier, serious differences arose between the Kremlin and the Albanians in the decade of the 1950s over such developments as Khrushchev's rapprochement with Yugoslavia, the "revisionist" Twentieth CPSU Congress in 1956, the campaign against Stalin, the Hungarian revolution, and the emergent Sino-Soviet dispute. Unable to win Albania's unquestioning acceptance of the Soviet general line, Moscow began to apply "all-round pressure" against Tiranë—a tactic which aggravated Soviet-Albanian relations all the more. Speaking at the Moscow November 1960 Conference, Hoxha revealed among other things that there were differences between Albania and the USSR over military matters as well, as, for example, Albania's place in the Warsaw Pact and the attitude of Soviet diplomats in Tiranë toward Albanian military leaders. He accused Marshal R. Malinovsky, then Soviet minister of defense, of threatening Albania with expulsion from the Warsaw Pact.[23] He said further that following the June 1960 Bucharest Conference, the Soviet ambassador in Tiranë attempted to incite the generals of Albania's army against the Albanian Party and state.[24] Reportedly, the ambassador asked General Balluku: Are you going to stand by the Soviet Union, or will you go against it, as your leadership is doing?[25] In effect, Moscow was asking for a military coup in Albania. Balluku took his stand with Hoxha. It was a fateful decision, not only for Hoxha's personal fortunes but in terms of resolving a larger question; namely, whether Albania would remain in the Soviet camp or cast her lot with China.

Relations with the Soviets continued to worsen, following the November 1960 Moscow Conference. As a result, in the spring of 1961, Moscow "arbitrarily annulled" the military agreements it had signed with Albania and cut off completely "all shipments of arms" and other equipment essential to Albania's defense.[26] By summer of that year, the Soviets had expelled all Albanian military students and personnel from the USSR, recalled their military advisers and specialists from Albania, and, after bitter negotiations with Tiranë, managed to remove eight of their twelve submarines from the Vlorë naval base in southern Albania.[27] Albania reacted with characteristic fury over these moves by the Soviets. The Vlorë base incident in particular proved to be the climactic and irreversible point in the deterioration of Soviet-Albanian military relations and for that reason deserves some elaboration.

It appears that the Soviets signed an agreement with Albania in September 1957—which was renewed in May 1959—to build a naval-military base in Vlorë. The base was built, as agreed, thus enhancing considerably Albania's defense capability and at the same time providing the Soviets with an important military toehold in the Mediterranean region. The Albanians contend, however, that in March 1961, owing to the deterioration of Soviet-Albanian relations, Moscow confronted the Albanian leadership, via a Warsaw Pact resolution, with a demand to evacuate all Albanian personnel from the base and to place it "solely under Soviet command; [otherwise] the Soviet Government would proceed to the liquidation of the base."[28] In an indignant reply, dated April 5, 1961, Albania alleged that the presence of Soviet military personnel in Vlorë was temporary and conditional; that is, they were there merely to train the Albanians in the use of Soviet military equipment and techniques, following which they were to phase out of the base. Albania also laid legal claim to "all warships" and other naval ordinance on the base. In the face of strong Soviet pressure, however, Albania agreed to let the Soviets evacuate most of their subs and other military equipment, including missile batteries. The Soviet vessels left Albanian waters on May 26, 1961, while the remaining Soviet naval personnel left Albania on June 5, 1961. Embittered by Albania's attitude, the Soviets addressed a strongly worded note to APL leaders, accusing them of engaging in "piracy."[29] Thus ended the Vlorë base episode and the Soviet naval presence in Albania and the Adriatic.

Eleven years later, on November 28, 1972, Hoxha recalled the visit to Albania of N. Khrushchev and Marshal Malinovsky in May of 1959. During the visit of the Soviet guests to Vlorë, Hoxha claimed to have overheard Malinovsky remark to Khrushchev that Soviet control of the Vlorë base in effect gave the Soviets control of the Mediterranean.[30]

The Vlorë episode revealed perhaps better than anything else the conflicting perceptions of the Albanians and the Soviets regarding the latter's military presence on Albanian soil. The Soviets apparently expected—in return for heavy economic, financial, and military aid to Albania—to gain overwhelming, if not total, political and military influence in that country. The Albanians, on the other hand, ever anxious over their nation's sovereignty and mindful moreover of the near military takeover of the country by Yugoslavia a few years earlier, distrusted Soviet motives and perceived a direct threat to Albania's independence from the growing military presence of the USSR at the

Vlorë base. The CPSU and the APL leadership evidently misread each other's motives and basic interests. The Soviets presumably believed that Hoxha could not afford to risk the loss of Moscow's military support and the tie to the Warsaw Pact. Accordingly, they expected Hoxha to bend under pressure and accede to Moscow's demands for ideological and political conformity in return for a reversal of the decision to dismantle the Vlorë base. Hoxha apparently calculated that Albania as a whole, and especially the Vlorë base, was of such importance to Moscow's strategic interests that Khrushchev would not actually carry out his threat to pull out of Vlorë. He therefore concluded that he could afford to resist Khrushchev's pressure and force the Soviet leader to back down on his demands.

These and other miscalculations led finally to the total break in Albanian-Soviet relations in December 1961. Militarily, the break weakened Albania's defense posture, not only because of the loss of Soviet aid but because it brought about her de facto exclusion from the collective security system of the Warsaw Pact. Albania's leaders appreciated the fact that the country was now exposed and angrily charged that the "hostile, anti-Albanian" actions of the "Khrushchev clique" whetted the appetites of imperialist states to commit aggression against Albania.[31] The break with the USSR was a blow also to Albania's economy, since it forced the Hoxha regime to allocate funds for defense that were badly needed for the development of the economy. Finally, it isolated Albania politically and ideologically from the mainstream of European socialism.

Perhaps the best summary of Albania's "bill of particulars" against the USSR, with regard to their military relations, appeared in an article in the Party daily in 1965. Addressing itself to the Soviet defense minister, Marshal Malinovsky, the article said, in part:

In a perfidious and crude manner, you arbitrarily tore up the bilateral agreements, and trampled over the obligations which you assumed in accordance with, and in the spirit of, the dispositions of the Warsaw Pact for arming the Albanian Army and defending the Albanian People's Republic. You pilfered from us eight submarines, as well as Albanian warships which were in Sebastopol for repairs. You dismantled the Vlorë base and did your best to weaken the defensive force of the socialist camp and Albania, and to incite imperialist covetousness toward us. You crudely chased away our military staff studying in the Soviet Union. . . . You never wanted to know what [our Army] thought about questions . . . of defense.[32]

The above passage not only illustrates well the substance of the Soviet-Albanian dispute over military matters but reveals the depth of bitterness in

Tiranë against the Soviet military leadership, following the crystallization of the Soviet-Albanian split.

As was true of developments during Albania's alliance with Yugoslavia, so during the twelve-year period of the Soviet-Albanian alliance, army-Party relations reflected the tensions and crises that developed within the APL, spawning new arrests, defections, trials, and purges of military personnel and Party officials connected with the army. In February 1950, the Fifth Party Plenum expelled from the Party's Central Committee Gjin Marku and Nexhip Vinçani, on the ground that they were destroying the Party's policy and "undermining its leadership in the Army."[33] A year later, Beqir Ndou, a member of the Central Committee of APL, was dismissed from the Party and arrested for "revealing military secrets."

The de-Stalinization process that began in the USSR with the Twentieth CPSU Congress then spread to East Europe, had a slight repercussion in Albania as well. Thus, at the Tiranë Party Conference—held in April 1956—an army officer, Maj. Iljaz Ahmeti, made strong attacks on the Hoxha leadership, complaining among other things that there was a great gap in the living standards of high Party officials and the Albanian masses. Ahmeti's remarks implied that the Party leadership had become an oppressive "new class" in Albania. He was promptly arrested and imprisoned, along with twenty-seven others who had voiced similar views at the conference.[34] The 1956 thaw in Eastern Europe apparently was a factor in the flight from Albania to Yugoslavia in May 1957 of Maj. Gen. Panajot Plaku, an oft-decorated officer and former deputy minister of national defense. Plaku had previously been in the USSR, where he had completed studies at the Soviet Military Academy (1948-1950). According to a Moscow radio broadcast on July 25, 1964, Plaku had fled because there was "no democracy in the Albanian Party" and because "Hoxha and the tiny group which he dominates constantly make decisions with no references to . . . party statutes, or Albanian law."[35] Hoxha subsequently called Plaku a traitor who favored normalization of relations with Yugoslavia and the rehabilitation of pro-Yugoslav and anti-Party elements, such as Koci Xoxe. Plaku's gravest offense, however, according to Hoxha, was that he was involved in a 1956 plot to overthrow the APL leadership.[36] In his speech at the November 1960 Moscow Conference, Hoxha alleged that Khrushchev himself was an accomplice of Plaku in a scheme to "eliminate the leadership of Albania . . . under the pretext that we were 'anti-Marxists and Stalinists.'"[37]

The growing differences between the Soviet Union and Albania in 1960 were apparently responsible, in part, for the arrest and subsequent purge of a number of officials in the Albanian army, Party, and government. The defendants reportedly were part of a joint Greek-Yugoslav-Italian-U S. Sixth Fleet counterrevolutionary plot to overthrow the Albanian government. The leader of the group was said to be Rear Adm. Teme Sejko, commander of Albania's naval forces. The defendants were tried in May 1961; Admiral Sejko was found guilty and sentenced to death and was executed forthwith.[38] The Albanians later implicated the Soviets as well in the alleged plot, stating they had documents that proved Moscow's complicity in the affair. According to Albania, the Soviets knew about the plot but kept silent about it, because they "intended to exploit it for their own purposes."[39]

The Teme Sejko trial came at the height of Albania's differences with Moscow over the Vlorë naval base and mirrored not only the severe tensions the Soviet-Albanian alliance was undergoing but also the continuing friction in Albanian army-Party relations. In October 1961, the Soviets held the Twenty-second Congress of the CPSU and publicly denounced the Albanian leadership. Albania's second close alliance with a communist nation—this time, with the world's first socialist state—had come to an end. Bitterly disillusioned with their alliances with European communist nations, Albania's Stalinist leaders turned their eyes toward the Far East, toward Mao Tse-tung and communist China.

Relations with China

Since Albania had already by 1961 drawn close to China on ideological and political issues, it was an easy step to develop similar military ties with the Chinese, following the split with the USSR. The Albanians had previously demonstrated their interest and leanings toward China in matters of military strategy and defense policies, at various interparty and international communist forums. In his speech to the November 1960 Moscow Conference, for example, Hoxha proposed that China be armed with atomic weapons. Taking issue with the Soviets on this point, he said: "We pose the question, why should Communist China not have the atomic bomb? We think that China should have it."[40] Hoxha's attempt to arm Peking with atomic weapons failed. But the Chinese nevertheless appreciated his efforts, and when Albania broke with the USSR, China began to fill the military vacuum created in Albania by the departure of the Soviets.

After 1962, Albanian-Chinese military cooperation became manifest in the exchange of messages of greetings and military delegations and in official statements on foreign policy and national defense. The Albanians responded with unrestrained enthusiasm to the news of China's advancements in military technology. When China exploded her first atomic bomb in October 1964, the Albanian Party daily announced the news in banner headlines and featured prominently the Chinese government's declaration on the successful test. Two years later (October 28, 1966), on the occasion of China's first successful test-firing of a guided nuclear missile, the Hoxha leadership wired a message to the Chinese leaders hailing the test as "an event of great historical importance" that further shattered the American-Soviet "plot" to maintain nuclear monopoly in the world.[42] On June 18, 1967, China succeeded in exploding her first hydrogen bomb—an event Albania called "an amazing success," which strengthened China's defense capability and increased her international prestige. "Let the American imperialists, Soviet revisionists and their servants tremble and be terrified by this colossal victory," warned Hoxha and Premier Shehu in their greetings to Mao.[42] In a similar vein, the Albanians spoke of China's launching of her first artificial satellite in March 1971 as "a shining new success" that proved their ally commanded all that was necessary "for the defense of the gains of the revolution and socialism."

The Albanians and the Chinese also dutifully exchanged fraternal messages on Albania's Army Day, July 10, and the anniversary of the Chinese People's Liberation Army (PLA) on August 1. When on March 4, 1966, Albania eliminated all military ranks and reinstated Party committees in the army, which had been eliminated after the war, and Party commissars, who were removed in 1956, China voiced warm approval. Marshal Lin Piao priased Albania's decision, saying that these were "important revolutionary measures, designed to place proletarian politics above all other things."[43]

Albanian-Chinese collaboration in the exchange of military delegations developed steadily since the mid-1960s and was apparently designed to serve Albania's military needs and at the same time advance her political and ideological ends. The prominent Albanian Party and government delegation that visited China in autumn of 1964 to attend the fifteenth anniversary of China's National Day was headed by Gen. Beqir Balluku. The delegation was in China from September 24 to October 12 and was received by Mao prior to its return to Tiranë. In late October 1966, one of the members of the high-level Chinese delegation that traveled to Tiranë to participate in the proceedings of the Fifth Congress of APL was Peng Shao-hue, deputy chief-of-staff of China's armed forces, an indication presumably that military matters were one of the items that concerned the Albanian and Chinese allies at the congress.[44] Two other members of the delegation were Kang Sheng and Li Hsien-nien, both of them members of the Politburo and Secretariat of the Communist Party of China (CPC). This was the time when the cultural revolution was in full swing in China and Albania, leaving China largely isolated from the rest of the world and causing widespread disruption within the country. It was a period when the Chinese leaders had an especially keen appreciation of the political and diplomatic value of frequent contacts with their Albanian allies.

Viewed in this context, it was not surprising that the following year three top-level Albanian delegations, including a military delegation headed by General Balluku, visited Peking and various parts of China. The Balluku delegation was in China for nearly a month (January 12 to February 7, 1967) and was met and feted in Peking by Yeh Chien-ying, CPC Politburo member and vice-president of the party's Military Council. Yeh said that Albania "symbolizes . . . the future of Europe," while Balluku priased "Mao's thought" and China's cultural revolution, which had shut the door to revisionist and bourgeois influences in that country. As in 1964, Balluku and the members of his delegation were received by Mao, with whom they had "an exceptionally cordial and warm discussion."[45]

The invasion of Czechoslovakia in August 1968 by a number of Warsaw Pact countries caused great indignation in Albania and alarm over her national security. The invasion prompted the Albanians to strengthen military ties with Peking and improve relations with Yugoslavia, with a view to enhancing the national security of their country. In September 1968, Albania formally withdrew from the Warsaw Pact, which she had joined in 1955, although she had ceased to attend pact meetings in 1961. The Albanians justified the withdrawal on the ground that the pact had abandoned its original purpose of affording security to its members and had become instead an instrument of aggression against them. The Chinese applauded Albania's action, and Mao Tse-tung wired a message to Hoxha and Shehu, assuring them that China would come to Albania's aid in case "American imperialists, Soviet modern revisionists and their servants" dared to attack it.[46]

To give substance to Mao's message, an Albanian Party and government delegation, headed by Defense Minister Balluku, arrived in Peking on September 29, 1968, at the invitation of the CPC and the Chinese government. The Albanians were given a warm welcome, with reassurances by the Chinese leaders, including Chou En-lai, that China and "other revolutionary peoples" in the world would aid Albania if the USSR were to attack it. On October 5, Balluku was reported to have had "very cordial talks" with Mao and Lin Piao.[47] The Balluku delegation left China on October 10, after a stay of two weeks.

Western press reports said that as a result of Balluku's talks with Chinese military leaders in Peking, China agreed to send Albania "more military material, including rockets."[48] The Chinese returned the visit in November 1968, when Huang Yung-sheng, chief-of-staff of the PLA, led a delegation to Albania to participate in festivities marking the twenty-fourth anniversary of her liberation.[49] This was the highest ranking Chinese military delegation ever to visit socialist Albania and served to underline China's growing interest and role in Albania's military affairs.

Some Western observers said at the time that Huang went to Tiranë to negotiate a Sino-Albanian defense agreement that would permit the Chinese to "establish naval and missile bases on the Adriatic coast" and "station troops" for the purpose of countering a possible Soviet naval attack on Albania from the Mediterranean.[50] It is true that the Huang delegation visited the Vlorë naval base early in December 1968, but no evidence has appeared to confirm reports that China and Albania had concluded a military pact. In view of China's great distance from Albania, and the absence of a Chinese naval fleet in the Mediterranean, it seemed implausible that Albania could have agreed to allow the Chinese to establish military bases on her soil and to "station troops" there. Far from acting as a deterrent to aggression, the establishment of a Chinese military presence in Albania was likely to have the opposite effect; namely, to operate as a magnet for attack by the Soviet Union. The Soviets for their part have pointed out to the Albanians that it would be unrealistic for them to rely on China for meaningful military help in case of a national emergency.[51] This is not to deny, however, that after 1961 Albania relied on China almost totally for military aid to meet her national defense needs. Accordingly, the Hoxha regime did not shrink from cultivating military relations with the Chinese, even after the Sino-Soviet border clashes in the spring and summer of 1969—which reportedly were a setback for China—and President Nixon's visit to Peking in February 1972, a development that Enver Hoxha did not welcome.[52]

On November 29, 1969, Albanian communists celebrated the twenty-fifth anniversary of their seizure of power. Their Chinese allies sent a high-powered delegation to Tiranë to commemorate the occasion. Headed by Li Hsien-nien, CPC Politburo member and deputy premier, the delegation included also Li Teh-sheng, a candidate member of the Politburo and member of the Party's Military Council; and Chang Tsai-chieh, the PLA artillery commander. The composition of the delegation demonstrated again the continuing interest of Hoxha and Mao in maintaining and developing their political as well as their military ties. This time, however, there were no foreign reports of any agreement by Albania to permit the Chinese to set up military bases on Albania's Adriatic coast. On the contrary, a Western journalist who visited Tiranë early in 1970 reported that the Albanians scoffed at the "idea of military cooperation with China"—in the sense, presumably, of signing a military pact, such as Albania had previously with Yugoslavia and the Soviet Union—for they remembered well "the lesson with the Russians."[53] He quoted an unnamed Albanian minister as saying: "We have no military agreement with China." This report found corroboration in a major foreign policy statement by Hoxha on October 3, 1974, when he said: "In our country there are no foreign military bases. . . ."[54]

Speculation on the above question became superfluous perhaps with the promulgation of Albania's new state Constitution in December 1976. The document rules out any foreign military presence in the country. It expressly says: "The establishment of foreign military bases and the stationing of foreign troops on the territory of the People's Socialist Republic of Albania is prohibited" (Art. 91). The main motive for this provision undoubtedly stemmed from Albania's desire to avoid a repetition of the unhappy consequences of her earlier military alliances with Yugoslavia and the Soviet Union. To a smaller extent, she was probably motivated also by the desire to quell the recurrence of reports that the country was becoming an advanced Chinese military outpost on the shores of the Adriatic.

On August 16, 1971, the highest ranking Chinese military delegation to visit Albania since November 1968 arrived in Tiranë. It was headed by Li Teh-sheng, chief of the Political Directorate of the Chinese army. Li arrived in Albania less than a month before the reported death of Lin Piao in a plane crash, following his fall from power. The Chinese spent a week in Albania and were received by Hoxha on August 20, but presumably Lin Piao did not enter their discussions. It appears that the Albanians were unaware at the time of Lin's declining fortunes, since in their speeches honoring the Li delegation they referred to him as "commander" of the Chinese army.[55] It was not until two months later that Albanian leaders eliminated all references to Marshal Lin.

At the invitation of the Chinese Ministry of National Defense, a top-level Albanian military delegation arrived in Peking on November 6, 1972, for a visit that lasted nearly five weeks. It was headed by Defense Minister Beqir Balluku and included the commanders of Albania's air force, navy, artillery, tank unit, and armored vehicles. Two other members of the delegation were Hito Çako, chief of the army's Political Directorate; and Gen. Rahman Perllaku,

Deputy chief-of-staff of the armed forces. The Balluku delegation traveled widely in China, stopping at half a dozen major cities, among them Shanghai, Naking, and Mukden. While in Peking, the delegation held several talks with Chou En-lai and top leaders of PLA.[56] Yet, unlike his visits to China in 1964, 1967, and 1968, this time Balluku was not received by Mao, suggesting possibly that the Chinese were disenchanted in some way with their Albanian allies. It was Balluku's last visit to China prior to his fall in July 1974.

When Albania celebrated the thirtieth anniversary of her army on July 10, 1973, China took an active part in observing the event. An editorial in PLA's organ, *Chieh-fang-chüng Pao*, dated July 10, expressed "hearty greetings" to the Albanian army, while the Ministry of Defense held a meeting in Peking at which the Chinese hailed the close ties between China and Albania. In the meantime, deputy chief of CPC's Military Commission Hsu Hsiang-chien, led a military delegation to Albania, accompanied by the vice-commander of the Chinese air force and marines. The Hsu delegation was feted by Balluku and later held talks with Premier Shehu (July 9) and Enver Hoxha (July 13). There was a possibly meaningful difference in the content and thrust of the speeches made by Hsu and his Albanian hosts, namely Balluku, Gen. Petrit Dume, and Hito Çako. For, whereas the Albanians were strongly militant and made vehement attacks against the United States and the Soviet Union, Hsu made no mention of the two superpowers but dwelt instead on domestic matters, particularly on army-Party relations in Albania.[57] At the same time, Hsu reaffirmed China's commitment to the preservation of her alliance with Albania: "We are brothers and close comrades-in-arms. Both in the long struggle against common enemies and in socialist . . . construction we support each other, inspire each other, and learn from each other."[58]

The Chinese delegation left Albania on July 14, after a stay of six days.

On November 26, 1973, the Chinese news agency, Hsinhua, announced that an Albanian military delegation had arrived in Peking for "a friendly visit." It was led by Gen. Petrit Dume, candidate member of the APL Politburo and chief-of-staff of Albania's armed forces. Dume was in China until December 27 but returned to Albania without being received by either Mao or Chou En-lai— a rather uncommon protocol, in view of the high-level character of the Albanian delegation. It is possible that Dume's trip to China was connected with the purges in the Albanian armed forces that occurred the following year.

For a period of about fifteen years following the break with the USSR, Albania was chiefly dependent on China for military aid. China was also seen as practically a guarantor of Albania's national security, as demonstrated by the statements of Albanian Party leaders on many occasions, as well as by the Chinese leaders' implicit, and sometimes explicit, offers to come to the aid of their Albanian ally in case of need. China's military might, backed by her substantial ideological and political authority, had served as a "protective umbrella" for Albania, or so at any rate it was perceived by the Hoxha leadership. It was in this context that Hysni Kapo, for example, who is said to be the third-ranking member of the Albanian hierarchy, made the remark in May 1966 that "If someone were to ask us how many people do we have, our answer is 701 millions."[59] As late as July 1975, the Albanian Party daily quoted Veli Llakaj, chief-of-staff of the country's armed forces, as saying that Albania was "not alone," for she was allied with the 800-million-strong Chinese People's Republic.[60]

In the course of one year, however, Albania's military relationship with communist China had undergone a significant change, as a consequence presumably of the ideological, political, and economic differences that had arisen between the two allies since 1969. The tone was reflected in the statements of Albanian officials and the information media on questions of national defense. Thus, an editorial in *Zëri i popullit* (July 9, 1976) said that APL did not rely on "international political configurations"—an esoteric phrase for Albania's heretofore military dependence on China—for Albania's defense but rather on the country's own armed forces and military capability. In subsequent months, the new policy on national defense, namely, "reliance on one's own forces," became one of the dominant themes of Albanian propaganda. The press now began to popularize the idea that Albania did not rely on any "umbrella" of the superpowers "or on any other power"—again an esoteric reference to Peking—for her national defense. Such reliance, the press now said, "would have dangerous consequences" for the country's independence and freedom.[61] The Albanian leadership appeared to be making a virtue of necessity, but it is possible also that Hoxha and Shehu had finally come to accept Chou En-lai's alleged remark to the Yugoslavs in August 1971 that "distant waters cannot quench a fire."

The Fall of General Balluku

The demise in July 1974 of Gen. Beqir Balluku, Albania's defense minister, member of the APL Politburo, and a deputy prime minister, came as a surprise to most, if not all, students of contemporary Albanian politics. The reason is that there was no public record of differences between him and Hoxha. On the contrary, as head of the Ministry of Defense since 1953, Balluku had a public record of unswerving loyalty and support of Hoxha and the Albanian Party line. He stood by Hoxha at the Tiranë Party Conference in April 1956—a critical time for the first secretary, owing to charges that he had ignored the conclusions of the Twentieth CPSU Congress.[62] He defended him in his struggle against Khrushchev in 1960-1961, and he supported the "dual adversary" theory that has been the cornerstone of Hoxha's foreign policy in the 1970s; namely, that American imperialism and Soviet revisionism are equally dangerous, and therefore communists must struggle against them with equal vigor and resolve until both are destroyed.

Balluku's fall marked the first shake-up in the Albanian Party Politburo since 1960, when Liri Belishova became a victim of the impending Soviet-Albanian split. It marked also the most serious incident of friction between the Party and army leadership in the thirty-year history of socialist Albania. What made Balluku's fall still more significant is that it was not an isolated incident but part of an action that brought down several army officers and officials of the Political Directorate of the army. As a result, army chief-of-staff and candidate member of the Politburo, General Dume, was replaced by Sami Meçollari, while Hito Çako, head of the army's Political Directorate, was replaced by Dilaver Poçi.[63] Deputy Chief-of-Staff Gen. Rahman Perllaku and deputy head of the army's Political Directorate, Halim Ramohito, apparently were purged along with their superiors, Dume and Çako. Balluku's post was officially taken over by Premier Mehmet Shehu in October 1974.[64]

The question arises: What led to this cleavage between the army and the Party in Albania, whose relationship was consistently portrayed by Albania's officialdom as one of unbreakable unity and harmony, by virtue of the army's unquestioned acceptance of the Party's leadership and guidance in all matters relating either to the military directly or to the country's domestic and foreign policy? Was the rift due to army-Party differences over Albania's foreign policy? What part, if any, did domestic conditions in Albania, particularly in the area of army-Party relations, play in the crisis?

A reading of Albanian sources, particularly certain editorials in *Zëri i popullit* and articles in *Rruga e Partisë* that touched on military matters, makes it possible to draw certain inferences that shed some light on the event. These sources suggest that there were high-level differences in the Politburo between the Balluku and Hoxha forces on the issue of defense—viewed in the narrow, technical sense—and on the larger issue of national security, which undoubtedly brought into question Albania's foreign policy or overall stance in international relations. Three main ingredients of Hoxha's foreign policy were (1) Albania, as a true Marxist-Leninist country, was engaged in an irreconcilable struggle against the two superpowers—U.S. imperialism and Soviet social-imperialism. (2) Albania was struggling to build socialism under conditions of "a fierce imperialist-revisionist encirclement"; hence, the country had to be ever vigilant against enemies, both external and internal. (3) Although Albania was a small country, surrounded by vicious enemies, she was neither isolated nor in mortal danger and would continue her polemical war against the United States and the Soviet Union until they and their lackeys met their inevitable doom.

The evidence suggested that Balluku and his top aides were not in full agreement with the Party's foreign policy and had attempted to use their influence to modify or reorient the policy. They had ventured to make their own appraisal of the international situation and Albania's place in it—an initiative that Hoxha and Shehu did not appreciate. This was rather plainly intimated by an editorial in *Rruga e Partisë* that claimed that only the Party "could understand the complex connections among phenomena."[65] A major point of contention was the issue of polemics. Army leaders seem to have argued that it was pretentious—and by implication, risky as well—for Albania to carry on a vitriolic polemical war against the United States and the Soviet Union. Hoxha hinted at this controversy in his speech on October 3, 1974, when he said:

It is utterly erroneous to sit back with folded arms and keep mum when others act to the detriment of peoples and nations, or to nod approval to such actions, as some people would like us to do, [claiming] that it is sheer arrogance for small nations to try to have their say . . . and come forward with their viewpoints in opposition to the "big ones."[66]

Balluku and his aides presumably argued also that Hoxha's policy of bitter hostility to both East and West had isolated Albania in the Balkans and Europe, thus creating a problem for her national security. Hoxha alluded to this dispute in his October 1974 speech when he rejected the thesis that Albania was isolated, saying that "hundreds and hundreds of millions are at one with us. . . ."[67] He added that, if Albania were to follow the advice of those who claimed she is isolated and seek an accommodation with imperialists and revisionists, the country would be "colonized" by foreigners and the Albanian people would be "enslaved."

Domestic factors, however, were probably more important than foreign policy considerations in Balluku's dismissal, although the two were related, since some of the domestic factors were obviously influenced by foreign developments and circumstances. These factors involved Army life, concepts of defense, and army-Party relations.

In the area of army life, there was evidently a serious breakdown of discipline at many levels, creating problems of morale and affecting the operational efficiency of the army. There were reports in the press of troops resisting officers, refusing to obey orders, going AWOL, and being generally indifferent to army regulations. There were complaints that Party cadres in the army had sought to conceal their defects and failures. It was also admitted, in an indirect fashion, that the study of Hoxha's teachings and Party materials had been neglected in some measure.[68] Party officials ascribed these weaknesses to the spread of liberal and bureaucratic attitudes within the armed forces, but that could hardly be considered a serious explanation of the roots of the discipline problem.

Another area of friction between the Balluku forces and Hoxha was the issue of defense. As in China, the official policy on national defense is based on the doctrine of "people's war," meaning the involvement of the entire able-bodied population in the defense of the homeland. It is the concept of the "citizen army," meaning that every citizen must assume the duties of the soldier and vice versa, thus fusing the armed forces and the civilian population into a single unit in matters of national defense. It is the doctrine of guerrilla warfare, which brought victory to the communists in Albania during World War II and convinced Hoxha and Shehu that it was an invincible strategy for warfare, valid for Albania even in the decade of the 1970s. According to this doctrine, the key element in national defense and victory is man rather than weapons, the revolutionary consciousness of the "citizen army" rather than military technology. Presumably, Balluku and his staff did not fully share this view. There were hints in the Albanian press that, as a result of "the great development in our time of technology and science," Balluku and his aides had come to believe that "people's war" no longer answered to the defense needs of Albania in the 1970s.[69] Lengthy commentaries on military matters in the nation's press left the impression that top army commanders had argued instead in favor of a defense policy based primarily on a "professional" army, well trained, relying heavily on the skillful use of modern weapons, and exercising a certain degree of independence from the Party and the masses.

The notion appears to have alarmed Hoxha and Shehu and prompted the former to say that "There is no stronger army than an armed and militarily trained nation."[70] Backers of the official defense policy attacked the notion of a professional army as "elitist." It was a notion, they said, that would spawn "an army of the barracks," a "military caste" that would be no different from the armies of bourgeois and revisionist countries.[71] They also denounced the notion—apparently nourished and practiced in the army—that the need for "military secrecy" made it "inadvisable" for nonmilitary personnel to control army activities.[72]

At this point, army-Party differences had reached a critical stage, since they went beyond the issues of discipline in the army and defense policy and touched directly on relations between the Party and army establishments. The widespread breakdown of discipline in the army signaled to Hoxha a disturbing lack of respect for the Party and its directives and a challenge to its organizational ability. Questioning of the Party's policy on national defense was even more serious, for it not only challenged the Party's claim to infallibility with regard to its general line but threatened the totalitarian exercise of its authority and power in Albanian society. This seems to have been at the heart of the Hoxha-Balluku feud and the primary cause of the purges that followed.

Party leaders grew uneasy over the Party's progressive loss of control over the army and over the creation of a "cult of the individual," presumably around Balluku. There were complaints in the media about complacency and the loss of revolutionary spirit in the army; of a slackening of loyalty to the Party and a consequent lessening of its prestige and authority; of putting army professionalism and specialized knowledge above politics; and of a plot to "separate" the army from the Party and the people. There were in addition attacks on those elements in the army who were afflicted by "conceit," "arrogance," and the "spirit of independence" or who demanded recognition and rewards for "special merits" they claimed to possess.

In an obvious reference to Balluku and his chief aides, an editorial in the Party's theoretical journal said: "Neither the minister . . . nor commander nor commissar can rise above the party," thus suggesting that the defense minister had tried to defy the Party and its authority.[73] The editorial further intimated that the deposed minister and his staff had resorted to "anti-Party methods" in their activity and equated them with "traitors and plotters." Albania's top army leader was also covertly attacked for his public professions of loyalty to the Party and its general line, on the ground that such professions were insincere and dangerous. An editorial in *Zëri i popullit* (Dec. 19, 1974) warned that "enemies are camouflaged, and strive to develop their activity under the cover of Party slogans, swearing [all the while] that they are defending the norms and decisions of the Party."[74]

In view of this situation, the Party leadership feared that the end result of the growing dissent within the army, and the widening gap between army and Party leaders, would be a military coup against the regime. More concretely, Hoxha feared a Zhukov-type coup in Albania. Thus, a revealing article by Ndreçi Plasari, leading historian and theoretician of the Partisan war, noted: "Comrade Enver Hoxha has said that the army of the barracks [allegedly favored by Balluku] is suited to hatching plots and military coups, such as the coup Khrushchev carried out with the aid of Zhukov in the Soviet Union, when he surrounded the Central Committee of the CPSU with the army and seized power by force."[75]

After keeping silent on the purge of General Balluku for nearly two and a half years, the Albanian leadership broke the silence in November 1976, on the occasion of the assembly of APL's Seventh Congress. Speaking at the congress, the Party's first secretary made a fierce attack on the deposed minister of defense and two of his top subordinates: Gen. Petrit Dume, former army chief-of-staff; and Hito Çako, former chief of the Political Directorate of the army. Hoxha accused the trio of being "a tratorous and putschist group," which operated as "a faction at the head of the army" and which intended "to overthrow by force the Central Committee . . . and annihilate the Party of Labor of Albania and the dictatorship of the proletariat."[76] He said that in this plot they relied also "on armed intervention from abroad" but gave no hint concerning the alleged foreign accomplice or accomplices to the "plot." Continuing his attack, Hoxha confirmed the indirect charges made against Balluku by the press in the preceding two years. He said that Balluku and his aides had "worked to weaken the Party organization and its leading role in the army," that they tried "to replace the Marxist-Leninist ideology" of APL with the revisionist ideology, and that they sought to undermine the defense capability of the country by introducing the methods of bourgeois and revisionist armies into Albania's military establishment.

Since Balluku's expulsion from his post and subsequent arrest, there have been reports that he as well as several other top army officers were executed.[77] Ironically, these reports, which were circulated by political enemies of the Albanian regime now living in exile, were confirmed indirectly by Enver Hoxha in his report to the November 1976 Party Congress. He said that traitors and enemies of the Party have always been attacked and punished by the Party, and "when necessary" also "by the laws of the dictatorship of the proletariat." This is an administrative phrase of the regime which, applied to Balluku and his associates, almost certainly means that they were executed.[78]

The weakening of Albania's military relationship with China, plus strong domestic pressures on the Party from dissidents in the army, account largely for the provisions on national defense and the armed forces in the new state Constitution. Article 88 of the document notes that "The Armed Forces are led by the Party," thus emphasizing the determination of the Party leadership to maintain strict control over the military, including unlimited review and veto power over all aspects of military life. The Constitution also authorized the creation of a Defense Council "to direct, organize and mobilize all the forces and resources of the country in the defense of the Homeland." The Council is headed by the first secretary of the Party, who is also the commander-in-chief of the country's armed forces (Art. 89). In brief, military power was thus almost entirely concentrated in the hands of Hoxha and Shehu.

Concluding Remarks

The history of the army in socialist Albania has on the whole been a history of harmonious relations with the Albanian Party of Labor. Both the Party and the army had their birth in wartime Albania and were tested and molded by the flames of the Partisan struggle, but the Party always claimed and exercised a leading role in the relationship. The army, as an institution, remained loyal to the Party and its first secretary, Enver Hoxha. Owing to the close tie between the two institutions, the army reflected the crises that have marked the course of the Party from the Partisan war to the midseventies.

But unlike previous shake-ups in Albania's armed forces, purges in the army in the summer of 1974 came practically without warning, in an ostensibly noncrisis situation. Yet this shake-up was more massive and graver in its implications than any previous shake-up in the army.

Hoxha and the Albanian Party have always sought to exercise uncontested power in Albania. The dismissal of Balluku manifested once again the regime's sense of insecurity, and extreme sensitivity to threats—whether real or imagined—to its power and position in Albanian society. The regime's final solution to such threats has been the purge mechanism. In 1967, seeing the religious establishment as an alternate source of loyalty and power, distinct from the Party, the regime abolished religion and proclaimed Alabania an atheist state. In 1973, the Party leaders suspected the intelligentsia of disloyalty and anti-Party activity, under the guise of liberalism, and promptly deposed the entire leadership of the League of Albanian Writers and Artists. In 1974, they detected the makings of a coup against the Party by Balluku and in characteristic fashion dismissed him and his staff.

It is perhaps not too strange that Hoxha viewed Balluku as a dangerous rival. He was greatly in debt to him, for on several occasions, especially in 1956 and 1961, Balluku used his post as head of Albania's armed forces to preserve Hoxha in power. Hoxha realized no doubt that if Balluku had the power to preserve him in his position he had the power also to destroy him. Hence, he turned against the defense minister, using the same basic arguments against him that his hated former enemy, Khrushchev, used against Marshal Zhukov back in 1957.

But with each such victory the Hoxha-Shehu leadership probably lost ground. When it abolished religion, it made enemies of numerous believers, especially among the older generation. When it moved against the intelligentsia, it alienated a large number of artists, scholars, and professionals. And now, by dispatching the leadership of the army, it lost the confidence and support of many in the army. One wonders how many more such victories the regime could stand.

While domestic considerations relating to the Party's maintenance of its leading position in Albania were the immediate cause of Balluku's fall, external factors were perhaps more important, in terms of creating the appropriate climate in which dissent in the army grew. The questioning of Albania's heavy dependence on China, the incongruence of Hoxha's anti-imperialist polemics with Albania's actual power in the world scene, Albania's pronounced political and ideological isolation in the Balkans and Europe, and above all the general mood of détente in Europe combined apparently to generate serious dissent in the army against Hoxha and the Party line.

To this one might also add the growing pressures on the Party for liberalization and reform, which came from a whole generation of highly educated technicians, professionals, and specialists who are pragmatically oriented and who seek to solve problems with the tools and techniques of modern science and technology, rather than by relying mainly on communist ideology, the dialectics of class struggle, and sundry political slogans. Ironically, the modernizing forces of technology and industry, which the Party itself labored mightily to create in order to develop the country, have now arisen to become a thorn in the Party's side. For the new technological intelligentsia, within both the army and Albanian society as a whole, seems no longer willing to accept the Party's judgment and decisions as infallible. Nor is it willing to pledge unquestioned loyalty to it.

While the Party succeeded in reinstating its control over the army, new outbreaks of resistance to the Party's Stalinist rule are almost certain to occur in the future.

A Note on Albania's Military Forces and Budget (1970-1976)

In 1969, as a result of the invasion of Czechoslovakia, Albania increased her defense budget 38 percent over 1968. Table 10.1 indicates Albania's military forces and budget over a six-year period, from 1970 to 1976.

A breakdown of Albania's armed forces in 1975-1976 presented the following picture: army—30,000; navy—3,000; air force—5,000. The defense establishment for the same year included: in the army—one tank brigade consisting of 125 tanks, eight infantry brigades, a variety of artillery guns ranging from 76mm to 152mm, and three coastal artillery battalions; in the navy—four submarines (Soviet), four coastal escort boats (Soviet), ten patrol boats (Soviet), forty-two torpedo boats (twelve Soviet, thirty Chinese), eight other boats; in the air force—ninety-six combat aircraft, including twenty-four MIG-17s, and twelve MIG-21s (Chinese), six transport planes, and twenty helicopters.[79]

Analysis of table 10.1 shows that while Albania's population increased by 18 percent from 1970 to 1976, her total regular forces decreased by about 7

Table 10.1
Military Forces and Budget

	1970-71	1972-73	1975-76	Change over 6-yr. Period
Population of Albania	2,100,000	2,250,000	2,490,000	+390,000 (18%)
Total regular forces	41,000	35,000	38,000	−3,000 (7.3%)
Paramilitary forces	37,000	15,000	13,000[a]	−24,000 (65%)
Defense budget (in millions of dollars)	84[b]	116[c]	127	+43 (51%)

Source: *The Military Balance*, annual study prepared by the International Institute for Strategic Studies (London), for the years shown.
[a] In addition to the paramilitary force, Albania in 1975-1976 had a *Sigurimi* (internal security) force of 4,000 and a frontier force of 9,000, making for a total of nearly 64,000 men and women under arms. An additional 100,000 civilians reportedly were in the reserve forces.
[b] 1969 figure.
[c] 1971 figure.

Table 10.2
Albania and Her Neighbors: A Comparison of Their Military Forces and Defense Budgets (1975-1976)

	Albania	Yugoslavia	Greece	Italy
Population	2,490,000	21,400,000	9,020,000	55,500,000
Armed forces	38,000	230,000	161,200	421,000
% of population	1.5	1.1	1.8	0.8
GNP (in billions)*	$1.1	$25.3	$18.6	$150.5
Defense budget (in millions)	$127.0	$1,705.0	$1,035.0	$3,891.0
% of GNP	11.5	6.7	5.6	2.6

Source: *The Military Balance*, 1975-76.
*1974 estimates.

percent, while the paramilitary forces registered a drastic decrease of 65 percent. These decreases were probably due to the belief of the Albanian leadership that the danger of an imminent attack by the USSR on Albania had subsided since 1968. The fact however that the defense budget increased by about 50 percent during the same period indicated that the leadership was greatly concerned about the country's national security but that the best way to assure such security under existing conditions was to allocate more funds for weapons and the military training of the Albanian population.

It is useful also to compare Albania's military position, in terms of the size of her military forces and defense budget, with that of her neighbors. For the comparison, see table 10.2.

As can be seen, Albania's military forces in 1975-1976 in relation to her population were almost double those of Italy and considerably higher than those of Yugoslavia, but smaller than those of Greece. On the other hand, her defense budget was nearly twice as large as that of Yugoslavia, more than twice that of Greece, and over four times that of Italy. It is obvious that Albania's military expenditures consumed a very large portion of her GNP and undoubtedly were a heavy burden on her economy. Hoxha himself said as much as far back as 1960 in his speech at the November Moscow Conference but placed the blame for it on the "imperialists and their lackeys."[80] One can argue more accurately that Albania's abnormally high defense budget was the logical consequence of the siege mentality fostered throughout the nation by her leaders, who proclaimed incessantly that Albania was building socialism in the face of "a fierce imperialist-revisionist encirclement."

11
The Albanian Minority in Yugoslavia

The Albanian Minority in Yugoslavia

In October, November, and December of 1968, violent demonstrations by Albanian nationals in Yugoslavia took place in at least nine cities, including Priština, capital of the Autonomous Socialist Province of Kosovo, and Tetovo in the Republic of Macedonia. The demonstrations involved an estimated 5,000 to 7,500 persons and resulted—according to official Yugoslav figures—in one death, some forty persons injured, and at least a score arrested, plus considerable destruction of property.[1]

A major demand of the demonstrators, most of whom were students, intellectuals, and professionals, concerned language rights. They called for the establishment of a "national" university in Priština, in which all instruction would be in the Albanian language. The demonstrators also called for language equality in matters of public administration, meaning that the Albanian language be used, alongside Serbo-Croatian, in all legal documents and other pertinent government communications.[2]

Other demands voiced by the Albanian nationals were explicitly political in character: They wanted self-determination for Kosovo, including a separate constitution, and republican status for the province; that is to say, the designation of Kosovo as the seventh republic of the Yugoslav federation. There were reports also of calls for the union of Kosovo and Albanian-populated areas of Macedonia and Montenegro with socialist Albania.[3]

The explosive events of 1968 in Kosovo caused Belgrade a measure of embarrassment, as they cast doubt on Yugoslavia's claim that under Tito's system of socialism the nationality problem had been solved. Belgrade's embarrassment was understandable, for Kosovo, with an area of 10,882 km^2 (4,127 mi^2), is larger than the states of Delaware and Rhode Island combined (3,271 mi^2) and has a population of over a million and a quarter, of whom approximately three-fourths (73.8%) or nearly one million (918,864) are Albanians.[4] Together with 280,000 other Albanians in Macedonia, and 35,000 in Montenegro, plus scattered elements in other republics, the total number of Albanian nationals in Yugoslavia in 1971 stood at 1,310,000. They are the largest ethnic minority by far in the Yugoslav nation.[5] Their number, therefore, is not merely an interesting demographic statistic but has important political implications in the present context of Yugoslav politics.

In discussing the Albanian minority in Yugoslavia, it seems advisable to consider the views of four parties: (1) the Albanian nationals, and how they see themselves in relation to Yugoslavia and Albania; (2) the federal government of Yugoslavia and its position on Kosovo, (3) the policy on Kosovo of the Albanian government; and (4) the view of Albanian émigrés from Kosovo and from communist Albania. This in itself shows the complexity of the subject under discussion and makes plain the fact that the Kosovo question is not simply an internal affair of Yugoslavia but, like all national minority problems, a matter of concern to the "kin-state" of the minority group, in this case, Albania, and also to Albanian political exiles.[6]

Moreover, to gain a better understanding of the current situation in Kosovo, it is useful to discuss the history of the region, since historic events that occurred centuries ago, as well as in the more recent past, still exercise considerable influence on the parties concerned.

The Historical Roots of the Problem

Looking at Kosovo from a long historical perspective, we perceive that the Albanians and the Slavs are divided over the question of the historic significance of the region to Slavs and Albanians and the manner in which the two ethnic groups settled there. From the Yugoslav point of view, Kosovo represents the heartland of the original Serbian nation and state. The Slavs are said to have settled there as early as the seventh century A.D. The medieval Serbian kings were crowned there. The great Serbian lord, Czar Stefan Dušan (1331-1355), established the seat of his empire in the town of Prizren in Kosovo. It was on the Kosovo plain that the Serbs engaged the Ottoman Turks in 1389 in the fateful battle of "The Field of the Blackbirds." That battle subsequently inspired the creation of Yugoslavia's great epic, *Kossovo Polje*. A monument stands in Priština today in memory of those who fell in the battle of Kosovo.

Kosovo, in addition, is associated in the minds of the Serbs with the Serbian Orthodox Church, which is practically synonymous with the history and destiny of the Serbian nation. In 1346–the year that Dušan was crowned emperor of the Serbs, Greeks, Bulgarians, and Albanians–the Serbian bishopric of Peć in Kosovo was proclaimed a patriarchate, thus making the Serbian church independent of the patriarch of Constantinople. It was a time when art and culture flourished in Yugoslavia.

For reasons of both church and state, Kosovo is "sacred ground" to the Serbs, who traditionally make pilgrimages there from all parts of Yugoslavia. Hence, the idea that Kosovo might some day be separated from Serbia causes what one observer has described as "an irrational emotional reaction" among the Serbs.[7]

According to Serb historians, the Albanians are late arrivals in Kosovo. They moved into the region in the seventeenth and eighteenth centuries, in consequence of the favor they enjoyed under the Turks, after large numbers of them had converted to the faith of Islam. The Serbs note that population pressures created by the "Albanian colonizers" in Kosovo caused the migration in 1690 of the Serbian patriarch Arsen Carnojević to Hungary, along with some 30,000 Serbian families. Other migrations of Serbs from Kosovo followed later, especially in the years 1736-1739.[8]

Such, in broad outline, is the Serbian argument in support of the claim that Kosovo is historically a part of Serbia.

The Albanians, for their part, insist that they have a stronger historical claim to Kosovo than the Slavs. It is common knowledge, they point out, that Kosovo was originally inhabited by the Illyrians, ancestors of present-day Albanians. They were there centuries before the Slavs appeared in the seventh century A.D. and proceeded to displace the Illyrians. Therefore, "If the issue [of original title to the land] were to be decided on historical grounds . . . then it is the Serbs who do not belong in Kosovo."[9] According to this thesis, the Albanians of Kosovo are native to the land; they have been there continuously from the time of the Illyrians to the present.

Nor can it be said that the Albanians moved into Kosovo in the seventeenth and eighteenth centuries because of the favor they enjoyed under the Turks, since no other people in the Balkans waged as fierce a struggle against the Ottomans as did the Albanians. During the more than 1,300 years that the Albanians and the Slavs have lived side by side in Kosovo—so goes the Albanian argument—the proportions of their respective populations have shifted with the tide of events. But documentary evidence from Catholic missionaries in the region, Turkish chroniclers, and West European travelers shows that there has always been a strong, if not always dominant, Albanian presence there.[10]

The first time Kosovo became a political issue in the modern history of Slavs and Albanians was in 1878, when the Congress of Berlin decreed that certain Albanian-populated areas of the region be given to the Slavic states. The Kosovo issue became much more acute in 1913 when the London Conference ceded the entire region to Yugoslavia. The lands lost to Yugoslavia on these occasions amount to well over one-half the territory of the present Albanian nation.

Albanians have felt keenly the loss of those lands, in part because of historical associations with Kosovo. The founding of the League of Prizren in 1878—generally considered as the starting point of the Albanian national awakening—and the armed struggle against the Turks in 1909-1912 were predominantly the work of the Albanians of Kosovo. Hence, it has been said that "Kosovo has been ... the cradle of the Albanian rebirth [and] the chief factor in the historic events that culminated in the founding of the Albanian state."[11]

If Kosovo then is sacred ground to the Serbs, because of past associations with the medieval Serbian church and state, the region is equally significant to the Albanians, not only as the home of their Illyrian ancestors but as the land that sparked the drive for freedom and national independence, after nearly five centuries of Turkish domination.

In sum, the Yugoslavs and the Albanians stand on opposite sides of the fence regarding Kosovo from a historical perspective, since both sides claim original title to the region, by virtue of right of possession and even more by virtue of the historic significance that Kosovo has for the two parties.

Kosovo between World Wars I and II

In his fine study of national minorities, Inis Claude writes that after World War I the new nations of Eastern and Central Europe were anxious to carry out policies of assimilation or elimination of the various ethnic groups living within their states. These nations, he remarks, were "obsessed by the ideal of national uniformity, . . . erected centralized administrative regimes, undertook to denationalize minorities, and in other ways used the power of the state to serve the interests of the majority nationality, at the expense of the rights of minorities."[12]

The appraisal fits well Yugoslavia's policy on her minorities between the two world wars, and Kosovo provides an unfortunate illustration of that policy. The Belgrade government, or more accurately the Serbs who controlled it, did not recognize the Albanian minority as a national group entitled to all the rights guaranteed to minorities under international law, as formulated by the League of Nations and formally acknowledged by Yugoslavia. Instead, the Albanians—along with other national groups in Yugoslavia—were treated as "second-class citizens" and subjected to "unbridled Serbian military and police rule."[13]

The Albanians were denied language equality, and as a result no Albanian schools were allowed in the country. All instruction in the schools was in Serbo-Croatian. Indeed, it was dangerous for Albanian nationals to possess Albanian-language books and similar literature. Belgrade's policy of repression of the Albanian language and general neglect of the educational system led a top-ranking communist official of Kosovo to remark years later that Kosovo was the only province in royalist Yugoslavia that "had more prisons and police stations than schools."[14]

The Albanians of Kosovo, the Albanian government, and Albanian émigré groups are in agreement that Belgrade's denial of language rights to the Albanian minority was part of an overall plan to change the ethnic composition of Kosovo, with a view to making the Serbs the dominant element there not only socially and politically but numerically as well. This meant, in effect, the implementation of a denationalization policy with regard to the Albanian minority. The policy spawned an administrative bureaucracy in Kosovo that Albania and Albanian émigré groups have characterized as a regime of terror. Persecution of Albanian intellectuals, clergy, and civic leaders became a common occurrence. There were arrests without cause and convictions without trial. The homes of Albanian nationals became targets of attack for Serbian chauvinists, their livestock was taken away from them, their freedom to travel was restricted, they were in many cases forced to work for the Serbs without compensation, and in some areas they were not permitted even to wear their customary Albanian dress.[15]

One of the methods used by Belgrade authorities to change the ethnic character of Kosovo was to manipulate national census figures in such a way as to show fewer Albanian nationals than there were in reality. This was done mostly by designating them as Turks or as Moslems.[16] Another method consisted of attempts to colonize the region with Slavs by means of an agrarian reform program. The program resulted in the confiscation of lands and properties owned by Albanians and the distribution of such holdings to Serbian and Montenegrin families. It is estimated that nearly 40,000 Slav families were brought into Kosovo in the course of carrying out the agrarian reform program. One of the most provocative methods used in the implementation of the denationalization plan was the "collection of arms" policy, which Belgrade initiated in 1938 and which authorized the police to search for arms among Albanian nationals, under the pretext that they were preparing to rise in revolt against the Yugoslav government. The intent of this policy, according to Albanian historians, was to create such an atmosphere of insecurity among Albanian nationals as to induce them to migrate from Kosovo.

Indeed, when it became obvious to Yugoslav authorities that the policy of assimilation through colonization of the Albanian minority was not producing the desired results, Belgrade undertook to solve the problem by eliminating the Albanian element altogether. The chief method chosen to accomplish this goal was deportation. Agreements signed between Turkish and Yugoslav officials in 1926 and 1938 envisioned the deportation of as many as 400,000 Albanians from Yugoslavia.[17] According to a recent issue of the Priština review *Përparimi*, "Hundreds of thousands" of Albanian nationals were deported to the desolate regions of Turkey between 1919 and 1941. The same review characterizes Belgrade's prewar treatment of the Albanian minority as "the crudest system of exploitation and oppression...."[18]

In the light of the foregoing discussion, it is evident that Serbian chauvinism was a deliberate and active policy of prewar Yugoslavia. It is not surprising, then, that all four of the principal parties directly involved with Kosovo— the Kosovo Albanians, the Yugoslav communists, the Albanian government, and Albanian political émigrés—concur in the view that the policy of royalist Yugoslavia toward her nationalities, including the Albanian minority, was unjust, unrealistic, and worthy of condemnation.

Kosovo during World War II

The picture of Kosovo during World War II remains unclear, owing to conflicting versions of the war in the region given by Yugoslav communists, spokesmen of the Albanian minority, the Albanian government, and Albanian anticommunist groups in exile.

Yugoslav communists appear to be divided in their appraisal of the wartime role of the Albanian minority. The official Belgrade view is generally sympathetic, even laudatory, but there were nevertheless influential leaders in Tito's Partisan movement, such as Svetozar Vukmanović-Tempo and Aleksandar Ranković, who distrusted the Albanian nationals, accused them of nourishing chauvinistic and hostile attitudes toward the Serbs, and could not overlook the fact that a portion of them had collaborated with the German occupiers.[19] The Tito leadership tried in various ways to build up support for the Partisan cause in Kosovo. Toward that end, it sought to assure Albanian nationals that, following the liberation of the country, Yugoslavia would be constituted as a federated state in which they, and all other national groups, would enjoy full equality.[20]

More relevant for our discussion are the conclusions of the local conference of the National Liberation movement of the Kosovo province, which convened from December 31, 1943, to January 2, 1944. The conference resolved that:

Kosovo and the Plateau of Dukagjin [i.e., Metohijë] are inhabited mostly by Albanians who as heretofore are eager to join up with Albania. . . . The only way by which the Albanians of Kosovo and the Dukagjin Plateau can unite with Albania is to make common cause with the other peoples of Yugoslavia and fight together against the criminal Nazi occupiers and their hirelings, for this is the only way to win liberty . . . [and] self-determination, even to the extent of seceding [from Yugoslavia].[21]

The resolution was an elaboration of the statement on nationalities issued in November 1943 by the national leadership of the Yugoslav Partisans. The resolution gave emphatic expression to the desire of Kosovo Albanians to unite with Albania. It showed that in order to realize that desire they made common cause with communist resistance groups in the struggle against Nazi occupation forces. Nationalism thus emerged as the primary motive in their deliberations and the focal point of their aspirations, while communism was to be the instrument for realizing those aspirations. The Kosovo resolution was not the first of its kind to encourage the idea of the union of Kosovo Albanians with their kin-state of Albania. The Yugoslav Communist Party had already, on two previous occasions—in 1928 and at the Fifth Party Congress in 1940—taken the stand that "Kosovo should be restored to Albania."[22] Such declarations had strong appeal to the national feelings of the Albanians of Kosovo and succeeded in activating many of them in the resistance movement against the German occupiers.

Albanian officials in Kosovo maintain that in spite of some Fascist elements in their midst, Albanian nationals as a whole supported the national-liberation struggle of the Yugoslav peoples and made an important contribution to the success of that struggle.[23] In support of this claim they point to the formation in 1942-1943 of the "Zenel Ajdini" and "Emin Duraku" guerrilla units, and later of the "Bajram Curri" battalion, all of which were made up of Partisans from Kosovo. As many as 40,000 Partisans from this region are said to have taken part in Yugoslavia's liberation struggle.

The official wartime position of the Albanian Communist Party in relation to Yugoslavia was one of close cooperation with Tito and the Albanians of Kosovo, in the common struggle to defeat the Axis powers. Accordingly, Albanian Party cadres were dispatched to Kosovo in 1943 to help organize the Albanian minority in the liberation struggle. In October 1944, at the request of the Yugoslav communist leadership, two units of the Albanian Partisan army, the Third and the Fifth Brigades, entered Kosovo and fought side by side with local communist contingents to wrest the province from the control of German and "local reactionary" forces. Hoxha's Partisans who fought in Kosovo later reported that there was widespread mistrust and fear of the Serbs, including Tito's Partisans, among the Albanian minority. Such apprehensions apparently were not without foundation. There had been violent clashes between Kosovo Albanians and Yugoslav Partisans in late 1944 and early 1945 when Tito's forces "were seeking to re-establish Yugoslav control of Albanian minority areas."[24]

The resistance of Kosovo Albanians to reincorporation into Yugoslavia is vividly described in the writings of Albanian émigrés who are united in their opposition to communist or Slavic domination of Kosovo and who remain steadfast in their commitment to the goal of an ethnic Albania. The dream of the émigrés became a reality, after a fashion, in 1941, when Germany occupied Yugoslavia and Italy proclaimed an ethnic Albanian state, including Kosovo. In general, however, anticommunist Albanians in Kosovo did not view this development as a satisfactory solution to the Kosovo question, since it compromised Albania's sovereignty and independence.

When Italy capitulated in September 1943, representatives of anticommunist Albanians in Kosovo met in the historic city of Prizren and on September 11, 1943, founded the Second League of Prizren, for the purpose of securing Kosovo's union with Albania.[25] The league proceeded to mobilize a military force of Albanian nationals, which reportedly fought a fierce and victorious battle against the Chetniks of Drago Mihailović in November-December 1943, though at a high cost in casualties.[26] According to émigré sources, toward the end of 1944, League forces clashed also with Tito's Partisans, when they attempted to extend their control over Kosovo, and succeeded in turning them back. At that point, Tito turned to "his apprentice in Tiranë," Enver Hoxha, and asked for the dispatch of two divisions to Yugoslaiva, "allegedly to fight the Germans." Hoxha complied, and it was only with the help of Albanian Partisans that Tito was able to "pacify" Kosovo, killing in the process "tens of thousands" of Kosovo Albanians. The émigrés have called Hoxha's action a "great betrayal" of the Albanians of Kosovo and contend that he and his coterie bear a heavy responsibility for the reversion of Kosovo to Yugoslav control at the end of the war.[27]

The armed resistance of Kosovo Albanians to Tito's forces had the characteristics of a rebellion and lasted until March 1945. The uprising "was ruthlessly suppressed"[28] and "is notable as the only instance of an armed rebellion against the communist government in Yugoslavia."[29] Later, Yugoslav authorities acknowledged that "atrocities were committed [by Yugoslav Partisans] against the Albanians in Kosovo and Macedonia" during the war.[30]

Events in wartime Kosovo made manifest several things worth noting: (1) Both procommunist and anticommunist factions of the Albanian minority were united in their desire to achieve the union of Kosovo with Albania. (2) They were divided over the means with which to achieve that goal, one faction believing that support of the communist-led national-liberation struggle of Yugoslavia held out the greatest promise, while the other thought that collaboration with the Axis powers was more likely to bring success. (3) Despite their declarations favoring self-determination for Kosovo, the conduct of the communist leaders of Yugoslavia showed that they were primarily motivated by nationalist feelings rather than communist class ideology; hence their interest in preserving intact Yugoslavia's prewar borders and their indifference to the expressed wishes of Albanian nationals for autonomy or merger with Albania. (4) The Communist Party of Albania showed no visible interest in furthering the goal of Kosovo Albanians for union with Albania. (5) The merger of Kosovo with Albania during the war years marked the first instance of such a union since 1913 and established a precedent that subsequently inspired many Albanians, both within and without Kosovo, to keep alive the dream of a final and stable union of the Kosovo province with Albania.

In summarizing this phase of the history of Kosovo, we can say that the Yugoslav and Albanian communist parties, guided by a supranational, class-oriented ideology, had a common policy on Kosovo, based on the priorities of the liberation struggle against the Fascist powers; that Kosovo Albanians, on the other hand, were split into two opposing factions, one procommunist and the other anticommunist; and lastly, that the émigré Albanians were generally sympathetic to the anticommunist faction and opposed to the communist-led Yugoslav and Albanian Partisans.

Kosovo in Postwar Yugoslavia

With the establishment of Yugoslavia as a federated state at the end of the war, the status of the Albanian minority changed in at least two important ways. First, Kosovo was recognized as a separate administrative area under the Republic of Serbia and on September 3, 1945, was officially established as an "autonomous region." This was the first time that the Albanian nationals in Yugoslavia were recognized as a distinct national group, living in a distinct geographical area within the state of Yugoslavia. Second, in 1945 the Albanian language was acknowledged by law as "one of the official languages of Kosovo." In accordance with this decree, the government affirmed the right of Kosovo

Albanians to teach their native tongue in school, and afterward a number of Albanian-language grade schools were opened in the province. This development was in dramatic contrast to the situation that existed in prewar Yugoslavia, when only Serbo-Croatian was taught in the schools. Albanian nationals had thus taken a potentially important step toward cultural and national affirmation.

Unfortunately, the rights granted by law to Kosovo Albanians in the use of their language, in education, and in other fields had more reality on paper than in practice. This state of affairs lasted for a period of some twenty years following the war. These were the years when Ranković, vice-president of Yugoslavia and heir-designate of Tito, exercised almost total authority over the Albanian minority, which he distrusted and despised. During most of this period, Belgrade, operating under the influence of Ranković, looked upon Kosovo Albanians as a political liability and as a "potentially subversive element."[31] Not surprisingly—in view of such a negative assessment of Albanian nationals—Belgrade set up a repressive security apparatus in Kosovo and ruled the Albanians "by the iron hand of the secret police."[32] Belgrade's hostility stemmed in part from lingering wartime resentment of Albanian elements who had collaborated with the Axis powers and who persisted in their resistance to communist rule in Yugoslavia even after the war. In part, it was nourished by the extremely bitter ideological polemics that broke out between Albania and Yugoslavia following their split in 1948.

For her part, Albania now assumed a position on Kosovo that was practically identical with that of the anticommunist émigré groups. The Hoxha leadership attacked first of all the creation of the autonomous province of Kosovo as an administrative scheme of the "Yugoslav revisionists," designed to weaken the sense of nationalism and the unity of Albanian nationals. In a furious editorial that appeared in September 1958, the Albanian Party daily said that the Albanians of Yugoslavia inhabit a compact region, yet they were split up administratively and apportioned to three different republics—Serbia, Macedonia, and Montenegro.[33] On the issue of language equality, Albanian polemicists accused Yugoslavia of discriminating against the Albanian language and of showing an anti-Albanian bias in public education. They complained, for example, that the Yugoslavs had distorted the truth about Albania's national hero, Skënderbeu; the League of Prizren; and the Albanian National Liberation struggle.

In general, the Albanian regime repeated all the arguments used to condemn royalist Yugoslavia's treatment of the Albanian minority, but with greater force than before. Particularly during the years 1957-1959, Albanian polemicists argued that the "Yugoslav renegades" were guilty of manipulating census figures to the disadvantage of the Albanian minority; behaved like colonizers in Kosovo; carried out a vicious "collection of arms" policy in 1955-1956; deported tens of thousands of Albanians to Turkey; and even resorted to genocide with a view to exterminating the Albanian element. "It is estimated," wrote the Albanian daily *Zëri i popullit* in 1958, "that the number of Albanians who fell under Titoite bullets, bayonets, and poison during the period from 1944 to 1948 reaches 36,000."[34] At the same time, the Albanians said, Yugoslavia had turned Kosovo into a center for subversion against Albania, using for this purpose Fascists and escapees from Albania, including war criminals. Kosovo had thus become a battleground in the relentless Cold War struggle between Tiranë and Belgrade.

As was the case during the Second World War, this time, too, the Albanians of Kosovo were divided, though along different lines and for different reasons from those of the war period. The split this time was between the Albanian communist leaders of Kosovo and lesser functionaries on the one hand, who willingly or not found it expedient to support Belgrade in its polemics against Albania, and the masses of the Albanian minority who resented Serbian domination and police brutality and consequently looked more or less sympathetically on Albania, inasmuch as she had assumed the role of protector and defender of their rights. The Kosovo leaders became the chief voice in Yugoslavia in the campaign to refute Albania's attacks on Belgrade's treatment of the Albanian minority. They accused the Hoxha leadership of pursuing an adventurist policy and of crudely interfering in the internal affairs of a sovereign state. On November 28, 1964, in a speech commemorating the anniversary of Yugoslavia's national day, Ali Sukrija, then regional Communist Party secretary for Kosovo, remarked that since 1948 Albania had pursued "nationalist, chauvinistic, and irredentist" aims toward Yugoslavia.[35] Indeed, the cry of irredentism, raised by Kosovo leaders, became the main element in Yugoslavia's counterattack against Albanian propaganda. Alluding to Albania's alleged irredentism, an article in the Priština daily, *Rilindja* (May 24, 1963) noted that Enver Hoxha and Mehmet Shehu wanted to include the Albanians of Yugoslavia "in the hell they have created for their people" but that Kosovo Albanians had rejected their chauvinistic propaganda. The same article also accused Albania of seeking in vain to incite the Albanian minority to rebel against Tito.

The fourth party involved directly with Kosovo, the anticommunist émigré groups, remained firm in their vehement criticism of Yugoslavia's treatment of Albanian nationals. They denounced the alleged forced migration to Turkey of "over 350,000 Kosovo Albanians" during the Ranković years and the killing of "at least 65,000" of their conationals in Yugoslavia by Tito's Partisans during and after the war.[36] Emigré publications referred to Kosovo as "an enslaved land" and reaffirmed their determination to press the fight for the ethnic unification of Albania.[37]

In summarizing postwar developments in Kosovo up to the mid-1960s, we find that national feelings and considerations proved stronger than the class ideology professed by the communist leaders of Yugoslavia and Albania. The strained atmosphere between the Tito and Hoxha leaderships degenerated into vitriolic polemics, as both sides exchanged charges of chauvinism, irredentism, and subversion, while Kosovo Albanians huddled in the resulting crossfire. This period was marked also by many pronouncements by Yugoslavia that she had solved the national question on the basis of Marxist-Leninist teachings, but in reality the situation in Kosovo remained much the same as it was before the war.

From the Midsixties to the Midseventies

Beginning with the midsixties, the situation of Albanian nationals in Kosovo took a turn for the better in some respects. The change in their fortunes can be attributed to a number of developments: A milestone event was the fall of Ranković in July of 1966 and the subsequent demolition of his police apparatus in the Kosovo province. Ranković's demise was a heavy moral and psychological blow to the "Greater Serbia" mentality of his supporters who worked actively to maintain Serbian supremacy in Kosovo. Also significant were the autumn 1968 demonstrations in Kosovo and Macedonia by the Albanian minority, which impelled Belgrade to take measures to eliminate at least some of the grievances of the demonstrators. A third factor was the improvement in relations with Albania, which began in the wake of the invasion of Czechoslovakia in 1968 by Warsaw Pact forces and culminated in the establishment of full diplomatic relations between Belgrade and Tiranë in February 1971. The normalization of Albanian-Yugoslav relations had the effect of converting Kosovo from an ideological battleground into a bridge of cooperation between the two neighbors. Lastly, Kosovo became a beneficiary of the 1968 and 1971 amendments to the federal constitution of Yugoslavia, which granted a greater measure of self-rule to the autonomous provinces than ever before.

The denunciation of Ranković by the Brioni Plenum of the League of Communists of Yugoslavia in July 1966 encouraged the Albanians to press for full recognition of their rights as a minority. Partly as a result of their agitation, they won the right in 1968 to fly the Albanian flag on their national holidays. The demand voiced by Albanian demonstrators in 1968 for a national university was largely fulfilled a year later with the inauguration of the University of Priština in November 1969. One yardstick of progress in education was the drop in the illiteracy rate in the province from an estimated 90 percent at the end of the war to about 41 percent in the late 1960s. Indeed, during this period in no other area of life did the Albanians of Kosovo make more progress than in the cultural field, including progress toward language equality, education, publications, the arts, radio and TV, the theater, and the cinema.

To a large extent, the cultural affirmation of Albanian nationals was due to the continuous development of cultural relations between Kosovo and Albania. For culturally and emotionally Kosovo Albanians are said to feel a strong pull toward their conationals in Albania. These contacts and ties covered sports events; tourism; the arts, including film exchanges, song and dance festivals, and performances by dramatic groups; the fostering of communications, such as radio and TV; and increasing cooperation between writers in Albania and in Kosovo. Above all, contacts with Albania were most numerous and productive in the academic field, as evidenced by the many protocols for educational cooperation that representatives of Tiranë State University and the University of Priština signed in the last decade. Professors from Albania taught in Priština, large quantities of textbooks and teaching aids were imported from Albania for use in Kosovo schools, and delegations of Kosovo scholars attended academic conferences on Albanian studies in Tiranë. Albanian scholars, in turn, attended symposia in Priština, Dubrovnik, and Bitola.

A historic event in the use of a uniform language by the Albanians of Kosovo and Albania proper occurred in April 1968 when a Conference on Language in Priština resolved to abandon the literary use of the Geg dialect—common in northern Albania and Kosovo—in favor of the Tosk dialect, which has been the official language of socialist Albania.[38] The decision was a significant manifestation of the desire of Albanians on both sides of the Yugoslav border to share more fully their common cultural heritage, through the use of a uniform literary language.

The Albanians of Yugoslavia also made gains in the field of politics and public administration. Unlike previous times, Kosovo now has its own constitution and along with it an independent High Court of Justice and a People's Assembly with power to promugate laws. Two representatives of the province, Veli Deva and Ilijaz Kurteši—the first, a former chairman of the Kosovo Party Committee; the second, a former chairman of the Provincial Assembly—hold membership in the twenty-three member body of the State Presidency, headed by President Tito. And an Albanian from Kosovo, Fadil Hoxha, a long-time member of the LCY Presidium, has been designated as a candidate to the nine-member State Presidency, which will become operative when Tito dies. Fadil Hoxha is in fact "the only non-Slav member in the supreme state collective leadership."[39] At the provincial level, the Albanians reportedly occupied the most important posts in the party and government organizations. Moreover, they were said to constitute the majority "in nearly all municipal councils."[40]

Summarizing this account of developments in Kosovo, we find a large measure of shared interests and objectives among three of the principal parties involved: the Yugoslav government, the Albanian government, and the people of Kosovo. The fourth party, the anticommunist Albanian émigrés, stood apart, denying that there had been meaningful improvement in the situation of Kosovo Albanians and continuing their attacks on Yugoslavia for "suppressing the rights of the Albanian minority."

Kosovo Today

While the autonomous province of Kosovo is said by some observers to possess nearly all the constitutional rights enjoyed by the republics of Yugoslavia, it is nevertheless true that the province is faced with such enormous problems of an economic, social, and also political nature as to greatly reduce the practical value of those rights. Despite the progress the province has made since the midsixties, it still lags far behind other regions and nationalities in Yugoslavia. Kosovo's economy is the most backward of any region in the country. The province is shackled with the highest rate of unemployment and the lowest per capita income in the nation. It has the highest illiteracy rate and the fastest population growth rate in Yugoslavia.[41] In addition, ethnic tensions continue to afflict the province. One reason for this is that Kosovo Albanians still lag behind the Serbs in competition for skilled jobs and top positions in industry and commerce, owing to their relative lack of education and training.

A combination of factors, including economic stagnation, high illiteracy, a galloping birth rate, and continuing ethnic rivalries make up the reality of Kosovo today. In other words, the national question has not been solved there. On the contrary, Kosovo seems to have become the new center of tension in Yugoslavia. The evidence suggests that the Albanians of Yugoslavia have become more active politically, more self-assertive socially, and more energetic and competitive economically than at any time since the war.

As in the past, the focus of political activity among Kosovo Albanians continued to be the delicate, decades-old question of attaining republican status for the province of Kosovo. There appeared to be wide sentiment among Albanian nationals for a republic of their own. One of their chief arguments in support of the demand for republican status was based on the population. Kosovo has both a large and compact Albanian population.[42] According to the 1971 Yugoslav census, Kosovo, with a population of 1,245,000, is two and a half times bigger than Montenegro, which numbers only 530,000; yet Montenegro is a republic, while Kosovo is not. The Albanians of Yugoslavia have sought republican status for Kosovo because the logic of their numbers supports such a demand, because it would be the fulfillment of the commitment made to them during the war by the leadership of the Yugoslav Partisans with regard to self-determination, and because of the added prestige they would acquire in the eyes of other nationalities in Yugoslavia, as well as abroad, through an upgrading of their current status.

Their aspirations, however, for the right of self-determination have consistently met with resistance on the part of the federal government of Yugoslavia. It has been reported that in early 1968 Tito "considered the idea of making Kosovo the seventh republic of Yugoslavia" but had to abandon it in view of the strong opposition voiced by the Serbs.[43] A major obstacle to granting Kosovo equal status with the other republics was its proximity to Albania. Belgrade officials were troubled by the suspicion that if they made Kosovo a republic, that action would inevitably lead to the next step—the merger of Kosovo with Albania. Such a development, it was feared, could trigger a chain reaction that might well end in the disintegration of the Yugoslav federation. The two main obstacles, therefore, to making Kosovo a republic were Serbian nationalism and Belgrade's fear of the dismemberment of Yugoslavia.

The aspirations, on the one hand, of ethnic Albanians for full national equality and the refusal, on the other hand, of the Tito leadership to grant such unconditional equality to the Albanians created the basic contradiction in the relations between the Albanian minority and the Yugoslav state. Since 1974, the tensions generated by this contradiction have led to a number of confrontations between Albanian nationals and Yugoslav authorities, some of which attracted international attention. In January 1975, Western press reports told of the arrest, trial, and imprisonment of four Kosovo Albanians on charges of "hostile anti-state activities," including the advocacy of "secession of Kosovo from Yugoslavia." The accused were sentenced to from five to nine years in prison.[44] The demonstration, which occurred in late December 1974 in Priština, was led mostly by students of the University of Priština and reportedly involved some 400 people. On April 3 and 4, 1975, President Tito paid a two-day visit to Priština to assess, among other things, the consequences of the December demonstration within the Kosovo province, as well as its repercussions in the world press.

As the year 1975 drew to a close, there were signs of a hardening of attitudes between Albania and Yugoslavia. While Belgrade officials did not openly accuse Albania of intervention in Kosovo's internal affairs, attacks by Yugoslavia's press on "Pan-Albanian irredentism" implied that the Albanian government was to some degree responsible for the revival of irredentist activity in Kosovo. Belgrade's indirect attacks on Albania came in the wake of several sharp attacks on Yugoslavia's foreign policy in the Albanian press in November of that year.[45]

The simmering nationality question in Kosovo, fed by the seemingly insoluble social, economic, political, language, and ethnic problems of the region, surfaced again early in 1976. Reports from Belgrade said that on February 7, 1976, a court in Priština sentenced at least nineteen Kosovo Albanians to prison terms ranging from four to fifteen years, on charges of belonging to an underground political organization known as the "Kosovo National Liberation Movement." The victims were accused of "irredentism," meaning that they advocated a union of Albanian-speaking areas of Yugoslavia with neighboring Albania.[46] The harsh punishment inflicted on the accused aroused indignation in some sections of the Albanian community in America. On May 3, 1976, Albanian-Americans from the states of Illinois, Wisconsin, and Michigan, under the leadership of Kosovo activists in America, demonstrated in front of the Yugoslav consulate in Chicago to protest Yugoslavia's treatment of Kosovo Albanians. Moreover, Congressman William S. Broomfield of Michigan—a state where the movement for the self-determination of Kosovo has strong adherents—dispatched a letter to the Yugoslav ambassador in Washington, expressing his concern over the sentencing of the nineteen ethnic Albanians in Kosovo.[47]

Albania's position on Kosovo in recent years has been much less vocal and militant than formerly. The two main features of the Albanian regime's position on Kosovo were first, to pose as the defender of Albanian nationals from real or alleged discrimination and persecution by the Slav majority; second, to support the struggle of the Albanian minority for full national equality. This position was reaffirmed by Enver Hoxha at the Seventh APL Congress in November 1976. Hoxha said that "fraternal ties of blood and language with the Albanians of Kosovo, Macedonia and Montenegro, [and] ties of tradition and national customs" gave the Albanian leaders and people the right to interest themselves in their conationals in Yugoslavia, in order that they may "enjoy all the rights, liberties, and opportunities that the other peoples of Federated Yugoslavia possess."[48] Hoxha denounced "the futile and very dangerous attempts" by "certain Yugoslav authorities" to create enmity between the Albanians of Yugoslavia and the Albanian republic. Presumably he was responding to implicit charges by the Yugoslav press that there was a linkage between Kosovo irredentists and the Albanian regime. Hoxha also said that there are "over one and a half million Albanians" in Yugoslavia at present—a much smaller figure than the two and a half million claimed by the Union of Kosovars in exile but higher than the figure of about 1,300,000 given in Yugoslavia's census of 1971.

Hoxha was totally silent on the question of a merger of Kosovo with Albania. This is perhaps not surprising, in view of the fact that Albania has not pressed any territorial claims on Kosovo. Indeed, APL's first secretary did not even lend support to the demands of Kosovo Albanians for a republic of their own. In brief, since normalizing diplomatic relations with Yugoslavia in 1971, Albania has been content to develop cultural relations with Kosovo and to ignore the larger and more pressing political questions which, in recent years, have been a source of increasing friction between the Albanians of Kosovo and the Yugoslav government.

As in the past, so also in recent years, the most fervent champion of the rights of Kosovo Albanians has been the anticommunist Albanian coalition of emigrés, known as *Lidhja Kosovare* or the Union of Kosovars. The coalition represents the major nationalist elements that competed for power in the last war against the communist forces of Enver Hoxha in Albania and Marshal Tito's forces in Kosovo.[49] But inasmuch as it is championing a national and patriotic Albanian cause, the coalition has begun to gather support in various

Albanian communities abroad, especially in the United States. At present the main centers of support in the country are Chicago, Detroit, and New York.

The Union of Kosovars openly proclaims that its objective is the union of Kosovo with "a free, independent, and democratic Albania." It thus stands for an ethnically unified Albanian nation, but at the same time a noncommunist Albania. The émigrés grouped in the union have maintained a consistent position on Kosovo at all times. They characterize Kosovo as an enslaved land, suffering under the double yoke of Slavic domination and communist oppression. Moreover, by Kosovo they mean not simply the autonomous province within the Republic of Serbia but the entire Albanian minority in Yugoslavia, including the Albanians in the republics of Macedonia and Montenegro. They claim that the number of Albanians in Yugoslavia is roughly equal to the population of Albania. It is for this reason that they refer to Kosovo as "the other half of Albania" and insist that without Kosovo Albania cannot be a viable nation.

The Kosovo activists won an important political victory in April 1977 when *Dielli* (The sun), organ of the historic and prestigious Pan-Albanian Federation of America (VATRA), undertook to make the cause of Kosovo its own.[50] VATRA won renown in the annals of the Albanians of America for its influential role in the preservation of Albanian independence and sovereignty from 1912 to 1920. Its alliance with the Kosovo activists was bound to influence Albanian public opinion regarding Kosovo, both within and outside the United States. Encouraged by these developments, the Union of Kosovars made plans to take its case to Washington, D.C. In early June 1977, it issued a call to all Americans of Albanian descent to gather in the Nation's capital on June 16—the day the Helsinki accords were to be reviewed in Belgrade—to "raise their voice against the injustices that are being committed against the Albanians of Kosovo" by the Yugoslav regime.

A Concluding Word

"Unity and Fraternity" of all nationalities in Yugoslavia—this has been one of the guiding principles and proud claims of the Tito regime ever since it came to power. But in the light of the preceding discussion, it is apparent that the Albanian minority in Yugoslavia has been a problem in that country for over sixty years. The "national question" of Albanian ethnics persists. Indeed, it has become more acute since 1974, owing to an increase in national fervor and militancy among the Albanians in the Kosovo province.

Table 11.1
Yugoslavia's Ethnic Minorities (As of March 31, 1971)

Nationalities	Yugoslavia	Bosnia-Herzegovina	Croatia	Macedonia	Montenegro	Serbia	Slovenia
Albanians	1,309,523	3,764	4,175	279,871	35,671	984,761	1,281
Hungarians	477,374	1,262	35,488	229	296	430,314	9,785
Turks	127,920	477	221	108,552	397	18,220	53
Slovaks	83,656	279	6,482	46	31	76,733	85
Gypsies	78,485	1,456	1,257	24,505	396	49,894	977
Bulgarians	58,627	284	676	3,334	394	53,800	139
Romanians	58,570	189	792	105	22	57,419	43
Ruthenians	24,640	141	3,728	59	38	20,608	66
Czechs	24,620	871	19,001	80	74	4,149	445
Walachians	21,990	52	13	7,190	6	14,724	5
Italians	21,791	673	17,433	48	70	566	3,001
Ukrainians	13,972	5,333	2,793	50	10	5,643	143
Germans	12,785	300	2,791	77	109	9,086	422
Russians	7,427	507	1,240	516	116	4,746	302
Jews	4,811	708	2,845	32	26	1,128	72
Poles	3,033	757	819	72	18	1,173	194
Greeks	1,564	48	93	536	23	840	24
Austrians	852	44	352	9	5	164	278
Others	21,722	174	759	16,702	96	3,684	307
Total	2,352,362	17,319	100,958	442,013	34,798	1,737,652	17,622

Source: Slobodan Stanković, "National Minorities in Yugoslavia," *RFE Research*, Feb. 21, 1974.

Table 11.2
Ethnic Minorities in Socialist Republic of Serbia (As of March 31, 1971)

Nationalities	Total	Serbia Proper	Kosovo	Voivodina
Albanians	984,761	65,507	916,168	3,086
Hungarians	430,314	6,279	169	423,866
Slovaks	76,733	3,912	26	72,975
Romanians	57,419	4,412	20	52,987
Bulgarians	53,800	49,791	264	3,745
Gypsies	49,894	27,541	14,593	7,760
Ruthenians	20,608	452	47	20,109
Turks	18,220	5,735	12,244	241
Walachians	14,724	14,653	5	66
Germans	9,086	1,825	18	7,243
Ukrainians	5,643	633	4	5,006
Russians	4,746	2,494	174	2,082
Czechs	4,149	1,341	37	2,771
Poles	1,173	453	16	704
Jews	1,128	603	12	513
Italians	566	330	25	211
Greeks	840	529	15	296
Austrians	164	118	8	38
Others	3,684	1,968	1,017	699

Source: Stanković, "National Minorities in Yugoslavia."

The future course of the Albanian minority in Yugoslavia is likely to be influenced by at least four factors: (1) how the national question in Yugoslavia as a whole is resolved, (2) the ever-shifting balance of power between the pro-Belgrade Albanian element and the pro-Tiranë element in the province, (3) the manner in which relations develop between Yugoslavia and Albania, (4) and probably most important, the effect that the death of Tito will have on Yugoslavia's domestic and foreign policy. At this juncture, the Kosovo question seems as insoluble as the Middle East and Northern Ireland questions. Nonetheless, the main trend of developments in Kosovo seems to be in the direction of greater autonomy, including republican status for the province.

12
The Foreign Policy Line

As with any country in the world today, Albania's foreign policy is the result primarily of her leaders' perception of the nation's fundamental interests. Their perception of those interests derives, of course, from their particular definition of them. And they have defined those interests, above all, in terms of national affirmation, with a view to assuring the country's political independence, terrirotial integrity, ethnic and cultural identity, economic development, and the survival of the present regime.

In spite of the ideological rhetoric that clothes Albania's foreign policy, the "general line" of Albanian Party leaders is not simply the expression of ideology or their peculiar interpretation of Marxism-Leninism. It is not exhuasted, in other words, by their conception of socialism, capitalism, the class struggle, the national liberation movement, and revisionism. The Party's general line is actually a composite of ideological, national, historical, geographic, and cultural forces.

The ideological component is obvious enough and has been rather well documented, especially in W. E. Griffith's book, *Albania and the Sino-Soviet Rift* (1963), and Nicholas Pano's *The People's Republic of Albania* (1968). Much less has been written about the national strand in socialist Albania's foreign policy. Yet nationalism is undoubtedly the most important factor in that policy. While professing fierce loyalty to proletarian internationalism and the interests of socialism and world revolution, Albania has always subordinated such loyalty to her national interests whenever the two have come into conflict with each other. It has been well said that Albania's foreign policy reflects, above all, a "concern to preserve . . . at all costs" the autonomy and integrity of the state.[1] The shifts in Albania's postwar alliances within the communist world become understandable when they are seen as the unceasing efforts of the country to regain political equilibrium and preserve national independence.[2]

The militant and verbally aggressive foreign policy of the Albanian state stems in part from historical and cultural factors. The Albanian people trace the beginnings of their nation to ancient times and point with pride to the fact that, in spite of their small numbers, they survived numerous conquests by foreign powers and maintained their national and ethnic identity through centuries of turmoil. In the course of the age-old struggle to preserve their national and cultural integrity, they developed a martial tradition which is honored and cherished in the country to this day. Albanian art and literature abound with works that extol the martial virtues and exploits of the Albanian people. The long history of foreign aggression, occupation, and oppression explains to some degree the isolationist posture and seeming paranoia of the Albanian regime, even at a time when the dominant political trend in Europe is détente, negotiation of East-West differences, and broadening of economic, technological, and cultural cooperation among nations and peoples.

Historical, national, and ideological forces have combined to produce a revolution-oriented foreign policy in socialist Albania. Accordingly, Albanian leaders reject the doctrine of peaceful coexistence among nations whose systems are "incompatible" with one another, such as capitalism and socialism, although occasionally they pay lip service to the doctrine. They also reject the notion of peaceful competition among socialist and capitalist countries, seeing it as a block to the cause of the revolution whose goal is the overthrow of the capitalist order by force. By the same line of reasoning, they dismiss the theory of peaceful transition to socialism, contending that history does not furnish a successful example of a country that achieved socialism by peaceful means. They continue to argue that it is only through armed struggle that oppressed people and the working masses can gain political power and establish a stable socialist society. They point to the victory of the Vietnamese people in 1975 in the war against the United States and the liquidation of the constitutional, nonviolent Allende government in Chile (1973) as irrefutable proofs of this thesis.

The grand strategy of Albania's Stalinist rulers calls for, and indeed requires, the maintenance and fueling of international tensions. The Hoxha-Shehu regime owes its durability in part to the tensions and crises that have gripped the communist world since World War II, as well as to an element of luck. The tensions between Stalin and Tito in 1948 that led to the expulsion of Yugoslavia from the Cominform, saved the Hoxha group from political and even physical liquidation. The tensions between the Soviet Union and the Hungarians, which culminated in the Hungarian revolution in 1956, again saved the Hoxha leadership from the growing threat posed by the increasing rapprochement between Khrushchev and Marshal Tito, Albania's archenemy at the time. The scenario was replayed in 1960-1961 when the defenders of Cold War politics in Tiranë felt increasingly threatened by Moscow's policy of peaceful coexistence with the Western powers. Then, too, Albania's Stalinist regime was saved by the mounting tensions between Mao Tse-tung and Nikita Khrushchev over Moscow's apparent abandonment of confrontation politics toward the West and other issues. It was a politically "propitious" development that made it possible for Albania's leaders to ally with Peking and thus once again save their regime from ruin.

If follows that international détente is the greatest external enemy of the Albanian regime. Peaceful coexistence, normalization of relations between the NATO and Warsaw Pact blocs, and all measures leading to a reduction of tensions between East and West, between socialist and capitalist countries, have the effect of continually eroding Albania's militant foreign policy, which still operates on the premises of the Cold War. The development of détente therefore means increasing isolationism for the maverick socialist country in southeastern Europe and mounting pressures on its militant regime for reform and change.

It is not surprising then that Albania has denounced all Soviet-American treaties for controlling nuclear arms, including the SALT pacts, and West Germany's *Ostpolitik* which led to the Moscow-Bonn and Warsaw-Bonn protocols in 1970 and subsequently to the Treaty on Basic Relations between the Two German States (1973). Unlike other countries in Europe, Albania stood alone in rejecting all multilateral conferences aimed at furthering European collective security. It was the only country that did not attend the all-European Security and Cooperation Conference, held in Helsinki in July 1975.[3]

Until 1960, the problem of isolationism with regard to Albania was more rhetorical than real, even though Party propagandists talked constantly of encirclement by Yugoslav "modern revisionists" and Greek "monarchofascists." Because of the outward unity of the communist bloc under the leadership of Moscow, the regime identified readily with the bloc and as a consequence projected an image of relative strength and stability to the outside world. The split with the USSR in 1961, however, brought about a sudden and drastic alteration in Albania's political situation, in that the country was now largely isolated from Western as well as from Eastern Europe. To offset the psychological effect on the Albanian population of this near-total isolation in Europe and to discourage a possible coup d'état by disaffected elements, the regime laid great stress on Albania's alliance with the 700-million-strong Chinese. The regime's conscious identification with the world's most populous nation—the "bulwark of the revolution" and the "invincible fortress of Marxism-Leninism"—was a sound and useful exercise in political craftsmanship. It enabled the Party and the government to achieve a remarkable degree of stability and to project an image of self-confidence abroad through most of the decade of the sixties. Indeed, Albania during this period became the nerve center or Mecca on the European Continent for "Marxist-Leninist" communist parties and groups from throughout the world. China's considerable economic support of her ideological ally, coupled with implicit commitments of military aid in case of need, made Albania feel fairly secure.

The invasion, however, of Czechoslovakia in 1968 by Soviet-led Warsaw Pact countries was a traumatic experience for Albania's rulers. The event made them fully aware of the geopolitical realities in Europe and painfully conscious of the fact that Albania was, at bottom, militarily exposed and could not really count on Chinese military support in case of a Soviet attack. The impression of Chinese impotence was no doubt reinforced in 1969, in the wake of the Sino-Soviet border clashes, which reportedly proved very costly to China. In sum, the closing of the 1960s left Albania not only politically isolated in Europe but with a heightened sense of her military vulnerability.

Ten years after the break with the Soviet Union, a dramatic new development occurred in international affairs, which could not but have repercussions on Albanian foreign policy. This was the announcement in Peking and Washington in July 1971 that President Richard Nixon planned to visit China. Nixon's historic trip to China in February 1972 met with a cool reception in Tiranë. In fact, on several occasions that Albanians made indirect attacks on China's sudden reversal of her heretofore bitterly hostile policy toward the United States. The most noted attack came in November 1971, when Hoxha delivered his report to the Sixth Congress of the Albanian Party. Hoxha warned that "any wavering in the struggle against [U.S.] imperialism is fraught with very dangerous consequences," that "you cannot rely on one imperialism to oppose the other," and finally that "one cannot successfully oppose [U.S.] imperialism without also fighting Soviet social-imperialism ... and vice versa."[4]

In the five years intervening between the Sixth and the Seventh APL Congresses, many dramatic political events occurred in both communist China and Albania. The more significant events in China were the death of Chou En-lai and Mao Tse-tung in 1976, the rise of Hua Kuo-feng to the top position of leadership in Peking, and the dramatic downfall of the "radicals" in the CPC Politburo, the so-called "Gang of Four," namely Mao's wife Chiang Ching, Wang Hung-wen, Chang Chun-chiao, and Yao Wen-yuan. There followed the spectacular rehabilitation of former Vice Premier Teng Hsiao-ping, who had twice fallen out of favor with Mao, and the holding of the historic Eleventh Chinese CP Congress in August 1977. Albania in turn was shaken by widespread dissent in the cultural, military, and economic sectors, forcing the regime to resort to purges of the leadership in those sectors in order to contain the dissent. The internal turmoil was to some degree the direct consequence of political and other events occurring in Europe and China, especially the changing relations between China and Albania. Nevertheless, these internal and external pressures for change had no visible effect on the men who formulate and implement Albania's foreign policy. This became apparent in the lengthy report that APL's first secretary, Enver Hoxha, presented to the Party's Seventh Congress.

Hoxha's remarks on Albania's foreign policy covered familiar ground, for the most part. He reiterated the Party's dogmatic faith in the revolution, saying that it is the only road of salvation from economic crises and the exploitation of capitalist and revisionist systems. He claimed that détente is a mere slogan rather than a political reality. The term "détente," along with such phrases as "general security," "equilibrium of forces," "spheres of influence," "limited sovereignty," and "dependent world" are only notions invented by enemies of peace and freedom of peoples in order to foster a capitulationist mentality among the working masses. The Helsinki Conference on European Security (1975) accomplished nothing, Hoxha said, in the way of strengthening peace. Neither SALT nor other disarmament agreements between East and West have advanced the cause of peace and security among nations. The numerous contacts and protocols between revisionist East Europe and the Western imperialist powers have not resulted in true dialogue or meaningful exchanges in the interest of peace and the welfare of European peoples. They have not contributed to a lowering of international tensions or the liquidation of the Cold War.

Hoxha's report to the congress followed the well-established Albanian pattern of presenting on the one hand a bleak picture of the capitalist world and insisting on the other hand that the trend of world events is favorable to the revolution. As in the past fifteen years, Albania's top leader attributed the present tensions and conflicts in the world to the two superpowers: the United States and the USSR. His report reaffirmed the fact that the keystone in Albania's foreign policy is total and unswerving opposition to the world's two leading powers. In the Albanian view, American "imperialism" and Soviet "modern revisionism" or "social imperialism" are the true and sole source of all the political, economic, social, and cultural dislocations and ills besetting contemporary nations and societies.

Hoxha thus left no doubt that Albania continues to adhere to what is commonly known as the "dual adversary" doctrine. The doctrine rests on the conviction that the United States and the Soviet Union are two equally aggressive and equally dangerous superpowers, bent on world hegemony. The two distinctive features of United States-Soviet relations are collaboration and rivalry. The superpowers are by nature aggressive, perfidious, and greedy for power. To maintain and expand their dominant position in world affairs, they continue to oppress, exploit, manipulate, threaten, and blackmail the smaller and weaker nations. In their headlong drive for world hegemony, they are building up their arsenals with increasingly destructive weapons and are preparing to unleash a third world war, fought with the most sophisticated atomic weapons.

The scenario of international affairs, as presented by Hoxha, is thus fairly simple. On the one side are the forces of imperialism, fascism, revisionism, and reaction, headed by the United States and the Soviet Union; on the other side are the Marxist-Leninist, revolutionary, and progressive forces of the world. In accordance with the law of dielectical materialism, the two sides are locked in a life-and-death struggle. And since the nature of the present epoch is the transition from the age of capitalism to the age of socialism and communism, the progressive pro-peace forces are destined to triumph. To speed the process of transition, the Albanian leadership considers it its proletarian internationalist duty to alert the peoples of the world to the dangerous politics of the superpowers and to make every effort toward the creation of a united front of "the peoples of the world" to oppose and defeat Soviet-American power. Such is the general outline of the world "balance of forces" so to speak, as seen by the Albanian leaders. It forms the basis for the revolutionary orientation of Albania's foreign policy.

Starting from this theoretical framework, Albania's position on other outstanding international questions follows more or less logically. The chief guiding principle for the proletariat, Marxist-Leninist revolutionaries, and the peoples of the world is to wage an open, vigorous, uncompromising and relentless struggle against the two superpowers, the United States and the Soviet Union, until their power and influence is totally destroyed. Consequently, it is erroneous and extremely dangerous for a socialist country—indeed, for any nation—to have contacts, enter into negotiations, and conclude agreements with the superpowers. To ignore this precept is to collaborate with the class enemy.

In conformity with this stance, Hoxha reaffirmed Albania's condemnation of NATO and the Warsaw Pact on the ground that both military blocs were under the control of the superpowers. He informed the Seventh APL Congress that the two blocs "have been and remain instruments for preparing and unleashing war."[5] On the economic front he reiterated Albania's opposition to regional economic groupings, such as the European Economic Community (Common Market) and its counterpart in East Europe, the COMECON. He said that both organizations served the "aggressive and exploitive" policies of the United States and the USSR rather than the economic and national interests of the member states. He also denounced the concept of a United Europe, alleging that it aims at "the elimination of the notion of nationality," and would result in "the extinction of the personality of the peoples and states of Western Europe."[6] Hoxha's remarks here reflected once again Albania's passionate attachment to nationalism.

Turning his attention to less developed regions of the world, Hoxha warned that terms such as "third world," "nonaligned states," or "developing" countries create illusions among the working masses in that they are led to believe they have found a shelter from the threats of the superpowers. But the fact is that most of those countries are closely tied to the superpowers and former colonial powers politically, ideologically, and economically. Hence the term "nonaligned" that is championed by the "Yugoslav revisionists" rings totally false and has no political validity. One must realize, Hoxha argued, that the bourgeoisie is a close ally of the superpowers in all countries where the United States and the USSR exert influence. The bourgeoisie is actually the main support of the imperialists in their efforts to prevent the people from rising in rebellion against their domestic and foreign oppressors. Therefore these two forces, namely the imperialists and the reactionary bourgeoisie, cannot be separated from each other. "You cannot fight one of them without fighting the other also."[7]

Reviewing Albania's relations with her Balkan neighbors, Hoxha said that they were developing satisfactorily with Greece, Yugoslavia, and Romania but, unfortunately, not with Bulgaria, inasmuch as she "has become a tool" in the hands of the Soviets and pursues a "hostile" policy toward Albania. Albania's continued attack on Bulgaria showed that fears of possible Soviet aggression against Balkan countries were still alive in Tiranë. In developing relations with other countries—with the exception of the United States and the USSR—Albania followed the principle of separating ideology from other considerations, such as trade and cultural matters. Accordingly, Albanian leaders felt free to carry on ideological polemics against Yugoslavia and other countries and at the same time pursue normal relations with them in the areas of diplomacy, trade, and culture. In his report to the Party congress, Hoxha said the Albanians had "irreconcilable contradictions of principle" with Yugoslavia in matters of ideology and politics and would continue to voice those differences in the future. He then launched a vitriolic attack on "Yugoslav revisionism," charging that it has supported world capitalism while zealously opposing the revolution and Marxism-Leninism. "Born as an opportunist ideological current to undermine the socialist society from within," Hoxha went on to say, Yugoslav revisionism "remains the favorite weapon of the internationalist imperialist bourgeoisie in the struggle against socialism and liberation movements."[8] Khrushchev, Palmiro Togliatti, and their followers were inspired by Yugoslav revisionism "to fight socialism and Marxist-Leninist ideology." Albania's attitude toward Tito's politics has been the most significant yardstick of her foreign policy ever since 1948, and Hoxha's report in November 1976 proved that the foundations of that policy had not changed. Tiranë was intent on pressing forward with its militant ideology in the true Cold War spirit that reigned over East Europe and the internationalist communist movement in the days of Stalin.

Tiranë's position on the USSR remained unchanged. Albanian Party leaders continued to regard Moscow as the center of modern revisionism and rejected with disdain all initiatives by Soviet leaders to normalize relations. Such was the enmity that Hoxha and Shehu felt toward the Soviet leadership that they belittled not only the enormous contribution of the USSR to the postwar reconstruction and development of Albania; they went so far as to denigrate the role of the Soviet Union in World War II in relation to Albania's liberation. Whereas previously Albania's leaders declared with pride and gratitude that the liberation of Albania was due "above all to the heroic struggle of the peoples of the Soviet Union,"[9] later they said that liberation was due primarily to the Partisan forces led by the Albanian Communist Party. To emphasize its total and undeviating hostility to Moscow, the Hoxha leadership published for the first time, in late 1975 and 1976, a number of documents on Hoxha's visit to Moscow in November 1960 and the talks he had there with Nikita Khrushchev and other Soviet Party leaders.[10] The documents received wide publicity in the West. They threw light on the differences that divided Soviet and Albanian Party leaders and depicted the stormy, even brutal, passions they engendered among them. Thoroughly disillusioned with the CPSU leadership's general line of peaceful coexistence with the West, the denigration of Stalin, the heavy-handed policy toward fraternal CPs, and above all its rapprochement with the "renegade Tito clique," Albanian leaders thereafter cut off all relations with Moscow and called repeatedly on the people of the Soviet Union to rise and overthrow their "traitorous revisionist" leaders and restore genuine socialism in their country. In the eyes of Hoxha and Shehu, the

USSR, like Yugoslavia, is no longer a socialist country but rather a country where capitalism has been fully restored and where life is bleaker than in the Russia of the Czars. In brief, as long as the Hoxha-Shehu team held power in Albania, the chances for a rapprochement with the Soviet Union were practically nil.

Hoxha's report to the Party's November 1976 Congress came barely two weeks after the official Chinese announcement of the purge of the "Gang of Four." The report contained no reference to the fallen quartet or to the succession of Hua Kuo-feng to the post of the late Chairman Mao. In general Hoxha's tone in discussing Albanian-Chinese relations was friendly. His report gave the impression that Albania's alliance with China was stable. He said that the Albanian Party and people were "loyal friends and allies" of the Chinese Party and people. He praised Mao—the chief architect of the Sino-Albanian entente—as "a great revolutionary" and "a distinguished Marxist-Leninist" who had enriched the theory and revolutionary practice of the proletariat. Indeed, when the Chinese leader died in September 1976, Albania declared a three-day mourning period in honor of his memory. Hoxha also had lavish praise for China's Great Proletarian Cultural Revolution, which had "strengthened the positions of socialism and the dictatorship of the proletariat" in China.

Nevertheless, some passages in Hoxha's report contrasted strongly with certain foreign policy positions of China and amounted to implicit attacks on Peking. They related to China's developing relations with the United States, her support for NATO and the Common Market, and her courting of the "reactionary bourgeoisie" of the countries of the Third World. Once again he spoke of Albania's "dual adversary" doctrine, reminding the Chinese that the two superpowers are equally dangerous and therefore "you can never lean on one imperialism in order to fight the other."[11] Using esoteric language, he attacked China for placing herself under the "defensive umbrella" of the United States in order to meet the challenge of Soviet military power. Such a policy, Hoxha contended, means making political and economic concessions to the United States that eventually could threaten China's national sovereignty.

It was fairly obvious also that Albania was not happy over the arrest of the "Gang of Four," since the militant politics of the fallen radicals were more congenial to Albanian leaders than the politics of the moderates, represented by Hua. In fact, one member of the "Gang of Four," Yao Wen-yuan, had been warmly received in Tiranë in November 1974 when Albania celebrated the thirtieth anniversary of her liberation. Hoxha's displeasure with the October 1976 events in Peking became manifest in his telegram of greetings to Hua upon his election as chairman of the CPC. He said, "We congratulate you on the occasion of your arrival [rather than election or appointment] to the post of Chairman."[12] The Albanians thus seemed to cast doubt on the legitimacy of Hua's authority and leadership of the Chinese Communist Party and nation.

APL's first secretary considered also the situation of communist parties in Europe and the international communist movement in general. Never before at a Party Congress had he devoted so much time to the discussion of this matter. As usual he separated the "revisionist" CPs from the "Marxist-Leninist" parties, heaping scorn on the former and praising the latter. Referring to the East Berlin Conference of European Communist Parties that was held on June 29-30, 1976, he called it an anti-Marxist conference that unmasked the revisionists as "incorrigible opportunists and anti-communists." The document issued by the conference, the so-called Declaration of Berlin, showed that the revisionist parties of Western Europe have renounced the dictatorship of the proletariat and the revolution and seek instead collaboration and eventual fusion with the bourgeoisie.

Hoxha lauded the role of Marxist-Leninist Parties and groups in the struggle for national liberation of peoples, revolution, and socialism. It has been the custom in Albania to invite Marxist-Leninist groups from all parts of the world to attend Party Congresses. A total of twenty-nine delegations of Marxist-Leninist CPs and groups attended the Seventh APL Congress. Hoxha said that the Albanian Party of Labor was in complete solidarity with such parties and stood ready to assist them in every way possible.

After the break with the USSR and the subsequent rift between China and the Soviet Union, Albania worked energetically to encourage the creation of revolutionary communist parties. For some fifteen years Tiranë has been the ideological center on the European continent for revolutionary groups. The Albanian Party served as a model party—along with the Chinese CP—for such groups, while Hoxha and Mao became for them model revolutionary leaders. At the Seventh APL Congress the idea apparently occurred to the Hoxha-Shehu leadership to transform Albania from an ideological center of revolution to an organizational center, in order to serve more effectively the cause of the revolution. In this connection Hoxha spoke of the positive role the Comintern played in the time of Lenin and Stalin, implying that Albania might fulfill a function at present similar to that of the Comintern in former times. He hinted that an international meeting of all Marxist-Leninist parties might be held in Albania in the near future.

Judging by the greetings to the congress of a number of the foreign delegations, it was evident that in their eyes Albania had replaced China as the bastion of world revolution and vanguard of Marxist-Leninist forces. It was in 1966 that Mao Tse-tung coined the slogan "Albania is the shining beacon of socialism in Europe." The phrase first appeared in his message of greetings to the Fifth APL Congress in November of that year. Yet ten years later Ernst Aust, head of the West German Marxist-Leninist CP, said in Tiranë that "Albania is not only the great beacon light of socialism for Europe, but for all the world."[13] The same sentiment was voiced by Raul Marco, head of the Spanish delegation to the congress. Fosco Dinucci, leader of the Italian delegation and General Secretary of the Italian Marxist-Leninist CP, said that Hoxha's report to the congress was a "contribution of great historical importance" not only for the construction of socialism in Albania but also "for the strategy and tactics of the international communist movement and the advancement of revolutionary practice."[14] Many of the delegations hailed Hoxha as a great Marxist-Leninist. The most enthusiastic appraisal came from the Brazilian delegation, which called Hoxha "the greatest and most enlightened Marxist-Leninist of the present time."

Continuing his report, Hoxha repeated one of the Party's favorite slogans, namely that Albania was building socialism in conditions of a vicious capitalist-revisionist encirclement. Paradoxically however, he denied that Albania was isolated and in support of his statement said that the country had diplomatic relations with seventy-four nations. To be sure, by autumn 1977 Albania had established diplomatic ties with a total of eighty nations, including all West European nations with the exception of Spain, West Germany, and Great Britain. Nonetheless, owing to her militant ideology, revolutionary stance, polemical warfare against both East and West Europe, and refusal to have broad cultural exchanges with European and other nations, Albania remained a Cold War island in the Balkans and Europe.

In sum, Hoxha's report to the Seventh APL Congress was significant and illuminating for several reasons. First, it reaffirmed the fact that Albania's dogmatic, Stalinist foreign policy continued on course, as before. Second, it sanctioned anew the Party's policy of keeping Albania isolated from nearly all countries. Third, it showed that Albania was taking an intense and unprecedented interest in promoting ties with Marxist-Leninist Communist Parties and groups. And fourth, the report revealed a widening of ideological differences between China and Albania.

Albania Launches Public Attack on China

On July 7, 1977, the Albanian Party daily, *Zëri i popullit*, came out with a 10,000-word editorial sharply attacking China's foreign policy. While it did not mention China by name, there was no doubt that the target of the stinging attack was Albania's heretofore closest ideological ally. Entitled "The Theory and Practice of Revolution," the editorial denounced China's policy toward the United States and the Third World. The Albanian statement accused China of "opportunism," "flagrant departure from the teachings of Marxism-Leninism," and attempts to "sabotage the revolution." The focus of the Albanian attack was on two key issues of Chinese foreign policy: (1) the view that one of the superpowers, the USSR, is more aggressive and more dangerous than the other, namely the United States; (2) the Chinese concept of three worlds: the world of the superpowers, the world of the industrialized countries, and the world of the developing nations. According to the *Zëri i popullit* editorial:

To speak about the so-called "third world" as the principal force of the struggle against imperialism, as do the supporters of the theory of the "three worlds," without making any distinction between the true anti-imperialist and revolutionary forces and the pro-imperialist, reactionary and fascist forces currently in power in a number of developing countries, means to depart in a flagrant manner from the teachings of Marxism-Leninism and to preach typically opportunistic viewpoints, thus causing confusion and disorientation among revolutionary forces. In essence, according to the theory of the "three worlds," the peoples in these countries must not struggle, for example, against the bloody fascits dictatorships of Geisel in Brazil and of Pinochet in Chile.

The editorial said the Chinese were in effect calling on peoples and revolutionaries to join forces with the reactionary regimes of the Third World; in short, "to renounce the revolution."

On the issue of the superpowers, the editorial noted: "Experience has verified that both superpowers represent, in the same measure and to the same degree, the chief enemy of socialism. [To] underestimate the danger posed by one or the other superpower and, worse still, to call for unity with one superpower in order to oppose the other, is to invite catastrophic consequences for the future of the revolution."

A third leading feature of the Albanian editorial is the linkage it made between the Chinese advocates of the Three Worlds theory and "the theoreticians of 'nonalignment,'" meaning the Yugoslav leadership. This was a serious charge, for Yugoslavia's concept of nonalignment has long been regarded as heresy by

Albania's leaders. They have viewed nonalignment as a cunning device to sabotage the national liberation movement and the revolution.

The July 7 attack on China was followed by half a dozen other attacks in July and August, most of them in the form of signed editorials in *Zëri i popullit*. Of special importance was the reprint in August of a lengthy document on a conversation Enver Hoxha had with Chou En-lai in Tiranë in March 1965.[15] In the light of the Sino-Albanian rift, the document could be read as an implicit attack on the present Chinese leadership for aiding and abetting the "Hitlerian policies" of Washington. It could also be interpreted as a call on all Marxist-Leninist parties to declare war on the Hua Kuo-feng leadership in Peking. The publication of this material presumably meant that Albanian leaders were determined to press their ideological offensive against the Chinese, despite several attempts by the Hua leadership to win their approval and support of the post-Mao line in Peking.

Actually Albania's rift with China was not surprising, although hardly anyone expected it to come so soon. The beginnings of the rift could be traced back to 1969, when China began to emerge from her diplomatic and political isolation, as a consequence of which Albania began to lose the political value she had for the Chinese up to that time. The potential rift began to take definite form in 1971-1972 with the start of the dialogue between China and the United States. It apparently reached a point of no return in 1976 with the death of Mao and Chou En-lai, the fall of the radicals (represented by the "Gang of Four"), and the rise of the moderates to leading positions of power in Peking.

Developments in China in 1977 very likely deepened Albanian displeasure and disillusionment with the direction of Chinese politics, on both the domestic and foreign planes. Foremost among these developments were probably the rehabilitation of Teng Hsiao-ping by the Third Plenary Session of the CPC Central Committee that was held on July 16-21, and the convening of the Eleventh Party Congress the following month (August 12-18). Teng was a hated name in Albania. On several occasions in 1976, Enver Hoxha denounced him—along with Liu Shao-chi and Lin Piao—as a "capitulationist," a "revisionist" and a "counterrevolutionary." Contrary to Albanian enthusiasm over previous Chinese Party Congresses, the Albanian press was eloquently silent about the Eleventh Congress, except for a brief communique from Peking that was printed without comment.[16] The Hoxha leadership was undoubtedly disconcerted by reports that a process of de-ideologization and even "de-Maoization" was taking place in China and that the principles and goals of the Cultural Revolution had been officially abandoned by the country's new leaders. Finally, Tito's nine-day visit to China (August 30–September 7, 1977) could not but infuriate the Albanians. For nearly three decades Tito has been the object of the greatest scorn on the part of Albanian leaders, who saw him as the leading revisionist renegade and betrayer of the communist cause. The invitation extended to Tito by China's new leaders, their open endorsement of Yugoslavia's nonalignment policy,[17] and their interest in Yugoslavia's self-management system[18] could be interpreted as a calculated Chinese rebuff to Albania, which Hoxha was not likely to ignore.

Concluding Remarks

Albania's sensational open rift with her sole ideological ally marks a watershed in Albanian-Chinese relations. In effect, it brought to an end the sixteen-year-old alliance between Albania and China.

The attack on China, on grounds of ideology, emphasizes once again the great importance the Albanian leaders attach to ideology, as opposed to pragmatism or the concern with practical questions of economics, technology, and management. China's contacts and cooperation with American capitalists and Yugoslav "revisionists" means, in the Albanian view, that she is no longer a genuine socialist state but rather a revisionist country. From Enver Hoxha's frame of reference, China has gone far down the road of collaboration with the class enemy and in principle is no different from the Soviet Union or Yugoslavia—the two "arch-revisionist" states in the world at present.

The initiative of the Albanian leadership in questioning China's international stance and challenging her claim to being a revolutionary country, proved conclusively—if such proof were needed—Albania's independence of China. It demonstrated that the Albanian Party was not a mere mouthpiece of Peking but follows a basically independent foreign policy.

By accusing China of abandoning revolutionary politics, Albania in effect lays claim to being the only genuine, revolutionary Marxist-Leninist state in the world today. According to Albania's intransigent Stalinist leadership, Albania is now the world center of revolution. In any event the rift with China means a further fragmentation of the socialist world and a historic split in the Marxist-Leninist forces. Instead of a unitary revolutionary world center, built around Peking and Tiranë, henceforth there will presumably be two distinct and competing centers: one in Peking and the other in Tiranë.

The open Sino-Albanian rift implies also an end to China's alleged plan to create a Balkan anti-Moscow entente, consisting of Tiranë, Belgrade, and Bucharest.

Epilogue

Disillusioned with Western diplomacy, which in 1878 and in 1913 cost Albania the loss of vast territory to the neighboring states of Serbia, Montenegro, and Greece; and embittered by the disastrous experience of close ties with a big Western power, namely Italy under the reign of Mussolini that ended with the occupation of the country in 1939, postwar Albania turned to the East in the long search for national security and economic wellbeing.

In three decades of tight, centralized communist rule, Albania was able to make remarkable strides in modernization. Compared with pre-World War II conditions in the country, Albanian society in the seventies had been transformed in every respect—economically, socially, culturally, and to some extent psychologically as well.

The economy of the country underwent a historic transition from private enterprise, of a rather primitive sort, to collectivism or a state-planned and state-directed economy. In the mid-seventies, Albania appeared to have the most orthodox and least flexible economic system in East Europe. Yet, under this system Albania had succeeded in laying the foundations of a modern industrial state and raising the standard of living of her impoverished people. The dominant goal of Albania's leaders in this respect was to transform the country from an agricultural to an industrial society. But the rigidity of the economic system generated wave upon wave of dissent among the people, creating a chronic problem for the leadership of the country.

Socially the country had come a long way toward overcoming age-old barriers to social progress. Using the communist formula for social change as a guide, Albania resorted to drastic steps in order to destroy deeply rooted medieval social structures and debilitating Oriental traditions. The complex struggle aimed at the elimination of tribal or semitribal social structures, blood feuds, superstitition, illiteracy, disease, and economic, social, and sexual inequality. In the course of thirty years, Albania succeeded in abolishing nearly all traces of the outmoded patriarchal social system, including the tradition of blood feuds. Similarly, the country apparently succeeded in abolishing illiteracy for all citizens under the age of forty, vastly expanding the system of education, securing the population from the ravages of epidemics, such as malaria, and instituting an extensive social welfare program. The determined campaign for the emancipation of women marked a historic change in the relations between men and women in the ancient Balkan nation. The campaign achieved a notable measure of success, but owing to the relatively undeveloped nature of Albanian society, Albanian women were still one or two steps behind their Western sisters in the struggle to attain equality with men.

In the area of culture, too, Albania made impressive advances, in spite of the ideological restrictions that were placed on artists and all cultural workers. Literature, painting, music, sculpture, the theater, the ballet, and other art forms developed to an unprecedented degree. Cultural activity reached even the humble cabins of peasants in the remote highlands of the country. Albania promoted the theory that art must be nationalist in form and socialist in content. She demanded that art subordinate itself to politics and that artists forego individual expression and personal gratification for the sake of serving the greater interests of society and the nation. She was eager to "export" her art and culture to other countries, especially Western Europe, but refused to open her doors to cultural influences from abroad, for fear that alien influences would undermine the national character and "communist purity" of her society. This one-sided cultural policy was a reflection of the country's traditional xenophobic tendencies. Many of the country's artists, however, complained that the Party's policy on art and culture was sectarian and oppressive. As a result the country's leadership was continually confronted with pressures from the intelligentsia to relax its control over the artistic community and to broaden cultural relations with the outside world.

Since 1944, Albania made valiant efforts to change the psychology and mentality of the population, with a view to overcoming the harmful legacy of Oriental fatalism and the notorious individualism of her citizens. While her top leaders were ruthless in the use of force in order to carry out their blueprint for modernization of the country, they nevertheless viewed education as the key in the long run to changing the consciousness of the people and building a new and progressive society. The primary objective of the Ideological and Cultural Revolution was to imbue the population with a new consciousness that stressed the values of self-denial and heroism in place of personal gain and comfort, and service to society in place of private advancement. But this teaching, like the teachings of the world's great religions, collided constantly with manifestations of egocentric and antisocial behavior on the part of numerous people, including communists.

Throughout its three-decades-old rule, the Albanian Party showed extraordinary concern to maintain its leading role in the Albanian state, which in practice meant dictatorial control over every phase of Albanian society. Over the years this led to a cult of the Party and of Enver Hoxha. The Party could not tolerate competing ideologies, even of a religious kind, and this was a major reason why Albania abolished the institution of religion in 1967. In this drastic social experiment, the Party leaders had the indispensable support of Albanian nationalism. They made nationalism an ally in the struggle against religion by successfully exploiting the antagonism between national aspirations and religion that developed during the movement for national independence. They also made effective use of the argument that religion—which they equated with malignant superstition—was an obstacle to the drive for modernization and a better standard of living for the people.

In the field of ideology and politics, Albania stood apart in the communist world for her unswerving loyalty to the memory of Stalin and to the Stalinist concept of statecraft. She remained the last outpost of Stalinism in Europe. Three decades after World War II, the country was still in the stage of revolutionary fervor and fanaticism and stubbornly resisted all pressures to decentralize authority and liberalize its social order. Its leaders continued to pursue Cold War politics, maintaining a "war psychosis" at home and fueling the polemics of class struggle and revolution on the international front.

Albania adhered to Stalinism in large part because Hoxha and Shehu were convinced believers in the classic communist dogma as interpreted by Stalin. Even the slogan that Albania was building socialism under a state of siege, imposed by her enemies, seemed to be modeled on Stalin's famous slogan that the Soviets were building "Socialism in one country" in the face of capitalist encirclement. Nationalism tinged with xenophobia was another powerful reason why Albania found it more congenial to remain faithful to Stalinism that to experiment with liberalism and abandon the policy of isolationism. A third reason for Albania's Stalinism was tied directly to the Party's leaders and the nearly absolute power they wielded in the country. Hoxha and Shehu were concerned about their positions and were persuaded that any relaxation of their Stalinist rule would ultimately threaten their own power and authority. Yet, in a Europe where détente was the dominant political trend in recent years, Albania's Stalinist politics seemed anachronistic and self-defeating. The extensive purges that swept the country in 1973-1976 were prompted in part by growing popular resistance to the Party's Stalinist domestic and foreign policy.

In foreign policy, Albania turned eastward at the close of World War II. Choosing the communist model as an instrument for modernization, Albania allied herself first with Yugoslavia (1944-1948), next with the Soviet Union (1948-1961), and then with communist China (1961-1977). Albania's relations with far-off China were the central factor in her foreign policy during

Epilogue 260

two decades in the nation's history, the sixties and the seventies. But whereas the decade of the sixties was one of seemingly ideal relations of friendship and all-round cooperation between a big and a small country, the decade of the seventies began to reveal cracks in the alliance. Beginning in 1971, the alliance suffered reverses in the areas of ideology, politics, the economy, and more recently the military.

The passing of Mao Tse-tung and Chou En-lai in 1976 closed an era for communist China, as well as a period in Albania's foreign relations, namely her special relationship with China. The rift with China took definite shape and apparently became irreversible in 1977, following the Eleventh Chinese Party Congress and Tito's trip to Peking. There are some noteworthy parallels between the dissolution of the Albanian-Soviet alliance and the widening rift between Albania and China. The Albanians were opposed to Khrushchev's trip to Belgrade in 1955; likewise they were unhappy about President Nixon's trip to Peking in 1972. They viewed these events as acts of collusion by their allies with notorious enemies of socialism and the revolution. Subsequently they condemned the Twentieth Congress of CPSU (1956) as the congress that put the USSR on a revisionist course. From Albania's point of view, the same could logically be said of China's Eleventh Party Congress (1977), which terminated the Cultural Revolution and reportedly set China on a revisionist footing. President Tito's trip to China in late August and September 1977 assuredly confirmed Albania's worst suspicions about China's post-Mao deviationism. Her leaders showed their strong disapproval of Tito's visit by reprinting in *Zëri i popullit* (September 2, 1977), a scathing 1963 article by Hoxha, under the title "Khrushchev on His Knees Before Tito"—an obvious reference to Chairman Hua Kuo-feng and his warm welcome of the Yugoslav leader in Peking. In brief, the ideological differences between Albania and China that emerged in 1971, became aggravated in 1975 by economic differences and evidently reached a point of no return in 1976-1977, with the rise to power in Peking of the "revisionist" Hua Kuo-feng, the rehabilitation of the "counter-revolutionary" Teng Hsiao-ping, and China's startling rapprochement with the "renegade" leadership of Yugoslavia.

What were the causes of the rift between the two "revolutionary vanguard" states in the socialist world? From the Albanian side, the leading cause seems to have been ideological. Hoxha has a distinguished record as a doctrinaire communist and was apparently willing to risk a rift with the Chinese comrades in defense of the communist faith, when in his view China embarked on a revisionist path. Furthermore, China's enthusiastic embrace of Tito presumably stirred old Albanian fears for the nation's independence and security, fears dating from the traumatic year of 1948 when Albania was almost annexed by Yugoslavia. Nationalism was thus another important factor in the rift. Economics also played a part. The Albanians resented the cutbacks of Chinese aid and credits.

The Chinese for their part had several reasons to downgrade the alliance with the Albanians. First, the Chinese presumably were disappointed with Albania's disapproval of their initiatives to normalize relations with America. Second, by the mid-1970s China had established diplomatic relations with a large number of countries throughout the globe and had gained admission also to the United Nations (October 1971). Having emerged from her previous isolation, she had much less need of Albania's political, ideological, and diplomatic support than in previous years. She could therefore more easily afford to risk a breach with Albania's foreign policy. Third, with the broadening of her political and economic relations, China's commitments of economic and technical aid to developing countries grew steadily. This development probably played a part in the Chinese decision to reduce economic support to Albania. Fourth, like the Soviets before them, the Chinese very likely considered that Yugoslavia carried more weight on the international scale than Albania and was potentially a more valuable ally to China than Albania.

In sum, by late 1977 the Sino-Albanian entente was well on the way to dissolution. The rift with China meant that socialist Albania would now be more isolated than ever before. The rift was expected to have an impact particularly on the economy of the Balkan country. Albania's weak economy had always been the Achilles' heel that in the past invited political dependency on a foreign power and created serious hazards for the nation's security and independence. Consequently, the current Five-Year Plan was critical for the country's economic well-being, and could test the strength of the Hoxha-Shehu leadership and force a modification in Albania's general line. China's ideological revisionism since 1971, and the readjustment of her economic policy on Albania in 1975, formed the backdrop for the domestic turmoil in Albania's economy, the military, and cultural life in the first part of the 1970s. It was "no accident"—as communist theoreticians are fond of saying—that the rising dissent and unprecedented purges of leading figures in these areas occurred during the period of widening ideological, political, and economic differences between the Albanian regime and China.

Under these circumstances, it was natural to ask about the direction Albania would take in the wake of her third disenchantment with a close communist ally since 1944? Would she turn again from East to West? At present, the indications are that Albania intends to "go it alone" and at the same time assume the leadership of the world's "genuine" Marxist-Leninist movement, in bitter opposition to Peking. Such a policy may sound quixotic, to be sure, but then many people thought that the Sino-Albanian alliance was quixotic and extravagant; yet it lasted for sixteen years. Developments of this sort are not really strange to the world of politics. Indeed, they are part of its fascination.

One can nevertheless predict that when Hoxha and Shehu are no longer in power in Tiranë, significant political, economic, and social changes will occur in Albania. Such changes occurred in the Soviet Union after the death of Stalin, and in China after the death of Mao. It is reasonable to expect that similar changes will take place in a post-Hoxha Albania. The country can be expected to emerge from its isolation, liberalize its regime, and finally lose its label as the last stronghold of Stalinism in Europe.

Regardless of the form and direction that Albania's future political orientation takes, we can assume that the country will survive, as it has done for thousands of years, and preserve its identity and character as well as its strange appeal to the outside world.

Notes

Notes to Chapter 1

1. As given in Faik Konitza, *Albania: The Rock Garden of Southeastern Europe*, ed. G. M. Panarity (Boston, Mass.); the name of publishing house and the date of publication are not given, but the book appeared ca. 1960.

2. As quoted by Konitza, *Rock Garden*, p. 12.

3. To be sure, part of the problem of inaccurate reportage on postwar Albania was due to the politics of isolation pursued by the country's Stalinist leadership.

4. In linear dimensions, Albania is 336 km (180 mi) long, north to south, and 148 km (85 mi) wide at her broadest part.

5. According to the 1970 U.S. census.

6. Ramadan Marmullaku, *Albania and the Albanians* (London: C. Hurst & Co., 1975), p. 3.

7. The terms "Geg" and "Tosk" are no longer in use in Albania. Being anxious to eliminate traditional linguistic, social, and other differences between the two groups, the postwar Albanian regime chose to use the terms "northern" and "southern" Albanians to designate the people in the two regions, instead of retaining the more or less politically polarized "Geg" and "Tosk" labels.

8. Charles and Barbara Jelavich, *The Balkans* (Englewood cliffs, N.J.: Prentice-Hall, 1965), p. 4; Wayne S. Vucinich, *Eastern Europe* (Lexington, Mass.: Ginn & Co., 1973), p. 11.

9. Marmullaku, *Albania*, p. 6.

10. See esp. *Ilirët dhe gjeneza e Shqiptarëve* [The Illyrians and the genesis of the Albanians] (Tiranë: Mihal Duri Press, 1969); and the two-volume publication, *Kuvendi i Studimeve Ilirë* [The Congress of Illyrian Studies], containing the proceedings of the congress, held in Tiranë Sept. 15–20, 1972, and published by the Mihal Duri Press in 1974.

11. Pockets of Arbëresh Italians exist currently in several cities in the United States, including a community of a few hundred in the town of Milford, Mass., not far from Wrocester and in Philadelphia, New Orleans, and San Francisco. See *Dielli* [The sun] (Boston), Oct. 1, 1976.

12. *Rock Garden*, p. 9.

13. Contemporary Albanian contains a considerable number of Latin, Turkish, Greek, and Slavic words.

14. Stuart E. Mann. *Albanian Literature* (London: Bernard Quaritch, 1955), p. 1.

15. Jup Kastrati, "The Beginnings of Albanian Grammatical Studies," *New Albania* (Tiranë), no. 2 (Mar.–Apr. 1974), p. 32.

16. *Rock Garden*, p. 22.

17. Kristo Frashëri, *The History of Albania* (Tiranë, 1964), pp. 29-30; Marmullaku, *Albania*, p. 6.

18. Eugene K. Keefe et al., eds., *Area Handbook for Albania*, Foreign Area Studies of American University, (Washington, D.C.: Government Printing Office, 1971), pp. 11-12.

19. Bishop Fan S. Noli, *George Castrioti Scanderbeg* (New York: International Universities Press, 1947), p. 2.

20. Ibid., p. 74.

21. Frashëri, *History*, p. 87; Noli, *Scanderbeg*, p. 74.

22. Marmullaku, *Albania*, p. 12; Stavro Skendi, *The Albanian National Awakening, 1878-1912* (Princeton, N.J.: Princeton University Press, 1967), p. 21.

23. In Skënderbeu's time, each Albanian feudal lord had his own emblem and banners. The banner of the Kastrioti family had a black, double-headed eagle on a field of red. This banner subsequently became the national flag of Albania.

24. Keefe, *Handbook*, p. 11.

25. Noli, *Scanderbeg*, p. 8.

26. *Rock Garden*, p. 55.

27. M. Edith Durham, *High Albania* (London, 1909), p. 56.

Notes to Chapter 2

1. *History of the Party of Labor of Albania* (Tiranë: Naim Frashëri Pub. Hse., 1971), p. 216, (hereafter cited as *History of APL*).

2. The Albanian Communist Party changed its name in 1948 to the Albanian Party of Labor (APL). Both names occur in this study.

3. Ndreçi Plasari and Thanas Leci, "The Great Patriotic War of the Soviet Union: Decisive Factor in the Victory over Fascism," *Rruga e Partisë* [The Party road], theoretical monthly of APL, 9, no. 6 (June 1962): 20-31, at p. 31.

4. For the most comprehensive Albanian communist account of the Partisans' seizure of power, consult the six-volume publication of the proceedings of the national conference on the war, held in Tiranë Nov. 8-11, 1974. See esp. vol. 1, *Konferenca Kombëtare e Studimeve për Luftën Antifashiste Nacionallirimtare të Popullit Shqiptar* [The National Conference on Studies of the Anti-Fascist National Liberation Struggle of the Albanian People] (Tiranë: 8 Nëntori Press, 1975).

5. Enver Hoxha's report to the First Congress of ACP (Nov. 1948), *Kongresi i Irë i Partisë Komuniste të Shqipërisë* (Tiranë: M. Duri Press, 1950), pp. 64-65.

6. *Partizanët tregojnë* [The Partisans speak], memoirs, diaries, and notes by participants in the National Liberation struggle (Tiranë: Institute of Party History, 1960), pp. 89, 168.

7. For a revealing glimpse of the political struggle and its impact among relatives and friends, see the correspondence between Halim Xhelo, commander of a communist guerrilla unit, and Skënder Muço, an attorney who later became a top leader of *BK*. H. Xhelo, *860 ditë lufte* [860 days of battle] (Tiranë: Department of Military History, 1960), pp. 99-101.

8. Ibid., pp. 56, 130, 156. We have an example of communist fanaticism in the diary of author-soldier Halim Xhelo, who later became a major general in the Albanian People's Army. Xhelo says that he was intent on killing his father, because he sided with *Balli*, and spared him only because of objections from Commissar Hysni Kapo, who thought that parricide would harm the Party politically.

9. Mehmet Shehu, *On the Experience of the National-Liberation War and on the Development of the National Army*, pamphlet in English (Tiranë, 1963), p. 40, (hereafter, Shehu, *N.L. War*).

10. Ibid., p. 40.

11. *Dokumenta kryesore të P.P.SH., I* [Main documents of APL, vol. 1] (Tiranë: Instituti i Historisë së Partisë pranë K.Q. të P.P.SH., 1960), p. 27; (hereafter, *D.K.*). *History of APL*, p. 97.

12. *History of APL*, p. 222.

13. In letter to Tito, dated Sept. 23,1944, *Rilindja* [Rebirth], Albanian-language daily published in Priština, Kosovo, Nov. 20, 1963. See also ibid., Feb. 23, 1965, for remarks of former APL Politburo member Tuk Jakova on the role of Miladin Popović in the formation of ACP.

14. Nicholas J. Costa, "Invasion—Action and Reaction: Albania, a Case Study," *East European Quarterly* 10 no. 4 (Spring 1976): 61.

15. Dr. Andrea Shuli, "The Democracy of the Communist Dictatorship," *Flamuri* [The flag] (Rome), Nov. 28, 1976.

16. For a lucid and detailed account of the subject, see Stephen Peters, "Ingredients of the Communist Takeover in Albania," *Studies on the Soviet Union* (Munich) 11, no. 4 (1971): 246-251.

17. *The National-Liberation Struggle of the Albanian People*, illus. vol. (Tiranë, n.d.), p. 3, (hereafter, *The N-L Struggle*).

18. Ibid., p. 9. However, Julian Amery of the British mission set the maximum Partisan strength at about one-third (slightly over 20,000) the figure given by the communists. Cf. Amery, *Sons of the Eagle* (London: Macmillan & Co., 1948).

19. *Kronikë e ditëve të stuhishme* [Chronicle of stormy days] (Tiranë: Department of Military History, 1962), pp. 82-83.

20. It is not surprising therefore that at the end of the war the total membership in the Party was a mere 2,800 as against the alleged total of 70,000 troops in the Partisan army. *History of APL*, pp. 221, 222.

21. Xhelo, *860 ditë lufte*, intro. to the diary, Dec. 31, 1942, p. 6.

22. *Kronikë*, p. 84.

23. Nationalist opponents of the communists, however, claim that *Balli Kombëtar* was created immediately after the Fascist invasion of Albania on April 7, 1939, by Midhat Frashëri, son of Abdyl Frashëri, noted patriot of the Albanian nationalist movement. See *The Struggle of the Kossovars*, no. 15 (July 10, 1974), p. 5. For the communist source, see *History of APL*, p. 130.

24. The communists were incensed by *Balli* reports that female Partisans were women of loose morals, an extremely offensive charge from the standpoint of the Albanian moral code.

25. See Enver Hoxha, letter to Ymer Dishnica, head of the NLF delegation to the Mukaj conference, Aug. 9, 1943, in *Vepra* [Works] (Tiranë: Naim Frashëri Pub. Hse. 1968), 1: 339-341.

26. *History of APL*, p. 174. This figure is disputed by Amery, who reports that the total German force in Albania numbered 25,000 troops, *Sons of the Eagle*, p. 103.

27. *D.K.*, 1: 176-181; *History of APL*, p. 177.

28. The civil war in Albania was fought almost entirely in the southern part of the country, birthplace of the Partisan movement and the base of operations of the nationalist *BK*.

29. Maj. Gen. Shefqet Peçi, "Memories of the War of National-Liberation," *Rruga e Partisë* 6, no. 7 (July 1959): 44-45; *Partisanët tregojnë*, pp. 83-84, 129.

30. Hoxha, *Vepra*, 2: 91-94, 110-114.

31. Shehu, *N.L. War*, p. 70.

32. *The N-L Struggle*, p. 5.

33. See his pamphlet, *Revolution and the Social System*, Hoover Institution Studies, no. 3 (Stanford, Cal.: Hoover Institution Press, 1964).

34. Lawrence Stone, "Theories of Revolution," *World Politics* 18 (Oct. 1965-July 1966): 163.

35. Hopper, "The Revolutionary Process," *Social Forces* 28 (Mar. 1950): 270-279.

36. This is not to deny, however, that the Partisans and *Balli* were motivated by strong feelings of patriotism and scorn for the Fascist invaders. Indeed, the presence of Italian occupation forces in Albania served as a catalyst for the founding of the two guerrilla resistance movements.

Notes to Chapter 3

1. Yugoslavia is an exception in the sense that she was never a member of the Warsaw Pact.

2. For the full account of Albania's position on détente and European security, see "The Conference of Insecurity of Europe," *Albania today*, no. 5 (Sept.-Oct. 1975), pp. 36-39.

3. *Zëri i popullit* [Voice of the people], daily organ of APL, Nov. 8, 1961; document 14 in William E. Griffith, *Albania and the Sino-Soviet Rift* (Cambridge, Mass.: MIT Press, 1963), p. 263.

4. A good collection of the principal APL statements on revisionism is to be found in Patrick Kessel, *Les communistes albanais contre le révisionisme* (Paris: Union Générale d'Editions, 1974); and in Gilbert Mury, ed., *Face au révisionisme*, containing selections from Enver Hoxha's writings (Paris: F. Maspero, 1972).

5. Even today Albanian officials become indignant when tourists take photographs of peasants riding donkeys or of quaint, dilapidated houses, instead of photographing the new railroads, factories, and apartments that have been built under the socialist regime.

6. Albania completed the collectivization of agriculture in 1967. In the same year, the regime abolished all ranks in the military forces and closed all public places of worship. Thus, 1967 stands out as the year of the greatest radicalization of Albanian life, under communist rule.

7. In 1938, at least 80% of the population was illiterate, and large areas of the lowlands were dangerous, malaria-infested marshes.

8. For a perceptive study of the nature of the Albanian state from a historical perspective, see the essay by Arshi Pipa, "Zhvillimi politik i shtetit Shqiptar, 1912-1962" [The political development of the Albanian state, 1912-1962], *Shqiptari i lirë* (New York), Nov.-Dec. 1962.

9. When the Party was founded in 1941, it had a total of only 200 members.

10. *Zëri i popullit*, Nov. 2, 1976.

11. *Statuti i Partisë së Punës të Shqipërisë* [The statutes of the Albanian Party of Labor](Tiranë, 1972), p. 66.

12. Stavro Skendi, ed., *Albania* (New York: Praeger, 1956), pp. 85-86; "History of the Albanian Communist Party II," *News from Behind the Iron Curtain* 5, no. 1 (Jan. 1956): 27-29.

13. See *History of the Party of Labor of Albania* (Tiranë: Naim Frashëri Pub. Hse., 1971), pp. 71-73; and Ramadan Marmullaku, *Albania and the Albanians* (London: C. Hurst & Co., 1975), pp. 67-71. Hoxha married Nexhmie Xhangolli in 1945, an APL-CC member since 1948 and currently director of the Institute of Marxism-Leninism. They have two sons and one daughter.

14. Skendi, *Albania*, pp. 341-343. Shehu is married to Fiqret Sanxhaktari, an APL-CC member since 1952 and presently director of the V. I. Lenin Party School in Tiranë.

15. E. Hoxha, *Speeches, 1971-1973* (Tiranë: 8 Nëntori Pub. Hse., 1974), pp. 394-395.

16. A total of 2,865 members, roughly 10% of the Party's membership, were expelled between 1945 and 1948; and another 12,000 (more than a fourth of the Party's members) were dropped from Nov. 1948 to the end of 1951. See *Kongresi i Irë i Partisë Komuniste të Shqipërisë* [First Congress of ACP] (Tiranë: M. Duri Press, 1950), p. 391; Skendi, *Albania*, p. 86.

17. Hoxha, *Report Submitted to the 6th Congress of the Party of Labor of Albania* (Tiranë: Naim Frashëri Pub. Hse., 1971), p. 180.

18. Hoxha, *Raporte e fjalime, 1965-1966* [Reports and speeches, 1965-1966] (Tiranë: Naim Frashëri Pub. Hse., 1971), p. 335.

19. Ibid., p. 230.

20. In the Ministries of Health, Commerce, and the State Planning Commission, the figures were 56.9%, 52.2%, and 50.5% respectively. See Hoxha, *Socialism Is Built by the Masses* (Tiranë: Political Book Pub. Hse., 1972), pp. 22-23. Communists also made up the majority of the cadres in the youth, labor, and women's organizations, the figures for these being 52.2%, 67.2%, and 65.8% respectively. Ibid., p. 26.

21. Ibid., p. 23.

22. Speech, Feb. 3-4, 1966, *Raporte 1965-66*, p. 217; *PPSH, mbi diktaturën e proletariatit dhe mbi demokracinë socialiste* [APL, on the dictatorship of the proletariat and socialist democracy] (Tiranë: M. Duri Press, presumed date of publication 1968), pp. 86-103, (hereafter, *Mbi diktaturën*).

23. Hoxha, *Speeches, 1971-1973*, pp. 136, 143-144.

24. Ibid., p. 134.

25. *Raporte 1965-66*, pp. 230, 228.

26. Ibid., p. 237.

27. Hoxha, *Speeches, 1971-1973*, pp. 132-133.

28. APL-CC "Open Letter," Mar. 4, 1966, in *Mbi diktaturën*, p. 72.

29. *Speeches, 1971-1973*, pp. 75-76.

30. Ibid., pp. 132–133; 152–153. It is possible, too, that there was a connection between these deliberations for some flexibility and moderation in the Party line and China's first significant steps toward better relations with the West.

31. The term "liberalism" was also used as a weapon to attack manifestations of laxity and complacent attitudes in the economic sector, the army, and other areas of Albanian life.

32. Report to the Fourth APL-CC Plenum, June 26, 1973, entitled, "Intensify the Ideological Struggle against Alien Manifestations and Liberal Attitudes toward Them," *Speeches, 1971–1973*, p. 392.

33. Ibid., pp. 238–269.

34. Ibid., p. 396.

35. Ibid., p. 240.

36. Ibid., p. 261.

37. Ibid., p. 334.

38. *Zëri i popullit*, Dec. 29, 1976; *Gazeta zyrtare* [The official gazette], no. 5 (Dec. 30, 1976).

Notes to Chapter 4

1. It is not surprising, therefore, that Albanian officials and economists make constant references to the economic situation of King Zog's Albania and that the year 1938 is used by them as the standard date of reference for making comparisons between socialist and monarchist Albania.

2. Data are from Besim Bardhoshi and Theodhor Kareco, *Zhvillimi ekonomiko-shoqëror në Shqipëri, 1944–1974* [Economic and social development in Albania, 1944–1974] (Tiranë: M. Duri Press, 1974); (hereafter, *Zhvillimi ekonomiko-shoqëror*); and L. V. Tyagunenko, *Razvitiye ekonomiki Narodnoy Respubliki Albanii* (Moscow, 1960), translated into English under the title, *Development of the Albanian Economy*, JPRS: 4568, Apr. 27, 1961.

3. This is not an apology for Zog's reign. The former monarch's attitude toward the impoverished Albanian masses was not unlike that of King Louis XVI toward his French subjects. Columnist and author C. L. Sulzberger, who was in Albania in 1938–1939, tells a story that supports this viewpoint. At a New Year's party given by Zog in Tiranë, which he attended, he was "astounded" to see the guests dine on "champagne, *foie gras*, salads, ice creams . . . beneath chandeliers of glittering lighted candles—and all in a famished land." See his book, *A Long Row of Candles* (New York: Macmillan Co., 1969), p. 58.

4. Michael Kaser and Janusz G. Zielinski, *Planning in East Europe* (London: Bodley Head, 1970), p. 17.

5. *History of the Party of Labor of Albania* (Tiranë: Naim Frashëri Pub. Hse., 1971), p. 281; (hereafter, *History of APL*).

6. Ibid., p. 328.

7. *Zhvillimi ekonomiko-shoqëror*, p. 36.

8. Kaser and Zielinski, *Planning in East Europe*, p. 10.

9. George W. Hoffman, *Regional Development Strategy in Southwest Europe* (New York: Praeger, 1972), pp. 108-109.

10. As quoted in *Zhvillimi ekonomiko-shoqëror*, p. 55.

11. *Dokumenta kryesore të P.P.SH., II* [Main documents of APL, vol. 2] (Tiranë: Instituti i Historisë së Partisë pranë K.Q. të P.P.SH., 1961), pp. 102-127.

12. Michael Kaser, *Comecon* (London: Oxford University Press, 1967), p. 86.

13. In 1958 Albania's production of this particular ore reportedly accounted for one-tenth of the world's total. Tyagunenko, *Development*, p. 24.

14. R. I. Dogonadze, *Sel'skoye Khozyaystvo Albanii* (Moscow, 1957), translated into English under the title, *Albanian Agriculture*, JPRS: 6662, Mar. 2, 1961, p. 139; *Rruga e Partisë* [The Party road] (Tiranë), no. 8 (Aug. 1958), p. 20.

15. *Kongresi IV i P.P.SH.* [Fourth Congress of APL] (Tiranë: Naim Frashëri Pub. Hse., 1961), p. 201.

16. For example, industrial production increased at an average annual rate of 6.8%, instead of the planned 8.6%.

17. M. Shehu report to the Fifth Party Congress, in *Kongresi i Pestë i P.P.SH.* (Tiranë: Naim Frashëri Pub. Hse., 1967), p. 244.

18. *Zëri i popullit* [Voice of the people], daily organ of the Albanian Party of Labor, May 1, 1976.

19. *30 vjet Shqipëri socialiste* [30 years of Albanian socialism] (Tiranë: M. Duri Press, 1974), pp. 66, 71, 75.

20. Pandi Geço, *Shqipëria, pamje fiziko-ekonomike* [Albania, physical and economic survey] (Tiranë: Mihal Duri Press, 1959), JPRS: 9945, Aug. 25, 1961, p. 6.

21. Dogonadze, *Albanian Agriculture*, p. 21.

22. *Zhvillimi ekonomiko-shoqëror*, p. 32.

23. Ibid.

24. *Kongresi i Pestë i P.P.SH.*, p. 61.

25. *Dokumenta kryesore të P.P.SH., II*, pp. 430-450, at p. 432.

26. Tyagunenko, *Development*, p. 53.

27. Geço, *Shqipëria*, p. 164. This was especially true of water buffalo, which had decreased to one-half their number in 1938; ibid., p. 177.

28. *Vjetari statistikor i R.P.SH., 1971-72* [Statistical yearbook of APR (Albanian People's Republic)] (Tiranë: M. Duri Press, 1973), p. 113.

29. Tyagunenko, *Development*, pp. 3–4.

30. Stavro Skendi, ed., *Albania* (New York: Praeger, 1956), p. 193.

31. Geço, *Shqipëria*, p. 135.

32. Skendi, *Albania*, p. 167.

33. Tyagunenko, *Development*, p. 51. Indeed, in 1955 the Soviets envisioned a "prospective plan" for the development of citrus fruit and olive production in Albania over a twenty-year period (1956–75), which was to catapult that country to "first place in Europe in the production of olives, tangerines, oranges and lemons"; ibid., p. 52.

34. Robert Owen Freedman, *Economic Warfare in the Communist Bloc* (New York: Praeger, 1970), p. 67; for material on Albania, see chap. 3, "Soviet Use of Economic Pressure against Albania," pp. 58–102.

35. M. Shehu, *Report on the 6th Five-Year Plan (1976–1980)* (Tiranë: 8 Nëntori Pub. Hse., 1976), p. 7; (hereafter, *Report on Sixth 5-YP*).

36. *30 vjet*, p. 133.

37. *Zhvillimi ekonomiko-shoqëror*, p. 111.

38. *30 vjet*, p. 180.

39. Kaser, *Comecon*, p. 11. COMECON held two of its sessions in Albania. In January 1958 the Agricultural Commission met in Tiranë; and the Eleventh Session of the council convened there May 13–16, 1959, to discuss matters concerning electricity, mining machinery, chemicals, etc.; ibid., pp. 45, 226.

40. Freedman, *Economic Warfare*, p. 80. In this respect, the triangular trade relationship between Albania, the Soviet Union, and East Europe differed from the relationship between the Soviet Union and Yugoslavia after 1948, when East Europe, following Moscow's lead, ceased to trade with Yugoslavia.

41. Geço, *Shqipëria*, p. 191.

42. *Rapport . . . au IIIe congrès du parti*, Enterprise d'éditions de L'état (Tiranë, 1956), p. 31. The complete text reads: "La coordination des plans économiques de nos pays dans le cadre du Conseil Economique et de l'assistance Mutuelle assure des avantages immenses, particulièrement à notre pays, parce que c'est de cette façon que vont se développer et progresser toutes les branches de notre économie et que les Etats amis nous donneront

une aide complete et profitable pour tout ce que nous ne pourrons pas construire ou produire chez nous, soit parce que les matières premières nous manquent, soit parce que cela demande de gros investissements non avantageux pour notre économie."

43. R. H. Osborne, *East-Central Europe* (London: Chatto & Windus, 1967), p. 89; for additional material, see chap. 3, "Albania," pp. 71-90.

44. Jan S. Prybyla, "Albania's Economic Vassalage," *East Europe* 16, no. 1 (Jan. 1967): 10.

45. Osborne, *East-Central Europe*, p. 89.

46. At the official rate of 50 leks to a dollar.

47. At the official rate of exchange of 50 dinars to a dollar.

48. Vladimir Dedijer, *Tito*, (New York: Simon & Schuster, 1953), pp. 300-303.

49. Ibid., pp. 302-303.

50. *Zhvillimi ekonomiko-shoqëror*, p. 41.

51. Skendi, *Albania*, p. 230; Freedman, *Economic Warfare*, pp. 59-60, 64.

52. For documentation of this claim, one has only to refer to published Albanian materials during the 1950s. Two useful Soviet sources are L. V. Tyagunenko and R. I. Dogonadze.

53. Tyagunenko, *Development*, p. 25.

54. In the same year, a Soviet author, R. Strelnikov, reflecting, it seems, the sentiments of Khrushchev, wrote a book entitled, *Albania stanet svjetushim sadom* [Albania will become a flourishing garden].

55. "Speech of Comrade Enver Hoxha to the Representatives of the Capital's Intelligentsia," *Zëri i popullit*, Nov. 4, 1962.

56. Louis Zanga, "The Albanian Way," *RFE Research*, Dec. 21, 1972, p. 7.

57. *Rruga e Partisë*, no. 3 (Mar. 1956), p. 59.

58. *Rapport . . . au IIIe congrès du parti* (Tiranë, 1956), p. 30; translated from the French.

59. Radio Tiranë, July 20, 1954, as given in Freedman, *Economic Warfare*, p. 66.

60. The calculated figure is $497.75 million. See Prybyla, "Albania's Economic Vassalage," pp. 9-14; Ramadan Marmullaku, *Albania and the Albanians* (London: C. Hurst & Co., 1975), p. 96.

61. In the midsixties Albania ceased publishing itemized, country-by-country breakdowns of data on foreign trade in her statistical yearbooks and since 1973 has not included data on imports—presumably because of concern that

revelation of such data would reflect unfavorably on the country's foreign trade.

62. *Raporte e fjalime, 1965-1966* [Reports and speeches, 1965-1966] (Tiranë: N. Frashëri Pub. Hse., 1971), p. 77.

63. Osborne, *East-Central Europe*, pp. 89-90.

64. Prybyla, "Albania's Economic Vassalage," p. 12; P. J. D. Wiles, ed., *The Prediction of Communist Economic Performance* (Cambridge: Cambridge University Press, 1971), p. 92.

65. *Peking Review*, no. 28 (July 11, 1975), p. 7; *Zëri i popullit*, July 4, 1975.

66. *Zëri i popullit*, Mar. 23, 1976. See also Louis Zanga, "Albania Reacts to Balkan Conference," *RFE Research* (Albania), Apr. 5, 1976.

67. M. Duverger, "Le socialisme albanais," *Le monde*, Sept. 5-6, 1971. An editorial in *Koha e jonë* [Our time], vol. 14, nos. 4-6 (Apr.-June, 1975)—an Albanian review with an anticommunist bias, published in Paris—acknowledged that the Albanian economy "has made demonstrable strides in a number of technological areas" (p. 16).

68. Talk at the 18th Tiranë Party Conference, Sept. 29, 1971, in Enver Hoxha, *Speeches, 1971-1973* (Tiranë: 8 Nëntori Pub. Hse., 1974), p. 55.

69. Qemal Xhaka, "For a Better Assimilation of Foreign Languages," *Zëri i popullit*, July 12, 1975.

70. *Zëri i popullit*, Feb. 7, 1976.

71. Priamo Bollano, "The Principle of Reliance on One's Own Forces in the Draft-Constitution," *Probleme ekonomike* [Economic problems] (Tiranë), organ of the Institute of Economic Studies, 23, no. 1 (Jan.-Mar. 1976): 126.

72. Ibid., p. 128.

73. Këllezi was replaced by Petro Dode, a member of the APL-CC Secretariat; while Theodhosi's place was filled by Pali Miska, a former district Party secretary. Ngjela's position was given to Nedin Hoxha, former president of the Executive Council of the town of Gjirokastër.

74. *Zëri i popullit*, Apr. 30, 1976. Deliana was replaced by a woman, Tefta Cami, a university graduate and former school director and district Party secretary. The post of Dodbiba was given to a woman, Themie Thomai, who was described as "an economist and agronomist of high education."

75. Ibid., Feb. 11, 1976.

76. Ibid.

77. Ibid., Apr. 1, 2, 1976.

78. See editorial, "Let Us Mobilize All Forces for the Realization of the Tasks

of the First Year of the Sixth Five-Year Plan," *Rruga e Partisë*, no. 1 (Jan. 1976), pp. 5-11; Pirro Dodbiba, "Let Us Mobilize All Our Energies to Achieve an Extraordinary Increase in the Production of Bread Grains in 1976," *Bujqësia socialiste* [Socialist agriculture] (Tiranë), monthly organ of the Ministry of Agriculture, 30, no. 1 (1976): 5-8; *Zëri i popullit*, Mar. 21, 31, Apr. 23, 1976.

79. See Hoxha's report to the congress, *Zëri i popullit*, Nov. 2, 1976; and Ndreçi Plasari's article, ibid., Feb. 20, 1977.

80. M. Shehu, *Report on the 5th 5-Year Plan*, (Tiranë: Naim Frashëri Pub. Hse., 1971), p. 147.

81. *Report on Sixth 5-YP*, p. 78.

82. Ibid., p. 5.

Notes to Chapter 5
1. *Answers to Questions about Albania* (Tiranë, 1969), p. 31.

2. *New Albania* (Tiranë), no. 3 (May-June 1961), pp. 18-19.

3. A. Buda, "The Noble Role of [Albanian] Women in History," ibid., Special Issue on Women (Mar. 1961), pp. 10-11.

4. Ibid., pp. 10-11. There is, however, another view on the question of who embroidered the flag that was raised in Vlorë. According to the late Qerim Panarity, former editor of *Dielli* [The sun], organ of the Pan-Albanian Federation of America (VATRA), Boston, Mass., the first Albanian flag was embroidered in Boston. Then, in 1911, it was taken to Corfu by a çetë (guerrilla band) of the Besa-Besën Society, whose intent was to land in Albania and join the struggle for independence. The çetë, however, disbanded, and the flag was left in the care of one Nuci Naci, a trade school instructor in Corfu from Korcë. Marigo Pozio (Poçi, according to Panarity), also from Korçë, had married a merchant in Vlorë who traded with Corfu. One day, while returning to Albania from Corfu, Marigo brought the flag to Vlorë, and it was this same flag that was subsequently placed at the disposal of Ismail Qemal for the flag-raising ceremony on November 28. (See also *The Albanian Struggle in the Old World and the New* [Boston: The Writer, 1939], pp. 48, 50-51.)

5. *Shqiptarja e re* [The new Albanian woman], monthly organ of UAW, no. 4 (Apr. 1960), p. 20.

6. For the condition of women in Albania up to the end of the Second World War, see the volumes of collected correspondence between Enver Hoxha and the people during 1967, especially the following: *Nuk ka liri të vërtetë shoqërore pa emancipimin e plotë të gruas* [There can be no true social freedom without the full emancipation of woman] (Tiranë: Naim Frashëri Pub. Hse., 1967); *Lufta kundër zakoneve prapanike dhe besimeve fetare: Shprehje e luftës së klasave* [The struggle against backward customs and religious beliefs:

An expression of class warfare] (Tiranë: Naim Frashëri Pub. Hse., 1967); *Në shekuj do të përjetësohen emrat e bijave dhe bijve të këtij trualli* [The names of the sons and daughters of this hearth will live through the centuries](Tiranë: Naim Frashëri Pub. Hse., 1968).

7. J. Swire, *King Zog's Albania* (New York: Liveright, 1937), p. 89.

8. Ibid., p. 89.

9. Rose Wilder Lane, *Peaks of Shala* (New York: Harper & Bros., 1923), p. 27.

10. These laws are also known as the canons of Lek Dukagjin, Lek being the name of the law giver and Dukagjin the region of his origin.

11. K. Gjoka and Ll. Pashko, "The Remnants of Patriarchy in the Family and in Society," *Rruga e Partisë* [The Party road], monthly theoretical journal of APL, 15, no. 7 (July 1968): 16.

12. *Zëri i popullit* [Voice of the people], Feb. 6, 1968.

13. *On Some Aspects of the Problem of the Albanian Women* (Tiranë: Naim Frashëri Pub. Hse., 1967), p. 15.

14. M. Hasluck, *The Unwritten Law in Albania* (Cambridge: Cambridge University Press, 1954), p. 25.

15. Ibid., p. 25. Hasluck discusses the position of women in Albanian society, especially in chap. 4, "The Albanian Household," pp. 25-33. See also Lane, *Peaks of Shala*, pp. 98-99, 146-147.

16. Swire, *King Zog's Albania*, p. 97.

17. *Bashkimi* [Unity], daily organ of the Albanian government, Apr. 1, 1967. See also Hulusi Hako, "Religion, Fierce Enemy of Women," in his book, *Akuzojmë fenë* [We accuse religion](Tiranë, 1968), pp. 94-104; *Shqiptarja e re*, no. 8 (Aug. 1974), p. 11.

18. *Zëri i popullit*, Feb. 11, 1968.

19. Gen. Beqir Balluku, former Albanian minister of defense, in his greetings to *Kongresi i 6të i BGSH* [6th Congress of UAW](Tiranë: Naim Frashëri Pub. Hse., 1967), p. 13.

20. Enver Hoxha, *Mbi problemin e gruas* [On the problem of woman], a volume of excerpts and speeches by Hoxha on the Albanian women, 1942-67 (Tiranë: Naim Frashëri Pub. Hse., 1967), p. 119. The deliberate effort of Albanian women activisits to influence Third World women was manifest in the speech of Vito Kapo, president of UAW, at the International Women's Year World Conference, held in Mexico City in late June 1975. The text of Kapo's speech was published in *Zëri i popullit*, June 26, 1975.

21. Hoxha, *Mbi problemin e gruas*, p. 9.

22. *On Some Aspects*, p. 30.

23. J Alibali, "Mara of Oroshi," *New Albania* (Tiranë), a bimonthly "political, social, and literary review," Special Issue on Women (Mar. 1961), pp. 14-15.

24. Hoxha, *Mbi problemin e gruas*, p. 27.

25. *On Some Aspects*, p. 47.

26. Report to the 6th UAW Congress, Oct. 1967, *Kongresi i 6të i BGSH*, p. 77.

27. Hoxha, *Mbi Problemin e gruas*, p. 22.

28. Ibid., p. 165.

29. Ibid., p. 164.

30. *Kongresi i 6të i BGSH*, p. 50.

31. Hoxha, *Mbi problemin e gruas*, p. 71.

32. *On Some Aspects*, p. 81.

33. For a study of the place of women in modern Albania, see Robert Schwanke, "Frauenemanzipation in Albanien," *East European Quarterly* 2, no. 1 (Mar. 1968): 57-73. For a succinct Albanian account, see the section, "The Movement for the Complete Emancipation of Women," in *History of the Party of Labor of Albania* (Tiranë: Naim Frashëri Pub. Hse., 1971), pp. 627-634.

34. Stavro Skendi, ed., *Albania* (New York: Praeger, 1956), p. 89.

35. The Third UAW Congress was held in Oct. 1950, the Fifth in Oct. 1961, the Sixth in Oct. 1967, and the Seventh in June 1973.

36. *Zëri i popullit*, Apr. 30, 1976.

37. *Shqipëria e re*, (New Albania), monthly newspaper (Tiranë), no. 11 (Nov. 1976), p. 1.

38. *Dokumenta kyresore të P.P.SH., III* [Main documents of APL, vol. 3] (Tiranë: Mihal Duri Press, 1970), p. 449.

39. Ibid., p. 435. It is ironic that a year earlier Hoxha had praised Belishova for "her ability and dynamism, her great loyalty to the Party and the people." See *Shqiptarja e re*, no. 1 (Jan. 1960), p. 8.

40. William E. Griffith, *Albania and the Sino-Soviet Rift* (Cambridge, Mass.: MIT Press, 1963), p. 235.

41. *Bashkimi*, May 10, 1964.

42. Skendi, *Albania*, p. 108.

43. *Bashkimi*, Aug. 17, 1947.

44. Hoxha, *Mbi problemin e gruas*, p. 216.

45. *Zëri i popullit*, Feb. 7, 1967.

46. *On Some Aspects*, p. 34.

47. Ibid., p. 70. Albania's leaders affirmed repeatedly that the struggle for the emancipation of women must not be conceived as something apart from the men's struggle to raise their consciousness and build a socialist society. They argued that every aspect of the women's struggle was inextricably bound up with the men's struggle, for both struggles had the same roots and the same objectives. See editorial, "Revolutionary Greetings to Our Mothers, Wives, and Sisters," *Zëri i popullit*, Mar. 8, 1975.

48. *On Some Aspects*, p. 9.

49. To substantiate Engel's views, Hoxha recommended to Albanian scholars the study of Father Shtjefën Gjeçov's work, *Kanuni i Lekë Dukagjinit* [The Canon of Lek Dukagjin], which shows "how private property holds woman in bondage" and "turns her into a simple commodity that can be bought and sold", ibid., p. 15.

50. Ibid., pp. 30-31.

51. *Kongresi i 6të i BGSH*, p. 34. The congress was attended by 34 delegations of women from foreign countries. Graphic accounts of the changing role of women in contemporary Albanian society appeared frequently in illustrated Albanian publications. Typical examples were the pictures of groups of young women dressed in pants and sporting short hairdos—a far cry from the traditional attire of prewar Albanian women. See *New Albania*, no. 4, (July-Aug. 1976), pp. 5, 10-11.

52. *Bashkimi*, Nov. 10, 1967.

53. The site has become a shrine for school children and youth. Moreover, she has been widely commemorated in literature, film, theater, and the plastic arts.

54. *Zëri i popullit*, Feb. 7, 1968.

55. For the proceedings of the congress, see ibid., June 12-16, 1973; *Shqiptarja e re*, no. 7 (1973); and Supplement on the congress (June 12, 1973), published by *Shqiptarja e re*.

56. *Zëri i popullit*, June 12, 1973.

57. For Kapo's report, see Supplement entitled *Kongresi i 7të i BGSH* [7th Congress of UAW], June 12, 1973; (hereafter, Supplement).

58. Enver Hoxha, *Report Submitted to the 7th Congress of the Party of Labor of Albania* (Tiranë: 8 Nëntori Pub. Hse., 1976), pp. 89-90; *Albania Report* (New York), no. 1 (Jan.-Mar. 1976), p. 1.

59. *Shqipëria e re*, no. 3 (Mar. 1977), p. 3.

60. *Nëndori* [November], monthly organ of the League of Writers and Albanian Artists, no. 6 (June 1970), pp. 8-28.

61. Hysni Kapo, "Social and Family Relations: A Broad Field of Class Struggle," *Rruga e Partisë* 8, no. 1 (Jan. 1970): 57-83.

62. *Zëri i popullit*, June 11, 1976.

63. *Kongresi i 6të i BGSH*, p. 28.

64. *Shqiptarja e re*, no. 1 (Feb. 1960), pp. 16-17.

65. Ibid., no. 10 (Oct. 1960), p. 23; no. 12 (Dec. 1960), pp. 20-21.

66. *Zëri i popullit*, Oct. 17, 1961. Exchanges between Albanian and Chinese women delegations continued through the first half of the 1970s. In Sept. 1974, a UAW delegation visited Peking at the invitation of the Chinese People's Society for Friendship with Foreign Countries. The delegation was headed by Eleni Pashko, vice-president of the General Council of UAW. Ibid., Sept. 5, 1974.

67. *Kongresi i 6të i BGSH*, p. 106.

68. Supplement, p. 10. Kapo repeated her attacks on the IFDW and Soviet and American foreign policies in an article entitled "A Free Woman Can Live Only in a Free Society," which appeared in *Albania today*, no. 3 (May-June 1975), pp. 15-19.

69. *On Some Aspects*, p. 28.

70. Meto Metaj, "The Family-Primary Center for Moulding a Human Being," *Zëri i popullit*, June 16, 1974.

Notes to Chapter 6

1. Enver Hoxha in speech given at a solemn meeting on the tenth anniversary of liberation, *Nëndori* [November], monthly organ of the League of Albanian Writers and Artists, 1, no. 12 (Dec. 1954): 5; *PPSH, mbi kulturën, letërsinë dhe artet* [APL, on culture, literature, and the arts](Tiranë: Naim Frashëri Pub. Hse., presumed date of publication 1968), 94 pp., at pp. 11-12.

2. *Nëndori* 19, no. 7 (July 1972): 199-202.

3. *New Albania* (Tiranë), 26, no. 3 (May-June 1972): 25.

4. See Th. Popa, *Piktorët mesjetarë shqiptarë* [Medieval Albanian painters] (Tiranë: Mihal Duri Press, 1961), 124 pp. Albanian's interest in preserving religious edifices and paintings is in a sense ironic, in view of the abolition of organized religion in the country in 1967. The regime, however, justifies its policy in terms of the value that such objects have in enhancing the general culture of the country.

5. *New Albania* 26, no. 3 (May-June 1972): 25, 36.

6. Ibid., no. 6 (Nov.-Dec. 1969): 42-43.

7. Ramadan Sokoli, "Sadefqar Mehmeti of Elbasan," *Nëndori* 19, no. 5 (May 1972): 75-84.

8. Ahmet Kondo, "Elena Gjika: An Outstanding Militant of the Albanian Question," *New Albania* 25, no. 1 (Jan.-Feb. 1971): 32-33.

9. Bardhyl Kosova, *Aleksandër Moisiu* (Tiranë: Naim Frashëri Pub. Hse., 1969): 118 pp.; *New Albania* 24, no. 2 (Mar.-Apr. 1970): 18-19.

10. *Zëri i popullit* [Voice of the people], June 25, 1971; *Shqipëria e re* (New Albania) monthly newspaper (Tiranë), 21, no. 7 (July 1971): 1, 4.

11. *Bashkimi* [Unity], Albanian government daily, Jan. 12, 13, 16, 17, and 20, 1968; *Nëndori* 16, no. 11 (Nov. 1969): 3-5; *Drita* [Light], weekly organ of LAWA, Dec. 5, 1971; *Zëri i popullit*, July 8, 1973; *Nëntori* 21, no. 11 (Nov. 1974): 23-222, and 22, no. 1 (Jan. 1975): 3-25. Note: the spelling of the name of the literary review was changed from *Nëndori* to *Nëntori*, in the wake of the purge of the leadership of LAWA in 1973.

12. The equestrian statue is the work of three sculptors: Odhise Paskali, Andrea Mana, and Janaq Paço.

13. *Zëri i popullit*, June 4, 1968.

14. Ibid., Nov. 14, 1968.

15. *Bashkimi*, Jan. 21, 1970.

16. *Nëndori* 17, no. 6 (June 1970): 87-127.

17. *Nëntori* 21, no. 6 (June 1974): 135-155; *Shqipëria e re*, nos. 6-7 (June-July 1974), pp. 1, 4.

18. *New Albania*, no. 5 (Sept.-Oct. 1976), p. 13.

19. *Zëri i popullit*, June 21, 1972.

20. *Shqipëria e re*, no. 3 (Mar. 1973), p. 5. Note: the spelling of the names of these scholars may not be correct in all cases, since it is based on Albanian sources which, unfortunately, are not always consistent in their spellings of proper names.

21. Ibid., no. 1 (Jan. 1973), p. 1.

22. Ibid., no. 3 (Mar. 1975), p. 5.

23. *New Albania*, no. 4 (July-Aug. 1976), p. 6. For an informative and currently the only extensive study in English of communist Albania's educational system, see John I. Thomas, *Education for Communism* (Stanford, Cal.: Hoover Institution Press, 1969).

24. *Zëri i popullit*, May 31, 1964.

25. *Nëndori* 7, no. 12 (Dec. 1960): 152; and Special Issue (1969), p. 41.

26. Fadil Paçrami, *Tri drama* [Three plays](Tiranë, 1968). Paçrami was denounced as an enemy of the Party and the people. See *Zëri i popullit*, July 28 and Aug. 3, 1973. Uruçi also came under attack, allegedly for making concessions to liberalism while he was editor-in-chief of the literary weekly *Drita*.

27. *Nëndori* 16, no. 3 (Mar. 1969): 121-154.

28. Ibid., no. 2 (Feb. 1969): 89-134.

29. The other winner was Naum Prifti, author of *Dasmë pa nuse* [*Wedding without bride*].

30. *Nëndori* 16, no. 6 (June 1969): 42-88.

31. Ibid., 12, no. 10 (Oct. 1965): 232.

32. Ibid., no. 8 (Aug. 1965): 220-223.

33. *Shqipëria e re*, no. 4 (Apr. 1974), p. 2; no. 9 (Sept. 1974), p. 3; and no. 9 (Sept. 1975), p. 3.

34. *Mbledhës të hershëm të folklorit shqiptar* [Early compilers of Albanian folklore](Tiranë: Instituti i Folklorit, 1961), 1: 504-505. A slightly different version of the story appears in the *Visaret e kombit* collection of folklore.

35. Kolë Jakova adapted the tale in a play entitled *Halili e Hajrija*, which has become a "classic" of the postwar Albanian theater.

36. *Arësimi popullor* [People's education](Tiranë), no. 11 (Nov. 1959), pp. 3-7.

37. See the illustrated volume, *Artet figurative në Republikën Popullore të Shqipërisë* [The figurative arts in the People's Republic of Albania](Tiranë: Naim Frashëri Pub. Hse., 1969), p. 11.

38. Ibid., p. 17.

39. Ibid., pp. 87, 88.

40. Ibid., p. 93.

41. Marko's work appears in numerous publications. A sample is the illustrated magazine for preschool children, *Yllkat* [Stars], (July 1971).

42. *Nëndori* 17, no. 6 (June 1970): 18.

43. *New Albania*, no. 1 (Jan.-Feb. 1976), pp. 20-21.

44. However, the general concept for the monument came from Hoxha, in a letter dated June 26, 1969, which he addressed to the sculptors. See *Nëndori* 16, no. 8 (Aug. 1969): 3-6.

45. *Drita*, Dec. 3, 1972, p. 13.

46. *Artet figurative*, p. 18.

47. Ibid., p. 49.

48. Ibid., p. 46.

49. Ibid., p. 53.

50. *Shqipëria e re*, no. 12 (Dec. 1972), p. 4.

51. *Arësimi popullor*, no. 11 (Nov. 1959), pp. 3–7.

52. *Albania Report* (New York), 2, no. 5 (Feb.–Mar. 1972): 4. *Shqipëria e re*, no. 4 (Apr. 1977), p. 6.

53. Ramiz Alia, Report to the 15th Party Plenum, "On the Growth of the Role of Literature and the Arts in the Communist Education of the Masses," *Dokumenta kryesore, të P.P.SH., IV* [Main documents of APL, vol. 4](Tiranë: Naim Frashëri Pub. Hse., 1970), pp. 558–602, at p. 588; (hereafter, *D.K.*).

54. *Shqipëria e re*, no. 12 (Dec. 1972), p. 4. The number of radio sets in operation in 1972 was placed at over 300,000.

55. *New Albania*, no. 4 (July–Aug. 1976), p. 23.

56. *Shqipëria e re*, no. 12 (Dec. 1972), p. 5. The same source notes that the library's oldest document was published in 1331.

57. *Answers to Questions about Albania* (Tiranë 1969), p. 395.

58. Jup Kastrati, *Bibliografi shqipe* [Albanian bibliography] (Tiranë: Naim Frashëri Pub. Hse., 1959), pp. 236–339. Over four dozen men of letters were engaged in translation work. The most prolific among them were Mitrush Kuteli, Vedat Kokona, Bedri Dedja, Sotir Caci, Hamit Kokalari, and Skënder Luarasi.

59. Report to the 15th Party Plenum on literature and the arts, *D.K.*, 4: 564.

60. Editorial, "May–Festival of Albanian Literature," *Nëndori* 12, no. 5 (May 1965): 10–11.

61. For a suggestive discussion of this subject, see A. Pipa, "For a Critical Appraisal of Albanian Literature," in *Përpjekja jonë* [Our effort](Jan. 1970), pp. 44–57.

62. *Nëndori* 17, no. 1 (Jan. 1970): 172. Other prominent women novelists are Eglantina Mandia and Lavdie Leka.

63. *Liria* [Liberty](Boston), July 10, 1970. Kadare described his very negative impressions of American life in a three-part article in *Zëri i popullit*, Sept. 4, 5, 6, 1970.

64. See his volume of collected poetry, *Shekulli im* [My century](Tiranë: Naim Frashëri Pub. Hse., 1961), p. 148.

65. See his article, "Panorama of Contemporary Albanian Literature," in *Zeitschrift für Balkanologie* (Munich), 7, nos. 1-2 (1969–70): 112.

66. *Drita*, Nov. 14, 1971, p. 6; *Shqipëria e re*, no. 6 (June 1975), p. 5.

67. *Zëri i popullit*, June 10, 1973.

68. Adriatik Kallulli, "Our Revolution and Poetry," *Nëndori* 17, no. 10 (Oct. 1970): 30-37.

69. *Nëndori* 16, no. 12 (Dec. 1969): 241.

70. *Rilindja* [rebirth], Sept. 6, 1969, p. 12.

71. For a very negative view of the state of literature in contemporary Albania, see Flaka [pseud.], "The Literature of the Communist Period," *Flamuri* [The flag] (Rome), May 15, 1972.

72. *Nëndori* 17, no. 10 (Oct. 1970): 216-217; *Zëri i popullit*, Sept. 8, 1970.

73. *New Albania*, no. 1 (Jan.-Feb. 1961), p. 2.

74. Editorial in *Arësimi popullor*, no. 11 (1959), pp. 3-7. To be sure, the Soviets began the construction of the Palace of Culture in June 1960 but abandoned work on it in April of the following year, owing to the aggravation of Soviet-Albanian relations. The Albanians then completed its construction themselves in 1966.

75. Kastrati, *Bibliografi*, pp. 236-339.

76. *Shqipëria e re*, no. 9 (Sept. 1971), p. 1; *New Albania*, no. 6 (Nov.-Dec. 1975), p. 10.

77. A. Uçi, "Subjective Idealism Is the Basis of the Revisionist Degeneration of Soviet Art," *Rruga e Partisë* [The Party road], monthly theoretical organ of APL, 14, no. 3 (Mar. 1967): 53-64, at p. 54.

78. *Drita*, June 11, 1967.

79. *Zëri i popullit*, Apr. 3, 1968.

80. *Drita*, Oct. 31, 1971.

81. Gjergj Zheji, "The Inundation of the Bourgeois 'Avant-Garde' Theater by Mysticism and Pornography," *Nëndori* 17, no. 6 (June 1970): 78-86.

82. Ilia Lengu, "Symptoms of the Agony of Bourgeois Society," *Zëri i popullit*, Apr. 20, 1973.

Notes to Chapter 7

1. *Kongresi IV i P.P.SH.* [Fourth Congress of APL] (Tiranë: N. Frashëri Pub. Hse., 1961), p. 16.

2. *Kongresi i Pestë i P.P.SH.* [Fifth Congress of APL] (Tiranë: Naim Frashëri Pub. Hse., 1967), p. 11.

3. *Kongresi IV i P.P.SH.* p. 171.

4. *Kongresi i Pestë i P.P.SH.* p. 301.

5. For an analysis of Albania's relations with the Warsaw Pact, see Robin Alison Remington, *The Changing Soviet Percpetion of the Warsaw Pact* (monograph), MIT Center for International Studies, C/67-24 (November 1967), pp. 111-128.

6. Jan S. Prybyla, "Albania's Economic Vassalage," *East Europe* 16, no. 1 (Jan. 1967): 9-14.

7. Enver Hoxha, "On the Role of the Tasks of the Democratic Front in the Struggle for the Complete Victory of Socialism in Albania," *Bashkimi* [Unity], Albanian government daily, Sept. 15, 1967.

8. See e.g., Mehmet Shehu, "Works of Comrade Enver," *Rruga e Partisë* [The Party road], 15, no. 6 (June 1968): 3-14. In the late 1960s Albania began to publish the complete works of Enver Hoxha. By the summer of 1977, a total of 24 volumes of speeches, letters, and other material had been published, covering the period from November 1941 to May 1963.

9. Charles Neuhauser, "The Chinese Communist Party in the 1960s: Prelude to the Cultural Revolution," *China Quarterly*, no. 32 (Oct.-Dec. 1967), pp. 3-36.

10. *Zëri i popullit* [Voice of the people], Mar. 8, 1966.

11. A Red Guard delegation visited Albania, June 21-July 10, 1967. See "Red Guard Delegation Returns from Albania, *Peking Review* 10, no. 30 (July 21, 1967): 7, 39.

12. Philip Bridgham, "Mao's 'Cultural Revolution': Origin and Development," *China Quarterly*, no. 29 (Jan.-Mar. 1967), pp. 1-35.

13. "Raising Still Higher the Banner of Socialist Realism," *Nëndori* [November], 13, no. 3 (Mar. 1966): 3-7.

14. Enver Hoxha, "For the Further Revolutionization of Our Education," *Zëri i popullit*, Mar. 10, 1968. In calling for a purge of textbooks containing harmful, antisocial materials, Hoxha did not spare even the classic works in Albanian literature; that is, the writings of such men as Naim Frashëri, Çajupi, and Ndre Mjeda, whom Albanian leaders had heretofore praised and honored for their strong proletarian sympathies and concern for social justice.

15. Beginning with the spring of 1967, Hoxha succeeded in carrying on a genuine and apparently fruitful dialogue with the masses through correspondence published in the daily press. One interesting by-product of this dialogue was that it broke down, to some extent, the traditional barrier between Gegs and Tosks (or northern and southern Albanians) and helped to foster a sense of unity and collaboration between the two regional groups. See *Zëri i popullit*, Feb. 7 and Mar. 7, 1968.

16. For a stimulating discussion of Albania's cultural revolution, viewed in

the broad context of the country's postwar developments, see Nicholas C. Pano, "The Albanian Cultural Revolution," *Problems of Communism* 23 (Jul.-Aug. 1974): 44-57.

Notes to Chapter 8

1. *East Europe* 16, no. 11 (Nov. 1967): 35. Speaking at the Seventh Congress of the Union of Albanian Women (held in Shkodër) on June 11, 1973, Premier Mehmet Shehu said: "It is a great historic merit of our party and people that they made Albania the first country in the world without religious rites". *Zëri i popullit* [Voice of the people], June 12, 1973.

2. *Zëri i popullit*, Nov. 2, 1971.

3. Pandi Geço, *Shqipëria, pamje fiziko-ekonomike* [Albania, a physical and economic survey] (Tiranë, 1959), JPRS: 9945, Aug. 25, 1961, p. 58.

4. Hulusi Hako, *Akuzojmë fenë* [We accuse religion] (Tiranë: Naim Frashëri Pub. Hse., 1968), p. 80.

5. *Të shkulim nga rrënjët besimet fetare* [Let us abolish religious beliefs, root and branch], published by the Central Committee of the Labor Youth Union of Albania (Tiranë: Naim Frashëri Pub. Hse., 1967), p. 61. Hako, *Akuzojmë*, pp. 81-82.

6. Hako, *Akuzojmë*, p. 71.

7. For simplicity, the term "Church," unless otherwise specified, is used in this study in a broad sense, so as to include both the Christian and the Moslem religious establishments.

8. Hako, *Akuzojmë*, p. 121.

9. *ACEN News* (New York), no. 128 (Mar.-Apr. 1967), p. 18.

10. Stavro Skendi, ed., *Albania*, (New York: Praeger, 1956), p. 297.

11. Hako, *Akuzojmë*, p. 75; *ACEN News*, no. 128 (Mar.-Apr. 1967), pp. 19-20.

12. Fishta's *Lahuta e malcis* [The lute of the mountains] is generally regarded as the greatest Albanian epic poem.

13. Hako, Akuzojmë, p. 52.

14. Ibid., p. 82.

15. *ACEN News*, no. 128 (Mar.-Apr. 1967), p. 19.

16. Hako, *Akuzojmë*, pp. 53, 79.

17. *Shqiptari i lirë* [The free Albanian] (New York), 12, nos. 1-2 (Jan.-Feb. 1968): 1.

18. *Dokumenta kryesore të P.P.SH., I* [Main documents of APL, vol. 1] (Tiranë: Instituti i Historisë së Partisë pranë K.Q. të P.P.SH., 1960), p. 329.

19. Ibid., p. 357.

20. *Report on the Role and Tasks of the Democratic Front for the Complete Triumph of Socialism in Albania* (Tiranë: Naim Frashëri Pub. Hse., 1967), p. 64.

21. Zihni Sako, *Populli dhe feja* [The people and religion] (Tiranë: Naim Frashëri Pub. Hse., 1967), p. 32.

22. Fehmi Xhuglini, *Mjekësia dhe feja* [Medicine and religion] (Tiranë: Naim Frashëri Pub. Hse., 1967), p. 3; *Të shkulim*, p. 17.

23. G. Konomi, *Darvinizmi dhe feja* [Darwinism and religion] (Tiranë: Naim Frashëri Pub. Hse., 1967).

24. Mina Qirici, *"Çudirat" e fesë* [The "miracles" of religion] (Tiranë: Naim Frashëri Pub. Hse., 1967).

25. Sotir Melka, *Dëmet e riteve dhe festave fetare* [The harm of religious rites and festivals] (Tiranë: Naim Frashëri Pub. Hse., 1967), p. 15.

26. Ahmed il Drrha, "Mission to Albania," *Nea politeia* (Athens), Dec. 1-5, 1968.

27. G. Konomi, *Mbi origjinën e fesë* [On the origin of religion] (Tiranë: Naim Frashëri Pub. Hse., 1967); Sako, *Populli dhe feja*, pp. 3-7.

28. *Të shkulim*, p. 8.

29. *Rruga e Partisë* [The Party road], 17, no. 2 (Feb. 1970): 104-105.

30. Hako, *Akuzojmë*, p. 85.

31. *Rruga e Partisë* 17, no. 2 (Feb. 1970): 104-105.

32. Hoxha, *Report on Democratic Front*, p. 65.

33. Skendi, "Skenderbeg and Albanian National Consciousness," *Südost-Forschungen* (Munich: R. Oldenbourg, 1968), p. 86.

34. Hoxha, *Report on Democratic Front*, p. 65. Hoxha's remark about "foreign invaders" refers to the Romans, during whose occupation of Albania (then known as Illyria) Christianity spread into the country in the first centuries of the Christian era, and to the Ottoman Turks who introduced Islam following their invasion of Albania in the fourteenth century.

35. *PPSH, mbi fenë dhe edukimin ateist-shkencor të punonjësve* [APL, on religion and the atheist-scientific education of the workers] (Tiranë, 1967), p. 5. It is interesting, for example, that among the Albanians in the United States, both Christians and Moslems attended mass in the churches of the Albanian Orthodox Diocese, which was founded in 1908, just four years prior

to Albania's independence from the Turks. This fact was not merely an indication of religious tolerance but an expression of national unity.

36. *Nëntori* [November], 21, no. 2 (Feb. 1974): 144.

37. *PPSH, mbi fenë*, p. 5.

38. Hoxha, *Mbi problemin e gruas* [On the problem of woman] (Tiranë: Naim Frashëri Pub. Hse., 1967), p. 71.

39. Mina Qirici, *Thelbi reaksionar i Muslimanizmit* [The reactionary core of Islamism] (Tiranë: Naim Frashëri Pub. Hse., 1967), p. 51.

40. Hako, *Akuzojmë*, p. 98.

41. G. Konomi, *Mbi festat dhe të kremtet fetare* [On religious festivals and holidays] (Tiranë: Naim Frashëri Pub. Hse., 1967), p. 9.

42. See esp. Petro Marko, *Urata, dhia dhe perëndia* [The priest, the goat, and god] (Tiranë: Naim Frashëri Pub. Hse., 1967)—a book that portrays the clergy as deceivers, gluttons, degenerates, and agents of Albania's enemies.

43. Hako, *Akuzojmë*, p. 76.

44. *Zëri i popullit*, Apr. 28, 1966.

45. Enver Muça, "Religion in the Service of the Ruling Bourgeois-Revisionist Dictatorship," *Bashkimi* [Unity], Nov. 19, 1969. For a particularly violent attack on the Kremlin's relations with the Vatican, see Hulusi Hako, "The Vatican and Modern Revisionism," *Rruga e Partisë* 11, no. 6 (June 1964): 61-75.

46. Hako, *Akuzojmë*, p. 73.

47. The testimonials and pledges made at these meetings were published in several volumes, including: *Lufta kundër zakoneve prapanike dhe besimeve fetare: Shprehje e luftës së klasave* [The struggle against backward customs and religious beliefs: An expression of class warfare] (Tiranë: Naim Frashëri Pub. Hse., 1967); and *Nuk ka liri të vërtetë shoqërore pa emancipimin e plotë të gruas* [There can be no true social freedom without the full emancipation of woman] (Tiranë: Naim Frashëri Pub. Hse., 1967).

48. *Rruga e Partisë* 17, no. 6 (June 1970): 44.

49. Bik Peap, *Feja lakuriq* [Religion stripped naked] (Tiranë: Naim Frashëri Pub. Hse., 1967), p. 4.

50. *Zëri i popullit*, Nov. 2, 1971.

51. *Të shkulim*, p. 31.

52. Hoxha, *Report on Democratic Front*, p. 66.

53. *The Vineyard* (Boston), 1, no. 2 (1970): 13.

54. *Shqiptari i lirë* 12, no. 1-2 (Jan.-Feb. 1968): 1.

55. Eric Bourne, "Albanian Leaders Admit Religion Lingers," *Christian Science Monitor*, Sept. 11, 1973; j.c.k. [Joseph C. Kun], "Tirana to Revamp Atheistic Propaganda," *RFE Research* (Albania), Nov. 29, 1973.

56. The Kurti incident became the point of departure for a lengthy article on religion in Albania, in German, with a broad historical perspective. See Bernhard Tönnes, "Religionen in Albanien," *Osteuropa* (Sept. 1974), pp. 661-675. For a detailed discussion of the incident, see Gjon Sinishta, *The Fulfilled Promise* (Santa Clara, Cal.: H & F Composing Service, 1976), pp. 150-157. Sinishta's book is subtitled *A Documentary Account of Religious Persecution in Albania*. Another book on religion in Albania, published in 1976, is that of Reona Peterson, entitled *Tomorrow You Die*. Printed by Bible Voice, Van Nuys, Cal., this work is an account of the author's rather naive, though well-meaning, attempt to smuggle religious literature into Albania while visiting there in 1973 and her subsequent arrest and release by Albanian authorities.

57. *Albania Report* (New York), no. 5 (Apr.-May 1973).

58. *Zëri i popullit*, Apr. 14, 1973.

59. See article, "Some Albanians Are Ordered to Change Names," *New York Times*, Feb. 27, 1976; *Economist*, Mar. 13, 1976, p. 56.

60. The text of the Constitution appears in *Albania today*, no. 1 (Jan.-Feb. 1977), pp. 1-17.

61. For an extensive analysis of this subject, see Bohdan R. Bociurkiw and John W. Strong, eds., *Religion and Atheism in the USSR and Eastern Europe* (New York: Macmillan Co., 1975).

Notes to Chapter 9

1. The term "intelligentsia," as used here, refers generally to the "artistic intelligentsia" or those members of society who are engaged in art and cultural activities, although in some contexts it includes the academic community and members of the professions as well.

2. The *Zëri i popullit* article was published in English in pamphlet form under the title, *The Working Class in Revisionist Countries Must Take the Field and Re-establish the Dictatorship of the Proletariat* (Tiranë, 1968), 40 pp.

3. Ibid., p. 7.

4. See *Dokumenta kryesore të P.P.SH., I* [Main documents of APL, vol. 1] (Tiranë: Instituti i Historisë së Partisë pranë K.Q. të P.P.SH., 1960), p. 14; (hereafter cited as *D.K.*).

5. Ibid., pp. 71, 264; *D.K., III* (Tiranë: Mihul Duri Press, 1970), p. 82.

6. Closing remarks to the Party Plenum of July 7-9, 1964, in *PPSH, mbi kulturën, letërsinë dhe artet* [APL, on culture, literature, and the arts] (Tiranë: Naim Frashëri Pub. Hse., presumed date of publication 1968), 94 pp., at p. 72.

7. For a discussion of events relating to this period, see Stavro Skendi, ed., *Albania* (New York: Praeger, 1956), pp. 312-314; and in particular a two-part article by Arshi Pipa on Albanian writers and communism in *Shqiptari i lirë* [The free Albanian] (New York), Feb. 28, 1959, and Mar. 31, 1959.

8. Skendi, *Albania*, p. 312.

9. Melëshova's alleged opportunism was attacked by the Party's Central Committee in a letter dated May 10, 1947, and bearing the signature of Hoxha, which was sent to all Party organizations. See *D.K., I*, pp. 334-340. See also editorial in *Nëndori* [November], 17, no. 10 (Oct. 1970): 3-6.

10. *D.K., I*, p. 334.

11. *PPSH, mbi kulturën*, p. 7.

12. Pipa, in *Shqiptari i lirë*, Feb. 28, 1959.

13. Ibid.

14. M. Kokalari was the director in 1944 of *Zëri i lirisë*, organ of the Albanian Social-Democrat group. She was arrested in 1946 for anticommunist activity. See Pipa, in *Shqiptari i lirë*, Mar. 31, 1959.

15. For a detailed account of the Party's repression of dissident intellectuals and an appraisal of Albanian communist writers, see the informative two-part article by Pipa, cited above. Pipa, who is now a professor of Romance languages in a Midwestern university, was editor of *Kritika* [Criticism] in Albania in 1944. He was one of those arrested in 1946 and was in prison for ten years. His book, *Libri i burgut* [The book of prison], a collection of poems published in 1959, is a product of his prison experience.

16. Petro Marko was one of a number of Albanians who fought in Spain during the Spanish Civil War. After their release from prison, Varfi and Marko became respectable writers and enjoyed considerable prestige as members of the old group of Albanian communist intellectuals.

17. Skendi, *Albania*, p. 313.

18. Editorial in *Nëndori* 17, no. 10 (Oct. 1970): 3-6.

19. Skendi, *Albania*, p. 313.

20. Pipa, in *Shqiptari i lirë*, Mar. 31, 1959; *Area Handbook for Albania*, Foreign Area Studies of American University (Washington, D.C.: Government Printing Office, 1971), pp. 76-77.

21. See appraisal of Fishta in Dh. S. Shuteriqi et al., eds., *Historia e letërsisë shqipe, II* [The history of Albanian literature, vol. 2] (Tiranë: Mihal Duri Press, 1959), pp. 25, 36, 35, 256, 257, 429.

22. *PPSH, mbi kulturën*, p. 5.

23. Ibid., p. 9.

24. Directive of APL-CC Plenum of April 30, 1949. *D.K., II* (Tiranë: Instituti i Historisë së Partisë pranë K.Q. të P.P.SH., 1961), p. 7.

25. *Nëndori* 1, no. 12 (Dec. 1954): 5.

26. For a discussion of Socialist Realism in the arts, see Dalan Shapllo, "One Year of Literature on the Road of Socialist Realism," *Nëndori* 12, no. 1 (Jan. 1965): 3-10; and the report on a meeting of artists and writers in Tiranë, Dec. 1964, *Nëndori* 12, no. 3 (Mar. 1965): 197-200. For a recent restatement of Shapllo's views, see "The Vitality of the Principles of Socialist Realism in Present-Day Albanian Art," *Albania today* (Tiranë), no. 2 (Mar.-Apr. 1976), pp. 32-37.

27. For example, Llazar Siliqi, "Concerning the Problem of the Positive Hero," *Drita* [Light] (Tiranë), Mar. 19, 1972, pp. 3-4; and the report of Dritëro Agolli to the pelnum of the Directing Committee of LAWA, held on Feb. 27-28, 1975, *Nëntori* 22, no. 4 (Apr. 1975): 13-18.

28. *D.K., I*, p. 456.

29. *Nëndori*, currently spelled *Nëntori*, is advertised as a "monthly literary, artistic, social, and political" publication.

30. R. Brahimi, "Some Problems of Characterization in Our Literature," *Nëndori* 2, no. 5 (May 1956): 135-136, passim.

31. Report to the Second Congress of LAWA, *Nëndori*, Special Issue (1969), p. 40.

32. *Nëndori*, Special Issue on the First LAWA Congress (1957), pp. 182-184.

33. Ibid.

34. Ibid., pp. 184-186.

35. Ibid.

36. Ibid., Special Issue on the Second LAWA Congress (1969), p. 120.

37. R. Brahimi, "The Writer and Reality," ibid., 12, no. 1 (Jan. 1965): 136-155; *Drita*, Apr. 18, 1965; *Christian Science Monitor*, July 12, 1965.

38. *Nëndori* 12, no. 5 (May 1965): 116.

39. R. Alia, "On the Growth of the Role of Literature and the Arts in the Communist Education of the Masses," *D.K., IV* (Tiranë: Naim Frashëri Pub. Hse., 1970), pp. 558-602, at p. 560.

40. See Shuteriqi report in *Nëndori* 13, no. 1 (Jan. 1966): 11-39.

41. Ibid., p. 4.

42. Ibid., 12, no. 3 (Mar. 1966): 4-7.

43. J. Malo, "A Work Which Slanders Our Reality," *Zëri i popullit* [Voice of the people], June 18, 1966.

44. *Kongresi i Pestë i P.P.SH.* [Fifth Congress of APL] (Tiranë: Naim Frashëri Pub. Hse., 1967), p. 146.

45. Ibid., p. 141.

46. *East Europe* 16, no. 11 (Nov. 1967): 35.

47. Ndoc Papleka, "The Party" (excerpts), *Nëndori* 18, no. 12 (Dec. 1971): 117.

48. Sulejman Mato, "Enver" (excerpts), ibid., no. 9 (Sept. 1971): 10-11.

49. Ibid., Special Issue (1969) on the proceedings of the congress, pp. 4-5.

50. Ibid., pp. 9-56.

51. See editorial, ibid., 17, no. 10 (Oct. 1970): 3-6.

52. Article by D. Agolli in *Zëri i popullit*, May 20, 1973.

53. Ibid., Nov. 2, 1969.

54. Ibid., Nov. 4, 1969.

55. "A Critique of the Drama 'Grey Stains,'" *Zëri i popullit*, Nov. 18, 1969. Strongly critical articles appeared also in the *Nëndori* review (Dec. 1969) by novelist Fatmir Gjata and playwright Kolë Jakova.

56. Papa has produced some good work. He is the author of *Cuca e maleve* [The mountain lassie], a classic of the dramatic theater of socialist Albania.

57. *Nëndori*, Special Issue (1971), p. 55; *Drita*, Nov. 26, 1972, p. 13.

58. *Zëri i popullit*, Nov. 23, 1969.

59. Dhimitër Xhuvani won first prize for his book, *Përsëri në këmbë* [Standing straight again], a work one critic called the most successful novel in recent Albanian literature. See Llazar Siliqi's comments in *Nëndori*, Special Issue (1971), pp. 43-44. Naum Prifti was given first prize for his volume of short stories, *Duar të fuqishme* [Powerful hands], and top prize for his play, *Dasmë pa nuse* [Wedding without bride], a comedy about old-fashioned engagements and weddings. The first prize for humor went to Qamil Buxheli for his work, *Faraonë dhe firaunë* [Faraone and Firaune], while Fatos Arapi won top awards for his novelette, *Patat e egra* [Wild geese], and his volume of collected poems entitled *Ritme të hekurta* [Iron rhythms], which sang the praises of the working class and socialist life.

60. *Zëri i popullit*, May 16, 1973.

61. *Nëndori* 19, no. 3 (Mar. 1972): 9.

62. Ibid., no. 8 (Aug. 1972): 3-25.

63. Xhevat Lloshi, "Fahionable Names," *Zëri i popullit*, Mar. 16, 1973.

64. K. Bihiku, "For a More Militant Spirit in Poetry," ibid., Apr. 22, 1973.

65. Ibid.

66. *Drita*, Mar. 11, 1973.

67. Tomor Drini, "Bourgeois Television: The Masses and Reality," *Zëri i popullit*, Mar. 25, 1973; *Drita* editorial, Apr. 8, 1973.

68. Kudret Velça, "Ideology and Tastes," *Zëri i popullit*, May 25, 1973.

69. See editorial in *Rruga e Partisë* [The Party road] (Tiranë), 20, no. 4 (Apr. 1973): 5-12; and M. Ahmati article on liberalism in ibid., pp. 13-25.

70. *Zëri i popullit*, Apr. 7, 1973.

71. Ibid., Apr. 15, 1973.

72. Ibid., May 16, 1973.

73. "Intensify the ideological struggle against alien manifestations and liberal attitudes toward them," *Speeches, 1971-1973* (Tiranë: 8 Nëntori Pub. Hse., 1974), pp. 309-406. The plenum lasted for three days, June 26-28.

74. *Zëri i popullit*, July 26, 1973; *Drita*, July 29, 1973, pp. 1-3.

75. *Zëri i popullit*, Aug. 3, 1973. See also Eric Bourne, "Albania Feels Deep Internal Strain," *Christian Science Monitor*, Aug. 17, 1973; David Binder, "Albania Reported Upset by China Thaw," *New York Times* Sept. 13, 1973; and *Albanian Resistance* (Paris), Sept. 8, 1973, pp. 5-6.

76. *Nëntori* 22, no. 1 (Jan. 1975): 17-25. The list of winners included many familiar names: D. Agolli, Ll. Siliqi, F. Arapi, and A. Çaçi (poets); K. Jakova and F. Kraja (playwrights); A. Kondo and N. Prifti (short-story writers); and H. Dule, Sh. Hadëri, and Ll. Nikolla (sculptors). But there were many new faces as well, including Vito Koçi who won a first prize for her novelette, *Borë në bjeshkë* [Snow on the mountain]; Mirash Markaj, also a first-prize winner for his play, *Gjergj Kastrioti*; and L. Cukalla who took first and second prizes in two categories for children's stories.

77. Ibid., pp. 13-14.

78. "Writers and Artists Are Helpers of the Party for the Communist Education of Our People," ibid., no. 2 (Feb. 1975): 3-27. For an English version of the speech, see *Albania today*, no. 2 (Mar.-Apr. 1975), pp. 2-15.

79. *Nëntori* 22, no. 2 (Feb. 1975): 18.

80. Ibid., no. 4 (Apr. 1975): 10.

81. "Congress of Magnificient Gains and Perspectives," ibid., 23, no. 11 (Nov. 1976): 21; Mumtaz Dhrami, "A Reflection of the Progress of Our Figurative Arts," *New Albania*, no. 6 (Nov.-Dec. 1976), pp. 17-18.

Notes to Chapter 10

1. The term "army" is used in this discussion to mean either the regular army or the entire military establishment, including the regular army, the navy, and the air force.

2. *Kongresi i Irë i Partisë Komuniste të Shqipërisë* [First Congress of ACP](Tiranë: M. Duri Press, 1950), pp. 608-609.

3. *Kongresi i Iltë i Partisë së Punës të Shqipërisë* [Second Congress of APL] (Tiranë: M. Duri Press, 1952), p. 267.

4. Eugene K. Keefe, et al., eds., *Area Handbook for Albania* (Washington, D.C.: Government Printing Office, 1971), p. 179.

5. Hoxha, *Speech Delivered at the Meeting of 81 Communist and Workers' Parties* . . . , pamphlet in English, (Tiranë, 1969), pp. 91-92; (hereafter, *Speech at Meeting of 81 CPs*).

6. Ibid., p. 92.

7. See *History of the Party of Labor of Albania* (Tiranë: Naim Frashëri Pub. Hse., 1971), pp. 223-226; (hereafter, *History of APL*).

8. Ibid., p. 222.

9. Ibid., p. 216.

10. Višegrad, according to Albanian documents, was liberated on Feb. 14, 1945. See *Zëri i popullit* [Voice of the people], Feb. 15, 1975.

11. *Rruga e Partisë* [The Party road], 21, no. 12 (Dec. 1974): 98; *The National-Liberation Struggle of the Albanian People*, illus. vol. (Tiranë, n.d.), illus. no. 102. Albanian figures on the number of Partisans who fought in Yugoslavia vary from 15,000 to 20,000; the figures on casualties range from 350 to 600.

12. l[ouis] z[anga], "Situation Report" on Albania and Kosovo, *RFE Research*, Oct. 4, 1972.

13. *Rilindja* [Rebirth], May 4, 1975.

14. *Rilindja*, May 9, 1975; Louis Zanga, "Kosovo: An Important Element in Yugoslav-Albanian Rapproachment," *RFE Research* (Albania), June 2, 1975. The *Ballists* were the main opponents of the communists in the struggle for power in wartime Albania.

15. *Zëri i popullit*, Mar. 4, 1975; *New Albania*, no. 6 (Nov.-Dec. 1975), p. 31.

16. See *The Truth about the Plight of the Albanians of Yugoslavia*, pamphlet in English (Tiranë, Publisher's name not given, 1961); and Hamit Kokalari, *Kosova: Djepi i shqiptarizmit* [Koxovo: Cradle of Albanian nationalism], published by the Union of Kosovars (Rome: APICE Press, 1962).

17. *Dokumenta kryesore të P.P.SH., I* [Main documents of APL, vol. 1], (Tiranë: Instituti i Historisë së Partisë pranë K.Q. të P.P.SH., 1960), p. 392.

18. Ibid., p. 391.

19. Ibid., p. 392.

20. M. Shehu, *On the Experience of the National-Liberation War and on the Development of the National Army*, pamphlet in English (Tiranë, 1963), p. 3.

21. *Kongresi i Irë*, p. 112.

22. Stavro Skendi, ed., *Albania* (New York: Praeger, 1956), p. 324. M. Shehu attended the Voroshilov Academy from Sept. 1945 to Aug. 1946.

23. *Speech at Meeting of 81 CPs*, p. 72.

24. Ibid., p. 68.

25. *History of APL*, p. 457.

26. Ibid., p. 493.

27. Leo Heiman, "Peking's Adriatic Stronghold," *East Europe* 13, no. 4 (Apr. 1964): 15–17.

28. For an extensive Albanian documentation of the Vlorë controversy, see the APL-CC letter of July 6, 1961, to the CPSU-CC, in *Dikumenta kryesore të P.P.SH., IV* [Main documents of APL, vol. 4] (Tiranë: Naim Frashëri Pub. Hse., 1970), pp. 41–51, and p. 46 for the preceding quote.

29. Ibid., p. 49. The letter is dated June 3, 1971.

30. *Zëri i popullit*, Nov. 29, 1972.

31. *History of APL*, p. 493.

32. *Zëri i popullit*, May 22, 1965.

33. *History of APL*, p. 355.

34. Hoxha, *Vepra* [Works] (Tiranë: Naim Frashëri Pub. Hse., 1973), 13: 228–231; *Rilindja*, Feb. 27, 1965.

35. *East Europe* 13, no. 9 (Sept. 1964): 29. See also *Borba*, the People's Front daily (Belgrade), May 28, 1961; William E. Griffith, *Albania and the Sino-Soviet Rift* (Cambridge, Mass.: MIT Press, 1963), p. 110.

36. *Zëri i popullit*, Nov. 8, 1961.

37. *Speech at Meeting of 81 CPs*, p. 105.

38. *Rilindja*, Mar. 4, 1965; Keefe, *Area Handbook for Albania*, pp. 190–191.

39. *History of APL*, p. 453; *Bashkimi* [Unity], Feb. 2, 1965. Admiral Sejko had been in the USSR for military training in 1947–49 and again in 1956–58,

a pattern followed also by Mehmet Shehu, General Plaku, and General Balluku.

40. *Speech at Meeting of 81 CPs*, p. 38.

41. *Bashkimi*, Oct. 30, 1966; *New York Times*, Oct. 28, 1966.

42. *Bashkimi*, June 20, 1967.

43. Ibid., July 10, 1966. Albanian sources explained that the move aimed at removing all formal divisions between officers and soldiers, thereby preventing "bossism" and elitism among army cadres and the alienation of the masses from the army. *Zëri i popullit*, Mar. 11, 1966; *Rruga e Partisë* 22, no. 2 (Feb. 1975): 45.

44. *Bashkimi*, Oct. 29, 1966.

45. Ibid., Jan. 13, Feb. 4, 1967.

46. *Zëri i popullit*, Sept. 19, 1968; *Peking Review*, Sept. 20, 1968, pp. 3-4.

47. *Zëri i popullit*, Oct. 6, 1968; *Bashkimi*, Oct. 8, 1968.

48. *New York Times*, Oct. 7, 1968.

49. *Peking Review*, Dec. 13, 1968, pp. 3-13.

50. Lajos Lederer, "Albania Allows Chinese Bases," *Boston Sunday Globe*, Dec. 8, 1968.

51. For example, Moscow Radio in Albanian to Albania, 1730 GMT, Sept. 9, 1968.

52. P. Prifti, "Albania and the Sino-Soviet Conflict," *Studies in Comparative Communism* 6, no. 3 (Autumn 1973): 257-261.

53. Leslie Gardiner, writing in *Christian Science Monitor*, Mar. 3, 1970.

54. Hoxha, *Our Policy Is an Open Policy* . . . , pamphlet in English, (Tiranë, 1974), p. 72.

55. Speech by General Balluku, *Zëri i popullit*, Aug. 22, 1971.

56. *Zëri i popullit*, Dec. 2, 1972.

57. Ibid., July 10, 13, 14, 1973.

58. Ibid., July 10, 1973.

59. *Peking Review* 9, no. 19 (May 6, 1966): 3.

60. *Zëri i popullit*, July 10, 1975.

61. Ibid., Mar. 15, 1977.

62. Hoxha, *Vepra*, 13: 232-233. For an earlier and longer account of the Balluku incident, see the author's "The Dismissal of General Beqir Balluku, Albania's Minister of Defense: An Analysis," in George W. Simmonds ed.,

Nationalism in the USSR and Eastern Europe in the Era of Brezhnev and Kosygin (Detroit, Mich.: University of Detroit Press, 1977), pp. 495-502. For a lengthy review of the military establishment in Albania, see Horst Dieter Topp, *Die albanische Militärführung und die Beziehungen zwischen der VR Albanien, der VR China and den USA* (Köln-Ehrenfeld, West Germany: Bundesinstitut für ostwissenschaftliche und internationale Studien, 1975), pp. 44.

63. *Zëri i popullit*, July 31, 1974. Later, however, Veli Llakaj was identified as chief-of-staff as well as a deputy minister of defense; ibid., May 7, 1975. The same issue referred to Llambi Gegprifti as deputy minister of defense. In addition to his new post, Gegprifti had attained the rank of a candidate member of the Politburo. The shifts in the personnel of the army leadership occurred during the convocation of the Fifth and Sixth Party Plenums (held in July and Dec. 1974), which dealt specifically with the situation in the armed forces.

64. Ibid., Oct. 30, 1974.

65. *Rruga e Partisë* 22, no. 2 (Feb. 1975): 26.

66. Hoxha, *Our Policy*, p. 31.

67. Ibid., pp. 50, 55-57.

68. *Zëri i popullit*, July 9, 1974; Feb. 4, 18, Mar. 4, 11, 1975.

69. Ibid., July 10, 1974.

70. Hoxha, *Our Policy*, p. 29.

71. Ndreçi Plasari, "The Strength and Invincibility of Our Army Lie in Its Popular and Revolutionary Character," *Rruga e Partisë* 22, no. 2 (Feb. 1975): 40.

72. *Zëri i popullit*, Jan. 3, 1975.

73. *Rruga e Partisë* 22, no. 1 (Jan. 1975): 9.

74. Ibid., no. 2 (Feb. 1975): 34.

75. Marshal Georgi Zhukov, the greatest hero of the Red Army during WWII, visited Albania in Oct. 1957. He was in Albania when Khrushchev ousted him as defense minister of the USSR, ostensibly for trying to limit the control of the party organization over the armed forces and for "abetting his own personality cult." See *New York Times*, Oct. 27, 1957. Viewed from this frame of reference, Balluku's fall was a curious example of history repeating itself, for the two main accusations lodged against him by the Hoxha-Shehu leadership were the same two accusations Khrushchev utilized to bring down Zhukov.

76. *Raport në Kongresin VII të PPSH* [Report to the Seventh APL Congress] (Tiranë: 8 Nëntori Pub. Hse., 1976), p. 144; (hereafter, *Raport*).

77. See *Flamuri* [The flag] (Rome), Nov. 28, 1974; and *The Albanian Resistance* (Paris), no. 104 (Apr. 28, 1976).

78. *Raport*, p. 95.

79. *The Military Balance*, 1975-76 (London: International Institute for Strategic Studies, 1975), p. 27.

80. *Speech at Meeting of 81 CPs*, p. 41.

Notes to Chapter 11

1. Unofficial reports put the death toll at five and the number of those arrested at several hundred. For a detailed account of the demonstrations, see the author's *Kosovo in Ferment*, monograph, (Cambridge, Mass.: MIT Center for International Studies, June 1969), 37 pp. The material in this chapter formed the basis for an article by the author entitled "Minority Politics: The Albanians in Yugoslavia," *Balkanistica II* (1975), pp. 7-18.

2. For a general study of Kosovo, see Thomas Adolph Roth, "Yugoslav (Socialist) Rule in Practice: A Survey of Developments in the Kosovo Region" (M.A. thesis, University of Oregon, 1970); (hereafter cited as Roth, "Survey").

3. Prifti, *Kosovo in Ferment*, p. 14.

4. The last national census, taken in 1971, showed Kosovo with a population of 1,244,755. See l[ouis] z[anga], "Sharp Growth in Kosovo Population," *RFE Research* (Yugoslavia), May 5, 1971. A comprehensive treatment of the question of national minorities in Yugoslavia is given in Nada Dragic, ed., *Nations and Nationalities in Yugoslavia* (Belgrade: Medjunarodna Politika, 1974).

5. See appendix to this chapter, tables 11.1 and 11.2.

6. The question of Kosovo has acquired a new dimension since the 1975 Helsinki accords and Pres. James Carter's campaign in behalf of human rights in all nations.

7. *Le monde*, Mar. 25, 1969.

8. Roth, "Survey," pp. 8-14; Zdenko Antic, *RFE Research* (Yugoslavia), Feb. 7, 1969.

9. Hamit Kokalari, *Kosova: Djepi i shqiptarizmit* [Kosovo: Cradle of Albanian nationalism], published by the Union of Kosovars (Rome: APICE Press, 1962), p. 12.

10. Ibid., pp. 41-45.

11. Ibid., p. 61.

12. Inis L. Claude, Jr., *National Minorities* (New York: Greenwood Press, 1969), p. 40.

13. Paul Lendvai, "Yugoslavia in Crisis," *Encounter* 39, no. 2 (Aug. 1972): 71; *Le monde*, Mar. 25, 1969.

14. Veli Deva, former president of the League of Communists of Kosovo, in *Rilindja* [Rebirth] (Pristina), Nov. 28-29-30, 1968, p. 6.

15. Kokalari, *Kosova*, pp. 165-166. See also *The Truth about the Plight of the Albanians of Yugoslavia* (Tiranë: n.p., 1961), 107 pp., at p. 5. Yugoslavia's policy of denationalization of the Albanian minority is substantiated also by Yugoslav sources, most notably by G. Krstic, who in 1928 published a book in Sarajevo on the colonization of southern Serbia. See Kokalari, *Kosova*, p. 52.

16. Kokalari, *Kosova*, pp. 85-102; Roth, "Survey," p. 25.

17. As reported in the Turkish press, *Milijet*, Apr. 17, 1926, and *Vatan*, July 7, 1938. "In official Yugoslav propaganda it was said that the evacuation to Turkey would [affect] 400,000 inhabitants under the condition ... that they be of Albanian nationality." Roth, "Survey," p. 24.

18. *Përparimi* [Progress] (Pristina), Jan.-Feb. 1974, p. 127.

19. *Frankfurter Allgemeine Zeitung*, Dec. 28, 1968; *Le monde*, Mar. 25, 1969. It is true that the Germans, playing on the Albanians' national feelings and memories of Slav oppression, had succeeded in mobilizing a division of Kosovo Albanians, known as the "SS Skanderbeg" and numbering about 12,000 troops, to fight against the Slavs; Roth, "Survey," p. 34.

20. Claude, *National Minorities*, p. 88; *Zëri i popullit* [Voice of the people], Albanian CP daily, Nov. 24, 1968.

21. *The Truth*, pp. 56-57.

22. Nicholas C. Pano, *The People's Republic of Albania* (Baltimore, Md.: John Hopkins Press, 1968), p. 40.

23. See comments by Ali Sukrija, at the time president of the Kosovo Executive Committee, in *Rilindja*, Oct. 28, 1963.

24. Robert R. King, *Minorities under Communism* (Cambridge, Mass.: Harvard University Press, 1973), p. 283, n. 59; Roth, "Survey," p. 39.

25. *Lidhja e Prizrenit* [The League of Prizren], organ of the League of Prizren in exile, Apr.-May-June 1972. The first League of Prizren was established in 1878 to resist Slavic "territorial encroachments" in Kosovo.

26. T. Zavalani, *Histori e Shqipnis, pjesa e dytë (1878-1965)* [History of Albania, part two] (London: Poets' and Painters' Press, 1966), p. 277.

27. Ibid., p. 278; Kokalari, *Kosova*, p. 53.

28. King, *Minorities*, p. 128.

29. Roth, "Survey," p. 39.

30. King, *Minorities*, p. 283, n. 59.

31. Paul Shoup, "The National Question in Yugoslavia," *Problems of Communism* 21, no. 1 (Jan.-Feb. 1972): 19.

32. Ilija Jukic, "Tito's Legacy," *Survey*, no. 77 (Autumn 1970), p. 100.

33. *Zëri i popullit*, Sept. 9, 1958. Albania's position on Kosovo is forcefully stated in *The Truth*.

34. *Zëri i popullit*, Sept. 9, 1958.

35. *Rilindja*, Nov. 28, 1964.

36. *The Struggle of the Kossovars*, no. 15 (July 10, 1974), p. 8; *Flamuri* [The flag] (Rome), organ of *Balli Kombëtar* [the National Front], Aug. 26, 1974.

37. One of the means the émigrés use to press their "Kosovo crusade" is their liaison with the Federalist Union of European National Minorities, in which their group, the Union of Kosovars, holds membership.

38. Ali Hadri, "One Nation—One Literary Language," *Përparimi* 14, no. 3 (Mar.-Apr. 1968): 323-324.

39. Slobodan Stanković, *RFE Research* (Yugoslavia), Mar. 18, 1974.

40. *Le monde*, Mar. 25, 1969; Dan Morgan, "Belgrade Aids Ethnic Albanians," *Washington Post*, Jan. 24, 1972.

41. l[ouis] z[anga], "Sharp Growth in Kosovo Population," *RFE Research* (Yugoslavia), May 5, 1971.

42. In view of the high birth rate among Albanian nationals, Kosovo threatens to overtake the Republic of Macedonia as well. At their current rate of population growth, it is estimated that in the next dozen years the Albanians will be the third largest national group in Yugoslavia, after the Serbs and the Croatians. See D. Morgan, *Washington Post*, Jan. 24, 1972.

43. Jukic, "Tito's Legacy," p. 101.

44. *New York Times*, Jan. 16, 1975; *Le monde*, Jan. 17, 1975.

45. *New York Times*, Nov. 24, 1975; *Zëri i popullit*, Nov. 7 and 16, 1975.

46. Dusko Doder, "Tension Mounts on Yugoslav-Albanian Border," *Washington Post*, Mar. 1, 1976; Malcolm W. Browne, "Albanians in Yugoslavia Demand a Better Deal," *New York Times*, Apr. 26, 1976.

47. *Flamuri*, July 25, 1976.

48. *Zëri i popullit*, Nov. 2, 1976.

49. The coalition is an active movement that includes members of such groups as *Lidhja e Prizrenit* and *Balli Kombëtar*. Its purpose, aims, and activities are reported in a number of Albanian publications in the West, among them *The*

Struggle of the Kossovars (U.S.A.), *Lidhja e Prizrenit* (U.S.A.), *Albanian Resistance* (branches in U.S.A. and other countries), *Flamuri* (Italy), *Koha e jonë* [Our time] (Paris), *Dielli* [The sun] and *Liria* [Liberty] (Boston).

50. Editorial, "The Banner of Kosovo in the Hands of 'Vatra,'" *Dielli*, Apr. 16, 1977; see also, May 1 and 16, 1977.

Notes to Chapter 12

1. Ramadan Marmullaku, *Albania and the Albanians* (London: C. Hurst & Co., 1975), p. 129. See also S. Peters, "Communist Seizure of Power and Nationalism in Eastern Europe," *Koha e jonë* [Our time] (Paris), 9, nos. 5-8 (May-Aug. 1970): 5-11, 22; Milovan Djilas has said that "Enver Hoxha is as much a nationalist as he is a power-loving dogmatist" (as quoted by Peters, p. 11).

2. For a perceptive study of the influence of nationalism on Albanian politics, see Arshi Pipa, "The Political Development of the Albanian State, 1912-1962," *Shqiptari i lirë* [The free Albanian] (New York), Nov.-Dec. 1962.

3. *Zëri i popullit* [Voice of the people], July 29, 1975. For a recent appraisal of Albania's historical struggle for independence and defiance of the great powers, see Jan Myrdal and Gun Kessle, *Albania Defiant* (New York: Monthly Review Press, 1976); translated from the original in Swedish, *Albansk utmaning* (1970), by Paul Britten Austin.

4. *Zëri i popullit*, Nov. 2, 1971; Hoxha, *Report Submitted to the 6th Congress of the Party of Labor of Albania* (Tiranë: Naim Frashëri Pub. Hse., 1971), pp. 21, 30, 45.

5. Enver Hoxha, *Raport në Kongresin VII të P.P.SH.* [Report to the Seventh APL Congress] (Tiranë: 8 Nëntori Pub. Hse., 1976), p. 199.

6. Ibid., p. 210.

7. Ibid., p. 227.

8. Ibid., p. 264.

9. *Kongresi i Irë i Partisë Komuniste të Shqipërisë* [First Congress of ACP] (Tiranë: M. Duri Press, 1950), p. 112.

10. *Albania today*, no. 6 (Nov.-Dec. 1975), pp. 1-51; and no. 4 (July-Aug. 1976), pp. 1-55.

11. *Raport në Kongresin VII*, p. 219. For a recent appraisal of the Albanian-Chinese alliance, see esp. Chap. 7 in Anton Logoreci, *The Albanians: Europe's forgotten survivors* (London: Victor Gollancz Ltd., 1977), pp. 115-138.

12. *Zëri i Popullit*, Oct. 26, 1976.

13. Ibid., Nov. 5, 1976.

14. Ibid., Nov. 4, 1976.

15. Ibid., Aug. 14, 1977.
16. Ibid., Aug. 21, 1977.
17. *Peking Review*, no. 2 (Jan. 7, 1977), pp. 4, 20.
18. *New York Times,* Aug. 28, 1977, Section One, p. 1.

Index

Abdihoxha, Ali, 134
Academy of Phonetic and Plastic Arts (Institute of Arts), 119
Actors' Academy, 119
Administration, 36, 37, 39
Adriatic Sea, 9, 49
Agathangjel, Bishop, 152
Agimi [The dawn], 124
Agolli, Dritëro, 125, 134, 136, 187, 190-191
  elected president of LAWA, 188
  literary work criticized, 177, 183
Agolli, Hiqmet, 128
Agrarian Reform Law, 65
Agriculture, 52, 58, 63-71, 85, 86
  and arable land area, 64, 69
  collectivization of, 28, 65-67
  mechanization of, 70
  politics of, 71
  and rural electrification, 69
Ahmeti, Iljaz, 205
Albanian Academy of Sciences, 118
Albanian-American Moslem Society, 165
Albanian Communist Party (ACP), 9, 10-11, 13-14. *See also* Albanian Party of Labor
Albanianism, 158
Albanian National Liberation Army (ANLA), 15, 16, 18-19, 200
Albanian Orthodox Church in America, 6, 163, 164
  and telegram to Lleshi, 162
Albanian Party of Labor (APL), 27, 46, 181, 182, 199, 216, 258. *See also* Albanian Communist Party.
  and the arts, 43, 178-179, 184-185
  and East European Communist Parties, 22-24
  general line of, 32, 39, 40, 43
  internal life of, 35-40
  mainsprings of politics of, 24-29
  membership of, 30, 31, 35
  Politburo of, 31, 50-51
  and relations with youth, 40-44, 177
  social composition of, 36
Albanian Studies Conference, Second (1968), 117
Albanian Unity, 151
Albanoi tribe, 3
Aleksi, Andrea, 115

Alia, Ramiz, 49, 97, 100, 134, 182, 186
  and report at Plenum on arts, 178-179
  and report at Plenum on women, 104-105
Allende, Salvador, 243
Allied Mediterranean Command, 14
Alphabet, 4
American Vocational School (Tiranë), 34
Andoni, Sotir, 136
Anti-Fascist National Liberation Congress, First (Përmet), 15
"Antonio Gramsci" battalion, 18
Apollonia (Pojan), 5
Aquinas, Saint Thomas, 105
Arapi, Fatos, 136, 177, 183, 185
Archeology, 114
Area, 2
Aristotle, 5
Armed forces, 72, 195, 209, 210, 211, 212, 216, 221. *See also* Balluku, Beqir
  and China, 206-212
  and "people's war," 215
  purge of leadership in (1974), 212-213
  role in liberation of Yugoslavia of, 197-199
  troop strength of, 220
  and USSR, 201-206
  Vlorë base incident, 202-204
  and Yugoslavia, 196-201
Artist of the People award, holders of, 116, 123, 124, 127, 191
Arts, 114, 116-118, 119, 171, 172-173. *See also* Culture
  attack on liberalism in, 184-189
  motives for development of, 113, 141
Atheism, state, 23, 154-157, 165
Attlee, Clement, 169
Aust, Ernst, 252
Avrazi, Gaqo, 176

"Bajram Curri" battalion, 228
Bala, Mantho, 187
Balkan anti-Moscow entente, 256
Balkan Federation, 197
Balkan Regional Economic Cooperation Conference (Athens), 83
Ballet. *See* Opera and ballet
Balli, Valentina, 129
Balliçi, Beatriçe, 136

Index

Balli Kombëtar [The National Front], 11, 14, 18, 19, 20, 34
   founding of, 17
Ballsh oil refinery system, 61, 87
Balluku, Beqir, 195-196, 201
   and Hoxha, 202, 213, 219
   purged, 212-218
   visits to China, 207-208, 209, 210-211
Balzac, Honoré de, 33
Barleti, Marin, 90
Bektashi sect, 152
Belishova, Liri, 102
Berat, 24, 57
Berlin, Congress of (1878), 224
Bihiku, Koço, 135, 186
Bilali, Selim, 128
Bino, Arsinoi, 122
Blood feuds, 257
Blue Mosque (Istanbul), 115
Boletini, Isa, 24, 117
Bolshoi Ballet, 128
Bota e re [The new world], 168, 174
Brahimi, Razi, 135, 174, 176
Brioni Plenum (1966), 234
Brocardus, Father, 4
Broomfield, William S., 237
Bruno, Giordano, 155
Bubani, Dionis, 122, 137
Buda, Aleks, 90, 119
Bulqizë, 55
Bureaucratism, 35-40, 54, 59
Buxheli, Qamil, 137, 177, 183, 185
Buza, Kujtim, 189
Buzuku, Dom Gjon, 4
Byron, George Gordon, 1, 8
Byzantine Empire, 5, 7

Çabej, Eqrem, 119
Çaçi, Aleks, 136, 176
Çajupi, A. Z., 134, 168, 176
Çajupi Theater, A. Z. (Korçë), 184
Çako, Gaqo, 127
Çako, Hito, 211
Calixtus III (pope), 6
Calvin, John, 189
Çamëria, 18
Çami, Foto, 84
Cami, Tefta, 101
Camus, Albert, 140, 141, 186
Carçani, Adil, 82

Canojević, Arsen, 224
Catholic Action, 151
Catholic Church, 152, 153, 154. *See also* Vatican
Çefa, Liljana, 128
Cemetery of the Martyrs (Tiranë), 199
Center for Computer Mathematics, 119
Centralism, 27-28, 46
Cërrik, 55, 57
Chang Chun-chiao, 245
Chang, Tsai-chieh, 209
Charles I of Anjou, 5
Chetniks, 229
Chiang Ching, 245
Chicago, 237
Childe Harold, 1
Chile, 243
China, Communist Party of (CPC), Eleventh Congress, 245, 254, 260
China, People's Republic of, 57, 66, 139, 176, 250
   and aid and credits to Albania, 80-81
   and five-year economic pact with Albania (1976-1980), 82, 89
   food shipments to Albania by, 81
   influence on Albanian economy of, 57, 58, 66
   and rift with Albania, 88-89, 250, 253-261
   and Yugoslavia, 253, 255
China Ballet, 139
Chinese Academy of Sciences, 62
Chinese-Albanian Maritime Association, Joint, 82
Chinese cultural revolution, 144-149, 255
Chou En-lai, 208, 212, 245, 260
   and conversation with Hoxha, 254
Christianity, 7, 155
Chromium, 62, 73
Church of Saint Nikolla (Berat), 114
Church of Saint Triadha (Berat), 114
Cinemas, 132
Civil war. *See* National Liberation War
Claude, Inis, 225
Climate, 2
Coal, 62, 73
Collectivization of agriculture, 65-67
COMECON, 74, 75, 248
Coninform, 243
Comintern, 251

Index

Communications
  telephone, 62
  television, 131
Communism
  in Moslem countries, 22
  puritanical, 24
Communist Party of the Soviet Union (CPSU), Twentieth Congress, 22, 260
Çomora, Spiro, 122-123, 125
Conservatism, 35, 37, 185
Constitution of 1946, 154
Constitution of 1976, 44-47, 84, 97, 218
  and ban on religion, 165
  on foreign military bases, 210
Copper 62, 73
Cosi fan tutte, 1
Council of Imams of North America, 165
Cuca e maleve [The mountain lassie]
  as a ballet, 125, 126
  as a play, 121
Çuko, Lenka, 101
Cultural Relations with the Outside World, Committee for, 137
Cultural revolution, 28, 35, 59, 149, 182, 192
  and abolition of religion, 147, 160, 165
  and comparison with China's cultural revolution, 144-149
  and educational system, 147-148
  and effect on arts, 179-181
  and intelligentsia, 147
  role of army in, 146
  role of Party in, 146
Culture, 114-116, 137, 157. *See also* Arts
  and character of Albanians, 7-8
  Chinese influence on, 139, 144, 175-176
  institutions of, 119, 132-133
  motives for development of, 113, 142-143
  new policy for 172-173
  and personal life-style, 187
  and polemics against USSR and West, 139-141 142
  Soviet influence on, 138, 141
  summary of developments in, 258
  Western influence on, 141-142
Czechoslovakia, invasion of, 22, 167, 208, 245

Daija, Tish, 125, 126
Darwin, Charles, 155
Dedja, Bedri, 119
Defense Council, 218
Deliana, Thoma, 85
De-Maoization, 254
Democratic Front, 100, 172
Détente, 23, 26, 43, 193. *See also* Foreign policy
Deva, Veli, 235
Dhrami, Lumturi, 128
Dhrami, Mumtaz, 129, 190
Dibra, Hafëz Ibrahim, 152
Dictatorship of proletariat, 46, 258
Dielli [The Sun], 165, 170, 239
Dijon International Fall Festival (1970), 138
Dilo, Ksenofon, 189
Dini, Xhemal, 189
Dinucci, Fosco, 252
Dishnica, Pullumb, 200
Ditari i një mësuesi [Diary of a teacher], 122
Dodbiba, Pirro, 85, 87
Dode, Petro, 85
Dolanć, Stane, 198, 199
Dora d'Istria. *See* Gjika, Elena
Drin River, 61
Drita [The light], 186
"Dual adversary" doctrine, 246, 250
Dukagjin, Lek, 8
Dule, Hektor, 129
Dume, Petrit, 211, 213
Durham, Edith, 8
Durrës, 57, 59, 161
  ancient, 4, 5, 7
Durrës-Elbasan railroad, 102
Dušan, Stefan, 223
Dy me zero [Two to nothing], 122-123

East Berlin Conference of European Communist Parties (1976), 251
Economy, 46, 261. *See also* Five-year plans
  conflict over policy and purges in, 84-85, 87-88
  foreign dependency in, 74, 76-77
  progress and problems in, 83-88, 257
  radicalization of, 52-55
  role of China in, 80-82, 88-89

Economy (*continued*)
  role of USSR in, 54-55, 57-58, 78-80
  role of Yugoslavia in, 77-78, 87
Education, 72, 118-120
  enrollment, 119, 120
  reform in, 40, 147-148, 172
Education and Culture, Ministry of, 49, 181 184
Efthimiu Viktor, 115
Elbasan metal works, 61, 86, 87
Electrification, 59, 69
Electronic computer center (Tiranë), 62
"Emin Duraku" guerrilla unit, 228
Encirclement doctrine. *See* Isolationism
Engjëlli, Pal, 4
Ethnic
  composition, 2
  origin, 3
Ethnic Albania, 18
  proclaimed by Italy, 229
Etymology of Albania, 3
European Economic Community (Common Market), 248
European Security and Cooperation Conference (1975), 22-23, 244, 246
Existentialism, 140, 167, 186, 193
Exports, 73-76

Factionalism, 11, 28, 32
Faja, Agim, 127
Fajo, Baba, 152
Fejzo, Baba, 152
Festival, 116-118
"Field of the Blackbirds," 223
Fier 56, 58
Fierzë hydroelectric power plant, 61, 87
Filipi, Lazar, 123
Films, 130-131, 190
  by foreigners on Albania, 1, 2
Fishta, Gjergj, 153, 168, 169, 171
Five-year plans
  First, 56-57
  Second, 57-58
  Third, 58-59
  Fourth, 59-61
  Fifth, 61-63, 87
  Sixth, 86
Flag, 6, 90, 234
Food
  imports, 68, 81

  industry, 62, 104, 108
  production, 68, 86
Foreign policy, 242-256, 259-262
  and diplomatic relations, 252
  on European communism, 251
  and isolationism, 243, 244, 252
  and Marxist-Leninist movement, 244-245, 251, 252, 254
  on nonalignment, 248, 253-254
  and rift with China, 250-251, 253-256, 259-262
  and superpowers, 246, 247, 249-250
  on United Europe concept, 248
Foreign trade, 73-77. *See also* Economy
  deficits, 76
  with Greece, 82, 89
  with Western Europe, 75-76
Frashëri, Abdyl, 24
Frashëri, Andon, 170
Frashëri, Midhat, 13, 17
Frashëri, Naim, 24, 176, 192
Frashëri, Sami, 117
Free Albania Committee (New York), 153, 163
Freud, Sigmund, 105, 140, 186, 193
Front, 198
Fulfilled Promise, The, 165

Gaci, Pjetër, 125
Galileo, 155
Gallery of Fine Arts (Tiranë), 127
"Gang of Four," 245, 250, 254
Gazeta zyrtare [The official gazette], 161, 164
Gega, Liri, 100, 102
Gegs, 2, 107
Geraldine, Queen, 7
Germany, Nazi, 9, 11, 28, 20, 153
Gibbon, Edward, 1
Gjata, Fatmir, 134, 135, 168, 176
Gjegjan, 59
Gjenerali i ushitrisë së vdekur [The general of the dead army], 135, 183
Gjika, Elena, 115
Gjirokastër folklore festival, 116
Gomulka, Wladyslaw, 167
Grameno, Mihal, 117, 192
Greece, 18, 82-83, 89
Griffith, William E., 242
Grillo, O., 122

Index

Gurakuqi, Luigj, 117

Hadëri, Shaban, 129, 190
Halili e Hajrija, 125-126
Harapi, Anton, 153, 170
Harapi, Tonin, 125
Hasluck, Margaret, 93
Haxhiademi, Etëhem, 170
Haxho, Zoica, 126, 190
Hazbiu, Kadri, 48
Health, 72, 104, 108
Helsinki, 23, 244, 246
Helvetii monastery (Berat), 114
High Regency, 153
Holbach, Paul Henri Dietrich d', 155
Hopper, Rex, 20
Hoshi, Kristina, 129
Hoxha, Enver, 14, 19, 25, 31, 37-40, 54, 102, 194
   and the Albanian minority in Yugoslavia, 229, 232, 238
   on armed forces, 196-197, 200, 205, 219, 221
   biography of, 33-34
   on bourgeois culture, 42-43
   on China's relations with the U.S., 245
   cult of, 181, 182
   February 6, 1967, speech, 103-104
   on foreign policy, 246-252
   on intelligentsia, 168, 169, 170, 180, 190, 192
   meeting with youth leaders, 41-42
   relations with Shehu, 34
   on religion, 150, 157-158, 159, 161, 162, 164
   on Soviet aid to Albania, 79
   on succession question, 47-49
   on women, 95-96, 97, 98, 99, 105, 109, 111
Hoxha, Fadil, 235
Hoxha, Nexhmije, 100, 101
Hsu Hsiang-chien, 211
Hua Kuo-feng, 245, 250-251, 254, 260
Huang Yung-sheng, 209
Hull, Cordell, 14
Hungarian revolution, 167, 243
Hydraulic Research Laboratory, 119
Hydroelectric power, 56, 57, 61, 87

Ideology, 25-26, 34, 45

Illyrians, 3, 224, 225
Imports, 73-76
Industrial towns, new, 55
Industry, 53, 73, 74
   development of, 55-63
   growth rates in, 62
   nationalization of, 28, 53, 54
   steel, 86
Institute for the Preservation of the Monuments of Culture, 115
Institute of Agriculture, 119
Institute of Arts (Academy of Phonetic and Plastic Arts), 119
Institute of Economic Studies, 119
Institute of Folklore, 113, 119
Institute of History, 119
Institute of Hydrology and Meteorology, 119
Institute of Language and Literature, 119
Institute of Marxist-Leninist Studies, 101
Institute of Nuclear Physics, 119
Institute of the Figurative Arts, 119
Intelligentsia
   campaign for rectification of, 179-180, 185-189
   dissent in ranks of, 168-171, 174, 176-179
   generation gap between Party leaders and, 177
   Party mistrust of, 167-168
   Western influence on, 186, 187, 193
International Democratic Federation of Women (IDFW), 100, 110
International Women's Day, 90, 100
Investments, 63
Irenei, Bishop, 152
Iron, 73
Islam, 7
Isolationism, 22, 42, 43, 170, 188, 243, 244
Italy, 18
   occupation of Albania by, 9, 10, 11, 17, 229
   and trade with Albania, 74

Jakova, Kolë, 134, 136, 168
Jakova, Prenk, 124
Jakova, Tuk, 31, 32
Jermilov, V. V., 175, 176
Jero, Minush, 123, 177, 183-185

Index   306

John Chrysostom, Saint, 105
Johnson, Chalmers, 20
Jorganxhi, Xhuljana, 136
Jorgaqi, Nasho, 190
Jovanović, Bllazho, 197
June 1924 "revolution," 117

Kadare, Elena, 135
Kadare, Ismail, 134, 135-136, 177, 183
Kallamata, Miço, 137
Kang Sheng, 208
Kapo Hysni, 31, 47, 48, 109
  on population of Albania, 212
Kapo, Vito, 97, 100, 101, 106, 109-110
  report at Seventh Congress of Women
    by, 107-108
Karl Marx hydroelectric plant, 57
Kaser, Michael, 55
Këlcyra, Ali, 13
Këllezi, Abdyl, 85, 87, 88
Këlliçi, Zija, 119
Khrushchev, Nikita, 8, 102, 243, 260
  talks with Hoxha in Moscow (1960),
    249
  visit to Albania (1959), 79, 203
Kilica, Vilson, 189, 127-128
Kisi, Kristofor, 152
Kodra, Klara, 136
Kokalari, Musine, 170
Kokoshi, Kudret, 170
Koleka, Spiro, 31
Kolgjini, Hafëz Tahir, 152
Kondo, Anastas, 189
Konitza, Faik, 3, 168, 169
Kono, Kristo, 124, 125
Ko Pau Chuan, 175, 176
Koran, 159
Kosovo
  and adoption of uniform Albanian language, 234
  Albania's position on, 238
  calls for self-determination in, 222, 230
  demonstrations in, 222, 233, 236, 237, 239
  economic and social conditions in, 235, 237
  historical background of, 223-225
  persecution of Albanians in, 229, 231, 232, 233
  population of, 222

prewar, 225-227
postwar, 230-235
and question of union with Albania, 18, 197, 227-228, 229, 232, 233, 237, 239
Kosovo National Liberation Conference (1943), 227-228
Kosovo National Liberation Movement, 237
Kossovo Polje, 223
Kostallari, Androkli, 119
Krabë, 55
Kraja, Fadil, 122
Kraja, Guljelm, 128
Krasniqi, Rexhep, 163
Kristoforidhi, Kostandin, 24, 168, 192
Krujë, 24, 129
Kupi, Abas, 13, 19
Kurteši, Ilijaz, 235
Kurti, Shtjefën, 163-164
Kurti, Tinka, 123
Kuteli, Mitrush [pseud. Dhimitër Pasko], 168, 170

Labinot Conference, 15
Labor Youth Union of Albania (LYAU), 44, 98, 100, 172
  and confrontation with Hoxha, 41-44
Laço, Teodor, 136
La Mettrie, Julien Offroy de, 155
Language
  earliest records of, 4
  origin of, 3-4
Lara, Kozma, 126
League of Albanian Writers and Artists (LAWA), 43, 179, 181, 186, 190
  First Congress, 174-176
  founding of, 174
  July 1973 Plenum, 188-189
  membership in, 182, 183
  Second Congress, 182-183
League of Nations, 225
League of Prizren (1878), 24, 117, 224
League of Prizren, Second (1943), 229
League of Writers and Artists Club, 132
Legaliteti [Legality], 11, 20
Lek, Law of, 93, 96, 99, 100, 125, 126
Leka (son of King Zog), 7
Lenin, V. I., power plant, 56
Lenin Party School, V. I., 101

Letërsia jonë [Our literature], 174
Lezhë 59, 103
L'humanité, 33
Li Teh-sheng, 209, 210
Liaonin Song and Dance Ensemble, 139
Liberalism, 35, 42, 177
  attack in art and literature, 185-189
  and détente, 43
Libraries, 132
Lidhja Kosovare [Union of Kosovars], 238
Li Hsien-nien, 208, 209
Lin Piao, 146, 207, 208, 210
Li Teh-sheng, 209, 210
Literature, 133-137, 138, 177, 185-189
  prominent postwar writers, 134
  radicalization of, 134, 169, 171
  translation of foreign works of, 133-134
Liu Shao-chi, 146
Llakaj, Veli, 212
Lleshi, Haxhi, 162
Logoreci, Marie, 123, 191
London Conference (1913), 224
Luarasi, Petro Nini, 158, 192
Lubonja, Todi, 189
Luca, Ndrekë, 121
Lulja e kujtimit [The flower of remembrance], 125
Lushnjë, Congress of (1920), 117
Lu Ting-yi, 146

Malëshova, Sejfulla, 32, 136, 170
  economic policy of, 54
  policy on art and culture of, 168-169
Malinovsky, R., 202, 203, 204
Maliq, 55
Mamaqi, Adelina, 136
Mamica (Castrioti), 90
Mana, Andrea, 129
Mao Tse-tung, 39, 89, 190, 243
  death of, 245, 260
  pledge to defend Albania of, 208
  slogan on Albanian socialism of, 252
Mao Tse-tung textile combine (Berat), 58
Marco, Raul, 252
Marko, Petro, 134, 135, 170, 183
Marko, Safo, 128
Marxism-Leninism, 25, 26, 45
Marxist-Leninist movement, 244-245, 251, 252, 254
  split in, 255, 262

Mat district, 106
Mat River, 57
Mehmeti, Sadefqar, 115
Memaliaj, 55
Mero, Agim, 43
Meshari [Missal], 4
Metallurgy, 61, 86, 87
Miçaço, Dionis, 170
Migjeni, Milosh Gjergj Nikolla, 134, 176
Mihailović, Drago, 229
Mindszenty, Cardinal, 160
Minorities in Albania, 2
Mio, Vangjush, 127
Mirditë district, 106
Mjeda, Ndre, 134
Modernization, 27, 45, 257-259
Moisiu, Aleksandër, 115-116
Moisiu, Spiro, 15
Molière, Jean Baptiste, 33
Monastir, Congress of (1908), 4, 24, 117
Montaigne, Michel de, 33
Montenegro, republic of, 236
Montpellier University, 33
Monuments, 129
Moscow November 1960 Conference
  on giving atom bomb to China, 206
  Hoxha speech at, 102, 221
  on wartime relations with Yugoslavia, 196-197
Moslem community, 152, 154
Mozart, Leopold, 1
Mrika, 124
Mugosa, Dusan, 14, 197
Mukaj Conference (1943), 17-18
Mula, Avni, 126, 127, 176, 191
Mula, Nina, 127
Musaraj, Shevqet, 134, 135, 136
Museum cities, 24-25
Museum of Ethnology, 132
Museums, 132
Muslin Organizations, international conference of (Philadelphia), 165
Mussolini, Benito, 7, 17
Myftiu, Manush, 179

Naim Frashëri High School (Durrës), 161
Napoleon Bonaparte, 105
"Narrow nationalism," 43, 84, 85
Nastradin Hoxha, 157
National Conference on Folklore, First, 113

National defense, 44
National Festival of the Dramatic Theater, Fourth (1969), 183
National Folklore Festival (Gjirokastër), 116
Nationalism, 113, 158, 243
  of Albanian communists, 24-25
  in conflict with religion, 157-159, 165, 259
Nationalization of industry, 28
National Liberation Conference (Pezë), 12-13
National Liberation Front (NLF), 13, 15, 19
National Liberation War, 10, 12, 17-21
  youth attitude toward, 41, 42
National Library, 132, 133
National Theater of Opera and Ballet, 124
NATO, 23, 244, 247
Negovani, Papa Kristo, 158, 159
Nëndori [November], 150, 174, 177
  attack on editorial board of, 186
New Albania Film Studio, 130
Newspapers, 131-132
New York Times, 163
Ngjela, Kiço, 85, 87
Nicholas V (pope), 6
Nietzsche, Friedrich, 105
Nixon, Richard, 139, 209, 245, 260
Njolla të murme [Gray stains], 183-184
Noli, Fan S., 134, 159, 163, 168
  term as prime minister of Albania, 6-7
Nonalignment, 248, 253-254, 255
Nora of Kelmend, 90
Novi Pazar, 198
Nuclear research laboratory (Tiranë), 62
Nushi, Gogo, 31

Oil, 61, 62, 73, 87
Onufri (The elder), 114
Onufri, Nikolla, 114
Opera and ballet, 124-127
  liberal influences in, 186, 187
  prominent artists in, 126-127
Order of Naim Frashëri, 116
Order of the Red Flag of Labor, 179
Osborne, R. H., 76
Orthodox Church, 152, 154
  and Uniate "plot," 160
Osservatore romano, 162

Ostpolitik, 244
Ottoman Empire, 5-6, 25, 27, 52
  and cultural stagnation, 113
  women during, 90

Paço, Janaq, 129
Paçrami, Fadil, 121, 179, 189, 191
Painting, 127-128
Paisi Vodica, 152
Palace of Culture, 132
Palaj, Bernardin, 153
Pan-Albanian Federation of America (VATRA), 170, 239
Pano, Nicholas, 243
Papa, Loni, 121, 125, 134, 184
Partisans
  ingredients of victory of, 21
  major goals of, 11
  military buildup and seizure of power by, 15-20
  social composition of, 12
Pashko Shkodrani, Vase, 158
Pasko, Dhimitër. *See* Kuteli, Mitrush
Pasternak, Boris, 139
Paul, Saint, 4
Paul VI (pope), 150
Pazari, Sheh Xhemal, 152
Pejo, Leonora, 127
Peng Chen, 146
Peng Shao-hue, 207
People's Army Ensemble, 132, 176
People's Dramatic Theater, 120, 132, 186
People's Festival of Light, 59
People's Liberation Army (of China), 146, 207
Perllaku, Rahman, 211
Përmet, 15
Përparimi [Progress], 227
Personal names, 161, 186
  decree on changing of, 164
Pezë, 13
Philharmonic Society, 127
Picasso, Pablo, 140
Pipa, Arshi, 135, 168
Pitarka, Sulejman, 121
Plaku, Panajot, 205
Plasari, Ndreçi, 217
Plumbi, Ollga, 100
Poetry, 136
Popović, Miladin, 14, 197

Population, 2, 107, 212
  of Albanian minority in Yugoslavia, 222
  percentage of communists in, 31
  ratio to armed forces, 221
  religious composition of, 60, 61
  urban-rural ratio in, 71
Postoli, Foqion, 125
Pozio, Marigo, 90
Prela, Kol, 170
Prenushi, Vinçenc, 153, 169, 170
Prifti, Naum, 125, 134, 136, 177, 183, 185
Priština Conference on Language (1968), 234
Priština University, 234
Prize of the Republic award, 128, 189-190
Prosi, Sandër, 123
Ptolemy, 3
Publications
  books, 133
  newspapers, 131-132

Qafëzezi, Luan, 176
Qemal, Ismail, 6, 24, 90
Qiriazi, Parashqevi, 90
Qiriazi, Sevasti, 90

Radicalism, 28-29, 46, 171
Radio and television, 116, 186, 189
Radovicka, Petrit, 118
Rafael, Stavri, 127, 176
Rama, Kristaq, 129, 130, 190
Ranković, Aleksandar, 199, 227, 231, 233, 234
Rectification of intelligentsia, 179-180, 185-89
Red Army, 9, 12, 21, 201
"Red Detachment of Women" ballet, 139
Red Guards, 146, 147, 148
Religion, 7, 150
  abolition of, 23, 160-161, 259
  and Albanianism, 158
  in confrontation with the state, 151-154
  and paganism, 157
  vs. nationalism, 157-159, 165
Religion Stripped Naked, 161
Revolution, "uninterrupted," 32, 36, 43, 145, 182

Revolution, world, 26-27, 45, 255
Rexha, Lumturi, 101
Relindja [Rebirth], 136, 198
Riza, Selman, 170
Roman Empire, 5, 7
Romanoff and Juliet, 1
Roshi, Kadri, 123
Rrogozhinë-Fier railroad, 106

Sako, Zihni, 113, 134, 157, 176
SALT, 244, 246
Sartre, Jean-Paul, 140, 141, 186, 193
Savonarola, Girolamo, 189
Schiro, Zef, 169
Sculpture, 129-130
Sebastopol naval base, 204
Seismological Center, 119
Sejko, Teme, 206
Selenica, David, 114
Serbia, ethnic minorities in republic of, 241
Serbian Orthodox Church, 223
Shakespeare, 1, 33
Shanto, Lazër, 170
Shapllo, Dalan, 135
Shehu, Fiqret, 101
Shehu, Mehmet, 15, 31, 47, 58, 143, 200
  on Albania's mountains, 19
  appointed minister of defense, 213
  biography of, 34
  report at Seventh Party Congress, 88-89
  report on Partisan war, 201
Shehu, Qerim, 152
Shkodër, 4, 57, 107
  armed attack on (1946), 153
Shkurte Pal Vata, 106-107
Shoshi, Zef, 127, 128
Shpati, Bexhet, 152
Shqipëri [Albania], 3
Shqiptarë [Albanians], 3
Shuteriqi, Dhimitër, 119, 134, 135, 168, 169, 176
  attack on deviationist writers, 174-175, 183
  election to presidency of LAWA, 174
  loss of presidency of LAWA, 188
  report at Second LAWA Congress, 182
Siliqi, Llazar, 134, 136
Sinishta, John, 165
Skënderbeu, 24, 130

Index

Skënderbeu (*continued*)
  biography of, 5-6
  five-hundredth-anniversary festival, 116-117
Skendi, Stavro, 157
Six-Day War (Mideast), 156
Socialism, stages in construction of, 29, 46, 57, 58
Socialist Realism, 134, 167, 171, 183, 185, 190
  definition of, 173
  Soviet view of, 175, 176
Solzhenitsyn, Aleksander, 140
Soviet Union, 12, 17, 32, 68, 246, 247, 249-250
  constitution of (1936), 30
  economic relations with Albania, 54, 57, 58, 68, 74, 78-80
  influence on Albanian culture, 138, 139-140, 141, 142, 171, 173
  military mission to wartime Albania, 9
  military relations with Albania, 201-206
  Nazi attack on, 10
  role in liberation of Albania, 201
Spahiu, Bedri, 32
Spanish Civil War, 34
Spasse, Sterjo, 134, 135, 176, 177
Stalin, Joseph, 47, 56, 139, 201
  and break with Toto, 200, 243
  monument in Tiranë, 117
Stalinism, 22, 29, 49, 189, 262
  Albanian loyalty to, 259
Stalin textile combine, 56, 102
State Conservatory of Music, 119
State Ensemble of Popular Songs and Dances, 132, 138
State Variety Theater, 132
Stojnić, Velimir, 14, 197
Stringa, Hamide, 189
Sufflay, Milan von, 1
Sukrija, Ali, 232
Surrealism, 140, 167, 193
Surrealist Manifesto (1924), 140

Tana, 130
Tasi, Arkile, 170
Taxes, 59
Teachers' Training Institute, 119
Telephones, 62
Television, 116, 131

Teng Hsiao-ping, 146, 245, 254, 260
Tepelenë, 109
Teuta, Queen, 90
Textiles, 56, 58, 61, 104, 108
Të Rinjtë [Youth], 11
Thaçi, Gasper, 153
Theater, 116, 120-124
  classic plays, 121
  houses, 132
  prominent artists in, 123
Theater Olympiad, 116
Themelko, Kristo, 200
Theodhosi, Koço, 85, 87
Thomai, Themie, 101
Thumanë, 59
Tiranë
  cultural institutions in, 132-133
  population of, 2
Tiranë Party Conference (1956), 205
Tiranë-Peking Airline, 82
Tiranë State University, 41, 62, 118
  cooperation with Priština University, 234
Tisserant, Cardinal, 160
Tito, J. B., 13, 47, 229, 237, 243
  on Albania's aid in liberation of Yugoslavia, 198, 199
  on question of a republic of Kosovo, 236
  trip to China (1977), 255, 260
Todorović, Vojo, 197
Togliatti, Palmiro, 249
Topography, 1, 2, 64
Topulli, Çerciz, 24
Tosks, 2, 107
Tourism, 23, 45
Trade Unions of Albania (TUA), 172
Treska, Misto, 138
Tropojë district, 106
Truman, Harry S., 169
Twelfth Night, 1
Tyagunenko, L. V., 79

UNESCO, 118
Uniates. *See* Orthodox Church
Union of Albanian Artists, 174
Union of Albanian Women (UAW), 95, 97, 100, 110, 172. *See also* Kapo, Vito; Women
  membership of, 104

Sixth Congress of (1967), 105
Seventh Congress of (1973), 107-108
Union of Albanian Writers, 168, 169, 172
Union of Kosovars, 238-239
United Europe, 248
United Nations, 163
Universiteti shtetëror i Tiranës. See Tiranë State University
Uruçi, Ibrahim, 121
Ustinov, Peter, 1

Varfi, Andrea, 168, 170
Varoshi, Mustafa effendi, 152
Varvitsiotis, Ioanis, 82
Vatican, 110, 152, 160, 187
Vehbi Ismail, Imam, 165
Velça, Kudret, 135, 183
Vendresha, Ganimet, 126
Via Egnatia, 5
Vietnam, 243
Višegrad, 198
Vlorë, 5, 56, 202-204
Vlorë, Battle of (1920), 24, 117
Voisava, Castrioti, 90
Volaj, Gjergj, 153
Voroshilov Military Academy, 201
Vukmanović-Tempo, S., 14, 197, 227
Vurg, 59

Wages, 86
Wang Hung-wen, 245
Warsaw Pact, 23, 244, 247
  Albania joins, 202
  Albania withdraws from, 22, 208
Washington, D.C., 239
West Europe, 41, 42, 43, 140
Wied, Wilhelm, 6
Women
  current leading personages, 101
  in education, 108
  heroines of Partisan war, 96
  historic figures, 90
  June 1967 Party Plenum on, 104-105
  in labor force, 104, 107
  main problems facing, 111-112
  Party members, 104, 108
  patriarchal system and, 93, 94, 106
  prewar condition of, 91-94
  in production, 97, 102, 104, 108

Workers' control, 39, 55, 59-60
Working class, growth of, 60
Writers' Conference
  Second (1946), 169, 173
  Third (1949), 173

Xhepa, Margarita, 123
Xhuvani, Dhimitër, 134, 135, 136, 180, 183, 185
Xhuxha, Roza, 123
Xoxa, Jakov, 134, 135
Xose, Koci, 169, 170

Yao Wen-yuan, 245, 250
Yeh Chien-ying, 208
Yevtushenko, Yevgeny, 140
Ylli i Mëngjezit [The morning star], 90
Yugoslav Communist Party (YCP), 11, 13-14, 228
Yugoslavia, 18, 87, 199, 225-227, 249, 255
  and Albanian intelligentsia, 170, 173
  Albanian population in, 222
  and establishment of full diplomatic relations with Albania, 233
  ethnic minorities in, 240
  1971 Constitution of, 233
  and plan to annex Albania, 200

Zadeja, Cesk, 126, 191
Zadeja, Ndre, 153
Zajmi, Nexhmedin, 127, 176
"Zenel Ajdini" guerrilla unit, 228
Zëri i popullit [Voice of the people]
  circulation of, 132
  July 7, 1977, attack on China, 253
Zheji, Gjergj, 134
Zhukov, Georgi Konstantinovich, 217, 219
Zielinski, Janusz G., 55
Zjarri [Fire], 11
Zog, Ahmed, 7, 10, 11, 19
  government of, 33, 52, 68, 74
Zoraqi, Nikolla, 125, 126, 190
Zylfo, Baba, 152

LIBRARY OF DAVIDSON COLLEGE